THE BERNARD SHAW LIBRARY
PLAYS POLITICAL

Bernard Shaw was born in Dublin in 1856. Essentially shy, yet he created the persona of G.B.S., the showman, satirist, controversialist, critic, pundit, wit, intellectual buffoon and dramatist. Commentators brought a new adjective into English: Shavian, a term used to embody all his brilliant qualities.

After his arrival in London in 1876 he became an active Socialist and a brilliant platform speaker. He wrote on many social aspects of the day: on *Commonsense about the War* (1914), *How to Settle the Irish Question* (1917) and *The Intelligent Woman's Guide to Socialism and Capitalism* (1928).

He undertook his own education at the British Museum and subsequently became keenly interested in cultural subjects.

His prolific output included music, art and theatre reviews, which were collected into several volumes: *Music in London 1890–1894* (3 vols., 1931); *Pen Portraits and Reviews* (1931); and *Our Theatres in the Nineties* (3 vols., 1931). He wrote five novels and some shorter fiction including *The Black Girl in Search of God and some Lesser Tales* and *Cashel Byron's Profession*, both published in Penguins.

He conducted a strong attack on the London theatre and was closely associated with the intellectual revival of British theatre. His many plays fall into several categories: 'Plays Pleasant'; 'Plays Unpleasant'; comedies; chronicle-plays; 'metabiological Pentateuch' (*Back to Methuselah*, a series of plays) and 'political extravaganzas'. G.B.S. died in 1950.

D1362751

BERNARD SHAW

PLAYS POLITICAL

•

THE APPLE CART

ON THE ROCKS

GENEVA

Definitive Text

UNDER THE EDITORIAL SUPERVISION

OF DAN H. LAURENCE

PENGUIN BOOKS

PENGUIN BOOKS

Published by the Penguin Group
27 Wrights Lane, London w8 5TZ, England
Viking Penguin Inc., 40 West 23rd Street, New York, New York 10010, USA
Penguin Books Australia Ltd, Ringwood, Victoria, Australia
Penguin Books Canada Ltd, 2801 John Street, Markham, Ontario, Canada L3R 1B4
Penguin Books (NZ) Ltd, 182–190 Wairau Road, Auckland 10, New Zealand

Penguin Books Ltd, Registered Offices: Harmondsworth, Middlesex, England

The Apple Cart published separately in Penguin Books 1956
This collection published in Penguin Books 1986

006

Printed in Great Britain by Clays Ltd, St Ives plc

Typeset in Plantin Light

All business connected with Bernard Shaw's plays is in the hands of The Society of Authors, 84 Drayton Gardens, London sw10 9sb (Telephone: 01-373 6642), to which all inquiries and applications for licences to perform should be addressed and performing fees paid. Dates and places of contemplated performances must be precisely specified in all applications.
Applications for permission to give stock and amateur performances of Bernard Shaw's plays in the United States of America and Canada should be made to Samuel French Inc., 45 West 25th Street, New York, New York 10010

www.greenpenguin.co.uk

Penguin Books is committed to a sustainable future for our business, our readers and our planet. This book is made from Forest Stewardship Council™ certified paper.

ALWAYS LEARNING   **PEARSON**

CONTENTS

The Apple Cart
A Political Extravaganza

WITH

Preface

Composition begun 5 November 1928; completed 29 December 1928. First published in German translation, as *Der Kaiser von Amerika*, 1929. Published in English, 1930. First presented in Polish at the Teatr Polski, Warsaw, on 14 June 1929. First presented in English at the Festival Theatre, Malvern, on 19 August 1929.

Pamphilius ⎱ Private Sec- ⎰ *Wallace Evennett*
⎰ retaries to ⎱
Sempronius ⎰ the King ⎱ *Scott Sunderland*

Boanerges (President of the Board of Trade) *Matthew Boulton*

Magnus (King of England) *Cedric Hardwicke*

Alice (The Princess Royal) *Eve Turner*

Proteus (Prime Minister) *Charles Carson*

Balbus (Home Secretary) *Frank Moore*

Nicobar (Foreign Secretary) *Clifford Marquand*

Crassus (Colonial Secretary) *Julian d'Albie*

Pliny (Chancellor of the Exchequer) *Aubrey Mallalieu*

Lysistrata (Powermistress-General) *Eileen Beldon*

Amanda (Postmistress-General) *Dorothy Holmes-Gore*

Orinthia *Edith Evans*

Queen Jemima *Barbara Everest*

Mr Vanhattan (American Ambassador) *James Carew*

Period—The Future

ACT I *An Office in the Royal Palace. A Summer Morning. 11 a.m.*

An Interlude: *Orinthia's Boudoir. The Same Day. 3.15 p.m.*
ACT II *A Terrace overlooking the Palace Gardens. Later in the Afternoon*

Preface

The first performances of this play at home and abroad provoked several confident anticipations that it would be published with an elaborate prefatory treatise on Democracy to explain why I, formerly a notorious democrat, have apparently veered round to the opposite quarter and become a devoted Royalist. In Dresden the performance was actually prohibited as a blasphemy against Democracy.

What was all this pother about? I had written a comedy in which a King defeats an attempt by his popularly elected Prime Minister to deprive him of the right to influence public opinion through the press and the platform: in short, to reduce him to a cipher. The King's reply is that rather than be a cipher he will abandon his throne and take his obviously very rosy chance of becoming a popularly elected Prime Minister himself. To those who believe that our system of votes for everybody produces parliaments which represent the people it should seem that this solution of the difficulty is completely democratic, and that the Prime Minister must at once accept it joyfully as such. He knows better. The change would rally the anti-democratic royalist vote against him, and impose on him a rival in the person of the only public man whose ability he has to fear. The comedic paradox of the situation is that the King wins, not by exercising his royal authority, but by threatening to resign it and go to the democratic poll.

That so many critics who believe themselves to be ardent democrats should take the entirely personal triumph of the hereditary king over the elected minister to be a triumph of autocracy over democracy, and its dramatization an act of political apostasy on the part of the author, convinces me that our professed devotion to political principles is only a mask for our idolatry of eminent persons. The Apple Cart exposes the unreality of both democracy and royalty as our idealists conceive them. Our Liberal democrats believe in a figment called a constitutional monarch, a sort of Punch puppet who cannot move until his Prime Minister's fingers are in his sleeves. They believe in another figment called a responsible minister, who moves only when similarly actuated by the million fingers of the electorate. But the most superficial inspection of any two such figures shews that they are not puppets but living men, and that the supposed control of one by the other and of both by the electorate amounts to no more than a not very deterrent fear of uncertain and under ordinary circumstances quite remote consequences. The nearest thing to a puppet in our political system is a Cabinet minister at the head of a great public office. Unless he possesses a very exceptional share of dominating ability and relevant knowledge he is helpless in the hands of his officials. He must sign whatever documents they present to him, and repeat whatever words they put into his mouth when answering questions in parliament, with a docility which cannot be imposed on a king who works at his job; for the king works continuously whilst his ministers are in office for spells only, the spells being few and brief, and often occurring for the first time to men of advanced age with little or no training for and experience of supreme responsibility. George the Third and Queen Victoria were not, like Queen Elizabeth, the natural superiors of their ministers in political genius and general capacity; but they were for many purposes of State necessarily superior to them in experience, in cunning, in exact knowledge of the limits of their responsibility and consequently of the limits of their irresponsibility: in short, in the authority and practical power that these superiorities produce. Very clever men who have come into contact with monarchs have been so impressed that they have attributed to them extraordinary natural qualifications which they, as now visible to us in historical perspective, clearly did not possess. In conflicts between monarchs and popularly elected ministers the monarchs win every time when personal ability and good sense are at all equally divided.

In The Apple Cart this equality is assumed. It is masked by a strong contrast of character and methods which has led my less considerate critics to complain that I have packed the cards by making the King a wise man and the minister a fool. But that is not at all the relation between the two. Both play with equal skill; and the King wins, not by greater astuteness, but because he has the ace of trumps in his hand and knows when to play it. As the prettier player of the two he has the sympathy of the audience. Not being as pampered and powerful as an operatic prima donna, and depending as he does not on some commercially valuable talent but on his conformity to the popular ideal of dignity and perfect breeding, he has to be trained, and to train himself, to accept good manners as an indispensable condition of his intercourse with his subjects, and to leave to the less highly placed such indulgences as tempers, tantrums, bullyings, sneerings, swearings, kickings: in short, the commoner violences and intemperances of authority.

His ministers have much laxer standards. It is open to them, if it will save their time, to get their own way by making scenes, flying into calculated

rages, and substituting vulgar abuse for argument. A
clever minister, not having had a royal training, will,
if he finds himself involved in a duel with his king,
be careful not to choose the weapons at which the
king can beat him. Rather will he in cold blood oppose
to the king's perfect behavior an intentional misbe-
havior and apparently childish petulance which he
can always drop at the right moment for a demeanor
as urbane as that of the king himself, thus employing
two sets of weapons to the king's one. This gives him
the advantages of his own training as a successful
ambitious man who has pushed his way from obscurity to celebrity: a process involving a considerable
use of the shorter and more selfish methods of dominating the feebly recalcitrant, the unreasonable, the
timid, and the stupid, as well as a sharp sense of the
danger of these methods when dealing with persons
of strong character in strong positions.

In this light the style of fighting adopted by the
antagonists in the scrap between King Magnus and
Mr Joseph Proteus is seen to be a plain deduction
from their relative positions and antecedents, and not
a manufactured contrast between democracy and
royalty to the disadvantage of the former. Those who
so mistook it are out of date. They still regard democracy as the under dog in the conflict. But to me it is
the king who is doomed to be tragically in that position
in the future into which the play is projected: in fact,
he is visibly at least half in it already; and the theory
of constitutional monarchy assumes that he is wholly
in it, and has been so since the end of the seventeenth
century.

Besides, the conflict is not really between royalty
and democracy. It is between both and plutocracy,
which, having destroyed the royal power by frank

force under democratic pretexts, has bought and swallowed democracy. Money talks: money prints: money broadcasts: money reigns; and kings and labor leaders alike have to register its decrees, and even, by a staggering paradox, to finance its enterprises and guarantee its profits. Democracy is no longer bought: it is bilked. Ministers who are Socialists to the backbone are as helpless in the grip of Breakages Limited as its acknowledged henchmen: from the moment when they attain to what is with unintentional irony called power (meaning the drudgery of carrying on for the plutocrats) they no longer dare even to talk of nationalizing any industry, however socially vital, that has a farthing of profit for plutocracy still left in it, or that can be made to yield a farthing for it by subsidies.

King Magnus's little tactical victory, which bulks so largely in the playhouse, leaves him in a worse plight than his defeated opponent, who can always plead that he is only the instrument of the people's will, whereas the unfortunate monarch, making a desperate bid for dictatorship on the perfectly true plea that democracy has destroyed all other responsibility (has not Mussolini said that there is a vacant throne in every country in Europe waiting for a capable man to fill it?), is compelled to assume full responsibility himself, and face all the reproaches that Mr Proteus can shirk. In his Cabinet there is only one friendly man who has courage, principle, and genuine good manners when he is courteously treated; and that man is an uncompromising republican, his rival for the dictatorship. The splendidly honest and devoted Die-hard lady is too scornfully tactless to help much; but with a little more experience in the art of handling effective men and women as distinguished from the art of handling mass meetings Mr Bill Boanerges might surprise those who, because he makes them laugh, see nothing in him but a caricature.

In short, those critics of mine who have taken The Apple Cart for a story of a struggle between a hero and a roomful of guys have been grossly taken in. It is never safe to take my plays at their suburban face value: it ends in your finding in them only what you bring to them, and so getting nothing for your money.

On the subject of Democracy generally I have nothing to say that can take the problem farther than I have already carried it in my Intelligent Woman's Guide to Socialism and Capitalism. We have to solve two inseparable main problems: the economic problem of how to produce and distribute our subsistence, and the political problem of how to select our rulers and prevent them from abusing their authority in their own interests or those of their class or religion. Our solution of the economic problem is the Capitalist system, which achieves miracles in production, but fails so ludicrously and disastrously to distribute its products rationally, or to produce in the order of social need, that it is always complaining of being paralysed by its "overproduction" of things of which millions of us stand in desperate want. Our solution of the political problem is Votes for Everybody and Every Authority Elected by Vote, an expedient originally devised to prevent rulers from tyrannizing by the very effectual method of preventing them from doing anything, and thus leaving everything to irresponsible private enterprise. But as private enterprise will do nothing that is not profitable to its little self, and the very existence of civilization now depends on the swift and unhampered public execution of enterprises that supersede private enterprise and are not merely profitable but vitally necessary to the whole community, this purely inhibitive check on tyranny has become a stranglehold on genuine democracy. Its painfully evolved machinery of parliament and Party System and Cabinet is so effective in obstruction that we take thirty years by constitutional methods to do thirty minutes work, and shall presently be forced to clear up thirty years arrears in thirty minutes by unconstitutional ones unless we pass a Reform Bill that will make a complete revolution in our political machinery and procedure. When we see parliaments like ours kicked into the gutter by dictators, both in kingdoms and republics, it is foolish to wait until the dictator dies or collapses, and then do nothing but pick the poor old things up and try to scrape the mud off them: the only sane course is to take the step by which the dictatorship could have been anticipated and averted, and construct a political system for rapid positive work instead of slow nugatory work, made to fit into the twentieth century instead of into the sixteenth.

Until we face this task and accomplish it we shall not be able to produce electorates capable of doing anything by their votes except pave the way to their own destruction. An election at present, considered as a means of selecting the best qualified rulers, is so absurd that if the last dozen parliaments had consisted of the candidates who were at the foot of the poll instead of those who were at the head of it there is no reason to suppose that we should have been a step more or less advanced than we are today. In neither case would the electorate have had any real choice of representatives. If it had, we might have had to struggle with parliaments of Titus Oateses and

Lord George Gordons dominating a few generals and artists, with Cabinets made up of the sort of orator who is said to carry away his hearers by his eloquence because, having first ascertained by a few cautious feelers what they are ready to applaud, he gives it to them a dozen times over in an overwhelming crescendo, and is in effect carried away by them. As it is, the voters have no real choice of candidates: they have to take what they can get and make the best of it according to their lights, which is often the worst of it by the light of heaven. By chance rather than by judgment they find themselves represented in parliament by a fortunate proportion of reasonably honest and public spirited persons who happen to be also successful public speakers. The rest are in parliament because they can afford it and have a fancy for it or an interest in it.

Last October (1929) I was asked to address the enormous audience created by the new invention of Wireless Broadcast on a range of political and cultural topics introduced by a previous speaker under the general heading of Points of View. Among the topics was Democracy, presented, as usual, in a completely abstract guise as an infinitely beneficent principle in which we must trust though it slay us. I was determined that this time Votes for Everybody and Every Authority Elected by Vote should not escape by wearing its imposing mask. I delivered myself as follows:

Your Majesties, your Royal Highnesses, your Excellencies, your Graces and Reverences, my Lords, Ladies and Gentlemen, fellow-citizens of all degrees: I am going to talk to you about Democracy objectively: that is, as it exists and as we must all reckon with it equally, no matter what our points of view may be. Suppose I were to talk to you not about Democracy, but about the sea, which is in some respects rather like Democracy! We all have our own views of the sea. Some of us hate it and are never well when we are at it or on it. Others love it, and are never so happy as when they are in it or on it or looking at it. Some of us regard it as Britain's natural realm and surest bulwark: others want a Channel Tunnel. But certain facts about the sea are quite independent of our feelings towards it. If I take it for granted that the sea exists, none of you will contradict me. If I say that the sea is sometimes furiously violent and always uncertain, and that those who are most familiar with it trust it least, you will not immediately shriek out that I do not believe in the sea; that I am an enemy of the sea; that I want to abolish the sea; that I am going to make bathing illegal; that I am out to ruin our carrying trade and lay waste all our seaside resorts and scrap the British Navy. If I tell you that you cannot breathe in the sea, you will not take that as a personal insult and ask me indignantly if I consider you inferior to a fish. Well, you must please be equally sensible when I tell you some hard facts about Democracy. When I tell you that it is sometimes furiously violent and always dangerous and treacherous, and that those who are familiar with it as practical statesmen trust it least, you must not at once denounce me as a paid agent of Benito Mussolini, or declare that I have become a Tory Die-hard in my old age, and accuse me of wanting to take away your votes and make an end of parliament, and the franchise, and free speech, and public meeting, and trial by jury. Still less must you rise in your places and give me three rousing cheers as a champion of medieval monarchy and feudalism. I am quite innocent of any such extravagances. All I mean is that whether we are Democrats or Tories, Catholics or Protestants, Communists or Fascists, we are all face to face with a certain force in the world called Democracy; and we must understand the nature of that force whether we want to fight it or to forward it. Our business is not to deny the perils of Democracy, but to provide against them as far as we can, and then consider whether the risks we cannot provide against are worth taking.

Democracy, as you know it, is seldom more than a long word beginning with a capital letter, which we accept reverently or disparage contemptuously without asking any questions. Now we should never accept anything reverently until we have asked it a great many very searching questions, the first two being What are you? and Where do you live? When I put these questions to Democracy the answer I get is "My name is Demos; and I live in the British Empire, the United States of America, and wherever the love of liberty burns in the heart of man. You, my friend Shaw, are a unit of Democracy: your name is also Demos: you are a citizen of a great democratic community: you are a potential constituent of the Parliament of Man, the Federation of the World." At this I usually burst into loud cheers, which do credit to my enthusiastic nature. Tonight, however, I shall do nothing of the sort: I shall say "Dont talk nonsense. My name is not Demos: it is Bernard Shaw. My address is not the British Empire, nor the United States of America, nor wherever the love of liberty burns in the heart of man: it is at such and such a number in such and such a street in London; and it will be time enough to discuss my seat in the Parliament of Man when that celebrated institution comes into existence. I dont believe your name is Demos: nobody's name is Demos; and all I can make of your address is that you have no address, and are just a tramp—if indeed you exist at all."

You will notice that I am too polite to call Demos a windbag or a hot air merchant; but I am going to ask you to begin our study of Democracy by considering it first as a big balloon, filled with gas or hot air, and sent up so that you shall be kept looking up at the sky whilst other people are picking your pockets. When the balloon comes down to earth every five years or so you are invited to get into the basket if you can throw out one of the people who are sitting tightly in it; but as you can afford neither the time nor the money, and there are forty millions of you and hardly room for six hundred in the basket, the balloon goes up again with much the same lot in it and leaves you where you were before. I think you will admit that the balloon as an image of Democracy corresponds to the parliamentary facts.

Now let us examine a more poetic conception of Democracy. Abraham Lincoln is represented as standing amid the carnage of the battlefield of Gettysburg, and declaring that all that slaughter of Americans by Americans occurred in order that Democracy, defined as government *of* the people *for* the people *by* the people, should not perish from the earth. Let us pick this famous peroration to pieces and see what there really is inside it. (By the way, Lincoln did not really declaim it on the field of Gettysburg; and the American Civil War was not fought in defence of any such principle, but, on the contrary, to enable one half of the United States to force the other half to be governed as they did not wish to be governed. But never mind that. I mentioned it only to remind you that it seems impossible for statesmen to make speeches about Democracy, or journalists to report them, without obscuring it in a cloud of humbug.)

Now for the three articles of the definition. Number One: Government *of* the people: that, evidently, is necessary: a human community can no more exist without a government than a human being can exist without a co-ordinated control of its breathing and blood circulation. Number Two: Government *for* the people, is most important. Dean Inge put it perfectly for us when he called Democracy a form of society which means equal consideration for all. He added that it is a Christian principle, and that, as a Christian, he believes in it. So do I. That is why I insist on equality of income. Equal consideration for a person with a hundred a year and one with a hundred thousand is impossible. But Number Three: Government *by* the people, is quite a different matter. All the monarchs, all the tyrants, all the dictators, all the Diehard Tories are agreed that we must be governed. Democrats like the Dean and myself are agreed that we must be governed with equal consideration for everybody. But we repudiate Number Three on the ground that the people cannot govern. The thing is a physical impossibility. Every citizen cannot be a ruler any more than every boy can be an engine driver or a pirate king. A nation of prime ministers or dictators is as absurd as an army of field marshals. Government by the people is not and never can be a reality: it is only a cry by which demagogues humbug us into voting for them. If you doubt this—if you ask me "Why should not the people make their own laws?" I need only ask you "Why should not the people write their own plays?" They cannot. It is much easier to write a good play than to make a good law. And there are not a hundred men in the world who can write a play good enough to stand daily wear and tear as long as a law must.

Now comes the question, If we cannot govern ourselves, what can we do to save ourselves from being at the mercy of those who *can* govern, and who may quite possibly be thoroughpaced grafters and scoundrels? The primitive answer is that as we are always in a huge majority we can, if rulers oppress us intolerably, burn their houses and tear them to pieces. This is not satisfactory. Decent people never do it until they have quite lost their heads; and when they have lost their heads they are as likely as not to burn the wrong house and tear the wrong man to pieces. When we have what is called a popular movement very few people who take part in it know what it is all about. I once saw a real popular movement in London. People were running excitedly through the streets. Everyone who saw them doing it immediately joined in the rush. They ran simply because everyone else was doing it. It was most impressive to see thousands of people sweeping along at full speed like that. There could be no doubt that it was literally a popular movement. I ascertained afterwards that it was started by a runaway cow. That cow had an important share in my education as a political philosopher; and I can assure you that if you will study crowds, and lost and terrified animals, and things like that, instead of reading books and newspaper articles, you will learn a great deal about politics from them. Most general elections, for instance, are nothing but stampedes. Our last but one was a conspicuous example of this. The cow was a Russian one.

I think we may take it that neither mob violence nor popular movements can be depended on as checks upon the abuse of power by governments. One might suppose that at least they would act as a last resort when an autocrat goes mad and commits outrageous excesses of tyranny and cruelty. But it is a curious fact that they never do. Take two famous cases: those of Nero and Tsar Paul the First of Russia. If Nero had been an ordinary professional fiddler he would probably have been no worse a man than any member of the wireless orchestra. If Paul had been a lieutenant in a line regiment we should never have heard of him. But when these two poor fellows were invested with absolute powers over their fellow-creatures they went mad, and did such appalling things that they had to be killed like mad dogs. Only, it was not the people that rose up and killed them. They were dispatched quite privately by a very select circle of their own bodyguards. For a genuinely democratic execution of unpopular statesmen we must turn to the brothers De Witt, who were torn to pieces by a Dutch mob in the seventeenth century. They were neither tyrants nor autocrats. On the contrary, one of them had been imprisoned and tortured for his resistance to the despotism of William of Orange; and the other had come to meet him as he came out of prison. The mob was on the side of the autocrat. We may take it that the shortest way for a tyrant to get rid of a trouble-some champion of liberty is to raise a hue and cry against him as an unpatriotic person, and leave the mob to do the rest after supplying them with a well tipped ringleader. Nowadays this is called direct action by the revolutionary proletariat. Those who put their faith in it soon find that proletariats are never revolutionary, and that their direct action, when it is controlled at all, is usually controlled by police agents.

Democracy, then, cannot be government by the people: it can only be government by consent of the governed. Unfortunately, when democratic statesmen propose to govern us by our own consent, they find that we dont want to be governed at all, and that we regard rates and taxes and rents and death duties as intolerable burdens. What we want to know is how little government we can get along with without being murdered in our beds. That question cannot be answered until we have explained what we mean by getting along. Savages manage to get along. Unruly Arabs and Tartars get along. The only rule in the matter is that the civilized way of getting along is the way of corporate action, not individual action; and corporate action involves more government than individual action.

Thus government, which used to be a comparatively simple affair, today has to manage an enormous development of Socialism and Communism. Our industrial and social life is set in a huge communistic framework of public roadways, streets, bridges, water supplies, power supplies, lighting, tramways, schools, dockyards, and public aids and conveniences, employing a prodigious army of police, inspectors, teachers, and officials of all grades in hundreds of departments. We have found by bitter experience that it is impossible to trust factories, workshops, and mines to private management. Only by stern laws enforced by constant inspection have we stopped the monstrous waste of human life and welfare it cost when it was left uncontrolled by the Government. During the war our attempt to leave the munitioning of the army to private enterprise led us to the verge of defeat and caused an appalling slaughter of our soldiers. When the Government took the work out of private hands and had it done in national factories it was at once successful. The private firms were still allowed to do what little they could; but they had to be taught to do it economically, and to keep their accounts properly, by Government officials. Our big capitalist enterprises now run to the Government for help as a lamb runs to its mother. They cannot even make an extension of the Tube railway in London without Government aid. Unassisted private capitalism is breaking down or getting left behind in all directions. If all our Socialism and Communism and the drastic taxation of unearned incomes which finances it were to stop, our private enterprises would drop like shot stags, and we should all be dead in a month. When Mr Baldwin tried to win the last election by declaring that Socialism had been a failure whenever and wherever it had been tried, Socialism went over him like a steam roller and handed his office to a Socialist Prime Minister. Nothing could save us in the war but a great extension of Socialism; and now it is clear enough that only still greater extensions of it can repair the ravages of the war and keep pace with the growing requirements of civilization.

What we have to ask ourselves, then, is not whether we will have Socialism and Communism or not, but whether Democracy can keep pace with the developments of both that are being forced on us by the growth of national and international corporate action.

Now corporate action is impossible without a governing body. It may be the central Government: it may be a municipal corporation, a county council, a district council, or a parish council. It may be the board of directors of a joint stock company, or of a trust made by combining several joint stock companies. Such boards, elected by the votes of the shareholders, are little States within the State, and very powerful ones, too, some of them. If they have not laws and kings, they have by-laws and chairmen. And you and I, the consumers of their services, are more at the mercy of the boards that organize them than we are at the mercy of parliament. Several active politicians who began as Liberals and are now Socialists have said to me that they were converted by seeing that the nation had to choose, not between governmental control of industry and control by separate private individuals kept in order by their competition for our custom, but between governmental control and control by gigantic trusts wielding great power without responsibility, and having no object but to make as much money out of us as possible. Our Government is at this moment having much more trouble with the private corporations on whom we are dependent for our coals and cotton goods than with France or the United States of America. We are in the hands of our corporate bodies, public or private, for the satisfaction of our everyday needs. Their powers are life and death powers. I need not labor this point: we all know it.

But what we do not all realize is that we are equally dependent on corporate action for the satisfaction of our religious needs. Dean Inge tells us that our general elections have become public auctions at which the contending parties bid against one another for our votes by each promising us a larger share than the other of the plunder of the minority. Now that is perfectly true. The contending parties do not as yet venture to put it exactly in those words; but that is

what it comes to. And the Dean's profession obliges
him to urge his congregation, which is much wider
than that of St. Paul's (it extends across the Atlantic),
always to vote for the party which pledges itself to go
farthest in enabling those of us who have great possessions to sell them and give the price to the poor. But
we cannot do this as private persons. It must be done
by the Government or not at all. Take my own case. I
am not a young man with great possessions; but I am
an old man paying enough in income tax and surtax
to provide doles for some hundreds of unemployed
and old age pensioners. I have not the smallest
objection to this: on the contrary, I advocated it
strongly for years before I had any income worth
taxing. But I could not do it if the Government did
not arrange it for me. If the Government ceased
taxing my superfluous money and redistributing it
among people who have no incomes at all, I could do
nothing by myself. What could I do? Can you suggest
anything? I could send my war bonds to the Chancellor of the Exchequer and invite him to cancel the
part of the National Debt that they represent; and he
would undoubtedly thank me in the most courteous
official terms for my patriotism. But the poor would
not get any of it. The other payers of surtax and
income tax and death duties would save the interest
they now have to pay on it: that is all. I should only
have made the rich richer and myself poorer. I could
burn all my share certificates and inform the secretaries
of the companies that they might write off that much
of their capital indebtedness. The result would be a
bigger dividend for the rest of the shareholders,
with the poor out in the cold as before. I might sell
my war bonds and share certificates for cash, and
throw the money into the street to be scrambled for;

but it would be snatched up, not by the poorest, but by the best fed and most able-bodied of the scramblers. Besides, if we all tried to sell our bonds and shares—and this is what you have to consider; for Christ's advice was not addressed to me alone but to all who have great possessions—the result would be that their value would fall to nothing, as the Stock Exchange would immediately become a market in which there were all sellers and no buyers. Accordingly, any spare money that the Government leaves me is invested where I can get the highest interest and the best security, as thereby I can make sure that it goes where it is most wanted and gives immediate employment. This is the best I can do without Government interference: indeed any other way of dealing with my spare money would be foolish and demoralizing; but the result is that I become richer and richer, and the poor become relatively poorer and poorer. So you see I cannot even be a Christian except through Government action; and neither can the Dean.

Now let us get down to our problem. We cannot govern ourselves; yet if we entrust the immense powers and revenues which are necessary in an effective modern Government to an absolute monarch or dictator, he goes more or less mad unless he is a quite extraordinary and therefore very seldom obtainable person. Besides, modern government is not a one-man job: it is too big for that. If we resort to a committee or parliament of superior persons, they will set up an oligarchy and abuse their power for their own benefit. Our dilemma is that men in the lump cannot govern themselves; and yet, as William Morris put it, no man is good enough to be another man's master. We need to be governed, and yet to control our governors. But the best governors will not accept any control except that of their own consciences; and, as we who are governed are also apt to abuse any power of control we have, our ignorance, our passions, our private and immediate interests are constantly in conflict with the knowledge, the wisdom, and the public spirit and regard for the future of our best qualified governors.

Still, if we cannot control our governors, can we not at least choose them and change them if they do not suit?

Let me invent a primitive example of democratic choice. It is always best to take imaginary examples: they offend nobody. Imagine then that we are the inhabitants of a village. We have to elect somebody for the office of postman. There are several candidates; but one stands out conspicuously, because he has frequently treated us at the public-house, has subscribed a shilling to our little flower show, has a kind word for the children when he passes, and is a victim of oppression by the squire because his late father was one of our most successful poachers. We elect him triumphantly; and he is duly installed, uniformed, provided with a red bicycle, and given a batch of letters to deliver. As his motive in seeking the post has been pure ambition, he has not thought much beforehand about his duties; and it now occurs to him for the first time that he cannot read. So he hires a boy to come round with him and read the addresses. The boy conceals himself in the lane whilst the postman delivers the letters at the house, takes the Christmas boxes, and gets the whole credit of the transaction. In course of time he dies with a high reputation for efficiency in the discharge of his duties; and we elect another equally illiterate successor on similar grounds. But by this time the boy has grown up and become an institution. He presents himself to the new postman as an established and indispensable feature of the postal system, and finally becomes recognized and paid by the village as such.

Here you have the perfect image of a popularly elected Cabinet Minister and the Civil Service department over which he presides. It may work very well; for our postman, though illiterate, may be a very capable fellow; and the boy who reads the addresses for him may be quite incapable of doing anything more. But this does not always happen. Whether it happens or not, the system is not a democratic reality: it is a democratic illusion. The boy, when he has ability enough to take advantage of the situation, is the master of the man. The person elected to do the work is not really doing it: he is a popular humbug who is merely doing what a permanent official tells him to do. That is how it comes about that we are now governed by a Civil Service which has such enormous power that its regulations are taking the place of the laws of England, though some of them are made for the convenience of the officials without the slightest regard to the convenience or even the rights of the public. And how are our Civil Servants selected? Mostly by an educational test which nobody but an expensively schooled youth can pass, thus making the most powerful and effective part of our government an irresponsible class government.

Now, what control have you or I over the Services? We have votes. I have used mine a few times to see what it is like. Well, it is like this. When the election approaches, two or three persons of whom I know nothing write to me soliciting my vote and enclosing a list of meetings, an election address, and a polling

card. One of the addresses reads like an article in
The Morning Post, and has a Union Jack on it.
Another is like The Daily News or Manchester
Guardian. Both might have been compiled from the
editorial waste paper baskets of a hundred years ago.
A third address, more up-to-date and much better
phrased, convinces me that the sender has had it
written for him at the headquarters of the Labor
Party. A fourth, the most hopelessly out of date of
them all, contains scraps of the early English translations of the Communist Manifesto of 1848. I have
no guarantee that any of these documents were
written by the candidates. They convey nothing
whatever to me as to their character or political
capacity. The half-tone photographic portraits which
adorn the front pages do not even tell me their ages,
having been taken twenty years ago. If I go to one of
the meetings I find a schoolroom packed with people
who find an election meeting cheaper and funnier than
a theatre. On the platform sit one or two poor men
who have worked hard to keep party politics alive in
the constituency. They ought to be the candidates;
but they have no more chance of such eminence than
they have of possessing a Rolls-Royce car. They move
votes of confidence in the candidate, though as the
candidate is a stranger to them and to everybody else
present nobody can possibly feel any such confidence.
They lead the applause for him; they prompt him
when questions are asked; and when he is completely
floored they jump up and cry "Let me answer that,
Mr Chairman!" and then pretend that he has
answered it. The old shibboleths are droned over; and
nothing has any sense or reality in it except the
vituperation of the opposition party, which is received
with shouts of relief by the audience. Yet it is nothing

but an exhibition of bad manners. If I vote for one of these candidates, and he or she is elected, I am supposed to be enjoying a democratic control of the government—to be exercising government *of* myself, *for* myself, *by* myself. Do you wonder that the Dean cannot believe such nonsense? If I believed it I should not be fit to vote at all. If this is Democracy, who can blame Signor Mussolini for describing it as a putrefying corpse?

The candidates may ask me what more they can do for me but present themselves and answer any questions I may put to them. I quite admit that they can do nothing; but that does not mend matters. What I should like is a real test of their capacity. Shortly before the war a doctor in San Francisco discovered that if a drop of a candidate's blood can be obtained on a piece of blotting paper it is possible to discover within half an hour what is wrong with him physically. What I am waiting for is the discovery of a process by which on delivery of a drop of his blood or a lock of his hair we can ascertain what is right with him mentally. We could then have a graded series of panels of capable persons for all employments, public or private, and not allow any person, however popular, to undertake the employment of governing us unless he or she were on the appropriate panel. At the lower end of the scale there would be a panel of persons qualified to take part in a parish meeting; at the higher end a panel of persons qualified to act as Secretaries of State for Foreign Affairs or Finance Ministers. At present not more than two per thousand of the population would be available for the highest panel. I should then be in no danger of electing a postman and finding that he could neither read nor write. My choice of candidates would be perhaps more restricted than at present; but I do not desire liberty to choose windbags and nincompoops to represent me in parliament; and my power to choose between one qualified candidate and another would give me as much control as is either possible or desirable. The voting and counting would be done by machinery: I should connect my telephone with the proper office; touch a button; and the machinery would do the rest.

Pending such a completion of the American doctor's discovery, how are we to go on? Well, as best we can, with the sort of government that our present system produces. Several reforms are possible without any new discovery. Our present parliament is obsolete: it can no more do the work of a modern State than Julius Cæsar's galley could do the work of an Atlantic liner. We need in these islands two or three additional federal legislatures, working on our municipal committee system instead of our parliamentary party system. We need a central authority to co-ordinate the federal work. Our obsolete little internal frontiers must be obliterated, and our units of local government enlarged to dimensions compatible with the recent prodigious advances in facility of communication and co-operation. Commonwealth affairs and supernational activities through the League of Nations or otherwise will have to be provided for, and Cabinet function to be transformed. All the pseudo-democratic obstructive functions of our political machinery must be ruthlessly scrapped, and the general problem of government approached from a positive viewpoint at which mere anarchic national sovereignty as distinguished from self-government will have no meaning.

I must conclude by warning you that when everything has been done that can be done, civilization will still be dependent on the consciences of the governors and the governed. Our natural dispositions may be good; but we have been badly brought up, and are full of anti-social personal ambitions and prejudices and snobberies. Had we not better teach our children to be better citizens than ourselves? We are not doing that at present. The Russians *are*. That is my last word. Think over it.

So much for my broadcast on Democracy! And now a word about Breakages, Limited. Like all Socialists who know their business I have an exasperated sense of the mischief done by our system of private Capitalism in setting up huge vested interests in destruction, waste, and disease. The armament firms thrive on war; the glaziers gain by broken windows; the operating surgeons depend on cancer for their children's bread; the distillers and brewers build cathedrals to sanctify the profits of drunkenness; and the prosperity of Dives costs the privation of a hundred Lazaruses.

The title Breakages, Limited, was suggested to me by the fate of that remarkable genius, the late Alfred Warwick Gattie, with whom I was personally acquainted. I knew him first as the author of a play. He was a disturbing man, afflicted—or, as it turned out, gifted—with chronic hyperæsthesia, feeling everything violently and expressing his feelings vehemently and on occasion volcanically. I concluded that he was not sufficiently cold-blooded to do much as a playwright; so that when, having lost sight of him for some years, I was told that he had made an invention of first-rate importance, I was incredulous, and concluded that the invention was only a Utopian

project. Our friend Henry Murray was so provoked
by my attitude that to appease him I consented to investigate the alleged great invention in person on
Gattie's promising to behave like a reasonable being
during the process, a promise which he redeemed with
the greatest dignity, remaining silent whilst an
engineer explained his miracles to me, and contenting
himself with the reading of a brief statement shewing
that the adoption of his plan would release from
industry enough men to utterly overwhelm the
Central Empires with whom we were then at war.

I approached the investigation very sceptically.
Our friend spoke of "the works." I could not believe
that Gattie had any works, except in his fervid
imagination. He mentioned "the company." That
was more credible: anyone may form a company; but
that it had any resources seemed to me doubtful.
However, I suffered myself to be taken to Battersea;
and there, sure enough, I found a workshop, duly
labelled as the premises of The New Transport
Company, Limited, and spacious enough to accom-
modate a double railway line with a platform. The
affair was unquestionably real, so far. The platform
was not provided with a station: its sole equipment
was a table with a row of buttons on it for making
electrical contacts. Each line of railway had on it a
truck with a steel lid. The practical part of the proceedings began by placing an armchair on the lid of
one of the trucks and seating me in it. A brimming
glass of water was then set at my feet. I could not
imagine what I was expected to do with the water or
what was going to happen; and there was a suggestion
of electrocution about the chair which made me
nervous. Gattie then sat down majestically at the
table on the platform with his hand hovering over the

buttons. Intimating that the miracle would take place when my truck passed the other truck, he asked me to choose whether it should occur at the first passage or later, and to dictate the order in which it should be repeated. I was by that time incapable of choosing; so I said the sooner the better; and the two trucks started. When the other truck had passed mine I found myself magically sitting on it, chair and all, with the glass of water unspilled at my feet.

The rest of the story is a tragi-comedy. When I said to Gattie apologetically (I felt deeply guilty of having underrated him) that I had never known that he was an engineer, and had taken him to be the usual amateur inventor with no professional training, he told me that this was exactly what he was: just like Sir Christopher Wren. He had been concerned in an electric lighting business, and had been revolted by the prodigious number of breakages of glass bulbs involved by the handling of the crates in which they were packed for transport by rail and road. What was needed was a method of transferring the crates from truck to truck, and from truck to road lorry, and from road lorry to warehouse lift without shock, friction, or handling. Gattie, being, I suppose, by natural genius an inventor though by mistaken vocation a playwright, solved the mechanical problem without apparent difficulty, and offered his nation the means of effecting an enormous saving of labor and smash. But instead of being received with open arms as a social bene-factor he found himself up against Breakages, Limited. The glass blowers whose employment was threatened, the exploiters of the great industry of repairing our railway trucks (every time a goods train is stopped a series of 150 violent collisions is propagated from end to end of the train, as those who live within earshot know to their cost), and the railway porters who dump the crates from truck to platform and then hurl them into other trucks, shattering bulbs, battering cans, and too often rupturing themselves in the process, saw in Gattie an enemy of the human race, a wrecker of homes and a starver of innocent babes. He fought them undauntedly; but they were too strong for him; and in due time his patents expired and he died almost unrecognized, whilst Unknown Soldiers were being canonized throughout the world. So far, The Apple Cart is his only shrine; and as it does not even bear his name, I have written it here pending its tardy appearance in the roll of fame.

I must not leave my readers to assume that Gattie was an easy man to deal with, or that he handled the opposition in a conciliatory manner with due allowance for the inertia of a somewhat unimaginative officialdom which had not, like myself, sat on his trucks, and probably set him down as a Utopian (a species much dreaded in Government departments) and thus missed the real point, which was that he was an inventor. Like many men of genius he could not understand why things obvious to him should not be so at once to other people, and found it easier to believe that they were corrupt than that they could be so stupid. Once, after I had urged him to be more diplomatic, he brought me, with some pride, a letter to the Board of Trade which he considered a masterpiece of tact and good temper. It contained not a word descriptive of his invention; and it began somewhat in this fashion: "Sir: If you are an honest man you cannot deny that among the worst abuses of this corrupt age is the acceptance of city directorships by retired members of the Board of Trade." Clearly it was not easy for the Board of Trade to deal with an inventor who wished to interest them, not in his new machines, but in the desirability of its abolishing itself as infamous.

The last time I saw him he called on me to unfold a new scheme of much greater importance, as he declared, than his trucks. He was very interesting on that occasion. He began by giving me a vivid account of the pirates who used to infest the Thames below London Bridge before the docks were built. He described how the docks had come into existence not as wharves for loading and unloading but as strongholds in which ships and their cargoes could be secure from piracy. They are now, he declared, a waste of fabulously valuable ground; and their work should be done in quite another way. He then produced plans of a pier to be built in the middle of the river, communicating directly by rail and road with the shore and the great main lines. The ships would come alongside the pier; and by a simple system of hoists the contents of their holds would be lifted out and transferred (like myself in the armchair) to railway trucks or motor lorries without being touched by a human hand and therefore without risk of breakage. It was all so masterly, so simple in its complexity, so convincing as to its practicability, and so prodigiously valuable socially, that I, taking it very seriously, proceeded to discuss what could be done to interest the proper people in it.

To my amazement Gattie began to shew unmistakeable signs of disappointment and indignation. "You do not seem to understand me," he said. "I have shewn you all this mechanical stuff merely by way of illustration. What I have come to consult you about is a great melodrama I am going to write, the scene of which will be the Pool of London in the seventeenth century among the pirates!"

What could I or anyone do with a man like that? He was naïvely surprised when I laughed; and he went away only half persuaded that his scheme for turning the docks into building land; expediting the Thames traffic; saving much dangerous and demoralizingly casual labor; and transfiguring the underpaid stevedore into a fullfed electrician, was stupendously more important than any ridiculous melodrama. He admitted that there was of course all that in it; but I could see that his heart was in the melodrama.

As it was evident that officialdom, writhing under his insults and shocked by his utter lack of veneration for bigwigs, besides being hampered as all our Government departments are by the vested interests of Breakages, Limited, would do nothing for him, I induced some less embarrassed public persons to take a ride in the trucks and be convinced that they really existed and worked. But here again the parallel between Gattie and his fellow-amateur Sir Christopher Wren came in. Wren was not content to redesign and rebuild St Paul's: he wanted to redesign London as well. He was quite right: what we have lost by not letting him do it is incalculable. Similarly, Gattie was not content to improve the luggage arrangements of our railways: he would not listen to you if your mind was not large enough to grasp the immediate necessity for a new central clearing house in Farringdon Market, connected with the existing railways by a system of new tubes. He was of course right; and we have already lost by sticking to our old ways more than the gigantic sum his scheme would have cost. But neither the money nor the enterprise was available just then, with the war on our hands.

The Clearing House, like the Thames pier, remains
on paper; and Gattie is in his grave. But I still hold
that there must have been something great in a man
who, having not only imagined them but invented
their machinery, could, far from being crushed by
their rejection, exclaim "Perish all my mechanical
trash if only it provides material for one bad play!"

This little history will explain how it actually did
provide material for Breakages, Limited, and for the
bitter cry of the Powermistress General. Not until
Breakages is itself broken will it cease to have a
message for us.

AYOT ST LAWRENCE, *March 1930*

$\lceil$ACT I$\rceil$

*An office in the royal palace. Two writing tables face
each other from opposite sides of the room, leaving
plenty of room between them. Each table has a chair by
it for visitors. The door is in the middle of the farthest
wall. The clock shews that it is a little past 11; and the
light is that of a fine summer morning.*

*Sempronius, smart and still presentably young, shews
his right profile as he sits at one of the tables opening the
King's letters. Pamphilius, middle aged, shews his left as
he leans back in his chair at the other table with a pile
of the morning papers at his elbow, reading one of them.
This goes on silently for some time. Then Pamphilius,
putting down his paper, looks at Sempronius for a
moment before speaking.*

PAMPHILIUS. What was your father?

SEMPRONIUS [*startled*] Eh?

PAMPHILIUS. What was your father?

SEMPRONIUS. My father?

PAMPHILIUS. Yes. What was he?

SEMPRONIUS. A Ritualist.

PAMPHILIUS. I dont mean his religion. I mean his
profession. And his politics.

SEMPRONIUS. He was a Ritualist by profession, a
Ritualist in politics, a Ritualist in religion: a raging
emotional Die Hard Ritualist right down to his boots.

PAMPHILIUS. Do you mean that he was a parson?

SEMPRONIUS. Not at all. He was a sort of spectacular
artist. He got up pageants and Lord Mayors' Shows

[43]

and military tattoos and big public ceremonies and things like that. He arranged the last two coronations. That was how I got my job here in the palace. All our royal people knew him quite well: he was behind the scenes with them.

PAMPHILIUS. Behind the scenes and yet believed they were all real!

SEMPRONIUS. Yes. Believed in them with all his soul.

PAMPHILIUS. Although he manufactured them himself?

SEMPRONIUS. Certainly. Do you suppose a baker cannot believe sincerely in the sacrifice of the Mass or in holy communion because he has baked the consecrated wafer himself?

PAMPHILIUS. I never thought of that.

SEMPRONIUS. My father might have made millions in the theatres and film studios. But he refused to touch them because the things they represented hadnt really happened. He didnt mind doing the christening of Queen Elizabeth in Shakespear's Henry the Eighth because that had really happened. It was a celebration of royalty. But not anything romantic: not though they offered him thousands.

PAMPHILIUS. Did you ever ask him what he really thought about it all? But of course you didnt: one cant ask one's father anything about himself.

SEMPRONIUS. My dear Pam: my father never thought. He didnt know what thought meant. Very few people do, you know. He had vision: actual bodily vision, I mean; and he had an oddly limited sort of imagination. What I mean is that he couldnt imagine anything he didnt see; but he could imagine that what he did see was divine and holy and omniscient and omnipotent and eternal and everything that is impossible if only it looked splendid enough, and the organ was solemn enough, or the military bands brassy enough.

PAMPHILIUS. You mean that he had to get everything from outside.

SEMPRONIUS. Exactly. He'd never have felt anything if he hadnt had parents to feel about in his childhood, and a wife and babies to feel about when he grew up. He'd never have known anything if he hadnt been taught at school. He couldnt amuse himself: he had to pay oceans of money to other people to amuse him with all sorts of ghastly sports and pleasures that would have driven me into a monastery to escape from them. You see it was all ritual: he went to the Riviera every winter just as he went to church.

PAMPHILIUS. By the way, is he alive? I should like to know him.

SEMPRONIUS. No. He died in 1962, of solitude.

PAMPHILIUS. What do you mean? of solitude?

SEMPRONIUS. He couldnt bear to be alone for a moment: it was death to him. Somebody had to be with him always.

PAMPHILIUS. Oh well, come! That was friendly and kindly. It shews he had something inside him after all.

SEMPRONIUS. Not a bit. He never talked to his friends. He played cards with them. They never exchanged a thought.

PAMPHILIUS. He must have been a rum old bird.

SEMPRONIUS. Not rum enough to be noticed. There are millions like him.

PAMPHILIUS. But what about his dying of solitude? Was he imprisoned?

SEMPRONIUS. No. His yacht struck a reef and sank somewhere off the north of Scotland; and he managed to swim to an uninhabited island. All the rest were drowned; and he was not taken off for three weeks. When they found him he was melancholy mad, poor old boy; and he never got over it. Simply from having no one to play cards with, and no church to go to.

PAMPHILIUS. My dear Sem: one isnt alone on an uninhabited island. My mother used to stand me on the table and make me recite about it.

[*He declaims*]

> To sit on rocks; to muse o'er flood and fell;
> To slowly trace the forest's shady scene
> Where things that own not man's dominion
>   dwell
> And mortal foot hath ne'er or rarely been;
> To climb the trackless mountain all unseen
> With the wild flock that never needs a fold;
> Alone o'er steeps and foaming falls to lean:
> This is not solitude: 'tis but to hold
> Converse with Nature's charms, and view her
>   stores unrolled.

SEMPRONIUS. Now you have hit the really funny thing about my father. All that about the lonely woods and the rest of it—what you call Nature—didnt exist for him. It had to be something artificial to get at him. Nature to him meant nakedness; and nakedness only disgusted him. He wouldnt look at a horse grazing in a field; but put splendid trappings on it and stick it into a procession and he just loved it. The same with men and women: they were nothing to him until they were dressed up in fancy costumes and painted and wigged and titled. To him the sacredness of the priest was the beauty of his vestment, the loveliness of women the dazzle of their jewels and robes, the charm of the countryside not in its hills and trees, nor in the blue smoke from its cottages in the winter evenings, but of its temples, palaces, mansions, park gates, and porticoed country houses. Think of the horror of that island to him! A void! a place where he was deaf and dumb and blind and lonely! If only there had been a peacock with its tail in full bloom it might have saved his reason; but all the birds were gulls; and gulls are not decorative. Our King could have lived there for thirty years with nothing but his own thoughts. You would have been all right with a fishing rod and a golf ball with a bag of clubs. I should have been as happy as a man in a picture gallery look-ing at the dawns and sunsets, the changing seasons, the continual miracle of life ever renewing itself. Who could be dull with pools in the rocks to watch? Yet my father, with all that under his nose, was driven mad by its nothingness. They say that where there is nothing the king loses his rights. My father found that where there is nothing a man loses his reason and dies.

PAMPHILIUS. Let me add that in this palace, when the king's letters are not ready for him at 12 o'clock, a secretary loses his job.

SEMPRONIUS [*hastily resuming his work*] Yes, devil take you: why did you start me talking before I had finished my work? You have nothing to do but pretend to read the newspapers for him; and when you say "Nothing particular this morning, Sir," all he says is "Thank Heaven!" But if I missed a note from one of his aunts inviting herself to tea, or a little line from Orinthia the Beloved marked "Strictly private and confidential: to be opened by His Majesty alone," I should never hear the end of it. He had six love letters yesterday; and all he said when I told him was "Take them to the Queen." He thinks they amuse her. I believe they make her as sick as they make me.

PAMPHILIUS. Do Orinthia's letters go to the Queen?

SEMPRONIUS. No, by George! Even I dont read Orinthia's letters. My instructions are to read everything; but I take care to forget to open hers. And I notice that I am not rebuked for my negligence.

PAMPHILIUS [*thoughtfully*] I suppose—

SEMPRONIUS. Oh shut up, Pam. I shall never get through if you go on talking.

PAMPHILIUS. I was only going to say that I suppose—

SEMPRONIUS. Something about Orinthia. Dont. If you indulge in supposition on that subject, you will lose your job, old chap. So stow it.

PAMPHILIUS. Dont cry out before Orinthia is hurt, young chap. I was going to say that I suppose you know that that bull-roarer Boanerges has just been taken into the Cabinet as President of the Board of Trade, and that he is coming here today to give the King a piece of his mind, or what he calls his mind, about the crisis.

SEMPRONIUS. What does the King care about the crisis? There has been a crisis every two months since he came to the throne; but he has always been too clever for them. He'll turn Boanerges inside out after letting him roar the palace down.

Boanerges enters, dressed in a Russian blouse and peaked cap, which he keeps on. He is fifty, heavily built and aggressively self-assertive.

BOANERGES. Look here. The King has an appointment with me at a quarter to twelve. How long more am I to be kept waiting?

SEMPRONIUS [*with cheerful politeness*] Good morning. Mr Boanerges, I think.

BOANERGES [*shortly, but a little taken aback*] Oh, good morning to you. They say that politeness is the punctuality of kings—

SEMPRONIUS. The other way about, Mr Boanerges. Punctuality is the politeness of kings; and King Magnus is a model in that respect. Your arrival cannot have been announced to His Majesty. I will see about it. [*He hurries out*].

PAMPHILIUS. Be seated, Mr Boanerges.

BOANERGES [*seating himself by Pamphilius's writing-table*] A nice lot of young upstarts you have in this palace, Mr—?

PAMPHILIUS. Pamphilius is my name.

BOANERGES. Oh yes: Ive heard of you. Youre one of the king's private secretaries.

PAMPHILIUS. I am. And what have our young upstarts been doing to you, Mr Boanerges?

BOANERGES. Well, I told one of them to tell the king I was here, and to look sharp about it. He looked at me as if I was a performing elephant, and took himself off after whispering to another flunkey. Then this other chap comes over to me and pretends he doesnt know who I am! asks me can he have my name! "My lad" I said: "not to know me argues yourself unknown. You know who I am as well as I do myself. Go and tell the king I'm waiting for him, d'ye see?" So he took himself off with a flea in his ear. I waited until I was fed up with it, and then opened the nearest door and came in here.

PAMPHILIUS. Young rascals! However, my friend Mr Sempronius will make it all right for you.

BOANERGES. Oh: that was Sempronius, was it. Ive heard of him too.

PAMPHILIUS. You seem to have heard of all of us. You will be quite at home in the palace now that you

are a Cabinet Minister. By the way, may I congratulate you on your appointment—or rather
congratulate the Cabinet on your accession?

SEMPRONIUS [*returning*] The King. [*He goes to his
table and takes the visitor's chair in his hand, ready for
the king's instructions as to where to place it*].

*Pamphilius rises. Boanerges turns to the door in his
chair without rising. King Magnus, a tallish studious
looking gentleman of 45 or thereabouts, enters, and
comes quickly down the middle of the room to Boanerges,
proffering his hand cordially.*

MAGNUS. You are very welcome to my little palace,
Mr Boanerges. Wont you sit down?

BOANERGES. I am sitting down.

MAGNUS. True, Mr Boanerges. I had not noticed it.
Forgive me: force of habit.

*He indicates to Sempronius that he wishes to sit near
Boanerges, on his right. Sempronius places the chair
accordingly.*

MAGNUS. You will allow me to be seated?

BOANERGES. Oh, sit down, man, sit down. Youre in
your own house: ceremony cuts no ice with me.

MAGNUS [*gratefully*] Thank you.

*The King sits. Pamphilius sits. Sempronius returns to
his table and sits.*

MAGNUS. It is a great pleasure to meet you at last,
Mr Boanerges. I have followed your career with
interest ever since you contested Northampton
twenty-five years ago.

BOANERGES [*pleased and credulous*] I should just
think you have, King Magnus. I have made you sit
up once or twice, eh?

MAGNUS [*smiling*] Your voice has shaken the throne
oftener than that.

BOANERGES [*indicating the secretaries with a jerk of*

[50]

his head] What about these two? Are they to over-
hear everything that passes?

MAGNUS. My private secretaries. Do they incommode you?

BOANERGES. Oh, they dont incommode me. I am
ready to have our talk out in Trafalgar Square if you
like, or have it broadcast on the wireless.

MAGNUS. That would be a treat for my people, Mr
Boanerges. I am sorry we have not arranged for
it.

BOANERGES [*gathering himself together formidably*]
Yes; but do you realize that I am going to say things
to you that have never been said to a king before?

MAGNUS. I am very glad indeed to hear it, Mr Boanerges. I thought I had already heard everything that
could possibly be said to a king. I shall be grateful
for the smallest novelty.

BOANERGES. I warn you it wont be agreeable. I am
a plain man, Magnus: a very plain man.

MAGNUS. Not at all, I assure you—

BOANERGES [*indignantly*] I was not alluding to my
personal appearance.

MAGNUS [*gravely*] Nor was I. Do not deceive yourself, Mr Boanerges. You are very far from being a
plain man. To me you have always been an Enigma.

BOANERGES [*surprised and enormously flattered: he
cannot help smiling with pleasure*] Well, perhaps I am
a bit of an enigma. Perhaps I am.

MAGNUS [*humbly*] I wish I could see through you, Mr
Boanerges. But I have not your sort of cleverness. I
can only ask you to be frank with me.

BOANERGES [*now convinced that he has the upper
hand*] You mean about the crisis. Well, frank is just
what I have come here to be. And the first thing I am
going to tell you frankly about it is that this country

has got to be governed, not by you, but by your ministers.

MAGNUS. I shall be only too grateful to them for taking a very difficult and thankless job off my hands.

BOANERGES. But it's not on your hands. It's on your ministers' hands. You are only a constitutional monarch. Do you know what they call that in Belgium?

MAGNUS. An indiarubber stamp, I think. Am I right?

BOANERGES. You are, King Magnus. An india-rubber stamp. Thats what you have got to be; and dont you forget it.

MAGNUS. Yes: thats what we are most of the time: both of us.

BOANERGES [*outraged*] What do you mean? both of us?

MAGNUS. They bring us papers. We sign. You have no time to read them, luckily for you. But I am expected to read everything. I do not always agree; but I must sign: there is nothing else to be done. For instance, death warrants. Not only have I to sign the death warrants of persons who in my opinion ought not to be killed; but I may not even issue death warrants for a great many people who in my opinion ought to be killed.

BOANERGES [*sarcastic*] Youd like to be able to say "Off with his head!" wouldnt you?

MAGNUS. Many men would hardly miss their heads, there is so little in them. Still, killing is a serious business: at least the person who is to be killed is usually conceited enough to think so. I think that if there were a question of killing me—

BOANERGES [*grimly*] There may be, someday. I have heard it discussed.

MAGNUS. Oh, quite. I have not forgotten King

Charles's head. Well, I hope it will be settled by a living person and not by an indiarubber stamp.

BOANERGES. It will be settled by the Home Secretary, your duly constituted democratic minister.

MAGNUS. Another indiarubber stamp, eh?

BOANERGES. At present, perhaps. But not when I am Home Secretary, by Jingo! Nobody will make an indiarubber stamp of Bill Boanerges: take that from me.

MAGNUS. Of course not. Is it not curious how people idealize their rulers? In the old days the king—poor man!—was a god, and was actually called God and worshipped as infallible and omniscient. That was monstrous—

BOANERGES. It was silly: just silly.

MAGNUS. But was it half so silly as our pretence that he is an indiarubber stamp? The ancient Roman emperor-god had not infinite wisdom, infinite knowledge, infinite power; but he had some: perhaps even as much as his ministers. He was alive, not dead. What man has ever approached either a king or a minister and been able to pick him up from the table and use him as one picks up and uses a piece of wood and brass and rubber? Permanent officials of your department will try to pick you up and use you like that. Nineteen times out of twenty you will have to let them do it, because you cannot know everything; and even if you could you cannot do everything and be everywhere. But what about the twentieth time?

BOANERGES. The twentieth time they will find they are up against Bill Boanerges, eh?

MAGNUS. Precisely. The indiarubber stamp theory will not work, Mr Boanerges. The old divine theory worked because there is a divine spark in us all; and the stupidest or worst monarch or minister, if not

wholly god, is a bit of a god—an attempt at a god—
however little the bit and unsuccessful the attempt.
But the indiarubber stamp theory breaks down in
every real emergency, because no king or minister is
the very least little bit like a stamp: he is a living soul.

BOANERGES. A soul, eh? You kings still believe in
that, I suppose.

MAGNUS. I find the word convenient: it is short and
familiar. But if you dislike being called a soul, let us
say that you are animate matter as distinguished
from inanimate.

BOANERGES [*not quite liking this*] I think I'd rather
you called me a soul, you know, if you must call me
anything at all. I know I have too much matter about
me: the doctor says I ought to knock off a stone or
two; but there's something more to me than beef.
Call it a soul if you like; only not in a superstitious
sense, if you understand me.

MAGNUS. Perfectly. So you see, Mr Boanerges, that
though we have been dealing with one another for
less than ten minutes, you have already led me into an
intellectual discussion which shews that we are something more than a pair of indiarubber stamps. You are
up against my brains, such as they are.

BOANERGES. And you are up against mine.

MAGNUS [*gallantly*] There can be no doubt of
that.

BOANERGES [*grinning*] Such as they are, eh?

MAGNUS. It is not for me to make that qualification,
except in my own case. Besides, you have given your
proofs. No common man could have risen as you have
done. As for me, I am a king because I was the nephew
of my uncle, and because my two elder brothers died.
If I had been the stupidest man in the country I
should still be its king. I have not won my position by

[54]

my merits. If I had been born as you were in the—in the—

BOANERGES. In the gutter. Out with it. Picked up by a policeman at the foot of Captain Coram's statue. Adopted by the policeman's grandmother, bless her!

MAGNUS. Where should *I* have been if the policeman had picked me up?

BOANERGES. Ah! Where? Not, mind you, that you mightnt have done pretty well for yourself. Youre no fool, Magnus: I will say that for you.

MAGNUS. You flatter me.

BOANERGES. Flatter a king! Never. Not Bill Boanerges.

MAGNUS. Yes, yes: everybody flatters the King. But everybody has not your tact, and, may I say? your good nature.

BOANERGES [*beaming with self-satisfaction*] Perhaps not. Still, I am a Republican, you know.

MAGNUS. That is what has always surprised me. Do you really think that any man should have as much personal power as the presidents of the republican States have? Ambitious kings envy them.

BOANERGES. What's that? I dont follow that.

MAGNUS [*smiling*] You cannot humbug me, Mr Boanerges. I see why you are a Republican. If the English people send me packing and establish a republic, no man has a better chance of being the first British president than you.

BOANERGES [*almost blushing*] Oh! I dont say that.

MAGNUS. Come come! You know it as well as I do. Well, if it happens you will have ten times more power than I have ever had.

BOANERGES [*not quite convinced*] How can that be? Youre King.

MAGNUS. And what is the King? An idol set up by a

group of plutocrats so that they can rule the country with the King as their scapegoat and puppet. Presidents, now, are chosen by the people, who always want a Strong Man to protect them against the rich.

BOANERGES. Well, speaking as a bit of a Strong Man myself, there may be something in that. But honestly, Magnus, as man to man, do you tell me youd rather be a president than what you are?

MAGNUS. By no means. You wouldnt believe me if I did; and you would be quite right. You see, my security is very comfortable.

BOANERGES. Security, eh? You admitted just now that even a modest individual like myself had given your throne a shake or two.

MAGNUS. True. You are quite right to remind me of it. I know that the monarchy may come to an end at any moment. But while the monarchy lasts—while it lasts, mark you—I am very secure. I escape the dreadful and demoralizing drudgery of electioneering. I have no voters to please. Ministers come and ministers go; but I go on for ever. The terrible precariousness of your position—

BOANERGES. What's that? How is my position precarious?

MAGNUS. The vote may go against you. Yours is a Trade Union seat, is it not? If the Hydro-Electric Workers Federation throw you over, where would you be?

BOANERGES [confidently] They wont throw me over. You dont know the workers, Magnus: you have never been a worker.

MAGNUS [lifts his eyebrows]!

BOANERGES [continuing] No king on earth is as safe in his job as a Trade Union Official. There is only one thing that can get him sacked; and that is drink. Not even that, as long as he doesnt actually fall down. I talk democracy to these men and women. I tell them that they have the vote, and that theirs is the kingdom and the power and the glory. I say to them "You are supreme: exercise your power." They say, "That's right: tell us what to do"; and I tell them. I say "Exercise your vote intelligently by voting for me." And they do. That's democracy; and a splendid thing it is too for putting the right men in the right place.

MAGNUS. Magnificent! I have never heard it better described. You certainly have a head on you, Mr Boanerges. You should write an essay on democracy. But—

BOANERGES. But what?

MAGNUS. Suppose a man with a bigger voice comes along! Some fool! Some windbag! Some upstart with a platform trick of gulling the multitude!

BOANERGES. Youre thinking of Iky Jacobus? He is only a talker. [*Snapping his fingers*] I dont give that for him.

MAGNUS. I never even heard of Mr Jacobus. But why do you say "only a talker." Talkers are very formidable rivals for popular favor. The multitude understands talk: it does not understand work. I mean brain work, like yours and mine.

BOANERGES. That's true. But I can talk Iky's head off.

MAGNUS. Lucky man: you have all the trumps in your hand. But I, who cannot pretend to your gifts, am very glad that Iky cannot upset me as long as I am the nephew of my uncle.

A young lady, dressed for walking, rushes in impetuously.

THE YOUNG LADY. Papa: I cannot find the address—

MAGNUS [*cutting her short*] No, no, no, dear: not now.

Go away. Dont you see that I am particularly engaged with the President of the Board of Trade? You must excuse my unruly daughter, Mr Boanerges. May I present her to you? Alice, my eldest girl. Mr Boanerges, dear.

ALICE. Oh! Are you the great Mr Boanerges?

BOANERGES [*rising in a glow of gratification*] Well, I dont call myself that, you know. But I believe the expression is in use, as you might say. I am very pleased indeed to make the aquaintance of the Princess Royal.

They shake hands.

ALICE. Why do you wear such awful clothes, Mr Boanerges?

MAGNUS [*remonstrating*] My dear—!

ALICE [*continuing*] I cant go out walking with you in that [*pointing to his blouse*].

BOANERGES. The uniform of Labor, your Royal Highness. I'm proud of it.

ALICE. Oh yes, I know all that, Mr Boanerges. But you dont look the part, you know. Anyone can see that you belong naturally to the governing class.

BOANERGES [*struck by this view*] In a way, perhaps. But I have earned my bread by my hands. Not as a laborer, though. I am a skilled mechanic, or was until my country called on me to lead it.

MAGNUS [*to Alice*] Well, my dear, you have broken up a most interesting conversation, and to me a most instructive one. It's no use our trying to go on, Mr Boanerges: I must go and find what my daughter wants, though I strongly suspect that what she really came in for was to see my wonderful new minister. We shall meet again presently: you know that the Prime Minister is calling on me today with some of his colleagues—including, I hope, yourself—to discuss the crisis. [*Taking Alice's arm and turning towards the door*] You will excuse us, wont you?

BOANERGES [*graciously*] Oh, thats all right. Thats quite all right.

The King and the Princess go out, apparently much pleased.

BOANERGES [*to Sempronius and Pamphilius comprehensively*] Well, say what you will, the King is no fool. Not when you know how to handle him.

PAMPHILIUS. Of course, that makes all the difference.

BOANERGES. And the girl hasnt been spoilt. I was glad to see that. She doesnt seem to know that she is the Princess Royal, eh?

SEMPRONIUS. Well, she wouldnt dream of giving herself any airs with you.

BOANERGES. What! Isnt she always like that?

SEMPRONIUS. Oh no. It's not everybody who is received as you have been. I hope you have enjoyed your visit.

BOANERGES. Well, I pulled Magnus through it pretty well: eh? Dont you think so?

SEMPRONIUS. He was pleased. You have a way with him, Mr President.

BOANERGES. Well, perhaps I have, perhaps I have.

A bevy of five Cabinet Ministers, resplendent in diplomatic uniforms, enters. Proteus the Prime Minister has on his left, Pliny, Chancellor of the Exchequer, good-humored and conciliatory, and Nicobar, Foreign Secretary, snaky and censorious. On his right Crassus, Colonial Secretary, elderly and anxious, and Balbus, Home Secretary, rude and thoughtless.

BALBUS. Holy snakes! look at Bill. [*To Boanerges*] Go home and dress yourself properly, man.

NICOBAR. Where do you think you are?

CRASSUS. Who do you think you are?

[59]

PLINY [*fingering the blouse*] Where did you buy it, Bill?

BOANERGES [*turning on them like a baited bear*] Well, if you come to that, who do you think you are, the lot of you?

PROTEUS [*conciliatory*] Never mind them, Bill: theyre jealous because they didnt think of it themselves. How did you get on with the King?

BOANERGES. Right as rain, Joe. You leave the King to me. I know how to handle him. If I'd been in the Cabinet these last three months there'd have been no crisis.

NICOBAR. He put you through it, did he?

BOANERGES. What do you mean? put me through it? Is this a police office?

PLINY. The third degree is not unknown in this palace, my boy. [*To Pamphilius*] Did the matron take a hand?

PAMPHILIUS. No. But the Princess Alice happened to drop in. She was greatly impressed by the President.

They all laugh uproariously at Boanerges.

BOANERGES. What in hell are you laughing at?

PROTEUS. Take no notice of them, Bill: they are only having their bit of fun with you as a new comer. Come, lads! enough of fooling: lets get to business. [*He takes the chair vacated by the King*].

Sempronius and Pamphilius at once rise and go out busily, taking some of their papers with them. Pliny takes Boanerges' chair, Balbus that of Sempronius, Boanerges that of Pamphilius, whilst Nicobar and Crassus take chairs from the wall and sit down at the ends of the writing tables, left and right of the Prime Minister respectively.

PROTEUS. Now to start with, do you chaps all fully realize that though we wiped out every other party at the last election, and have been in power for the last three years, this country has been governed during that time by the King?

NICOBAR. I dont see that. We—

PROTEUS [*impatiently*] Well, if you dont, then for Heaven's sake either resign and get out of the way of men who can see facts and look them in the face, or else take my job and lead the party yourself.

NICOBAR. The worst of you is that you wont face the fact that though youre Prime Minister youre not God Almighty. The king cant do anything except what we advise him to do. How can he govern the country if we have all the power and he has none?

BOANERGES. Dont talk silly, Nick. This indiarubber stamp theory doesnt work. What man has ever approached a king or a minister and been able to pick him up from the table and use him as youd use a bit of wood and brass and rubber? The King's a live man; and what more are you, with your blessed advice?

PLINY. Hullo, Bill! You have been having your mind improved by somebody.

BOANERGES. What do you mean? Isnt it what I have always said?

PROTEUS [*whose nerves are on edge*] Oh, will you stop squabbling. What are we going to say to the King when he comes in? If you will only hold together and say the same thing—or let me say it—he must give way. But he is as artful as the very devil. He'll have a pin to stick into the seat of every man of you. If you all start quarrelling and scolding and bawling, which is just what he wants you to do, it will end in his having his own way as usual, because one man that has a mind and knows it can always beat ten men who havnt and dont.

PLINY. Steady, Prime Minister. Youre overwrought

PROTEUS. It's enough to drive a man mad. I am sorry

PLINY [*changing the subject*] Where's Mandy?

NICOBAR. And Lizzie?

PROTEUS. Late as usual. Come! Business, business, business.

BOANERGES [*thunderously*] Order order!

PROTEUS. The King is working the Press against us. The King is making speeches. Things have come to a head. He said yesterday on the opening of the new Chamber of Commerce building that the king's veto is the only remaining defence of the people against corrupt legislation.

BOANERGES. So it is, by Jingo. What other defence is there? Democracy? Yah! We know what Democracy is worth. What we need is a Strong Man.

NICOBAR [*sneering*] Yourself for instance.

BOANERGES. I should stand a better chance than you, my lad, if we were a Republic, and the people could choose. And let me tell you that a republican president has more power than a king because the people know that they need a Strong Man to protect them against the rich.

PROTEUS [*flinging himself back in his chair in desperation*] This is a nice thing. Two Labor papers have leading articles this morning supporting the King; and the latest addition to the Cabinet here is a King's man. I resign.

General consternation except on the part of Nicobar, who displays cheerful unconcern, and of Boanerges, who squares himself with an iron face.

PLINY. ⎫ No: dont do that, Joe.
BALBUS. ⎬ What! Now! You cant. You mustnt.
CRASSUS. ⎭ Of course not. Out of the question.

PROTEUS. No use. [*Rising*] I resign, I tell you. You

can all go to the devil. I have lost my health, and almost lost my reason, trying to keep this Cabinet together in the face of the cunningest enemy popular government has ever had to face. I have had enough of it. [*Sitting down again*] I resign.

CRASSUS. But not at such a moment as this. Dont let us swop horses when crossing a stream.

NICOBAR. Why not, if the horse you have got is subject to hysterics?

BOANERGES. Not to mention that you may have more than one horse at your disposal.

PROTEUS. Right you are. Perfectly true. Take my job, Nick. It's vacant for you, Bill. I wish you joy of it.

PLINY. Now boys, boys, boys: be good. We cant make a new Cabinet before Magnus comes in. You have something in your pocket, Joe. Out with it. Read it to them.

PROTEUS [*taking a paper from his pocket*] What I was going to propose—and you can take it or leave it—is an ultimatum.

CRASSUS. Good!

PROTEUS. Either he signs this, or—[*he pauses significantly*]—!

NICOBAR. Or what?

PROTEUS [*disgusted*] Oh, you make me sick.

NICOBAR. Youre sick already, by your own account. I only ask, suppose he refuses to sign your ultimatum?

PROTEUS. You call yourself a Cabinet Minister, and you cant asnwer that!

NICOBAR. No I cant. I press my question. You said he must sign, OR. I ask, or what?

PROTEUS. Or we resign and tell the country that we cant carry on the King's Government under conditions which destroy our responsibility.

BALBUS. Thatll do it. He couldnt face that.

CRASSUS. Yes: thatll bunker him.

PROTEUS. Is that agreed?

PLINY.
CRASSUS. } Yes, yes, yes, 'greed 'greed 'greed.
BALBUS.

BOANERGES. I retain an open mind. Let us hear the ultimatum.

NICOBAR. Yes: lets hear it.

PROTEUS. Memorandum of understanding arrived at—

The King enters, with Amanda, Postmistress General, a merry lady in uniform like the men, on his left, and Lysistrata, Powermistress General, a grave lady in academic robes, on his right. All rise. The Prime Minister's face darkens.

MAGNUS. Welcome, gentlemen. I hope I am not too early. [*Noting the Prime Minister's scowl*] Am I intruding?

PROTEUS. I protest. It is intolerable. I call a conference of my Cabinet to consider our position in regard to the prerogative; and I find the two lady members, the Postmistress General and the Powermistress General, closeted with your Majesty instead of being in their places to confer with me.

LYSISTRATA. You mind your own business, Joe.

MAGNUS. Oh no: really, really, my dear Lysistrata, you must not take that line. Our business is to meddle in everybody's business. A Prime Minister is a busybody by profession. So is a monarch. So are we all.

LYSISTRATA. Well, they say everybody's business is nobody's business, which is just what Joe is fit for. [*She takes a chair from the wall with a powerful hand, and swings it forward to the inside corner of Sempronius's table, where she stands waiting for the King to sit down.*]

[64]

PROTEUS. This is what I have to put up with when I am on the verge of a nervous breakdown [*he sits down distractedly, and buries his face in his hands*].

AMANDA [*going to him and petting him*] Come, Joe! dont make a scene. You asked for it, you know.

NICOBAR. What do you go provoking Lizzie for like that? You know she has a temper.

LYSISTRATA. There is nothing whatever wrong with my temper. But I am not going to stand any of Joe's nonsense; and the sooner he makes up his mind to that the smoother our proceedings are likely to be.

BOANERGES. I protest. I say, let us be dignified. I say, let us respect ourselves and respect the throne. All this Joe and Bill and Nick and Lizzie: we might as well be hobnobbing in a fried fish shop. The Prime Minister is the prime minister: he isnt Joe. The Powermistress isnt Lizzie: she's Lysis Traitor.

LYSISTRATA [*who has evidently been a schoolmistress*] Certainly not, Bill. She is Ly Sistrata. You had better say Lizzie: it is easier to pronounce.

BOANERGES [*scornfully*] Ly Sistrata! A more foolish affectation I never heard: you might as well call me Bo Annerjeeze [*he flings himself into his chair*].

MAGNUS [*sweetly*] Shall we sit, ladies and gentlemen!

Boanerges hastily rises and sits down again. The King sits in Pliny's chair. Lysistrata and the rest of the men resume their seats, leaving Pliny and Amanda standing. Amanda takes an empty chair in each hand and plants them side by side between the King and the table of Pamphilius.

AMANDA. There you are, Plin. [*She sits next the table*].

PLINY. Ta ta, Mandy. Pardon me: I should have said Amanda. [*He sits next the King*].

AMANDA. Don't mention it, darling.

BOANERGES. Order, order!

AMANDA [*waves him a kiss*]!!

MAGNUS. Prime Minister: the word is with you. Why have you all simultaneously given me the great pleasure of exercising your constitutional right of access to the sovereign?

LYSISTRATA. Have I that right, sir; or havnt I?

MAGNUS. Most undoubtedly you have.

LYSISTRATA. You hear that, Joe?

PROTEUS. I—

BALBUS. Oh for Heaven's sake dont contradict her, Joe. We shall never get anywhere at this rate. Come to the crisis.

NICOBAR.		Yes yes: the crisis!
CRASSUS.	[*together*]	Yes yes: come along!
PLINY.		The crisis: out with it!

BALBUS. The ultimatum. Lets have the ultimatum.

MAGNUS. Oh, there is an ultimatum! I gathered from yesterday's evening papers that there is a crisis —another crisis. But the ultimatum is new to me. [*To Proteus*] Have you an ultimatum?

PROTEUS. Your Majesty's allusion to the royal veto in a speech yesterday has brought matters to a head.

MAGNUS. It was perhaps indelicate. But you all allude so freely to your own powers—to the supremacy of Parliament and the voice of the people and so forth—that I fear I have lost any little delicacy I ever possessed. If you may flourish your thunderbolts why may I not shoulder my little popgun of a veto and strut up and down with it for a moment?

NICOBAR. This is not a subject for jesting—

MAGNUS [*interrupting him quickly*] I am not jesting, Mr Nicobar. But I am certainly trying to discuss our differences in a goodhumored manner. Do you wish me to lose my temper and make scenes?

[66]

AMANDA. Oh please no, your Majesty. We get enough of that from Joe.

PROTEUS. I pro—

MAGNUS [*his hand persuasively on the Prime Minister's arm*] Take care, Prime Minister: take care: do not let your wily Postmistress General provoke you to supply the evidence against yourself.

All the rest laugh.

PROTEUS [*coolly*] I thank your Majesty for the caution. The Postmistress General has never forgiven me for not making her First Lady of the Admiralty. She has three nephews in the navy.

AMANDA. Oh you— [*She swallows the epithet, and contents herself with shaking her fist at the Premier*].

MAGNUS. Tch-tch-tch! Gently, Amanda, gently. Three very promising lads: they do you credit.

AMANDA. I never wanted them to go to sea. I could have found them better jobs in the Post Office.

MAGNUS. Apart from Amanda's family relations, am I face to face with a united Cabinet.

PLINY. No, sir. You are face to face with a squabbling Cabinet; but, on the constitutional question, united we stand: divided we fall.

BALBUS. That is so.

NICOBAR. Hear hear!

MAGNUS. What is the constitutional question? Do you deny the royal veto? or do you object only to my reminding my subjects of its existence?

NICOBAR. What we say is that the king has no right to remind his subjects of anything constitutional except by the advice of the Prime Minister, and in words which he has read and approved.

MAGNUS. Which Prime Minister? There are so many of them in the Cabinet.

BOANERGES. There! Serves you all right! Arnt you

ashamed of yourselves? But I am not surprised, Joseph Proteus. I own I like a Prime Minister that knows how to be a Prime Minister. Why do you let them take the word out of your mouth every time?

PROTEUS. If His Majesty wants a Cabinet of dumb dogs he will not get it from my party.

BALBUS. Hear, hear, Joe!

MAGNUS. Heaven forbid! The variety of opinion in the Cabinet is always most instructive and interesting. Who is to be its spokesman today?

PROTEUS. I know your Majesty's opinion of me; but let—

MAGNUS [*before he can proceed*] Let me state it quite frankly. My opinion of you is that no man knows better than you when to speak and when to let others speak for you; when to make scenes and threaten resignation; and when to be as cool as a cucumber.

PROTEUS [*not altogether displeased*] Well, sir, I hope I am not such a fool as some fools think me. I may not always keep my temper. You would not be surprised at that if you knew how much temper I have to keep. [*He straightens up and becomes impressively eloquent*]. At this moment my cue is to shew you, not my own temper, but the temper of my Cabinet. What the Foreign Secretary and the Chancellor of the Exchequer and the Home Secretary have told you is true. If we are to carry on your government we cannot have you making speeches that express your own opinions and not ours. We cannot have you implying that everything that is of any value in our legislation is your doing and not ours. We cannot have you telling people that their only safeguard against the political encroachments of big business whilst we are doing nothing but bungling and squabbling is your power of veto. It has got to stop, once for all.

BALBUS.
NICOBAR. } Hear hear!

PROTEUS. Is that clear?

MAGNUS. Far clearer than I have ever dared to make it, Mr Proteus. Except, by the way, on one point. When you say that all this of which you complain must cease once for all, do you mean that henceforth I am to agree with you or you with me?

PROTEUS. I mean that when you disagree with us you are to keep your disagreement to yourself.

MAGNUS. That would be a very heavy responsibility for me. If I see you leading the nation over the edge of a precipice may I not warn it?

BALBUS. It is our business to warn it, not yours.

MAGNUS. Suppose you dont do your business! Suppose you dont see the danger! That has happened. It may happen again.

CRASSUS [*insinuating*] As democrats, I think we are bound to proceed on the assumption that such a thing cannot happen.

BOANERGES. Rot! It's happening all the time until somebody has the gumption to put his foot down and stop it.

CRASSUS. Yes: I know. But that is not democracy.

BOANERGES. Democracy be— [*he leaves the word unspoken*]! I have thirty years experience of democracy. So have most of you. I say no more.

BALBUS. Wages are too high, if you ask me. Anybody can earn from five to twenty pounds a week now, and a big dole when there is no job for him. And what Englishman will give his mind to politics as long as he can afford to keep a motor car?

NICOBAR. How many voted at the last election? Not seven per cent of the register.

BALBUS. Yes; and the seven per cent were only a parcel of sillies playing at ins and outs. To make democracy work in Crassus's way we need poverty and hardship.

PROTEUS [*emphatically*] And we have abolished poverty and hardship. That is why the people trust us. [*To the King*] And that is why you will have to give way to us. We have the people of England in comfort —solid middle class comfort—at our backs.

MAGNUS. No: we have not abolished poverty and hardship. Our big business men have abolished them. But how? By sending our capital abroad to places where poverty and hardship still exist: in other words, where labor is cheap. We live in comfort on the imported profits of that capital. We are all ladies and gentlemen now.

NICOBAR. Well, what more do you want?

PLINY. You surely dont grudge us our wonderful prosperity, sir.

MAGNUS. I want it to last.

NICOBAR. Why shouldnt it last? [*Rising*] Own the truth. You had rather have the people poor, and pose as their champion and savior, than have to admit that the people are better off under our government— under our squabbling and bungling, as you call it.

MAGNUS. No: it was the Prime Minister who used those expressions.

NICOBAR. Dont quibble: he was quoting them from your reptile press. What I say is that we stand for high wages, and you are always belittling and opposing the men that pay them. Well, the voters like high wages. They know when they are well off; and they dont know what you are grumbling about; and thats what will beat you every time you try to stir them against us [*he resumes his seat*].

PLINY. There is no need to rub it in like that, Nick. We're all good friends. Nobody objects to prosperity.

MAGNUS. You think this prosperity is safe?

NICOBAR. Safe!

PLINY. Oh come, sir! Really!

BALBUS. Safe! Look at my constituency: Northeast-by-north Birmingham, with its four square miles of confectionery works! Do you know that in the Christmas cracker trade Birmingham is the workshop of the world?

CRASSUS. Take Gateshead and Middlesbrough alone! Do you know that there has not been a day's unemployment there for five years past, and that their daily output of chocolate creams totals up to twenty thousand tons?

MAGNUS. It is certainly a consoling thought that if we were peacefully blockaded by the League of Nations we could live for at least three weeks on our chocolate creams.

NICOBAR. You neednt sneer at the sweets: we turn out plenty of solid stuff. Where will you find the equal of the English golf club?

BALBUS. Look at the potteries: the new crown Derby! the new Chelsea! Look at the tapestries! Why, Greenwich Goblin has chased the French stuff out of the market.

CRASSUS. Dont forget our racing motor boats and cars, sir: the finest on earth, and all individually designed. No cheap mass production stuff there.

PLINY. And our live stock! Can you beat the English polo pony?

AMANDA. Or the English parlormaid? She wins in all the international beauty shows.

PLINY. Now Mandy, Mandy! None of your triviality.

MAGNUS. I am not sure that the British parlormaid is not the only real asset in your balance sheet.

AMANDA [*triumphant*] Aha! [*To Pliny*] You go home to bed and reflect on that, old man.

PROTEUS. Well, sir? Are you satisfied that we have the best paid proletariat in the world on our side?

MAGNUS [*gravely*] I dread revolution.

All except the two women laugh uproariously at this.

BOANERGES. I must join them there, sir. I am as much against chocolate creams as you are: they never agree with me. But a revolution in England!!! Put that out of your head, sir. Not if you were to tear up Magna Carta in Trafalgar Square, and light the fires of Smithfield to burn every member of the House of Commons.

MAGNUS. I was not thinking of a revolution in England. I was thinking of the countries on whose tribute we are living. Suppose it occurs to them to stop paying it! That has happened before.

PLINY. Oh no, sir: no, no, no. What would become of their foreign trade with us?

MAGNUS. At a pinch, I think they could do without the Christmas crackers.

CRASSUS. Oh, thats childish.

MAGNUS. Children in their innocence are sometimes very practical, Mr Colonial Secretary. The more I see of the sort of prosperity that comes of your leaving our vital industries to big business men as long as they keep your constituents quiet with high wages, the more I feel as if I were sitting on a volcano.

LYSISTRATA [*who has been listening with implacable contempt to the discussion, suddenly breaks in in a sepulchral contralto*] Hear hear! My department was perfectly able and ready to deal with the supply of power from the tides in the north of Scotland, and you gave it away, like the boobs you are, to the Pentland Firth Syndicate: a gang of foreign capitalists who will make billions out of it at the people's expense while we are bungling and squabbling. Crassus worked that. His uncle is chairman.

CRASSUS. A lie. A flat lie. He is not related to me. He is only my stepson's father-in-law.

BALBUS. I demand an explanation of the words bungling and squabbling. We have had quite enough of them here today. Who are you getting at? It was not I who bungled the Factory Bill. I found it on my desk when I took office, with all His Majesty's suggestions in the margin; and you know it.

PROTEUS. Have you all done playing straight into His Majesty's hand, and making my situation here impossible?

Guilty silence.

PROTEUS [*proceeding deliberately and authoritatively*] The question before us is not one of our manners and our abilities. His Majesty will not press that question, because if he did he would oblige us to raise the question of his own morals.

MAGNUS [*starts*] What!

BALBUS. Good, Joe!

CRASSUS [*aside to Amanda*] Thats got him.

MAGNUS. Am I to take that threat seriously, Mr Proteus?

PROTEUS. If you try to prejudice what is a purely constitutional question by personal scandal, it will be easy enough for us to throw your mud back. In this conflict we are the challengers. You have the choice of weapons. If you choose scandal, we'll take you on at that. Personally I shall deplore it if you do. No good will come of washing our dirty linen in public. But dont make any mistake as to what will happen. I will be plain with you: I will dot the Is and cross the Ts. You will say that Crassus is a jobber.

CRASSUS [*springing up*] I—

PROTEUS [*fiercely crushing him*] Sit down. Leave this to me.

CRASSUS [*sits*] I a jobber! Well!

PROTEUS [*continuing*] You will say that I should never have given the Home Office to a bully like Balbus—

BALBUS [*intimidated by the fate of Crassus, but unable to forbear a protest*] Look here, Joe—

PROTEUS. You shut up, Bert. It's true.

BALBUS [*subsides with a shrug*]!

PROTEUS. Well, what will happen? There will be no denials, no excuses, no vindications. We shall not fall into that trap, clever as you are at setting it. Crassus will say just simply that you are a freethinker. And Balbus will say that you are a libertine.

THE MALE CABINET [*below their breaths*] Aha-a-a-a-h!!!

PROTEUS. Now, King Magnus! Our cards are on the table. What have you to say?

MAGNUS. Admirably put! People ask how it is that with all these strong characters around you hold your own as the only possible Prime Minister, in spite of your hysterics and tantrums, your secretiveness and your appalling laziness—

BALBUS [*delighted*] Hear hear! Youre getting it now, Joe.

MAGNUS [*continuing*] But when the decisive moment comes, they find out what a wonderful man you are.

PROTEUS. I am not a wonderful man. There is not a man or woman here whose job I could do as well as they do it. I am Prime Minister for the same reason

that all Prime Ministers have been Prime Ministers:
because I am good for nothing else. But I can keep to
the point—when it suits me. And I can keep you to
the point, sir, whether it suits you or not.

MAGNUS. At all events you do not flatter kings. One
of them, at least, is grateful to you for that.

PROTEUS. Kings, as you and I very well know, rule
their ministers by flattering them; and now that you
are the only king left in the civilized half of Europe
Nature seems to have concentrated in you all the
genius for flattery that she used to have to divide
between half a dozen kings, three emperors, and a
Sultan.

MAGNUS. But what interest has a king in flattering a
subject?

AMANDA. Suppose she's a goodlooking woman, sir!

NICOBAR. Suppose he has a lot of money, and the
king's hard up!

PROTEUS. Suppose he is a Prime Minister, and you
can do nothing except by his advice.

MAGNUS [*smiling with his utmost charm*] Ah, there you
have hit the nail on the head. Well, I suppose I
must surrender. I am beaten. You are all too clever for
me.

BOANERGES. Well, nothing can be fairer than that.

PLINY [*rubbing his hands*] You are a gentleman, sir.
We shant rub it in, you know.

BALBUS. Ever the best of friends. I am the last to
kick a man when he's down.

CRASSUS. I may be a jobber; but nobody shall say
that I am an ungenerous opponent.

BOANERGES [*suddenly overwhelmed with emotion,
rises and begins singing in stentorian tones*]

  Should auld acquaintance be forgot,
   And never brought to mind—

[75]

Amanda bursts into uncontrollable laughter. The King looks reproachfully at her, struggling hard to keep his countenance. The others are beginning to join in the chorus when Proteus rises in a fury.

PROTEUS. Are you all drunk?

Dead silence. Boanerges sits down hastily. The other singers pretend that they have disapproved of his minstrelsy.

PROTEUS. You are at present engaged in a tug of war with the King: the tug of your lives. You think you have won. You havnt. All that has happened is that the King has let go the rope. You are sprawling on your backs; and he is laughing at you. Look at him! [*He sits down contemptuously*].

MAGNUS [*making no further attempt to conceal his merriment*] Come to my rescue, Amanda. It was you who set me off.

AMANDA [*wreathed with smiles*] You got me so nicely, sir. [*To Boanerges*] Bill: you are a great boob.

BOANERGES. I dont understand this. I understood His Majesty to give way to us in, I must say, the handsomest manner. Cant we take our victory like gentlemen?

MAGNUS. Perhaps I had better explain. I quite appreciate the frank and magnanimous spirit—may I say the English spirit?—in which my little concession has been received, especially by you, Mr Boanerges. But in truth it leaves matters just where they were; for I should never have dreamt of entering on a campaign of recrimination such as the Prime Minister suggested. As he has reminded you, my own character is far too vulnerable. A king is not allowed the luxury of a good character. Our country has produced millions of blameless greengrocers, but not one blameless monarch. I have to rule over more religious sects than I can count. To rule them impartially I must not belong to any of them; and they all regard people who do not belong to them as atheists. My court includes several perfectly respectable wives and mothers whose strange vanity it is to be talked about as abandoned females. To gain the reputation of being the king's mistress they would do almost anything except give the unfortunate monarch the pleasure of substantiating their claim. Side by side with them are the ladies who are really unscrupulous. They are so careful of their reputations that they lose no opportunity of indignantly denying that they have ever yielded to solicitations which have in fact never been made to them. Thus every king is supposed to be a libertine; and as, oddly enough, he owes a great part of his popularity to this belief, he cannot deny it without deeply disappointing his subjects.

There is a rather grim silence, during which the King looks round in vain for some encouraging response.

LYSISTRATA [*severely*] Your Majesty's private affairs do not concern us, in any case.

AMANDA [*splutters into an irrepressible laugh*]!!

MAGNUS [*looks reproachfully at Amanda*]!

AMANDA [*composing her features as best she can*] Excuse me.

CRASSUS. I hope your Majesty recognizes that kings are not the only people to whom certain sorts of mud always stick, no matter what fool throws them. Call a minister a jobber—

BALBUS. Or a bungler.

CRASSUS. Yes, or a bungler, and everybody believes it. Jobbery and incompetence are the two sorts of mud that stick to us, no matter how honest or capable we are; and we havnt the royal advantage that you enjoy, that the more the ladies take away your character the better the people like you.

BOANERGES [*suddenly*] Prime Minister: will you tell me what the Postmistress General is sniggering at?

AMANDA. This a free country, Bill. A sense of humor is not a crime. And when the King is not setting me off, you are.

BOANERGES. Where is the joke? I dont see it.

AMANDA. If you could see a joke, Bill, you wouldnt be the great popular orator you are.

BOANERGES. Thank Heaven, I am not a silly giggler like some I could mention.

AMANDA. Thanks, dearest Bill. Now, Joe: dont you think you have let us run loose long enough? What about that ultimatum?

MAGNUS [*shaking his head at her*] Traitor!

PROTEUS. I am in no hurry. His Majesty's speeches are very wise and interesting; and your back chat amuses both you and him. But the ultimatum is here all the time; and I shall not leave this room until I have His Majesty's signed pledge that its conditions will be observed.

All become gravely attentive.

MAGNUS. What are its terms?

PROTEUS. First, no more royal speeches.

MAGNUS. What! Not even if you dictate them?

PROTEUS. Not even if we dictate them. Your Majesty has a way of unrolling the manuscript and winking—

MAGNUS. Winking!

PROTEUS. You know what I mean. The best speech in the world can be read in such a way as to set the audience laughing at it. We have had enough of that. So, in future, no speeches.

MAGNUS. A dumb king?

PROTEUS. Of course we cannot object to such

[78]

speeches as "We declare this foundation stone well and truly laid" and so forth. But politically, yes: a dumb king.

PLINY [*to soften it*] A constitutional king.

PROTEUS [*implacably*] A dumb king.

MAGNUS. Hm! What next?

PROTEUS. The working of the Press from the palace back stairs must cease.

MAGNUS. You know that I have no control of the Press. The Press is in the hands of men much richer than I, who would not insert a single paragraph against their own interests even if it were signed by my own hand and sent to them with a royal command.

PROTEUS. We know that. But though these men are richer than you, they are not cleverer. They get amusing articles, spiced with exclusive backstairs information, that dont seem to them to have anything to do with politics. The next thing they know is that their pet shares have dropped fifteen points; that capital is frightened off their best prospectuses; and that some of the best measures in our party program are made to look like city jobs.

MAGNUS. Am I supposed to write these articles?

NICOBAR. Your man Sempronius does. I can spot his fist out of fifty columns.

CRASSUS. So can I. When he is getting at me he always begins the sentence with "Singularly enough."

PLINY [*chuckling*] Thats his trademark. "Singularly enough." Ha! ha!

MAGNUS. Is there to be any restriction on the other side? I have noticed, for instance, that in a certain newspaper which loses no opportunity of disparaging the throne, the last sentence of the leading article almost invariably begins with the words "Once for all." Whose trademark is that?

[79]

PROTEUS. Mine.

MAGNUS. Frank, Mr Proteus.

PROTEUS. I know when to be frank. I learnt the trick from Your Majesty.

AMANDA [*tries not to laugh*]!

MAGNUS [*gently reproachful*] Amanda: what is the joke now? I am surprised at you.

AMANDA. Joe frank! When I want to find out what he is up to I have to come and ask Your Majesty.

LYSISTRATA. That is perfectly true. In this Cabinet there is no such thing as a policy. Every man plays for his own hand.

NICOBAR. It's like a game of cards.

BALBUS. Only there are no partners.

LYSISTRATA. Except Crassus and Nicobar.

PLINY. Good, Lizzie! He! he! he!

NICOBAR. What do you mean?

LYSISTRATA. You know quite well what I mean. When will you learn, Nicobar, that it is no use trying to browbeat me. I began life as a schoolmistress; and I can browbeat any man in this Cabinet or out of it if he is fool enough to try to compete with me in that department.

BOANERGES. Order! order! Cannot the Prime Minister check these unseemly personalities?

PROTEUS. They give me time to think, Bill. When you have had as much parliamentary experience as I have you will be very glad of an interruption occasionally. May I proceed?

Silence.

PROTEUS. His Majesty asks whether the restriction on press campaigning is to be entirely onesided. That, I take it, sir, is your question.

MAGNUS [*nods assent*]!

PROTEUS. The answer is in the affirmative.

BALBUS. Good!

MAGNUS. Anything more?

PROTEUS. Yes: one thing more. The veto must not be mentioned again. That can apply to both sides, if you like. The veto is dead.

MAGNUS. May we not make a historical reference to the corpse?

PROTEUS. No. I cannot carry on the King's government unless I can give pledges and carry them out. What is my pledge worth if our constituents are reminded every day that the King may veto anything that Parliament does? Do you expect me to say, when I am asked for a pledge, "You must ask the king"?

MAGNUS. I have to say "You must ask the Prime Minister."

PLINY [*consoling him*] Thats the constitution, you know.

MAGNUS. Quite. I only mention it to shew that the Prime Minister does not really wish to kill the veto. He only wishes to move it next door.

PROTEUS. The people live next door. The name on the brass plate is Public Opinion.

MAGNUS [*gravely*] Admirably turned, Mr Prime Minister; but unreal. I am far more subject to public opinion than you, because, thanks to the general belief in democracy, you can always pretend that what you do is done by the will of the people, who, God knows, never dreamt of it, and would not have understood it if they had; whereas, for what a king does, he, and he alone, is held responsible. A demagogue may steal a horse where a king dare not look over a hedge.

LYSISTRATA. I doubt if that is any longer true, sir. I know that I get blamed for everything that goes wrong in my department.

MAGNUS. Ah! But what a despot you are, Lysistrata!

Granted, however, that the people have found out long ago that democracy is humbug, and that instead of establishing responsible government it has abolished it, do you not see what this means?

BOANERGES [*scandalized*] Steady, steady! I cannot sit here and listen to such a word as humbug being applied to democracy. I am sorry, sir; but with all respect for you, I really must draw the line at that.

MAGNUS. You are right, Mr Boanerges, as you always are. Democracy is a very real thing, with much less humbug about it than many older institutions. But it means, not that the people govern, but that the responsibility and the veto now belong neither to kings nor demagogues as such, but to whoever is clever enough to get them.

LYSISTRATA. Yourself, sir, for example?

MAGNUS. I think I am in the running. That is why I do not feel bound to accept this ultimatum. By signing it I put myself out of the running. Why should I?

BALBUS. Because youre the king: thats why.

MAGNUS. Does it follow?

PROTEUS. If two men ride the same horse, one must ride behind.

LYSISTRATA. Which?

PROTEUS [*turning to her sharply*] What was that you said?

LYSISTRATA [*with placid but formidable obstinacy and ironical explicitness*] I said Which? You said that if two men rode the same horse one of them must ride behind. I said Which? [*Explanatorily*] Which man must ride behind?

AMANDA. Got it, Joe?

PROTEUS. That is exactly the question that has to be settled here and now.

AMANDA. "Once for all."

Everybody laughs except Proteus, who rises in a fury.

PROTEUS. I will not stand this perpetual tomfooling. I had rather be a dog than the Prime Minister of a country where the only things the inhabitants can be serious about are football and refreshments. Lick the King's boots: that is all you are fit for. [*He dashes out of the room*].

BALBUS. Youve done it now, Mandy. I hope youre proud of yourself.

MAGNUS. It is you, Amanda, who should go and coax him back. But I suppose I must do it myself, as usual. Excuse me, ladies and gentlemen.

He rises. The rest rise. He goes out.

BOANERGES. I told you. I told you what would come of conducting a conference with His Majesty as if it were a smoking concert. I am disgusted. [*He flings himself back into his chair*].

BALBUS. We'd just cornered the old fox; and then Amanda must have her silly laugh and lets him out of it [*he sits*].

NICOBAR. What are we to do now? thats what I want to know.

AMANDA [*incorrigible*] I suggest a little community singing [*she makes conductorlike gestures*].

NICOBAR. Yah!! [*he sits down very sulkily*].

AMANDA [*sits down with a little splutter of laughter*]!

CRASSUS [*thoughtful*] Take it easy, friends. Joe knows what he is about.

LYSISTRATA. Of course he does. I can excuse you, Bill, because it's your first day in the Cabinet. But if the rest of you havnt found out by this time that Joe's rages are invariably calculated, then nothing will ever teach you anything [*she sits down contemptuously*].

BOANERGES [*in his grandest manner*] Well, madam, I know I am a newcomer: everything must have a beginning. I am open to argument and conviction. The Prime Minister brought this conference, in what I admit was a very able and resolute manner, to the verge of a decision. Then, in a fit of childish temper he breaks up the conference, leaving us looking like fools with nothing done. And you tell me he did it on purpose! Where was the advantage to him in such a display? answer me that.

LYSISTRATA. He is settling the whole business with the King behind our backs. That is what Joe always contrives to do, by hook or crook.

PLINY. You didnt arrange it with him, Mandy: did you?

AMANDA. There wasnt any need to arrange it. Joe can always depend on one or other of us saying something that will give him an excuse for flying out.

CRASSUS. In my opinion, ladies and gentlemen, we have done our bit, and may leave the rest to Joe. Matters had reached a point at which it was yes or no between the Cabinet and the Crown. There is only one sort of committee that is better than a committee of two; and that is a committee of one. Like the family in Wordsworth's poem, we are seven—

LYSISTRATA. Eight.

CRASSUS. Well, seven or eight, we were too many for the final grapple. Two persons sticking to the point are worth eight all over the shop. So my advice is that we just sit here quietly until Joe comes back and tells us whats been settled. Perhaps Amanda will oblige with a song. [*He resumes his seat*].

The King returns with Proteus, who looks glum. All rise. The two resume their seats in silence. The rest sit down.

MAGNUS [*very grave*] The Prime Minister has been good enough to pursue the discussion with me in private to a point at which the issue is now clear. If I do not accept the ultimatum I shall receive your resignations and his; and the country will learn from his explanatory speech in the House of Commons that it is to choose between Cabinet government and monarchical government: an issue on which I frankly say that I should be very sorry to win, as I cannot carry on without the support of a body of ministers whose existence gives the English people a sensation of self-government.

AMANDA [*splutters*]!

CRASSUS [*whispers*] Shut up, will you?

MAGNUS [*continuing*] Naturally I want to avert a conflict in which success would damage me and failure disable me. But you tell me that I can do so only by signing pledges which would make me a mere Lord Chamberlain, without even the despotism which he exercises over the theatre. I should sink below the level of the meanest of my subjects, my sole privilege being that of being shot at when some victim of misgovernment resorts to assassination to avenge himself. How am I to defend myself? You are many: I oppose you single-handed. There was a time when the king could depend on the support of the aristocracy and the cultivated bourgeoisie. Today there is not a single aristocrat left in politics, not a single member of the professions, not a single leading personage in big business or finance. They are richer than ever, more powerful than ever, more able and better educated than ever. But not one of them will touch this drudgery of government, this public work that never ends because we cannot finish one job without creating ten fresh ones. We get no thanks for it because ninety-nine hundredths of it is unknown to the people, and the remaining hundredth is resented by them as an invasion of their liberty or an increase in their taxation. It wears out the strongest man, and even the strongest woman, in five or six years. It slows down to nothing when we are fresh from our holidays and best able to bear it, and rises in an overwhelming wave through some unforeseen catastrophe when we are on the verge of nervous breakdown from overwork and fit for rest and sleep only. And this drudgery, remember, is a sweated trade, the only one now left in this country. My civil list leaves me a poor man among multi-millionaires. Your salaries can be earned ten times over in the city by anyone with outstanding organizing or administrative ability. History tells us that the first Lord Chancellor who abandoned the woolsack for the city boardroom struck the nation with amazement: today the nation would be equally amazed if a man of his ability thought it worth his while to prefer the woolsack even to the stool of an office boy as a jumping-off place for his ambition. Our work is no longer even respected. It is looked down on by our men of genius as dirty work. What great actor would exchange his stage? what great barrister his court? what great preacher his pulpit? for the squalor of the political arena in which we have to struggle with foolish factions in parliament and with ignorant voters in the constituencies? The scientists will have nothing to do with us; for the atmosphere of politics is not the atmosphere of science. Even political science, the science by which civilization must live or die, is busy explaining the past whilst we have to grapple with the present: it leaves the ground before our feet in black darkness whilst it lights up every corner of the landscape behind us. All the talent and genius of the country is bought up by the flood of unearned money.

On that poisoned wealth talent and genius live far more luxuriously in the service of the rich than we in the service of our country. Politics, once the centre of attraction for ability, public spirit, and ambition, has now become the refuge of a few fanciers of public speaking and party intrigue who find all the other avenues to distinction closed to them either by their lack of practical ability, their comparative poverty and lack of education, or, let me hasten to add, their hatred of oppression and injustice, and their contempt for the chicaneries and false pretences of commercialized professionalism. History tells us of a gentleman-statesman who declared that such people were not fit to govern. Within a year it was discovered that they could govern at least as well as anyone else who could be persuaded to take on the job. Then began that abandonment of politics by the old governing class which has ended in all Cabinets, conservative no less than progressive, being what were called in the days of that rash statesman Labor Cabinets. Do not misunderstand me: I do not want the old governing class back. It governed so selfishly that the people would have perished if democracy had not swept it out of politics. But evil as it was in many ways, at least it stood above the tyranny of popular ignorance and popular poverty. Today only the king stands above that tyranny. You are dangerously subject to it. In spite of my urgings and remonstrances you have not yet dared to take command of our schools and put a stop to the inculcation upon your unfortunate children of superstitions and prejudices that stand like stone walls across every forward path. Are you well advised in trying to reduce me to your own slavery to them ? If I do not stand above them there is no longer any reason for my existence at all. I stand for the future and the past, for the posterity that has no vote and the tradition that never had any. I stand for the great abstractions: for conscience and virtue; for the eternal against the expedient; for the evolutionary appetite against the day's gluttony; for intellectual integrity, for humanity, for the rescue of industry from commercialism and of science from professionalism, for everything that you desire as sincerely as I, but which in you is held in leash by the Press, which can organize against you the ignorance and superstition, the timidity and credulity, the gullibility and prudery, the hating and hunting instinct of the voting mob, and cast you down from power if you utter a word to alarm or displease the adventurers who have the Press in their pockets. Between you and that tyranny stands the throne. I have no elections to fear; and if any newspaper magnate dares offend me, that magnate's fashionable wife and marriageable daughters will soon make him understand that the King's displeasure is still a sentence of social death within range of St James's Palace. Think of the things you dare not do! the persons you dare not offend! Well, a king with a little courage may tackle them for you. Responsibilities which would break your backs may still be borne on a king's shoulders. But he must be a king, not a puppet. You would be responsible for a puppet: remember that. But whilst you continue to support me as a separate and independent estate of the realm, I am your scapegoat: you get the credit of all our popular legislation whilst you put the odium of all our resistance to ignorant popular clamor on me. I ask you, before you play your last card and destroy me, to consider where you will be without me. Think once: think twice: for your danger is, not that I may defeat you, but that your success is certain if you insist.

LYSISTRATA. Splendid!

AMANDA. You did speak that piece beautifully, sir.

BALBUS [*grumbling*] All very well; but what about my brother-in-law Mike?

LYSISTRATA [*maddened*] Oh, confound your brother-in-law Mike!

BOANERGES. Order! order!

LYSISTRATA [*to the King*] I beg your pardon, sir; but really—at a moment like this—[*words fail her*].

MAGNUS [*to Balbus*] If I had not put my foot down, Mr Balbus, the Prime Minister would have been unable to keep your brother-in-law out of the Cabinet.

BALBUS [*aggressively*] And why should he not be in the Cabinet?

AMANDA. Booze, my Balby: booze. Raising the elbow!

BALBUS [*bullying*] Who says so?

AMANDA. I do, darling.

BALBUS [*subsiding*] Well, perhaps it would surprise you all to know that Mike doesnt drink as much as I do.

AMANDA. You carry it better, Bert.

PLINY. Mike never knows when to stop.

CRASSUS. The time for Mike to stop is before he begins, if you ask me.

LYSISTRATA [*impetuously*] What sort of animals are you—you men? The King puts before us the most serious question of principle we shall ever have to deal with; and off you start discussing whether this drunken wretch takes honest whisky like Balbus or methylated spirit or petrol or whatever he can lay his hands on when the fit takes him.

BALBUS. I agree with that. What does it matter what Mike drinks? What does it matter whether he drinks or not? Mike would strengthen the Cabinet because he represents Breakages, Limited, the biggest industrial corporation in the country.

LYSISTRATA [*letting herself go*] Just so! Breakages, Limited! just so! Listen to me, sir; and judge whether I have not reason to feel everything you have just said to the very marrow of my bones. Here am I, the Powermistress Royal. I have to organize and administer all the motor power in the country for the good of the country. I have to harness the winds and the tides, the oils and the coal seams. I have to see that every little sewing machine in the Hebrides, every dentist's drill in Shetland, every carpet sweeper in Margate, has its stream of driving power on tap from a switch in the wall as punctually as the great thundering dynamos of our big industrial plants. I do it; but it costs twice as much as it should. Why? Because every new invention is bought up and suppressed by Breakages, Limited. Every breakdown, every accident, every smash and crash, is a job for them. But for them we should have unbreakable glass, unbreakable steel, imperishable materials of all sorts. But for them our goods trains could be started and stopped without battering and tearing the vitals out of every wagon and sending it to their repair shops once a week instead of once a year. Our national repair bill runs up to hundreds of millions. I could name you a dozen inventions within my own term of office which would have effected enormous economies in breakages and breakdowns; but these people can afford to pay an inventor more for his machine or his process or whatever it may be than he could hope to make by a legitimate use of it; and when they have bought it they smother it. When the inventor is poor and not good at defending himself they make bogus trials of his machine and report that it is no use. I have been shot at twice by inventors driven crazy by this sort of thing: they blamed me for it—as if I could stand up against this monster with its millions and its newspapers and its fingers in every pie. It is heartbreaking. I love my department: I dream of nothing but its efficiency: with me it comes before every personal tie, every happiness that common women run after. I would give my right hand to see these people in the bankruptcy court with half their business abolished and the other half done in public workshops where public losses are not private gains. You stand for that, sir; and I would be with you to the last drop of my blood if I dared. But what can I do? If I said one word of this in public, not a week would pass in the next two years without an article on the inefficiency and corruption of all Government departments, especially departments managed, like mine, by females. They would dig up the very machines they have buried, and make out that it is my fault that they have never been brought into use. They would set their private police to watch me day and night to get something against my private character. One of their directors told me to my face that by lifting up his finger he could get my windows broken by the mob; and that Breakages, Limited, would get the job of putting in new glass. And it is true. It is infamous; it is outrageous; but if I attempt to fight them I shall be hounded out of public life, and they will shove Mouldy Mike into the Cabinet to run my department in their interests: that is, to make such a failure of it that Joe will have to sell it to Breakages, Limited, at scrap iron prices. I—I—oh, it is beyond bearing [*she breaks down*].

There is a troubled silence for a moment. Then the

*voice of the Prime Minister breaks it impressively as he
addresses the King.*

PROTEUS. You hear that, sir. Your one supporter in
the Cabinet admits that the industrial situation is too
strong for her. I do not pretend to be able to control
the women in my Cabinet; but not one of them dare
support you.

AMANDA [*springing up*] Whats that? Not dare! What
do you bet that I dont go down to Mouldy Mike's
constituency and say everything that Lizzie has said
and a lot more too, if I choose? I tell you, Breakages,
Limited, never interferes in my department. I'd like
to catch them at it.

MAGNUS. I am afraid that that is only because the
efficiency of the Post Office is as important to them as
to the general public.

AMANDA. Stuff! They could get rid of me without
shutting up the Post Office. Theyre afraid of me—of
me, Amanda Postlethwaite.

MAGNUS. You coax them, I am afraid.

AMANDA. Coax! What do you think they care for
coaxing? They can have all the coaxing they want
from younger and prettier women than I by paying
for it. No use trying to coax that lot. Intimidate them:
thats the way to handle them.

LYSISTRATA [*her voice still broken*] I wish I could
intimidate them.

MAGNUS. But what can Amanda do that you cannot do?

AMANDA. I'll tell you. She cant mimic people. And she
cant sing funny songs. I can do both; and that—with all
respect, sir—makes me the real queen of England.

BOANERGES. Oh, come! Disgraceful! Shame!

AMANDA. If you provoke me, Bill, I'll drive you out
of your constituency inside of two months.

BOANERGES. Ho! You will, will you? How?

AMANDA. Just as I drove the Chairman of Breakages out of my own constituency when he came down there and tried to take my seat from me.

MAGNUS. I never quite understood why he turned tail. How did you do it?

AMANDA. I'll tell you. He opened his campaign with a great Saturday night speech against me in the Home Lovers' Hall to five thousand people. In that same hall a week later, I faced a meeting of the very same people. I didnt argue. I mimicked him. I took all the high-falutin passages in his speech, and repeated them in his best manner until I had the whole five thousand laughing at him. Then I asked them would they like me to sing; and their Yes nearly lifted the roof off. I had two songs. They both had choruses. One went "She lets me go out on Saturday night, on Saturday night, on Saturday night"—like that. The other went "Boo! Hoo! I want Amanda's Teddy bear to play with." They sang it under the windows of his hotel next time he came. He cancelled his meeting and left. And thats how England is governed by yours truly, sir. Lucky for England that Queen Amanda is a good sort, in spite of some surface faults. [*She resumes her seat with triumphant self-satisfaction*].

BALBUS. Lucky for England theres only one of you: thats what *I* say.

AMANDA [*wafts him a kiss*]!

MAGNUS. Should not the Queen support the King, your Majesty?

AMANDA. Sorry, sir; but there isnt room for two monarchs in my realm. I am against you on principle because the talent for mimicry isnt hereditary.

PROTEUS. Now, anybody else? We have heard why the two ladies cannot support the King. Is there anybody who can?

Silence.

MAGNUS. I see that my appeal has been in vain. I do not reproach you, ladies and gentlemen, because I perceive that your situation is a difficult one. The question is, how to change it.

NICOBAR. Sign the ultimatum: that is how.

MAGNUS. I am not quite convinced of that. The Home Secretary's brother-in-law was quite willing to sign the pledge of total abstinence if I would admit him to the Cabinet. His offer was not accepted, because, though none of us doubted that he would sign the pledge, we were not equally certain that the infirmities of his nature would allow him to keep it. My nature is also subject to infirmity. Are you satisfied, Mr Proteus, that if I sign this ultimatum, I shall not inevitably relapse into the conduct that my nature dictates?

PROTEUS [*his patience strained*] What is the use of going on like this? You are a man on the scaffold, spinning out his prayers to put off the inevitable execution as long as possible. Nothing that you can say will make any difference. You know you must sign. Why not sign and have done with it?

NICOBAR. Now youre talking, Joe.

BALBUS. Thats the stuff to give him.

PLINY. Gulp it down, sir. It wont get any sweeter by keeping: what?

LYSISTRATA. Oh, for God's sake, sign, sir. This is torture to me.

MAGNUS. I perceive, gentlemen, that I have come to the end of your patience. I will tax it no further: you have been very forbearing; and I thank you for it. I will say no more by way of discussion; but I must have until five o'clock this evening to consider my decision. At that hour, if I can find no other way out, I will sign

[94]

without another word. Meanwhile, ladies and gentlemen, au revoir!

He rises. All rise. He marches out.

PROTEUS. His last wriggle. Never mind: we have him safe enough. What about lunch? I am starving. Will you lunch with me, Lizzie.

LYSISTRATA. Dont speak to me. [*She rushes out distractedly*].

AMANDA. Poor darling Lizzie! She's a regular old true blue Diehard. If only I had her brains and education! or if she had my variety talent! what a queen she'd make! Like old Queen Elizabeth, eh? Dont grieve, Joe: I'll lunch with you since youre so pressing.

CRASSUS. Come and lunch with me—all of you.

AMANDA. What opulence! Can you afford it?

CRASSUS. Breakages will pay. They have a standing account at the Ritz. Over five thousand a year, it comes to.

PROTEUS. Right. Let us spoil the Egyptians.

BOANERGES [*with Roman dignity*] My lunch will cost me one and sixpence; and I shall pay for it myself [*he stalks out*].

AMANDA [*calling after him*] Dont make a beast of yourself, Bill. Ta ta!

PROTEUS. Come on, come on: it's ever so late.

They all hurry out. Sempronius and Pamphilius, entering, have to stand aside to let them pass before returning to their desks. Proteus, with Amanda on his arm, stops in the doorway on seeing them.

PROTEUS. Have you two been listening, may I ask?

PAMPHILIUS. Well, it would be rather inconvenient wouldnt it, if we had to be told everything that passed?

SEMPRONIUS. Once for all, Mr Proteus, the King's

private secretaries must hear everything, see everything, and know everything.

PROTEUS. Singularly enough, Mr Sempronius, I havnt the slightest objection [*he goes*].

AMANDA [*going with him*] Goodbye, Semmy. So long, Pam.

SEMPRONIUS.
PAMPHILIUS. } [*seating themselves at their writing tables and yawning prodigiously*] Ou-ou-ou-ou-ou-fff!!!

Orinthia's boudoir at half-past fifteen on the same day.
She is at her writing-table scribbling notes. She is
romantically beautiful, and beautifully dressed. As the
table is against the wall near a corner, with the other
wall on her left, her back alone is visible from the
middle of the room. The door is near the corner dia-
gonally opposite. There is a large settee in the middle of
the room.

The King enters and waits on the threshold.

ORINTHIA [*crossly, without looking round*] Who is
that?

MAGNUS. His Majesty the King.

ORINTHIA. I dont want to see him.

MAGNUS. How soon will you be disengaged?

ORINTHIA. I didnt say I was engaged. Tell the king
I dont want to see him.

MAGNUS. He awaits your pleasure [*he comes in and
seats himself on the settee*].

ORINTHIA. Go away. [*A pause*]. I wont speak to you.
[*Another pause*]. If my private rooms are to be broken
into at any moment because they are in the palace, and
the king is not a gentleman, I must take a house outside. I am writing to the agents about one now.

MAGNUS. What is our quarrel today, belovéd?

ORINTHIA. Ask your conscience.

MAGNUS. I have none when you are concerned. You
must tell me.

She takes a book from the table and rises; then sweeps
superbly forward to the settee and flings the book into
his hands.

ORINTHIA. There!

MAGNUS. What is this?

ORINTHIA. Page 16. Look at it.

MAGNUS [*looking at the title on the back of the book*] "Songs of our Great Great Grandparents." What page did you say?

ORINTHIA [*between her teeth*] Six-teen.

MAGNUS [*opening the book and finding the page, his eye lighting up with recognition as he looks at it*] Ah! The Pilgrim of Love!

ORINTHIA. Read the first three words—if you dare.

MAGNUS [*smiling as he caresses the phrase*] "Orinthia, my belovéd".

ORINTHIA. The name you pretended to invent specially for me, the only woman in the world for you. Picked up out of the rubbish basket in a secondhand bookseller's! And I thought you were a poet!

MAGNUS. Well, one poet may consecrate a name for another. Orinthia is a name full of magic for me. It could not be that if I had invented it myself. I heard it at a concert of ancient music when I was a child; and I have treasured it ever since.

ORINTHIA. You always have a pretty excuse. You are the King of liars and humbugs. You cannot understand how a falsehood like that wounds me.

MAGNUS [*remorsefully, stretching out his arms towards her*] Belovéd: I am sorry.

ORINTHIA. Put your hands in your pockets: they shall not touch me ever again.

MAGNUS [*obeying*] Dont pretend to be hurt unless you really are, dearest. It wrings my heart.

ORINTHIA. Since when have you set up a heart? Did you buy that, too, secondhand?

MAGNUS. I have something in me that winces when you are hurt—or pretend to be.

[98]

ORINTHIA [*contemptuously*] Yes: I have only to squeal, and you will take me up and pet me as you would a puppy run over by a car. [*Sitting down beside him, but beyond arm's length*] That is what you give me when my heart demands love. I had rather you kicked me.

MAGNUS. I should like to kick you sometimes, when you are specially aggravating. But I shouldnt do it well. I should be afraid of hurting you all the time.

ORINTHIA. I believe you would sign my death warrant without turning a hair.

MAGNUS. That is true, in a way. It is wonderful how subtle your mind is, as far as it goes.

ORINTHIA. It does not go as far as yours, I suppose.

MAGNUS. I dont know. Our minds go together half way. Whether it is that your mind stops there or else that the road forks, and you take the high road and I take the low road, I cannot say; but somehow after a certain point we lose one another.

ORINTHIA. And then you go back to your Amandas and Lysistratas: creatures whose idea of romance is a minister in love with a department, and whose bedside books are blue books.

MAGNUS. They are not always thinking of some man or other. That is a rather desirable extension of their interests, in my opinion. If Lysistrata had a lover I should not be interested in him in the least; and she would bore me to distraction if she could talk of nothing else. But I am very much interested in her department. Her devotion to it gives us a topic of endless interest.

ORINTHIA. Well, go to her: I am not detaining you. But dont tell her that I have nothing to talk about but men; for that is a lie; and you know it.

MAGNUS. It is, as you say, a lie; and I know it. But I did not say it.

ORINTHIA. You implied it. You meant it. When those ridiculous political women are with us you talk to them all the time, and never say a word to me.

MAGNUS. Nor you to me. We cannot talk to one another in public: we have nothing to say that could be said before other people. Yet we find enough to say to one another when we are alone together. Would you change that if you could?

ORINTHIA. You are as slippery as an eel; but you shall not slip through my fingers. Why do you surround yourself with political bores and frumps and dowdy busybodies who cant talk: they can only debate about their dull departments and their fads and their election chances. [Rising impatiently] Who could talk to such people? If it were not for the nonentities of wives and husbands they drag about with them, there would be nobody to talk to at all. And even they can talk of nothing but the servants and the baby. [Suddenly returning to her seat] Listen to me, Magnus. Why can you not be a real king?

MAGNUS. In what way, belovédest?

ORINTHIA. Send all these stupid people packing. Make them do their drudgeries in their departments without bothering you about it, as you make your servants here sweep the floors and dust the furniture. Live a really noble and beautiful life—a kingly life—with me. What you need to make you a real king is a real queen.

MAGNUS. But I have got one.

ORINTHIA. Oh, you are blind. You are worse than blind: you have low tastes. Heaven is offering you a rose; and you cling to a cabbage.

MAGNUS [laughing] That is a very apt metaphor, belovéd. But what wise man, if you force him to choose between doing without roses and doing without cabbages, would not secure the cabbages? Besides, all these old married cabbages were once roses; and, though young things like you dont remember that, their husbands do. They dont notice the change. Besides, you should know better than anyone else that when a man gets tired of his wife and leaves her it is never because she has lost her good looks. The new love is often older and uglier than the old.

ORINTHIA. Why should I know it better than anyone else?

MAGNUS. Why, because you have been married twice; and both your husbands have run away from you to much plainer and stupider women. When I begged your present husband to come back to court for a while for the sake of appearances he said no man could call his soul his own in the same house with you. And yet that man was utterly infatuated with your beauty when he married you. Your first husband actually forced a good wife to divorce him so that he might marry you; but before two years were out he went back to her and died in her arms, poor chap.

ORINTHIA. Shall I tell you why these men could not live with me? It was because I am a thoroughbred, and they are only hacks. They had nothing against me: I was perfectly faithful to them. I kept their houses beautifully: I fed them better than they had ever been fed in their lives. But because I was higher than they were, and greater, they could not stand the strain of trying to live up to me. So I let them go their way, poor wretches, back to their cabbages. Look at the old creature Ignatius is living with now! She gives you his real measure.

MAGNUS. An excellent woman. Ignatius is quite happy with her. I never saw a man so changed.

ORINTHIA. Just what he is fit for. Commonplace.
Bourgeoise. She trots through the streets shopping.
[*Rising*] *I* tread the plains of Heaven. Common women cannot come where I am; and common men find
themselves out and slink away.

MAGNUS. It must be magnificent to have the con-
sciousness of a goddess without ever doing a thing to
justify it.

ORINTHIA. Give me a goddess's work to do; and I
will do it. I will even stoop to a queen's work if you
will share the throne with me. But do not pretend that
people become great by doing great things. They do
great things because they are great, if the great things
come along. But they are great just the same when the
great things do not come along. If I never did anything but sit in this room and powder my face and tell
you what a clever fool you are, I should still be heavens high above the millions of common women who
do their domestic duty, and sacrifice themselves, and
run Trade departments and all the rest of the vul-
garities. Has all the tedious public work you have done
made you any the better? I have seen you before and
after your boasted strokes of policy; and you were the
same man, and would have been the same man to me
and to yourself if you had never done them. Thank
God my self-consciousness is something nobler than
vulgar conceit in having done something. It is what I
am, not what I do, that you must worship in me. If
you want deeds, go to your men and women of action,
as you call them, who are all in a conspiracy to pretend that the mechanical things they do, the fool-
hardy way they risk their worthless lives, or their
getting up in the morning at four and working
sixteen hours a day for thirty years, like coral insects,
make them great. What are they for? these dull

slaves? To keep the streets swept for me. To enable
me to reign over them in beauty like the stars without
having anything to do with their slavery except to
console it, to dazzle it, to enable them to forget it in
adoring dreams of me. Am I not worth it? [*She sits,
fascinating him*]. Look into my eyes and tell the truth.
Am I worth it or not?

MAGNUS. To me, who love beauty, yes. But you
should hear the speeches Balbus makes about your
pension.

ORINTHIA. And my debts: do not forget my debts,
my mortgages, the bill of sale on my furniture, the
thousands I have had from the moneylenders to save
me from being sold up because I will not borrow from
my friends. Lecture me again about them; but do not
dare pretend that the people grudge me my pension.
They glory in it, and in my extravagance, as you call it.

MAGNUS [*more gravely*] By the way, Orinthia, when
your dressmakers took up that last bill for you, they
were speculating, were they not, in your chances of
becoming my queen some day?

ORINTHIA. Well, what if they were?

MAGNUS. They would hardly have ventured on that
without a hint from somebody. Was it from you?

ORINTHIA. You think me capable of that! You have a
very low side to you, Magnus.

MAGNUS. No doubt: like other mortal fabrics I have
a wrong side and a right side. But it is no use your
giving yourself airs, belovédest. You are capable of
anything. Do you deny that there was some suggestion of the kind?

ORINTHIA. How dare you challenge me to deny it? I
never deny. Of course there was a suggestion of the
kind.

MAGNUS. I thought so.

ORINTHIA. Oh, stupid! stupid! Go keep a grocer's shop: that is what you are fit for. Do you suppose that the suggestion came from me? Why, you great oaf, it is in the air: when my dressmaker hinted at it I told her that if she ever dared to repeat such a thing she should never get another order from me. But can I help people seeing what is as plain as the sun in the heavens? [*Rising again*] Everyone knows that I am the real queen. Everyone treats me as the real queen. They cheer me in the streets. When I open one of the art exhibitions or launch a new ship they crowd the place out. I am one of Nature's queens; and they know it. If you do not, you are not one of Nature's kings.

MAGNUS. Sublime! Nothing but genuine inspiration could give a woman such cheek.

ORINTHIA. Yes: inspiration, not cheek. [*Sitting as before*] Magnus: when are you going to face my destiny, and your own?

MAGNUS. But my wife? the queen? What is to become of my poor dear Jemima?

ORINTHIA. Oh, drown her: shoot her: tell your chauffeur to drive her into the Serpentine and leave her there. The woman makes you ridiculous.

MAGNUS. I dont think I should like that. And the public would think it illnatured.

ORINTHIA. Oh, you know what I mean. Divorce her. Make her divorce you. It is quite easy. That was how Ronny married me. Everybody does it when they need a change.

MAGNUS. But I cant imagine what I should do without Jemima.

ORINTHIA. Nobody else can imagine what you do with her. But you need not do without her. You can see as much of her as you like when we are married. I shall not be jealous and make scenes.

MAGNUS. That is very magnanimous of you. But I am afraid it does not settle the difficulty. Jemima would not think it right to keep up her present intimacy with me if I were married to you.

ORINTHIA. What a woman! Would she be in any worse position then than I am in now?

MAGNUS. No.

ORINTHIA. You mean, then, that you do not mind placing me in a position that you do not think good enough for her?

MAGNUS. Orinthia: I did not place you in your present position. You placed yourself in it. I could not resist you. You gathered me like a daisy.

ORINTHIA. Did you want to resist me?

MAGNUS. Oh no. I never resist temptation, because I have found that things that are bad for me do not tempt me.

ORINTHIA. Well, then, what are we talking about?

MAGNUS. I forget. I think I was explaining the impossibility of my wife changing places with you.

ORINTHIA. Why impossible, pray?

MAGNUS. I cannot make you understand: you see you have never been really married, though you have led two captives to the altar, and borne children to one of them. Being your husband is only a job for which one man will do as well as another, and which the last man holds subject to six months notice in the divorce court. Being my wife is something quite different. The smallest derogation to Jemima's dignity would hit me like the lash of a whip across the face. About yours, somehow, I do not care a rap.

ORINTHIA. Nothing can derogate from my dignity: it is divine. Hers is only a convention: that is why you tremble when it is challenged.

MAGNUS. Not a bit. It is because she is a part of my real workaday self. You belong to fairyland.

ORINTHIA. Suppose she dies! Will you die too?

MAGNUS. Not immediately. I shall have to carry on as best I can without her, though the prospect terrifies me.

ORINTHIA. Might not carrying on without her include marrying me?

MAGNUS. My dear Orinthia, I had rather marry the devil. Being a wife is not your job.

ORINTHIA. You think so because you have no imagination. And you dont know me because I have never let you really possess me. I should make you more happy than any man has ever yet been on earth.

MAGNUS. I defy you to make me more happy than our strangely innocent relations have already made me.

ORINTHIA [*rising restlessly*] You talk like a child or a saint. [*Turning on him*] I can give you a new life: one of which you have no conception. I can give you beautiful, wonderful children: have you ever seen a lovelier boy than my Basil?

MAGNUS. Your children are beautiful; but they are fairy children; and I have several very real ones already. A divorce would not sweep them out of the way of the fairies.

ORINTHIA. In short, when your golden moment comes—when the gates of heaven open before you, you are afraid to come out of your pigsty.

MAGNUS. If I am a pig, a pigsty is the proper place for me.

ORINTHIA. I cannot understand it. All men are fools and moral cowards when you come to know them. But you are less of a fool and less of a moral coward than any man I have ever known. You have almost the

makings of a first rate woman in you. When I leave
the earth and soar up to the regions which are my
real eternal home, you can follow me: I can speak to
you as I can speak to no one else; and you can say
things to me that would just make your stupid wife
cry. There is more of you in me than of any other man
within my reach. There is more of me in you than of
any other woman within your reach. We are meant
for oneanother: it is written across the sky that you
and I are queen and king. How can you hesitate?
What attraction is there for you in your common
healthy jolly lumps of children and your common
housekeeper wife and the rabble of dowdies and
upstarts and intriguers and clowns that think they are
governing the country when they are only squabbling
with you? Look again at me, man: again and again.
Am I not worth a million such? Is not life with me as
high above them as the sun is above the gutter?

MAGNUS. Yes yes yes yes, of course. You are lovely:
you are divine [*she cannot restrain a gesture of triumph*].
And you are enormously amusing.

*This anti-climax is too much for Orinthia's exaltation;
but she is too clever not to appreciate it. With another
gesture, this time of deflation, she sits down at his left
hand with an air of suffering patience, and listens in
silence to the harangue which follows.*

MAGNUS. Some day perhaps Nature will graft the
roses on the cabbages and make every woman as
enchanting as you; and then what a glorious lark life
will be! But at present, what I come here for is to
enjoy talking to you like this when I need an hour's
respite from royalty: when my stupid wife has been
worrying me, or my jolly lumps of children bothering
me, or my turbulent Cabinet obstructing me: when,
as the doctors say, what I need is a change. You see,

my dear, there is no wife on earth so precious, no children so jolly, no Cabinet so tactful that it is impossible ever to get tired of them. Jemima has her limitations, as you have observed. And I have mine. Now if our limitations exactly corresponded I should never want to talk to anyone else; and neither would she. But as that never happens, we are like all other married couples: that is, there are subjects which can never be discussed between us because they are sore subjects. There are people we avoid mentioning to oneanother because one of us likes them and the other doesnt. Not only individuals, but whole sorts of people. For instance, your sort. My wife doesnt like your sort, doesnt understand it, mistrusts and dreads it. Not without reason; for women like you are dangerous to wives. But I dont dislike your sort: I understand it, being a little in that line myself. At all events I am not afraid of it; though the least allusion to it brings a cloud over my wife's face. So when I want to talk freely about it I come and talk to you. And I take it she talks to friends of hers about people of whom she never talks to me. She has men friends from whom she can get some things that she cannot get from me. If she didnt do so she would be limited by my limitations, which would end in her hating me. So I always do my best to make her men friends feel at home with us.

ORINTHIA. A model husband in a model household! And when the model household becomes a bore, I am the diversion.

MAGNUS. Well, what more can you ask? Do not let us fall into the common mistake of expecting to become one flesh and one spirit. Every star has its own orbit; and between it and its nearest neighbor there is not only a powerful attraction but an infinite distance. When the attraction becomes stronger than the distance the two do not embrace: they crash together in ruin. We two also have our orbits, and must keep an infinite distance between us to avoid a disastrous collision. Keeping our distance is the whole secret of good manners; and without good manners human society is intolerable and impossible.

ORINTHIA. Would any other woman stand your sermons, and even like them?

MAGNUS. Orinthia: we are only two children at play; and you must be content to be my queen in fairyland. And [*rising*] I must go back to my work.

ORINTHIA. What work have you that is more important than being with me?

MAGNUS. None.

ORINTHIA. Then sit down.

MAGNUS. Unfortunately, this silly business of government must be carried on. And there is a crisis this evening, as usual.

ORINTHIA. But the crisis is not until five: I heard all about it from Sempronius. Why do you encourage that greedy schemer Proteus? He humbugs you. He humbugs everybody. He even humbugs himself; and of course he humbugs that Cabinet which is a disgrace to you: it is like an overcrowded third class carriage. Why do you allow such riffraff to waste your time? After all, what are you paid for? To be a king: that is, to wipe your boots on common people.

MAGNUS. Yes: but this king business, as the Americans call it, has got itself so mixed up with democracy that half the country expects me to wipe my perfectly polished boots on the Cabinet, and the other half expects me to let the Cabinet wipe its muddy boots on me. The Crisis at five o'clock is to decide which of us is to be the doormat.

ORINTHIA. And you will condescend to fight with Proteus for power?

MAGNUS. Oh no: I never fight. But I sometimes win.

ORINTHIA. If you let yourself be beaten by that trickster and poseur, never dare to approach me again.

MAGNUS. Proteus is a clever fellow: even on occasion a fine fellow. It would give me no satisfaction to beat him: I hate beating people. But there would be some innocent fun in outwitting him.

ORINTHIA. Magnus: you are a mollycoddle. If you were a real man you would just delight in beating him to a jelly.

MAGNUS. A real man would never do as a king. I am only an idol, my love; and all I can do is to draw the line at being a cruel idol. [*He looks at his watch*] Now I must really be off. Au revoir.

ORINTHIA [*looking at her wrist watch*] But it is only twenty-five minutes past four. You have heaps of time before five.

MAGNUS. Yes; but tea is at half-past four.

ORINTHIA [*catching him by the arm with a snakelike dart*] Never mind your tea. I will give you your tea.

MAGNUS. Impossible, belovéd. Jemima does not like to be kept waiting.

ORINTHIA. Oh, bother Jemima! You shall not leave me to go to Jemima [*she pulls him back so vigorously that he falls into the seat beside her*].

MAGNUS. My dear, I must.

ORINTHIA. No, not today. Listen, Magnus. I have something very particular to say to you.

MAGNUS. You have not. You are only trying to make me late to annoy my wife. [*He tries to rise, but is pulled back*]. Let me go, please.

ORINTHIA [*holding on*] Why are you so afraid of your

wife? You are the laughing stock of London, you poor henpecked darling.

MAGNUS. Henpecked! What do you call this? At least my wife does not restrain me by bodily violence.

ORINTHIA. I will not be deserted for your old Dutch.

MAGNUS. Listen, Orinthia. Dont be absurd. You know I must go. Do be good.

ORINTHIA. Only ten minutes more.

MAGNUS. It is half-past already.

He tries to rise; but she holds him back.

MAGNUS [*pausing for breath*] You are doing this out of sheer devilment. You are so abominably strong that I cannot break loose without hurting you. Must I call the guard?

ORINTHIA. Do, do. It will be in all the papers to-morrow.

MAGNUS. Fiend. [*Summoning all his dignity*] Orinthia: I command you.

ORINTHIA [*laughs wildly*]!!!

MAGNUS [*furious*] Very well, then, you she-devil: you shall let go.

He tackles her in earnest. She flings her arms round him and holds on with mischievous enjoyment. There is a tapping at the door; but they do not hear it. As he is breaking loose she suddenly shifts her grip to his waist and drags him on to the floor, where they roll over one another. Sempronius enters. He stares at the scandalous scene for a moment; then hastily slips out; shuts the door; clears his throat and blows his nose noisily; and knocks loudly and repeatedly. The two combatants cease hostilities and scramble hastily to their feet.

MAGNUS. Come in.

SEMPRONIUS [*entering*] Her Majesty sent me to remind you that tea is waiting, sir.

MAGNUS. Thank you. [*He goes quickly out*].

ORINTHIA [*panting but greatly pleased with herself*]
The King forgets everything when he is here. So do
I, I am afraid. I am so sorry.

SEMPRONIUS [*stiffly*] No explanations are needed. I
saw what happened. [*He goes out*].

ORINTHIA. The beast! He must have looked through
the keyhole. [*She throws her hand up with a gesture of
laughing defiance, and dances back to her seat at the
writing-table*].

[ACT II]

Later in the afternoon. The Terrace of the Palace. A low balustrade separates it from the lawn. Terrace chairs in abundance, ranged along the balustrade. Some dining room chairs also, not ranged, but standing about as if they had just been occupied. The terrace is accessible from the lawn by a central flight of steps.

The King and Queen are sitting apart near the corners of the steps, the Queen to the King's right. He is reading the evening paper: she is knitting. She has a little work table on her right, with a small gong on it.

THE QUEEN. Why did you tell them to leave the chairs when they took away the tea?

MAGNUS. I shall receive the Cabinet here.

THE QUEEN. Here! Why?

MAGNUS. Well, I think the open air and the evening light will have a quieting effect on them. They cannot make speeches at me so easily as in a room.

THE QUEEN. Are you sure? When Robert asked Boanerges where he learnt to speak so beautifully, he said "In Hyde Park."

MAGNUS. Yes; but with a crowd to stimulate him.

THE QUEEN. Robert says you have tamed Boanerges.

MAGNUS. No: I have not tamed him. I have taught him how to behave. I have to valet all the beginners; but that does not tame them: it teaches them how to use their strength instead of wasting it in making fools of themselves. So much the worse for me when I have to fight them.

THE QUEEN. You get no thanks for it. They think you are only humbugging them.

MAGNUS. Well, so I am, in the elementary lessons. But when it comes to real business humbug is no use: they pick it up themselves too quickly.

Pamphilius enters along the terrace, from the Queen's side.

MAGNUS [*looking at his watch*] Good Heavens! They havnt come, have they? It's not five yet.

PAMPHILIUS. No, sir. It's the American ambassador.

THE QUEEN [*resenting this a little*] Has he an audience?

PAMPHILIUS. No, maam. He is rather excited about something, I think. I cant get anything out of him. He says he must see His Majesty at once.

THE QUEEN. Must!! An American must see the King at once, without an audience! Well!

MAGNUS [*rising*] Send him in, Pam.

Pamphilius goes out.

THE QUEEN. *I* should have told him to write for an audience, and then kept him waiting a week for it.

MAGNUS. What! When we still owe America that old war debt. And with a mad imperialist president like Bossfield! No you wouldnt, my dear: you would be crawlingly civil to him, as I am going to be, confound him!

PAMPHILIUS [*re-appearing*] His Excellency the American Ambassador. Mr Vanhattan.

He retires as Mr Vanhattan enters in an effusive condition, and, like a man assured of an enthusiastic welcome, hurries to the Queen, and salutes her with a handshake so prolonged that she stares in astonishment, first at him, and then appealingly at the King, with her hands being vigorously wrung and waved up and down all the time.

MAGNUS. What on earth is the matter, Mr Vanhattan? You are shaking Her Majesty's rings off.

VANHATTAN [*desisting*] Her Majesty will excuse me when she learns the nature of my errand here. This, King Magnus, is a great historic scene: one of the greatest, perhaps, that history has ever recorded or will ever again record.

MAGNUS. Have you had tea?

VANHATTAN. Tea! Who can think of tea at such a moment as this?

THE QUEEN [*rather coldly*] It is hard for us to share your enthusiasm in complete ignorance of its cause.

VANHATTAN. Thát is true, maam. I am just behaving like a crazy man. But you shall hear. You shall judge. And then you shall say whether I exaggerate the importance—the immensity—of an occasion that cannot be exaggerated.

MAGNUS. Goodness gracious! Wont you sit down?

VANHATTAN [*taking a chair and placing it between them*] I thank your Majesty. [*He sits*].

MAGNUS. You have some exciting news for us, apparently. Is it private or official?

VANHATTAN. Official, sir. No mistake about it. What I am going to tell you is authentic from the United States of America to the British Empire.

THE QUEEN. Perhaps I had better go.

VANHATTAN. No, maam: you shall not go. Whatever may be the limits of your privileges as the consort of your sovereign, it is your right as an Englishwoman to learn what I have come here to communicate.

MAGNUS. My dear Vanhattan, what the devil is the matter?

VANHATTAN. King Magnus: between your country and mine there is a debt.

MAGNUS. Does that matter, now that our capitalists

[115]

have invested so heavily in American concerns that after paying yourselves the interest on the debt you have to send us two thousand million dollars a year to balance the account.

VANHATTAN. King Magnus: for the moment, forget figures. Between your country and mine there is not only a debt but a frontier: the frontier that has on it not a single gun nor a single soldier, and across which the American citizen every day shakes the hand of the Canadian subject of your throne.

MAGNUS. There is also the frontier of the ocean, which is somewhat more expensively defended at our joint expense by the League of Nations.

VANHATTAN [*rising to give his words more impressiveness*] Sir: the debt is cancelled. The frontier no longer exists.

THE QUEEN. How can that be?

MAGNUS. Am I to understand, Mr Vanhattan, that by some convulsion of Nature the continent of North America has been submerged in the Atlantic?

VANHATTAN. Something even more wonderful than that has happened. One may say that the Atlantic Ocean has been submerged in the British Empire.

MAGNUS. I think you had better tell us as succinctly as possible what has happened. Pray sit down.

VANHATTAN [*resuming his seat*] You are aware, sir, that the United States of America at one time formed a part of your empire.

MAGNUS. There is a tradition to that effect.

VANHATTAN. No mere tradition, sir. An undoubted historical fact. In the eighteenth century—

MAGNUS. That is a long time ago.

VANHATTAN. Centuries count for but little in the lifetimes of great nations, sir. Let me recall the parable of the prodigal son.

[116]

MAGNUS. Oh really, Mr Vanhattan, that was a very very long time ago. I take it that something important has happened since yesterday.

VANHATTAN. It has. It has indeed, King Magnus.

MAGNUS. Then what is it? I have not time to attend to the eighteenth century and the prodigal son at this moment.

THE QUEEN. The King has a Cabinet meeting in ten minutes, Mr Vanhattan.

VANHATTAN. I should like to see the faces of your Cabinet ministers, King Magnus, when they hear what I have to tell you.

MAGNUS. So should I. But I am not in a position to tell it to them, because I dont know what it is.

VANHATTAN. The prodigal, sir, has returned to his father's house. Not poor, not hungry, not ragged, as of old. Oh no. This time he returns bringing with him the riches of the earth to the ancestral home.

MAGNUS [*starting from his chair*] You dont mean to say—

VANHATTAN [*rising also, blandly triumphant*] I do, sir. The Declaration of Independence is cancelled. The treaties which endorsed it are torn up. We have decided to rejoin the British Empire. We shall of course enjoy Dominion Home Rule under the Presidency of Mr Bossfield. I shall revisit you here shortly, not as the Ambassador of a foreign power, but as High Commissioner for the greatest of your dominions, and your very loyal and devoted subject, sir.

MAGNUS [*collapsing into his chair*] The devil you will! [*He stares haggardly into futurity, now for the first time utterly at a loss*].

THE QUEEN. What a splendid thing, Mr Vanhattan!

VANHATTAN. I thought your Majesty would say so.

The most splendid thing that has ever happened. [*He resumes his seat*].

THE QUEEN [*looking anxiously at the King*] Dont you think so, Magnus?

MAGNUS [*pulling himself together with a visible effort*] May I ask, Mr Vanhattan, with whom did this—this —this masterstroke of American policy originate? Frankly, I have been accustomed to regard your President as a statesman whose mouth was the most efficient part of his head. He cannot have thought of this himself. Who suggested it to him?

VANHATTAN. I must accept your criticism of Mr Bossfield with all doo reserve, but I may mention that we Americans will probably connect the good news with the recent visit to our shores of the President of the Irish Free State. I cannot pronounce his name in its official Gaelic form; and there is only one typist in our bureau who can spell it; but he is known to his friends as Mick O'Rafferty.

MAGNUS. The rascal! Jemima: we shall have to live in Dublin. This is the end of England.

VANHATTAN. In a sense that may be so. But England will not perish. She will merge—merge, sir—into a bigger and brighter concern. Perhaps I should have mentioned that one of our conditions will be that you shall be Emperor. King may be good enough for this little island; but if we come in we shall require something grander.

MAGNUS. This little island! "This little gem set in a silver sea!" Has it occurred to you, Mr Vanhattan, that rather than be reduced to a mere appendage of a big American concern, we might raise the old warcry of Sinn Fein, and fight for our independence to the last drop of our blood?

VANHATTAN. I should be right sorry to contemplate

such a reversion to a barbarous past. Fortunately, it's impossible—immpawsibl. The old warcry would not appeal to the cosmopolitan crews of the fleet of the League of Nations in the Atlantic. That fleet would blockade you, sir. And I fear we should be obliged to boycott you. The two thousand million dollars a year would stop.

MAGNUS. But the continental Powers! Do you suppose they would consent for a moment to such a change in the balance of power?

VANHATTAN. Why not? The change would be only nominal.

MAGNUS. Nominal! You call an amalgamation of the British Commonwealth with the United States a nominal change! What will France and Germany call it?

VANHATTAN [shaking his head indulgently] France and Germany? These queer old geographical expressions which you use here from old family habit do not trouble us. I suppose you mean by Germany the chain of more or less Soviet Republics between the Ural Mountains and the North Sea. Well, the clever people at Moscow and Berlin and Geneva are trying to federate them; and it is fully understood between us that if we dont object to their move they will not object to ours. France, by which I take it you mean the Government at New Timgad, is too busy in Africa to fuss about what is happening at the ends of your little Channel Tube. So long as Paris is full of Americans, and Americans are full of money, all's well in the west from the French point of view. One of the great attractions of Paris for Americans is the excursion to Old England. The French want us to feel at home here. And so we do. Why shouldnt we? After all, we are at home here.

MAGNUS. In what sense, may I ask?

VANHATTAN. Well, we find here everything we are accustomed to: our industrial products, our books, our plays, our sports, our Christian Science churches, our osteopaths, our movies and talkies. Put it in a small parcel and say our goods and our ideas. A political union with us will be just the official recognition of an already accomplished fact. A union of hearts, you might call it.

THE QUEEN. You forget, Mr Vanhattan. We have a great national tradition.

VANHATTAN. The United States, maam, have absorbed all the great national traditions, and blended them with their own glorious tradition of Freedom into something that is unique and universal.

THE QUEEN. We have a civilized culture which is peculiar to ourselves. It may not be better than yours; but it is different.

VANHATTAN. Well, is it? We found that culture enshrined in British material works of art: in the stately country homes of your nobility, in the cathedrals our common forefathers built as the country houses of God. What did you do with them? You sold them to us. I was brought up in the shade of Ely cathedral, the removal of which from the county of Cambridge to New Jersey was my dear old father's first big professional job. The building which stands on its former site is a very fine one: in my opinion the best example of reinforced concrete of its period; but it was designed by an American architect, and built by the Synthetic Building Materials Trust, an international affair. Believe me, the English people, the real English people who take things as they come instead of reading books about them, will be more at home with us than they are with the old English notions which our tourists try to keep alive. When you find some country gentleman keeping up the old English customs at Christmas and so forth, who is he? An American who has bought the place. Your people get up the show for him because he pays for it, not because it is natural to them.

THE QUEEN [*with a sigh*] Our own ·best families go so much to Ireland nowadays. People should not be allowed to go from England to Ireland. They never come back.

VANHATTAN. Well, can you blame them, maam? Look at the climate!

THE QUEEN. No: it is not the climate. It is the Horse Show.

The King rises very thoughtfully; and Vanhattan follows his example.

MAGNUS. I must think over this. I have known for years past that it was on the cards. When I was young, and under the influence of our family tradition, which of course never recognized the rebellion of the American colonies as valid, I actually dreamt of a reunited English speaking empire at the head of civilization.

VANHATTAN. Fine! Great! And now come true.

MAGNUS. Not yet. Now that I am older and wiser I find the reality less attractive than the dream.

VANHATTAN. And is that all I am to report to the President, sir? He will be disappointed. I am a little taken aback, myself.

MAGNUS. For the present, that is all. This may be a great idea—

VANHATTAN. Surely, surely.

MAGNUS. It may also be a trap in which England will perish.

VANHATTAN [*encouragingly*] Oh, I shouldnt look at

[121]

it that way. Besides, nothing—not even dear old England—can last for ever. Progress, you know, sir, progress, progress!

MAGNUS. Just so, just so. We may survive only as another star on your flag. Still, we cling to the little scrap of individuality you have left us. If we must merge, as you call it—or did you say submerge?— some of us will swim to the last. [*To the Queen*] My dear.

The Queen strikes her gong.

Pamphilius returns.

MAGNUS. You shall hear from me after the Cabinet meets. Not tonight: you must not sit up waiting for a message. Early tomorrow, I hope. Thank you for bringing me the news before the papers got it: that seldom happens now. Pamphilius: you will reconduct his Excellency. Good evening. [*He shakes hands*].

VANHATTAN. I thank your Majesty. [*To the Queen*] Good evening, maam. I look forward to presenting myself in court dress soon.

THE QUEEN. You will look very nice in it, Mr Vanhattan. Good evening.

The Ambassador goes out with Pamphilius.

MAGNUS [*striding grimly to and fro*] The scoundrels! That blackguard O'Rafferty! That booby bullroarer Bossfield! Breakages, Limited, have taken it into their heads to mend the British Commonwealth.

THE QUEEN [*quietly*] I think it is a very good thing. You will make a very good emperor. We shall civilize these Americans.

MAGNUS. How can we when we have not yet civilized ourselves? They have come to regard us as a mere tribe of redskins. England will be just a reservation.

THE QUEEN. Nonsense, dear! They know that we are their natural superiors. You can see it by the way their women behave at court. They really love and reverence royalty; while our English peeresses are hardly civil —when they condescend to come at all.

MAGNUS. Well, my dear, I do many things to please you that I should never do to please myself; and I suppose I shall end as American Emperor just to keep you amused.

THE QUEEN. I never desire anything that is not good for you, Magnus. You do not always know what is good for you.

MAGNUS. Well, well, well, well! Have it your own way, dearest. Where are these infernal ministers? Theyre late.

THE QUEEN [*looking out into the garden*] Coming across the lawn with Sempronius.

The Cabinet arrives. The men take off their hats as they come up the steps. Boanerges has taken advantage of the interval to procure a brilliant uniform and change into it. Proteus, with Sempronius, heads the procession, followed immediately by the two lady ministers. The Queen rises as Proteus turns to her. Sempronius moves the little table quickly back to the balustrade out of the way, and puts the Queen's chair in the centre for the King.

THE QUEEN [*shaking hands*] How do you do, Mr Proteus?

PROTEUS. May I present the President of the Board of Trade, Mr Boanerges?

THE QUEEN. I remember seeing you, Mr Boanerges, at the opening of the Transport Workers' Summer Palace. You wore a most becoming costume then. I hope you have not given it up.

BOANERGES. But the Princess told me I looked ridiculous in it!

THE QUEEN. That was very naughty of the Princess.

You looked particularly well in it. However, you look well in anything. And now I leave you all to your labors.

She goes out along the terrace. Sempronius follows with her knitting.

MAGNUS [*sitting down*] Be seated, ladies and gentlemen.

They take chairs of one sort or another where they can find them, first leaving their hats on the balustrade. When they are seated, their order from the King's right to his left is Nicobar, Crassus, Boanerges, Amanda, the King, Proteus, Lysistrata, Pliny, and Balbus.

A pause, Proteus waiting for the King to begin. He, deep in thought, says nothing. The silence becomes oppressive.

PLINY [*chattily*] Nice weather we're having, these evenings.

AMANDA [*splutters*] !!!

MAGNUS. There is rather a threatening cloud on the western horizon, Mr Pliny. [*To Proteus*] Have you heard the news from America?

PROTEUS. I have, sir.

MAGNUS. Am I to be favored with the advice of my ministers on that subject?

PROTEUS. By your Majesty's leave, we will take the question of the ultimatum first.

MAGNUS. Do you think the ultimatum will matter much when the capital of the British Commonwealth is shifted to Washington?

NICOBAR. We'll see it shifted to Melbourne or Montreal or Johannesburg first.

MAGNUS. It would not stay there. It will stay at a real centre of gravity only.

PROTEUS. We are agreed about that. If it shifts at all it will shift either west to Washington or east to Moscow.

BOANERGES. Moscow thinks a lot of itself. But what has Moscow to teach us that we cannot teach ourselves? Moscow is built on English history, written in London by Karl Marx.

PROTEUS. Yes; and the English king has side-tracked you again. [*To Magnus*] What about the ultimatum, sir? You promised us your decision at five o'clock. It is now a quarter past.

MAGNUS Are you inexorably determined to force this issue to its logical end? You know how unEnglish it is to do that?

PROTEUS. My people came from Scotland.

LYSISTRATA. I wish they had stayed there. I am English: every bone in my body.

BOANERGES [*vociferously*] Same here!

PROTEUS. God help England if she had no Scots to think for her!

MAGNUS. What does the Cabinet say to that?

AMANDA. All their people came from Scotland or Ireland or Wales or Jerusalem or somewhere, sir. It is no use appealing to English sentiment here.

CRASSUS. Politics are not suited to the English, if you ask me.

MAGNUS. Then I, the only Englishman left in politics, apparently, am to be reduced to complete nullity?

PROTEUS [*bluntly*] Yes. You cannot frighten us out of our position by painting it red. I could paint your position black if I liked. In plain terms we require from you an unconditional surrender. If you refuse it then I go to the country on the question whether England is to be an absolute monarchy or a constitutional one. We are all agreed on that: there will be no resignations. I have letters from the absent members of the Government: those present will speak for themselves.

ALL THE OTHER MEN. Agreed, agreed.

PROTEUS. Now, what is your answer?

MAGNUS. The day for absolute monarchies is past. You think you can do without me; and I know that I cannot do without you. I decide, of course, in favor of a constitutional monarchy.

THE MEN [*greatly relieved and delighted*] Hear! hear!

MAGNUS. Wait a moment.

Sudden silence and mistrust.

PROTEUS. So! There is a catch in it, is there?

MAGNUS. Not exactly a catch. But you have driven me to face the fact that I am unfitted to be a constitutional monarch. I am by nature incapable of the necessary self-effacement.

AMANDA. Well, thats true, at all events. You and I are a pair, sir.

MAGNUS. Thank you. Therefore, whilst accepting your constitutional principle without the slightest reserve, I cannot sign your ultimatum, because by doing so I should be making personal promises which I know I should break—which in fact I m u s t break because I have forces within me which your constitutional limits cannot hold in check.

BALBUS. How can you accept our principle if you dont sign the ultimatum?

MAGNUS. Oh, there is no difficulty about that. When an honest man finds himself incapable of discharging the duties of a public post, he resigns.

PROTEUS [*alarmed*] Resigns! What are you driving at?

CRASSUS. A king cannot resign.

NICOBAR. You might as well talk of beheading yourself. You cant behead yourself.

BOANERGES. Other people can, though.

MAGNUS. Do not let us quarrel about words, gentlemen. I cannot resign. But I can abdicate.

ALL THE REST [*starting to their feet*] Abdicate! [*They stare at him in consternation*].

AMANDA [*whistling a descending minor scale very expressively*] !!!!!!!! [*She sits down*].

MAGNUS. Of course, abdicate. Lysistrata: you have been a teacher of history. You can assure your colleagues that there is nothing unprecedented in an abdication. The Emperor Charles the Fifth, for instance—

LYSISTRATA. Oh, Charles the Fifth be—be bothered! he's not good enough. Sir: I have stood by you as far as I dared. Dont throw me over. You must not abdicate. [*She sits down, distressed*].

PROTEUS. You cannot abdicate except by my advice.

MAGNUS. I am acting upon your advice.

PROTEUS. Nonsense! [*He sits down*].

BALBUS. Ridiculous! [*He sits down*].

PLINY. Youre not serious, you know. [*He sits down*].

NICOBAR. You cant upset the apple cart like this. [*He sits down*].

CRASSUS. I must say this is not playing the game. [*He sits down*].

BOANERGES [*powerfully*] Well, why not? Why not? Though as an old Republican I have no respect for His Majesty as a King, I have a great respect for him as a Strong Man. But he is not the only pebble on the beach. Why not have done with this superstition of monarchy, and bring the British Commonwealth into line with all the other great Powers today as a republic? [*He sits down*].

MAGNUS. My abdication does not involve that, Mr Boanerges. I am abdicating to save the monarchy, not to destroy it. I shall be succeeded by my son Robert, Prince of Wales. He will make an admirable constitutional monarch.

PLINY. Oh, come! Dont be hard on the lad, sir. He has plenty of brains.

MAGNUS. Oh yes, yes, yes: I did not mean that he is a nonentity: quite the contrary: he is much cleverer than I am. But I have never been able to induce him to take any interest in parliamentary politics. He prefers intellectual pursuits.

NICOBAR. Dont you believe it. He is up to his neck in business.

MAGNUS. Just so. He asks me why I waste my time with you here pretending to govern the country when it is really governed by Breakages, Limited. And really I hardly know how to answer him.

CRASSUS. Things are like that nowadays. My son says just the same.

LYSISTRATA. Personally I get on very well with the Prince; but somehow I do not feel that he is interested in what I am doing.

BALBUS. He isnt. He wont interfere with you as long as you dont interfere with him. Just the right king for us. Not pig-headed. Not meddlesome. Thinks that nothing we do matters a rap. What do you say, Joe?

PROTEUS. After all, why not? if your Majesty is in earnest.

MAGNUS. I assure you I am very much in earnest.

PROTEUS. Well, I confess I did not foresee this turn of events. But I ought to have foreseen it. What your Majesty proposes is the straightforward, logical, intellectually honest solution of our difficulty. Consequently it is the last solution I could have expected in politics. But I reckoned without your Majesty's character. The more I think of it the more clearly I see that you are right—that you are taking the only course open to you.

CRASSUS. I never said I was against it, Joe.

BALBUS. Neither did I.

NICOBAR. I think theres a great deal to be said for it. *I* have no objection.

PLINY. One king is no worse than another, is he?

BOANERGES. Is he any better? The way you fellows scuttle backward and forward from one mind to another whenever Joe holds up his finger is disgusting. This is a Cabinet of sheep.

PROTEUS. Well, give the flock a better lead if you can. Have you anything else to propose?

BOANERGES. I dont know that I have on the spur of the moment. We should have had notice of this. But I suppose the King must do as he thinks right.

PROTEUS. Then the goat goes with the sheep; so thats all right.

BOANERGES. Who are you calling a goat?

NICOBAR. If you come to that, who are you calling sheep?

AMANDA. Steady there, children! steady! steady! [*To the King*] You have brought us all round, sir, as usual.

PROTEUS. There is nothing more to be said.

AMANDA. That means another half hour at least.

BOANERGES. Woman: this is not the moment for your tomfooleries.

PROTEUS [*impressively*] Bill is right, Amanda. [*He rises and becomes the conventional House of Commons orator*].

Ministers compose themselves to listen with grave attention, as if in church; but Lysistrata is contemptuous and Amanda amused.

PROTEUS [*continuing*] It is a solemn moment. It is a moment in which an old tie is being broken. I am not ashamed to confess that it is a tie from which I have learned something.

MALE MINISTERS [*murmur*] Hear hear! Hear hear!

PROTEUS. For my own part—and I think I may speak for others here as well—it has been no mere political tie, but a tie of sincere friendship.

Renewed murmurs of sympathy. Increasing emotion.

PROTEUS. We have had our disagreements—as which of us has not?—but they have been family quarrels.

CRASSUS. Thats all. Nothing more.

PROTEUS. May I say lovers' quarrels?

PLINY [*wiping his eyes*] You may, Joe. You may.

PROTEUS. My friends, we came here to a meeting. We find, alas! that the meeting is to be a leavetaking. [*Crassus sniffs tearfully*]. It is a sad leavetaking on our part, but a cordial one. [Hear Hear *from Pliny*]. We are cast down, but not discouraged. Looking back to the past with regret, we can still look forward to the future with hope. That future has its dangers and its difficulties. It will bring us new problems; and it will bring us face to face with a new king. But the new problems and the new king will not make us forget our old counsellor, monarch, and—he will allow me to say—comrade. [Hear Hears *ad libitum*]. I know my words will find an echo in all your hearts when I conclude by saying that whatsoever king shall reign—

AMANDA. Youll be the Vicar of Bray, Joe.

Uproar. Proteus flings himself into his chair indignantly.

BALBUS. Shame!

NICOBAR. Shut up, you b—

PLINY. A joke's a joke; but really—

CRASSUS. Too bad, Amanda! Behave yourself.

LYSISTRATA. She has a perfect right to speak. You are a parcel of sentimental fools.

BOANERGES [*rising*] Silence. Order.

AMANDA. Sorry.

BOANERGES. So you ought to be. Where's your manners? Where's your education? King Magnus: we part; but we part as strong men part: as friends. The Prime Minister has correctly represented the sentiments of all the men present. I call on them to express those sentiments in the good old English fashion. [*Singing in stentorian tones*] Fo-o-o-o-r-r-r

MALE MINISTERS EXCEPT PROTEUS [*rising and singing*]

> — he's a jolly good fel-low
> For he's a jolly good fel-low
> For he's—

MAGNUS [*peremptorily*] Stop. Stop.

Sudden silence and misgiving. They sit down furtively.

MAGNUS. I thank you with all my heart; but there is a misapprehension. We are not taking leave of one another. I have no intention of withdrawing from an active part in politics.

PROTEUS. What!!

MAGNUS. You are looking on me, with an emotion which has deeply touched me, as a man with a political past. But I look on myself rather as a man with a political future. I have not yet told you my plans.

NICOBAR. What plans?

BALBUS. A retired king cant have plans and a future.

MAGNUS. Why not? I am looking forward to a most exciting and enjoyable time. As I shall of course dissolve parliament, the fun will begin with a general election.

BOANERGES [*dismayed*] But Ive only just been elected. Do you mean that I shall have to stand two elections in one month? Have you thought of the expenses?

MAGNUS. Surely your expenses will be paid by the State.

BOANERGES. Paid by the State! Is that all you know about electioneering in England?

PROTEUS. You will get your whack out of the party funds, Bill; and if you cant find the extras you must put up with straight votes. Go on, sir: we want to hear about those plans of yours.

MAGNUS. My last act of royal authority will be to divest myself of all titles and dignities; so that I may step down at once into the position of a commoner.

BOANERGES. Step up, you mean. The common man is the superior, not the inferior, of the titled man.

MAGNUS. That is why I am going to make myself a common man, Mr Boanerges.

PLINY. Well, it does you honor.

CRASSUS. Not all of us would be capable of a sacrifice like that.

BOANERGES. A fine gesture, sir. A fine gesture. I admit it.

PROTEUS [*suspicious*] And since when, pray, has your Majesty taken to making gestures? Whats the game this time?

BOANERGES. Shame!

PROTEUS. Shut up, you gaby. [*To the King*] I say, whats the game?

MAGNUS. There is no imposing on you, Prime Minister. The game is, of course, that when I come back into politics I shall be in a better position as a commoner than as a peer. I shall seek a parliamentary seat.

PROTEUS. You in the House of Commons!

MAGNUS [*blandly*] It is my intention to offer myself to the Royal Borough of Windsor as a candidate at the forthcoming General Election.

All the rest except Boanerges and the ladies rise in consternation.

PROTEUS. This is treachery.

BALBUS. A dirty trick.

NICOBAR. The meanest on record.

PLINY. He'll be at the top of the poll.

CRASSUS. There wont be any poll: it will be a walk-over.

BALBUS. This shews what all your fine manners and friendly ways are worth.

NICOBAR. Hypocrite!

CRASSUS. Humbug!

LYSISTRATA. I wish your Majesty every success.

AMANDA. Hear hear! Fair play, boys. Why shouldnt he go into parliament with us?

BOANERGES. Well said! well said! Why not?

THE OTHER MALE MINISTERS. Ya-a-a-ah! [*They sit down in utter disgust*].

PROTEUS [*very sullen*] And when you are in Parliament, what then?

MAGNUS. There are several possibilities. I shall naturally endeavor to form a party. My son King Robert will have to call on some Party leader who can depend on the support of the House of Commons to form a Government. He may call on you. He may even call on me.

AMANDA [*breaks the glum silence by whistling a bar or two of the National Anthem*]!!

MAGNUS. Whatever happens, it will be a great relief to us to be able to speak out quite frankly about one-another in public. You have never been able to tell the British people what you really think of me: no real criticism of the King is possible. I have never been able to speak my mind as to your various capacities and characters. All that reserve, that tedious affectation, that unwholesome concealment will end. I hope you look forward to our new footing as pleasurably as I do.

[133]

LYSISTRATA. I am delighted, sir. You will fight Breakages for me.

AMANDA. It will be awful fun.

BOANERGES. Now, Mr Prime Minister, we are waiting for you. What have you to say about it?

PROTEUS [*rising and speaking slowly, with his brows deeply knitted*] Has Your Majesty got that ultimatum on you?

MAGNUS [*produces it from his breast pocket and presents it to him*]!

PROTEUS [*with measured emphasis, after tearing the paper up into four pieces at two deliberate strokes, and throwing the pieces away*] There is not going to be any abdication. There is not going to be any general election. There is not going to be any ultimatum. We go on as before. The crisis is a washout. [*To the King, with deadly concentration*] I will never forgive you for this. You stole your ace of trumps from the hand I played this morning. [*He takes his hat from the balustrade and goes away through the park*].

BOANERGES [*rising*] That was a very deplorable exhibition of temper on the part of the Prime Minister, sir. It was not the gesture of a Strong Man. I will remonstrate with him. You may depend on me. [*He takes his hat and follows Proteus in a serious and dignified manner*].

NICOBAR [*rising*] Well, I shall not say what I think. [*He is taking his hat when the King addresses him*].

MAGNUS. So I have not upset the apple cart after all, Mr Nicobar.

NICOBAR. You can upset it as soon as you like for all I care. I am going out of politics. Politics is a mug's game. [*He goes*].

CRASSUS [*rising reluctantly and taking his hat*] If Nick goes, I shall have to go too.

MAGNUS. Can you really tear yourself away from politics?

CRASSUS. Only too glad to be well out of them, if Breakages will let me. They shoved me into it; and I daresay theyll find another job for me. [*He goes*].

PLINY [*cheerful to the last as he, too, goes for his hat*] Well, I am glad nothing's happened. You know, sir, nothing ever really does happen in the Cabinet. Never mind their bit of temper. Theyll feed out of your hand tomorrow. [*He goes*].

BALBUS [*after taking his hat*] Now that theyre all gone I dont mind saying that if anything should ever happen to the throne, and your Majesty should become a President with a Cabinet to pick, you might easily find a worse Home Secretary than me, with all my faults.

MAGNUS. I shall bear it in mind. By the way, if you should happen to overtake the Prime Minister, will you be so good as to remind him that we quite forgot to settle that little affair of the proposal of America to annex the British Commonwealth.

BALBUS. By the Lord, so we did! Well, thats a good one! Ha ha! Ha ha ha ha ha! [*He goes out laughing heartily*].

MAGNUS. They dont take it in, Lizzie: not one bit. It is as if another planet were crashing into us. The kingdom and the power and the glory will pass from us and leave us naked, face to face with our real selves at last.

LYSISTRATA. So much the better, if by our real selves you mean the old English stock that was unlike any other. Nowadays men all over the world are as much alike as hotel dinners. It's no use pretending that the America of George Washington is going to swallow up the England of Queen Anne. The America of George Washington is as dead as Queen Anne. What they call an American is only a wop pretending to be a Pilgrim Father. He is no more Uncle Jonathan than you are John Bull.

MAGNUS. Yes: we live in a world of wops, all melting into one another; and when all the frontiers are down London may be outvoted by Tennessee, and all the other places where we still madly teach our children the mentality of an eighteenth century village school.

LYSISTRATA. Never fear, sir. It is not the most ignorant national crowd that will come out on top, but the best power station; for you cant do without power stations, and you cant run them on patriotic songs and hatred of the foreigner, and guff and bugaboo, though you can run nationalism on nothing else. But I am heartbroken at your not coming into the House with us to keep old England in front and lead a new Party against Breakages [*tears come into her eyes*].

MAGNUS [*patting her consolingly on the back*] That would have been splendid, wouldnt it? But I am too old fashioned. This is a farce that younger men must finish.

AMANDA [*taking her arm*] Come home with me, dear. I will sing to you until you cant help laughing. Come.

Lysistrata pockets her handkerchief; shakes the King's hands impulsively; and goes with Amanda. The King plunges into deep thought. Presently the Queen comes back.

THE QUEEN. Now Magnus: it's time to dress for dinner.

MAGNUS [*much disturbed*] Oh, not now. I have something very big to think about. I dont want any dinner.

THE QUEEN [*peremptorily*] No dinner! Did anyone ever hear of such a thing! You know you will not sleep if you think after seven o'clock.

[136]

MAGNUS [*worried*] But really, Jemima—

THE QUEEN [*going to him and taking his arm*] Now, now, now! dont be naughty. I musnt be late for dinner. Come on, like a good little boy.

The King, with a grimace of hopeless tenderness, allows himself to be led away.

On the Rocks: A Political Comedy

WITH

Preface

Composition begun 6 February 1933; completed 4 July 1933. Published in *Too True to be Good, Village Wooing & On the Rocks*, 1934. First presented at the Winter Garden Theatre, London, on 25 November 1933.

Sir Arthur Chavender (Prime Minister)
 Nicholas Hannen

Hilda Hanways (His Secretary) *Phyllis Thomas*

Sir Broadfoot Basham (Chief Commissioner of Police) *Walter Hudd*

Flavia Chavender *Marjorie Playfair*

Lady Chavender *Margaret Macdona*

David Chavender *Lewis Shaw*

Tom Humphries (Mayor of the Isle of Cats)
 Charles Sewell

Alderwoman Aloysia Brollikins *Ellen Pollock*

Alderman Blee *George E. Bancroft*

Viscount Barking *Emerton Court*

Mr Hipney *Edward Rigby*

The Lady *Fay Davis*

Sir Dexter Rightside (Foreign Secretary)
 Charles Carson

Admiral Sir Bemrose Hotspot (First Lord of the Admiralty) *Matthew Boulton*

Mr Glenmorison (President of the Board of Trade) *Norman MacOwan*

Sir Jafna Pandranath *Lewis Casson*

The Duke of Domesday *Lawrence Hanray*

Period—The Present

ACT I *The Cabinet Room at No. 10 Downing Street, London, S.W.1. July*

ACT II *The Same. 10 November, 9.30 a.m.*

Preface

Contents

EXTERMINATION

In this play a reference is made by a Chief of Police to the political necessity for killing people: a necessity so distressing to the statesmen and so terrifying to the common citizen that nobody except myself (as far as I know) has ventured to examine it directly on its own merits, although every Government is obliged to practise it on a scale varying from the execution of a single murderer to the slaughter of millions of quite innocent persons. Whilst assenting to these proceedings, and even acclaiming and celebrating them, we dare not tell ourselves what we are doing or why we are doing it; and so we call it justice or capital punishment or our duty to king and country or any other convenient verbal whitewash for what we instinctively recoil from as from a dirty job. These childish evasions are revolting. We must strip off the whitewash and find out what is really beneath it. Extermination must be put on a scientific basis if it is ever to be carried out humanely and apologetically as well as thoroughly.

KILLING AS A POLITICAL FUNCTION

That killing is a necessity is beyond question by any thoughtful person. Unless rabbits and deer and rats and foxes are killed, or "kept down" as we put it, mankind must perish; and that section of mankind which lives in the country and is directly and personally engaged in the struggle with Nature for a living has no sentimental doubts that they must be killed. As to tigers and poisonous snakes, their incompatibility with human civilization is unquestioned. This does not excuse the use of cruel steel traps, agonizing poisons, or packs of hounds as methods of extermination. Killing can be cruelly or kindly done; and the deliberate choice of cruel ways, and their organization as popular pleasures, is sinful; but the sin is in the cruelty and the enjoyment of it, not in the killing.

THE SACREDNESS OF HUMAN LIFE

In law we draw a line between the killing of human animals and non-human ones, setting the latter apart as brutes. This was founded on a general belief that humans have immortal souls and brutes none. Nowadays more and more people are refusing to make this distinction. They may believe in The Life Everlasting and The Life to Come; but they make no distinction between Man and Brute, because some of them believe that brutes have souls, whilst others refuse to believe that the physical materializations and personifications of The Life Everlasting are themselves everlasting. In either case the mystic distinction between Man and Brute vanishes; and the murderer pleading that though a rabbit should be killed for being mischievous he himself should be spared because he has an immortal soul and a rabbit has none is as hopelessly out of date as a gentleman duellist pleading his clergy. When the necessity for killing a dangerous human being arises, as it still does daily, the only distinction we make between a man and a snared rabbit is that we very quaintly provide the man with a minister of religion to explain to him that we are not killing him at all, but only expediting his transfer to an eternity of bliss.

The political necessity for killing him is precisely like that for killing the cobra or the tiger: he is so ferocious or unscrupulous that if his neighbors do not kill him he will kill or ruin his neighbors; so that there is nothing for it but to disable him once for all by making an end of him, or else waste the lives of useful and harmless people in seeing that he does no mischief, and caging him cruelly like a lion in a show.

Here somebody is sure to interject that there is the alternative of teaching him better manners; but I am not here dealing with such cases: the real necessity arises only in dealing with untameable persons who are constitutionally unable to restrain their violent or acquisitive impulses, and have no compunction about sacrificing others to their own immediate convenience. To punish such persons is ridiculous: we might as reasonably punish a tile for flying off a roof in a storm and knocking a clergyman on the head. But to kill them is quite reasonable and very necessary.

PRESENT EXTERMINATIONS

All this so far is mere elementary criminology, already dealt with very fully by me in my Essay on Prisons, which I recommend to those readers who may feel impelled to ramble away at this point into the prosings about Deterrence beloved by our Prison commissioners and judges. It disposes of the dogma of the unconditional sacredness of human life, or any other incarnation of life; but it covers only a corner of the field opened up by modern powers of extermination. In Germany it is suggested that the Nordic race should exterminate the Latin race. As both these lingual stocks are hopelessly interbred by this time, such a sacrifice to ethnological sciolism is not practicable; but its discussion familiarizes the idea and clears the way for practicable suggestions. The extermination of whole races and classes has been not only advocated but actually attempted. The extirpation of the Jew as such figured for a few mad moments in the program of the Nazi party in Germany. The extermination of the peasant is in active progress in Russia, where the extermination of the class of ladies and gentlemen of so-called independent means has already been accomplished; and an attempt to exterminate the old Conservative professional class and the kulak or prosperous farmer class has been checked only by the discovery that they cannot as yet be done without. Outside Russia the extermination of Communists is widely advocated; and there is a movement in the British Empire and the United States for the extermination of Fascists. In India the impulse of Moslems and Hindus to exterminate one another is complicated by the impulse of the British Empire to exterminate both when they happen to be militant Nationalists.

PREVIOUS ATTEMPTS MISS THE POINT

The novelty and significance of these instances consists in the equal status of the parties. The extermination of what the exterminators call inferior races is as old as history. "Stone dead hath no fellow" said Cromwell when he tried to exterminate the Irish. "The only good nigger is a dead nigger" say the

Americans of the Ku-Klux temperament. "Hates any man the thing he would not kill?" said Shylock naïvely. But we white men, as we absurdly call ourselves in spite of the testimony of our looking glasses, regard all differently colored folk as inferior species. Ladies and gentlemen class rebellious laborers with vermin. The Dominicans, the watchdogs of God, regarded the Albigenses as the enemies of God, just as Torquemada regarded the Jews as the murderers of God. All that is an old story: what we are confronted with now is a growing perception that if we desire a certain type of civilization and culture we must exterminate the sort of people who do not fit into it. There is a difference between the shooting at sight of aboriginal natives in the back blocks of Australia and the massacres of aristocrats in the terror which followed the foreign attacks on the French Revolution. The Australian gunman pots the aboriginal natives to satisfy his personal antipathy to a black man with uncut hair. But nobody in the French Republic had this feeling about Lavoisier, nor can any German Nazi have felt that way about Einstein. Yet Lavoisier was guillotined; and Einstein has had to fly for his life from Germany. It was silly to say that the Republic had no use for chemists; and no Nazi has stultified his party to the extent of saying that the new National Socialist Fascist State in Germany has no use for mathematician-physicists. The proposition is that aristocrats (Lavoisier's class) and Jews (Einstein's race) are unfit to enjoy the privilege of living in a modern society founded on definite principles of social welfare as distinguished from the old promiscuous aggregations crudely policed by chiefs who had no notion of social criticism and no time to invent it.

KING CHARLES'S HEAD

It was, by the way, the English Revolution which introduced the category of Malignant or Man of Blood, and killed the King as an affirmation that even kings must not survive if they are malignant. This was much more advanced than the execution in the following century of Louis XVI as an ordinary traitor, or of the Tsar in our own time to prevent his being captured by the Tchekoslovakian contingent and used as a standard to rally the royalist reaction. Charles affirmed a divine personal right to govern as against the parliament and would keep no bargain with it. Parliament denied his right, and set up against it a divine right of election winners to govern. They fought it out; and the victorious election winners exterminated the king, very logically. Finding that their authority still needed a royal disguise they drove a hard bargain for a crown with his son, and, after ejecting the next king who broke it, a still harder one with his Dutch grandson before they allowed the title of king, with nine tenths of the meaning knocked out of it, to be used as a matter of convenience again in England. Nobody had a word to say against Charles's private character. It was solely for incompatibility of politics that he was eliminated, or "liquidated" as we say now. There was a real novelty in the transaction. The Church had for centuries before compelled the secular State to liquidate heretics; and the slaughter of rebels who tried to substitute one dynasty for another, or to seize the throne for themselves, was common routine. But Charles was neither a heretic nor a rebel. He was the assertor of a divine right to govern without winning elections; and because that right could not co-exist with the supremacy of a much richer and more powerful plutocracy off went his head.

Charles was only the first victim. After Culloden the defeated Highland chiefs and their clansmen were butchered like sheep on the field. Had they been merely prisoners of war, this would have been murder. But as they were also Incompatibles with British civilization, it was only liquidation.

RIGHT TO EXTERMINATE CONFERRED BY PRIVATE PROPERTY

Having disposed of the divine right of kings the political liquidators turned their attention slowly to its derivatory the divine right of landlords, which had gradually disguised itself as private property in land. For when a tract of land becomes the private property of an individual who has to depend on it for his subsistence, the relation between him and the inhabitants of that tract becomes an economic one; and if they become economically superfluous or wasteful, he must exterminate them. This is continually happening wherever private property in land exists. If I possess land and find it profitable to grow wheat on it, I need many agricultural laborers to enable me to do it; and I tolerate their existence accordingly. If I presently find that it is more profitable to cover my land with sheep and sell their wool, I have to tolerate the existence of the sheep; but I no longer need tolerate the existence of the laborers; so I drive them off my land, which is my legal method of extermination, retaining only a few to act as shepherds. Later on I find that it is more profitable to cover my land with wild deer, and collect money from gentlemen and ladies who enjoy shooting them. I then exterminate my shepherds and keep only a few gamekeepers. But I may do much better by letting my land to industrialists for the erection of factories. They exterminate the sheep and the deer; but they need far more men than I needed even when I grew wheat. The driven-offs crowd into the factories and multiply like rabbits; and for the moment population grows instead of diminishing. But soon machines come along and make millions of proletarians economically superfluous. The factory owner accordingly sacks them, which is his legal method of extermination. During these developments the exterminated, or, as we call them, the evicted and sacked, try to avoid starvation partly by emigration, but mostly by offering themselves for all sorts of employment as soldiers, servants, prostitutes, police officers, scavengers, and operators of the immense machinery of amusement and protection for the idle rich classes created by the private property system. By organization in trade unions, municipal and parliamentary Labor Parties, and the like, and maintaining a sort of continual civil war consisting of strikes and riots, they extort from the proprietors enough to reduce the rate of extermination (shewn by the actuarial expectation of life of the unpropertied) for periods described as progressive, until the proprietors, by engaging in suicidal wars, are forced to intensify their economies, and the rate of extermination rises again.

DISGUISES UNDER WHICH PRIVATE EXTERMINATION OPERATES

Note that during all this the Registrar General's returns do not give us the deaths of the exterminated as such, because the exterminated do not starve as lost travellers starve in the desert. Their starvation is more or less protracted; and when the final catastrophe arrives, it is disguised under an imposing array of doctors' names for moribundity. The victims die mostly in their first year, and subsequently at all ages short of the age at which properly nourished people die. Sometimes they are starved into attaining an age at which people with well filled pockets eat themselves to death. Either way and all ways the extermination is a real and permanent feature of private property civilization, though it is never mentioned as such, and ladies and gentlemen are carefully educated to be unconscious of its existence and to talk nonsense about its facts when they are too obvious or become too scandalous to be ignored, when they often advocate emigration or Birth Control or war as remedies. And against the facts there is a chronic humanitarian revolt expressing itself either underground or overground in revolutionary movements; making our political constitutions very unstable; and imposing an habitual disingenuousness on conservative statesmen.

PRIVATE POWERS OF LIFE AND DEATH

Now the central fact of all these facts is that the private proprietors have irresponsible powers of life and death in the State. Such powers may be tolerated as long as the Government is in effect a committee of private proprietors; yet if such a committee be widened into or superseded by a Government acting in the interest of the whole people, that Government will not suffer any private class to hold the lives of the citizens at its mercy and thereby become their real masters. A popular Government, before it fully grasps the situation, usually begins by attempting to redistribute property in such a manner as to make everyone a petty proprietor, as in the French Revolution. But when the impossibility of doing this (except in the special case of agricultural land) becomes apparent, and the question is probed to the bottom by unpropertied political philosophers like Proudhon and Marx, private property is sooner or later excommunicated and abolished; and what was formerly called "real property" is replaced by ordinary personal property and common property administrated by the State.

All modern progressive and revolutionary movements are at bottom attacks on private property. A Chancellor of the Exchequer apologizing for an increase in the surtax, a Fascist dictator organizing a Corporate State, a Soviet Commissar ejecting a kulak and adding his acres to a collective farm, are all running the same race, though all of them except the Commissar may be extremely reluctant to win it. For in the long run the power to exterminate is too grave to be left in any hands but those of a thoroughly Communist Government responsible to the whole community. The landlord with his writ of ejectment and the employer with his sack, must finally go the way of the nobleman with his sword and his benefit of clergy, and of Hannibal Chollop with his bowie knife and pistol.

Let us then assume that private property, already maimed by factory legislation, surtax, and a good deal of petty persecution in England, and in Russia tolerated only provisionally as a disgraceful necessity pending its complete extirpation, is finally discarded by civilized communities, and the duty of maintaining it at all costs replaced by the duty of giving effect to the dogma that every ablebodied and ableminded and ablesouled person has an absolute right to an equal share in the national dividend. Would the practice of extermination thereupon disappear? I suggest that, on the contrary, it might continue much more openly and intelligently and scientifically than at present, because the humanitarian revolt against it would probably become a humanitarian support of it; and there would be an end of the hypocrisy, the venal special pleading, and the concealment or ignoring of facts which are imposed on us at present because extermination for the benefit of a handful of private persons against the interests of the race is permitted and practised. The old doctrine of the sacredness of human life, which in our idiot asylums at Darenth and elsewhere still terrifies us into wasting the lives of capable people in preserving the lives of monsters, was a crude expedient for beginning civilization. At present we discard it in dealing with murderers, heretics, traitors, and (in Scotland) vitriol throwers, who can be legally killed. A runaway convict can also be summarily shot by a warder to save the trouble of pursuing and recapturing him; and although the convict is not under capital sentence and the case is therefore clearly one of wilful murder, coroners' juries persist in treating it as a harmless and necessary incident in prison routine.

Unfortunately the whole question is bedevilled by our anti-Christian vice of punishment, expiation, sacrifice, and all the cognate tribal superstitions which are hammered into us in our childhood by barbarous scripturists, irascible or sadist parents, and a hideous criminal code. When the horrors of anarchy force us to set up laws that forbid us to fight and torture one another for sport, we still snatch at every excuse for declaring individuals outside the protection of law and torturing them to our hearts content.

CRUELTY'S EXCUSES

There have been summits of civilization at which heretics like Socrates, who was killed because he was wiser than his neighbors, have not been tortured, but ordered to kill themselves in the most painless manner known to their judges. But from that summit there was a speedy relapse into our present savagery. For Wallace, whom the Scots adored as a patriot and the English executed as a traitor, the most cruel and obscene method of killing that the human imagination could conceive at its vilest was specially invented to punish him for being a traitor (or "larn him to be a toad"); and this sentence has been passed, though not carried out, within the memory of persons now living. John of Leyden, for being a Communist, was tortured so frightfully before being hung up in a cage on the church tower to starve to death in sight of all the citizens and their little children, that the bishop who was officially obliged to witness it died of horror. Joan of Arc, for wearing men's clothes and being a Protestant and a witch, was burnt alive, after a proposal to torture her had been barely defeated. The people who saw her burnt were quite accustomed to such spectacles, and regarded them as holiday attractions. A woman's sex was made an excuse for burning her instead of more mercifully hanging her. Male criminals were broken on the wheel: that is, battered to death with iron bars, until well into the nineteenth century. This was a public spectacle; and the prolongation of the victim's suffering was so elaborately studied and arranged that Cartouche, one of the kings of scoundrelism, was bribed to betray his accomplices by the promise that he should be killed by the sixth blow of the bar. The wheel and the stake have lately gone out of use; but the Sadist mania for flogging seems ineradicable; for after a partially successful attempt to discard it in Victorian times it has revived again with redoubled ferocity: quite recently a criminal was sentenced to a flogging and ten years penal servitude; and although the victim escaped his punishment and gave a sensational advertisement to its savagery by committing suicide, nobody protested, though thirty years ago there would have been a strenuous outcry against it, raised by the old Humanitarian League, and voiced in Parliament by the Irish Nationalists. Alas! the first thing the Irish did when they at last enjoyed self-government was to get rid of these sentimental Nationalists and put flogging on their statute book in a series of Coercion Acts that would have horrified Dublin Castle. In a really civilized state flogging would cease because it would be impossible to induce any decent citizen to flog another. Among us a perfectly respectable official will do it for half a crown, and probably enjoy the job.

LEADING CASE OF JESUS CHRIST

I dislike cruelty, even cruelty to other people, and should therefore like to see all cruel people exterminated. But I should recoil with horror from a proposal to punish them. Let me illustrate my attitude by a very famous, indeed far too famous, example of the popular conception of criminal law as a means of delivering up victims to the normal popular lust for cruelty which has been mortified by the restraint imposed on it by civilization. Take the case of the extermination of Jesus Christ. No doubt there was a strong case for it. Jesus was from the point of view of the High Priest a heretic and an impostor. From the point of view of the merchants he was a rioter and a Communist. From the Roman Imperialist point of view he was a traitor. From the commonsense point of view he was a dangerous madman. From the snobbish point of view, always a very influential one, he was a penniless vagrant. From the police point of view he was an obstructor of thoroughfares, a beggar, an associate of prostitutes, an apologist of sinners, and a disparager of judges; and his daily companions were tramps whom he had seduced into vagabondage from their regular trades. From the point of view of the pious he was a Sabbath breaker, a denier of the efficacy of circumcision and the advocate of a strange rite of baptism, a gluttonous man and a winebibber. He was abhorrent to the medical profession as an unqualified practitioner who healed people by quackery and charged nothing for the treatment. He was not anti-Christ: nobody had heard of such a power of darkness then; but he was startlingly anti-Moses. He was against the priests, against the judiciary, against the military, against the city (he declared that it was impossible for a rich man to enter the kingdom of heaven), against all the interests, classes, principalities and powers, inviting everybody to abandon all these and follow him. By every argument, legal, political, religious, customary, and polite, he was the most complete enemy of the society of his time ever brought to the bar. He was guilty on every count of the indictment, and on many more that his accusers had not the wit to frame. If he was innocent then the whole world was guilty. To acquit him was to throw over civilization and all its institutions. History has borne out the case against him; for no State has ever constituted itself on his principles or made it possible to live according to his commandments: those States who have taken his name have taken it as an alias to enable them to persecute his followers more plausibly.

It is not surprising that under these circumstances, and in the absence of any defence, the Jerusalem community and the Roman government decided to exterminate Jesus. They had just as much right to do so as to exterminate the two thieves who perished with him. But there was neither right nor reason in torturing him. He was entitled to the painless death of Socrates. We may charitably suppose that if the death could have been arranged privately between Pilate and Caiaphas Jesus would have been dispatched as quickly and suddenly as John the Baptist. But the mob wanted the horrible fun of seeing somebody crucified: an abominably cruel method of execution. Pilate only made matters worse by trying to appease them by having Jesus flogged. The soldiers, too, had to have their bit of sport, to crown him with thorns and, when they buffeted him, challenge him ironically to guess which of them had struck the blow.

"CROSSTIANITY"

All this was cruelty for its own sake, for the pleasure of it. And the fun did not stop there. Such was and is the attraction of these atrocities that the spectacle of them has been reproduced in pictures and waxworks and exhibited in churches ever since as an aid to piety. The chief instrument of torture is the subject of a special Adoration. Little models of it in gold and ivory are worn as personal ornaments; and big reproductions in wood and marble are set up in sacred places and on graves. Contrasting the case with that of Socrates, one is forced to the conclusion that if Jesus had been humanely exterminated his memory would have lost ninetynine per cent of its attraction for posterity. Those who were specially susceptible to his morbid attraction were not satisfied with symbolic crosses which hurt nobody. They soon got busy with "acts of faith" which consisted of great public shows at which Jews and Protestants or Catholics, and anyone else who could be caught out on a point of doctrine, were burnt alive. Cruelty is so infectious that the very compassion it rouses is infuriated to take revenge by still viler cruelties.

The tragedy of this—or, if you will, the comedy—is that it was his clearness of vision on this very point that set Jesus so high above his persecutors. He taught that two blacks do not make a white; that evil should not be countered by worse evil but by good; that revenge and punishment only duplicate wrong; that we should conceive God, not as an irascible and vindictive tyrant but as an affectionate father. No doubt many private amiabilities have been inspired by this teaching; but politically it has received no more quarter than Pilate gave it. To all Governments it has remained paradoxical and impracticable. A typical acknowledgement of it was the hanging of a crucifix above the seat of the judge who was sentencing evildoers to be broken on the wheel.

CHRISTIANITY AND THE SIXTH COMMANDMENT

Now it is not enough to satirize this. We must examine why it occurred. It is not enough to protest that evildoers must not be paid in their own coin by treating them as cruelly as they have treated others. We still have to stop the mischief they do. What is to be done with them? It is easy to suggest that they should

be reformed by gentleness and shamed by non-resist-
ance. By all means, if they respond to that treatment.
But if gentleness fails to reform them and non-resist-
ance encourages them to further aggression, what
then? A month spent in a Tolstoyan community will
convince anybody of the soundness of the nearest
police inspector's belief that every normal human
group contains not only a percentage of saints but
also a percentage of irreclaimable scoundrels and good-
for-noughts who will wreck any community unless
they are expensively restrained or cheaply exterminated. Our Mosaic system of vindictive punishment,
politely called "retributory" by Prison Commissioners, disposes of them temporarily; but it wastes the
lives of honest citizens in guarding them; sets a
horrible example of cruelty and malicious injury;
costs a good deal of money that might be better spent;
and, after all, sooner or later lets the scoundrel loose
again to recommence his depredations. It would be
much more sensible and less cruel to treat him as we
treat mad dogs or adders, without malice or cruelty,
and without reference to catalogues of particular
crimes. The notion that persons should be safe from
extermination as long as they do not commit wilful
murder, or levy war against the Crown, or kidnap, or
throw vitriol, is not only to limit social responsibility
unnecessarily, and to privilege the large range of
intolerable misconduct that lies outside them, but to
divert attention from the essential justification for
extermination, which is always incorrigible social incompatibility and nothing else.

THE RUSSIAN EXPERIMENT

The only country which has yet awakened to this

extension of social responsibility is Russia. When the Soviet Government undertook to change over from Capitalism to Communism it found itself without any instruments for the maintenance of order except a list of crimes and punishments administered through a ritual of criminal law. And in the list of crimes the very worst offences against Communist society had no place: on the contrary they were highly honored and rewarded. As our English doggerel runs, the courts could punish a man for stealing the goose from off the common, but not the man who stole the common from the goose. The idler, that common enemy of mankind who robs everybody all the time, though he is so carefully protected from having his own pocket picked, incurred no penalty, and had actually passed the most severe laws against any interference with his idling. It was the business of the Soviet to make all business public business and all persons public servants; but the view of the ordinary Russian citizen was that a post in a public service was an exceptional stroke of good luck for the holder because it was a sinecure carrying with it the privilege of treating the public insolently and extorting bribes from it. For example, when the Russian railways were communized, some of the local stationmasters interpreted the change as meaning that they might now be as lazy and careless as they pleased, whereas in fact it was of life-or-death importance that they should redouble their activity and strain every nerve to make the service efficient. The unfortunate Commissar who was Minister of Transport found himself obliged to put a pistol in his pocket and with his own hand shoot stationmasters who had thrown his telegrams into the dustbin instead of attending to them, so that he might the more impressively ask the rest of the staff whether they yet grasped the fact that orders are meant to be executed.

INADEQUACY OF PENAL CODES

Now being Minister of Transport, or Minister of any other public service, is a whole time job: it cannot be permanently combined with that of amateur executioner, carrying with it the reputation in all the capitalist papers of the west of being a ferocious and coldblooded murderer. And no conceivable extension of the criminal code nor of the service disciplines, with their lists of specific offences and specific penalties, could have provided for instant exemplary exterminations of this kind, any more than for the growing urgency of how to dispose of people who would not or could not fit themselves into the new order of things by conforming to its new morality. It would have been easy to specify certain offences and certain penalties in the old fashion: as, for instance, if you hoard money you will be shot; if you speculate in the difference in purchasing power of the rouble in Moscow and Berlin you will be shot; if you buy at the Co-operative to sell at the private trader's shop you will be shot; if you take bribes you will be shot; if you falsify farm or factory balance sheets you will be shot; if you exploit labor you will be shot; and it will be useless to plead that you have been brought up to regard these as normal business activities, and that the whole of respectable society outside Russia agrees with you. But the most elaborate code of this sort would still have left unspecified a hundred ways in which wreckers of Communism could have sidetracked it without ever having to face the essential questions: are you pulling your weight in the social boat? are you giving more trouble than you are worth? have you earned the privilege of living in a civilized community? That is why the Russians were forced to set up an Inquisition or Star Chamber, called at first the Cheka and now the Gay Pay Oo (Ogpu), to go into these questions and "liquidate" persons who could not answer them satisfactorily. The security against the abuse of this power of life and death was that the Cheka had no interest in liquidating anybody who could be made publicly useful, all its interests being in the opposite direction.

LIMITED LIABILITY IN MORALS

Such a novelty is extremely terrifying to us, who are still working on a system of limited liability in morals. Our "free" British citizens can ascertain exactly what they may do and what they may not do if they are to keep out of the hands of the police. Our financiers know that they must not forge share certificates nor overstate their assets in the balance sheets they send to their shareholders. But provided they observe a few conditions of this kind they are free to enter upon a series of quite legitimate but not the less nefarious operations. For example, making a corner in wheat or copper or any other cornerable commodity and forcing up prices so as to make enormous private fortunes for themselves, or making mischief between nations through the Press to stimulate the private trade in armaments. Such limited liability no longer exists in Russia, and is not likely to exist in the future in any highly civilized state. It may be quite impossible to convict a forestaller or regrator under a criminal code of having taken a single illegal step, but quite easy to convince any reasonable body of judges that he is what the people call "a wrong one." In Russia such a conviction would lead to his disappearance and the receipt by his family of a letter to say that they need not wait up for him, as he would not return home any more.* In our country he would enjoy his gains in high honor and personal security, and thank his stars that he lived in a free country and not in Communist Russia.

But as the new tribunal has been forced on Russia by pressure of circumstances and not planned and thought out at leisure, the two institutions, the Ogpu and the ordinary police administering the criminal code, work side by side, with the odd result that the surest way to escape the Ogpu is to commit an ordinary crime and take refuge in the arms of the police and the magistrate, who cannot exterminate you because capital punishment has been abolished in Russia (liquidation by the Ogpu is not punishment: it is only "weeding the garden"); and the sentence of imprisonment, though it may seem severe to us in view of the cruelty of our treatment of criminals, will be carried out with comparative leniency, and probably, if the culprit behaves well be remitted after a while. As four years imprisonment is considered enough for any reasonable sort of murder, a cornerer who finds himself in imminent danger of detection and liquidation by the Ogpu would be well advised to lose his temper and murder his mother-in-law, thereby securing a lease of life for at least four years.

Sooner or later this situation will have to be thoroughly studied and thought out to its logical conclusion in all civilized countries. The lists of crimes

* Note, however, that a sentence of extermination should never be so certain as to make it worth the delinquent's while to avoid arrest by murdering his or her pursuers.

and penalties will obsolesce like the doctors' lists of diseases and medicines; and it will become possible to be a judge without ceasing to be a Christian. And extermination, my present subject, will become a humane science instead of the miserable mixture of piracy, cruelty, vengeance, race conceit, and superstition it now is.

NATURAL LIMIT TO EXTERMINATION

Fortunately the more frankly and realistically it is faced the more it detaches itself from the associations with crude slaughter which now make it terrible. When Charlemagne founded the Holy Roman Empire (as far as anyone can be said to have founded it) he postulated that all its subjects must be Catholic Christians, and made an amateurish attempt to secure this condition of social stability by killing everyone who fell into his power and refused to be baptized. But he cannot ever have got very far with it, because there is one sort of bird you must not kill on any pretext whatever: namely, the goose that lays the golden eggs. In Russia the Soviet Government began by a Charlemagnesque attempt to exterminate the bourgeoisie by classing them as intelligentsia, restricting their rations, and putting their children at the foot of the overcrowded educational list. They also proscribed the kulak, the able, hardheaded, hardfisted farmer who was richer than his neighbors and liked to see them poorer than himself. Him they rudely took by the shoulders and threw destitute into the lane. There were plausible reasons for this beginning of selection in population; for the moral outlook of the bourgeoisie and the kulaks was dangerously antisocial. But the results were disastrous. The bourgeoisie contained the professional class and the organizing business class. Without professional men and business organizers nothing could be done in the industries; and the hope that picked members of the proletariat could take up professional and organizing work on the strength of their native talent in sufficient numbers was crushingly disappointed. When the kulak was thrown out of his farm, and his farming ability paralyzed, food ran short. Very soon the kulak had to be thrown back into his farm and told to carry on until his hour had come; and a pleasant convention was established whereby all educated persons, however obviously ladies or gentlemen, who were willing to assure the authorities that their fathers had "worked on the land with their hands" were accepted as genuine proletarians, and transferred from the infamous category of intelligentsia to the honourable one of "the intellectual proletariat." Even Lenin and his colleagues, all ultra-bourgeois (otherwise they would never have so absurdly overestimated the intellectual resources of the proletariat and been so contemptuous of the pretension of their own class to be indispensable), allowed their parents to be described as hornyhanded cultivators of the soil. The pretence has now become a standing joke; but you will still come up against it if you accuse any Russian of being a lady or gentleman.

INCOMPATIBILITY OF PEASANTRY WITH MODERN CIVILIZATION

These, however, are merely expedients of transition. The Russian proletariat is now growing its own professional and organizing class; and the ex-bourgeois is dying out, after seeing his children receive a sound

Communist education and being lectured by them on his oldfashioned prejudices. And the planners of the Soviet State have no time to bother about moribund questions; for they are confronted with the new and overwhelming necessity for exterminating the peasants, who still exist in formidable numbers. The notion that a civilized State can be made out of any sort of human material is one of our old Radical delusions. As to building Communism with such trash as the Capitalist system produces it is out of the question. For a Communist Utopia we need a population of Utopians; and Utopians do not grow wild on the bushes nor are they to be picked up in the slums: they have to be cultivated very carefully and expensively. Peasants will not do; yet without the peasants the Communists could never have captured the Russian Revolution. Nominally it was the Soviets of peasants and soldiers who backed Lenin and saved Communism when all Western Europe set on him like a pack of hounds on a fox. But as all the soldiers were peasants, and all the peasants hungry for property, the military element only added to the peasants' cry of Give us land, the soldiers' cry of Give us peace. Lenin said, in effect, Take the land; and if feudally minded persons obstruct you, exterminate them; but do not burn their houses, as you will need them to live in. And it was the resultant legions of petty landed proprietors that made Lenin's position impregnable, and provided Trotsky and Stalin with the Red soldiers who defeated the counter-revolutionists of 1918. For the counter-revolution, in which we, to our eternal shame, took part (England sets the example of revolution and then attacks all other countries which presume to follow it), meant bringing the old landlords back; and the peasant fought against that as the

mercenaries and conscripts of the Capitalist armies
would not fight in favour of it.

A PEASANT VICTORY IS A VICTORY FOR
PRIVATE PROPERTY

So far so good for Lenin; but the war against the
counter-revolutionists, when it ended in victory for
the peasant proprietor, was really a victory for private
property, and was therefore succeeded by a fiercer
struggle between the fanatically Communist Government and the fiercely individualist peasant proprietor,
who wanted the produce of his plot for himself, and
had no notion of pooling it with anybody, least of all
with the urban proletarians who seemed like another
species to him. Left to themselves the moujiks would
have reproduced Capitalist civilization at its American
worst in ten years. Thus the most urgent task before
the victorious Communist Government was the extermination of the moujik; and yet the moujik, being
still the goose that laid the golden eggs, could not be
exterminated summarily without incidentally exterminating the whole Russian nation.

The way out of this deadlock was obvious enough,
though very expensive and tedious. You can exterminate any human class not only by summary violence
but by bringing up its children to be different. In the
case of the Russian peasantry the father lives in a
lousy kennel, at no man's call but his own, and extracts
a subsistence by primitive methods from a strip of
land on which a tractor could hardly turn even if he
could afford such a luxury, but which is his very own.
His book is a book of Nature, from which all wisdom
can be gathered by those who have been taught to
read it by due practice on printed books; but he has

not been so practised, and for cultural purposes has to be classed as ignorant, though he knows things that university professors do not know. He is brutalized by excessive muscular labor; he is dirty; his freedom from civilized control leaves him so unprotected from the tyranny of Nature that it becomes evident to his children that the highly regulated people in the nearest collectivist farm, where thousands of acres are cultivated by dozens of tractors, and nobody can put his foot on one of the acres or his hand on one of the tractors and say "This is my own to do what I like with," are better fed and housed, nicer, and much more leisured, and consequently free, than he ever is.

PREVENTIVE EXTERMINATION:
ITS DIFFICULTIES

In short, you exterminate the peasant by bringing up his children to be scientifically mechanized farmers and to live a collegiate life in cultivated society. It sounds simple; but the process requires better planning than is always forthcoming (with local famines and revolts as the penalty); for while the grass grows the steed starves; and when education means not only schools and teachers, but giant collective farms equipped with the most advanced agricultural machinery, which means also gigantic engineering works for the production of the machinery, you may easily find that you have spent too much on these forms of capitalization and are running short of immediately consumable goods, presenting the spectacle of the nation with the highest level of general culture running short of boots and tightening its belt for lack of sufficient food.

I must not suggest that this has occurred all over

Russia; for I saw no underfed people there; and the children were remarkably plump. And I cannot trust the reports; for I have no sooner read in The Times a letter from Mr Kerensky assuring me that in the Ukraine the starving people are eating one another, than M. Herriot, the eminent French statesman, goes to Russia and insists on visiting the Ukraine so that he may have ocular proof of the alleged cannibalism, but can find no trace of it. Still, between satiety and starvation mitigated by cannibalism there are many degrees of shortage; and it is no secret that the struggle of the Russian Government to provide more collective farms and more giant factories to provide agricultural machinery for them has to be carried on against a constant clamor from the workers for new boots and clothes, and more varied food and more of it: in short, less sacrifice of the present to the future. As Stalin said quaintly "They will be demanding silver watches next." The constant correction of the inevitable swerves towards one extreme or the other, analogous to the control of the Bank rate by the Bank of England (only enormously more laborious), strains all the wit and industry of the Russian rulers; and occasional sideslips must be inevitable during these years when the ablest and oldest Communists are still learners.

TEMPERAMENTAL DIFFICULTIES

Even when the extinction of the bourgeoisie and the kulaks and the old aristocracy is complete, and the Russian population consists of citizens educated as Communists, there will still be questions to settle which are bottom questions as to the sort of civilization that is desirable; and this involves a decision as to the sort of people that are desirable and undesirable. Some of us, believing that a more primitive life than ours would be happier and better, advocate "a return to nature." Others dream of a much more mechanized, specialized, and complicated life. Some of us value machinery because it makes a shorter working day possible for us: others value it because it enriches us by increasing the product per hour. Some of us would like to take things easy and retire at 60: others would like to work their utmost and retire at 40. Some of us will say Let us be content with £200 a year: others No: let us live at the rate of £20,000 a year and strain every faculty to earn it. Some of us want a minimum of necessary work and a maximum of liberty to think and discover and experiment in the extension of science and art, philosophy and religion, sport and exploration: others, caring for none of these things, and desiring nothing more than to be saved the trouble of thinking and to be told what to do at every turn, would prefer thoughtless and comfortable tutelage and routine, not knowing what to do with themselves when at liberty. A life filled with scientific curiosity would be hell for the people who would not cross the street to find out whether the earth is flat or round; and a person with no ear for music would strenuously object to work for the support of municipal bands, whilst people of Shakespear's tastes would agitate for the extermination of the unmusical.

IMPORTANCE OF LAZINESS FOR FALLOWING

Some of these differences could be settled on give-and-take lines. The division of society into classes with different tastes and capacities—different natures, as folks call it—would not shake social stability provided everyone had an equal share of the national dividend. It is not true that it takes all sorts to make a world; for there are some sorts that would destroy any world very soon if they were suffered to live and have their way; but it is true that in the generations of men continuous high cultivation is not expedient; there must be fallows, or at least light croppings, between the intense cultivations; for we cannot expect the very energetic and vital Napoleon to be the son of an equally energetic father or the father of an equally vital son. Nobody has yet calculated how many lazy ancestors it takes to produce an indefatigable prodigy; but it is certain that dynasties of geniuses do not occur, and that this is the decisive objection to hereditary rulers (though not, let me hasten to add, to hereditary figure heads). There is a large field for toleration here: the clever people must suffer fools gladly, and the easygoing ones find out how to keep the energetic ones busy. There may be as good biological reasons for the existence of the workshy as of the workmad. Even one and the same person may have spells of intense activity and slackness varying from weeks to years.

STANDARD RELIGION INDISPENSABLE

Nevertheless there will be conflicts to the death in the creation of artificial humanity. There is nothing that can be changed more completely than human nature when the job is taken in hand early enough. Such artificial products as our agricultural laborers and urban mechanics, our country gentlemen and city plutocrats, though they are from the same human stock, are so different that they cannot live together without great discomfort, and are practically not intermarriageable. It is possible to get rid of their social incompatibility by giving them all the same education and income, and ranking them all in the same class. For example, Lord Lonsdale is not in the least socially incompatible with Dean Inge, though a really critical naturalist would as soon class Shetland ponies with zebras as lump these two gentlemen under the same heading. But the question remains, what is this same education to be? The training of the scholar and the sportsman may split and diverge as they adolesce; but they must start from a common training and a common morality as children. And when the state has to prescribe a uniform moral curriculum the variety of our temperaments makes it impossible to please everybody. The Quaker and the Ritualist, the Fundamentalist and the Freethinker, the Vegetarian and the flesh eater, the missionary and the cannibal, the humanitarian and the sportsman-hunter, the military terrorist and the Christian, will not agree as to the faiths and habits to be inculcated upon the children of the community in order that they may be good citizens. Each temperament will demand the extermination of the other through the schools and nurseries, and the establishment of its temperamental faith and habits as standard in these factories of future citizens. All will agree to exterminate illiteracy by compulsory reading, writing, and arithmetic: indeed they have already done so. But all will not agree on a standard religion. Yet a standard religion is indispensable, however completely it may shed the old theologies. Every attempt to banish religion from the schools proves that in this respect Nature abhors a vacuum, and that the community must make up its mind, or have its mind made up for it by its official thinkers, as to what its children are to be taught to believe and how they should be trained to behave.

Compromise is ruled out by the nature of the case. What compromise is possible between myself, for instance, who believe in the religion of Creative Evolution, the economics of Socialism, and a diet from which the dead bodies of men, fish, fowls, and animals are rigidly excluded, and my Fundamentalist neighbors who believe that all Evolutionists go to hell; that children languish and die without beefsteaks; and that without private property civilization must perish ? We cannot exterminate oneanother at present; but the time cannot be very far off when the education authorities will have to consider which set of beliefs is the better qualification for citizenship in Utopia.

ECLECTIC RELIGIONS

They will probably pigeon-hole both, and proceed eclectically to compile several creeds suitable to the several capacities and ages of the children. For there is clearly no sense in offering the religion of a mature and scholarly philosopher to a child of five, nor attempting to bring the cosmogonies of Dante and Aquinas, Hegel and Marx, within the comprehension of a village dunce. Nurses rule their little charges by threatening them with bogies in whose existence no nurse believes, exactly as Mahomet ruled his Arabs by promises of a paradise and threats of a hell the details of which he must have known to be his own invention even if he did believe generally in a post mortem life of rewards and punishments for conduct in this world. Therefore I do not suggest that the education authorities in Utopia will seek for absolute truth in order to inculcate it though the heavens fall. Nor do I advise a return to Queen Elizabeth's plan of

39 Articles to please everybody by alternately affirm-
ing and denying all the disputed beliefs. The likeliest
outcome is an elaborate creed of useful illusions, to be
discarded bit by bit as the child is promoted from
standard to standard or form to form, except such of
them as adults may be allowed to comfort themselves
with for the sake of the docility they produce.

There would be nothing new in this: it is what our
authorities do at present, except that they do it un-
systematically and unconsciously, being mostly more
or less duped themselves by the illusions. Unfortunately they allow the illusions to fall behind the times
and become incredible, at which point they become
exceedingly dangerous; for when people are brought
up on creeds which they cannot believe, they are left
with no creeds at all, and are apt to buy pistols and
take to banditry bag snatching and racketeering when
employment fails and they find themselves short of
money. It is the importance of keeping our inculcated
illusions up to date that throws our higher professional
classes into wild alarm when the individual liberty of
thought, speech, and conscience which they think
they possess (this is one of their inculcated illusions)
is threatened by the dictatorships which are springing
up all over the world as our pseudo-democratic parliamentary institutions reduce themselves more and
more disastrously to absurdity.

IMPORTANCE OF FREE THOUGHT

Let me try to straighten this out for them. It was very
generally believed as lately as in Victorian times that
religious education consisted in imparting to children
certain eternal, final, and absolute truths. I, for instance, being the son of an Irish Protestant gentleman,

found myself, at the dawn of my infant conscience, absolutely convinced that all Roman Catholics go to hell when they die, a conviction which involved not only a belief in the existence of hell but a whole series of implications as to the nature and character of God. Now that I am older I cannot regard this as anything more than a provisional hypothesis which, on consideration, I must definitely reject. As the more pious of my uncles would have put it, I have lost my religious faith and am in peril of damnation as an Apostate. But I do not present my creed of Creative Evolution as anything more than another provisional hypothesis. It differs from the old Dublin brimstone creed solely in its greater credibility: that is, its more exact conformity to the facts alleged by our scientific workers, who have somehow won that faith in their infallibility formerly enjoyed by our priests. No future education authority, unless it is as badly educated as our present ones, will imagine that it has any final and eternal truths to inculcate: it can only select the most useful working hypotheses and inculcate them very much as it inculcates standard behaviour throughout that vast field of civilized conduct in which it does not matter in the least how people act in particular situations provided they all act in the same way, as in the rule of the road. All the provisional hypotheses may be illusions; but if they conduce to beneficial conduct they must be inculcated and acted on by Governments until better ones arrive.

TOLERATION MOSTLY ILLUSORY

But, cry the professors, are the hypotheses never to be questioned? Is disillusion to be punished as a crime? That will always depend a good deal on circumstances.

One of the best religious brains in England has said that the war of 1914–18 was foolish and unnecessary; and nobody now dreams of prosecuting him; but he would not have been allowed to go through the trenches from platoon to platoon saying so just before zero hour, with or without the addition "Sirs, ye are brethren: why do ye wrong one to another?" I have no illusion of being free to say and write what I please. I went round the world lately preaching that if Russia were thrust back from Communism into competitive Capitalism, and China developed into a predatory Capitalist State, either independently or as part of a Japanese Asiatic hegemony, all the western States would have to quintuple their armies and lie awake at nights in continual dread of hostile aeroplanes, the obvious moral being that whether we choose Communism for ourselves or not, it is our clear interest, even from the point of view of our crudest and oldest militarist diplomacy, to do everything in our power to sustain Communism in Russia and extend it in China, where at present provinces containing at the least of many conflicting estimates eighteen millions of people, have adopted it. Now I was not physically prevented from saying this, nor from writing and printing it. But in a western world suffering badly from Marxphobia, and frantically making itself worse like a shrew in a bad temper, I could not get a single newspaper to take up my point or report my utterance. When I say anything silly, or am reported as saying anything reactionary, it runs like wildfire through the Press of the whole world. When I say anything that could break the carefully inculcated popular faith in Capitalism the silence is so profound as to be almost audible. I do not complain, because I do not share the professorial illusion that there is any more freedom for disillusionists in the British Empire and the United States of North America than in Italy, Germany, and Russia. I have seen too many newspapers suppressed and editors swept away, not only in Ireland and India but in London in my time, to be taken in by Tennyson's notion that we live in a land where a man can say the thing he will. There is no such country. But this is no excuse for the extravagances of censorship indulged in by jejune governments of revolutionists, and by Churches who imagine they possess the eternal truth about everything, to say nothing of hereditary autocrats who conceive that they are so by divine right. Our papers are silent about the suppression of liberty in Imperialist Japan, though in Japan it is a crime to have "dangerous thoughts." In my native Ireland, now nominally a Free State, one of my books is on the index; and I have no doubt all the rest will follow as soon as the clerical censorship discovers their existence. In Austria my chronicle play St Joan had to be altered to please Catholic authorities who know much less about Catholicism than I do. In America books which can be bought anywhere in Europe are forbidden. The concentration of British and American attention on the intolerances of Fascism and Communism creates an illusion that they do not exist elsewhere; but they exist everywhere, and must be met, not with ridiculous hotheaded attacks on Germany, Italy, and Russia, but by a restatement of the case for Toleration in general.

LEADING CASES: SOCRATES AND JESUS

It is a historical misfortune that the most world-famous victims of persecution made no valid defence.

Socrates and Jesus are the most talked of in Christian countries. Socrates at his trial was in full possession of his faculties, and was allowed to say everything he had to say in his defence; but instead of defending his right to criticize he infuriated his accusers by launching at them a damning contrast between their infamous corruption and mendacity and his own upright disinterestedness and blameless record as citizen and soldier. Jesus made no defence at all. He did not regard himself as a prisoner being tried for a vulgar offence and using all his wit to escape condemnation. He believed that he was going through a sacrificial rite in which he should be slain, after which he should rise from the dead and come again in glory to establish his kingdom on earth for ever. It does not matter to our present purpose whether this was the delusion of a madman or a hard and holy fact: in either case the question of toleration was not at issue for him; therefore he did not raise it.

THE CASE OF GALILEO

In the epoch which Jesus inaugurated, or at least in which his name was habitually taken in vain, we have Joan of Arc and John of Leyden, Giordano Bruno and Galileo, Servetus and John Hus and the heroes of Foxe's Book of Martyrs standing out in our imagination from thousands of forgotten martyrdoms. Galileo is a favoured subject with our scientists; but they miss the point because they think that the question at issue at his trial was whether the earth went round the sun or was the stationary centre round which the sun circled. Now that was not the issue. Taken by itself it was a mere question of physical fact without any moral significance, and therefore no concern of the Church. As Galileo was not burnt and certainly not abhorred, it is quite credible that both his immediate judges and the Pope believed with at least half their minds that he was right about the earth and the sun. But what they had to consider was whether the Christian religion, on which to the best of their belief not only the civilization of the world but its salvation depended, and which had accepted the Hebrew scriptures and the Greek testament as inspired revelations, could stand the shock of the discovery that many of its tales, from the tactics of Joshua in the battle of Gibeon to the Ascension, must have been written by somebody who did not know what the physical universe was really like. I am quite familiar with the pre-Galileo universe of the Bible and St Augustine. As a child I thought of the earth as being an immense ground floor with a star studded ceiling which was the floor of heaven, and a basement which was hell. That Jesus should be taken up into the clouds as the shortest way to heaven seemed as natural to me as that, at the Opera, Mephistopheles should come up from hell through a trap in the floor. But if instead of telling me that Jesus was taken up into the clouds and that the disciples saw him no more, which still makes me feel quite holy, you tell me that he went up like a balloon into the stratosphere, I do not feel holy: I laugh obstreperously. The exalting vision has suddenly become a ribald joke. That is what the Church feared; and that is what has actually happened. Is it any wonder that the Pope told Galileo that he really must keep his discoveries to himself, and that Galileo consented to deny them? Possibly it was the Pope who, to console him, whispered "E pur se muove."

FIGMENT OF THE SELFREGARDING ACTION

St Joan did not claim toleration: she was so far from believing in it that she wanted to lead a crusade of extermination against the Husites, though she was burnt for sharing their heresy. That is how all the martyrs have missed the point of their defence. They all claimed to possess absolute truth as against the error of their persecutors, and would have considered it their duty to persecute for its sake if they had had the power. Real toleration: the toleration of error and falsehood, never occurred to them as a principle possible for any sane government. And so they have left us no model defence. And there is no modern treatise known to me which quite supplies this need. Stuart Mill's Essay on Liberty satisfied the nineteenth century, and was my own first textbook on the subject; but its conclusion that selfregarding actions should not be interfered with by the authorities carries very little weight for socialists who perceive that in a complex modern civilization there are no purely selfregarding actions in the controversial sphere. The color of a man's braces or a woman's garters may concern the wearers alone; but people have never been burnt for wearing black underclothes instead of white; and the notion that preaching a sermon or publishing a pamphlet can be classed as a selfregarding action is manifestly absurd. All great Art and Literature is propaganda. Most certainly the heresies of Galileo were not selfregarding actions: his feat of setting the earth rolling was as startling as Joshua's feat of making the sun stand still. The Church's mistake was not in interfering with his liberty, but in imagining that the secret of the earth's motion could be kept, and fearing that religion could not stand the shock of its disclosure, or a thousand such. It was idiotic to try to adapt Nature to the Church instead of continually adapting the Church to Nature by changing its teaching on physical matters with every advance made in our knowledge of Nature. In treating the legend of Joshua's victory as a religious truth instead of insisting that it did not make the smallest difference to religion whether Joshua was any more real than Jack the Giant Killer, and that Galileo might play skittles with the whole solar system without moving the Eternal Throne and the Papal Chair which was its visible tangible symbol on earth a single inch, it lost a great opportunity, as it has since lost many others, leaving itself open to the reproach of stupidity in not understanding Galileo's argument, of pride in not having humility enough to admit that it had been wrong in its astronomy, and of feebleness of faith and confusion of the temporal with the spiritual as aforesaid, laying itself open to much damaging Protestant and scientific disparagement, both mostly open to precisely the same reproaches.

INCOMPLETENESS OF THE GREAT TRIALS

No doubt Galileo missed the real point at issue as completely as Socrates or Jesus. For this we need not blame him: he was a physicist and not a politician; and to him the only questions at issue were whether the earth moved or not, and whether a ten pound cannon ball would fall twice as fast as a five pound one or only just as fast and no faster. But Socrates was by vocation and habit a solver of problems of conduct, both personal and political; and Jesus, who had spent his life in propounding the most staggering paradoxes on the same subject, not by any means always in the abstract, but as personal directions to his followers, must, if he had any sense of moral responsibility, have been challenged by his own conscience again and again as to whether he had any right to set men on a path which was likely to lead the best of them to the cross and the worst of them to the moral destruction described by St Augustine. No man could expressly admit that his word would bring not peace but a sword without having satisfied himself that he was justified in doing so. He must have been told as frequently as I have been told that he was giving pain to many worthy people; and even with the fullest allowance for the strain of impishness with which the Life Force endows those of us who are destined by it to *épater le bourgeois*, he cannot have believed that the mere satisfaction of this Punchesque *Schadenfreude* could justify him in hurting anyone's feelings. What, then, would have been his defence if, at his trial, he had been his old self, defending himself as an accused man threatened with a horrible penalty, instead of a god going through an inevitable ordeal as a prelude to the establishment of his kingdom on earth?

A MODERN PASSION PLAY IMPOSSIBLE

The question is of such importance at the present crisis, when the kingdoms are breaking up, and upstart rulers are sowing their wild oats by such grotesque persecutions that Galileo's great successor Einstein is a plundered fugitive from officially threatened extermination, that I must endeavor to dramatize the trial of Jesus as it might have proceeded had it taken

place before Peter uttered his momentous exclama-
tion "Thou art the Christ." I have been asked
repeatedly to dramatize the Gospel story, mostly by
admirers of my dramatization of the trial of St Joan.
But the trial of a dumb prisoner, at which the judge
who puts the crucial question to him remains un-
answered, cannot be dramatized unless the judge is to
be the hero of the play. Now Pilate, though perhaps a
trifle above the average of colonial governors, is not a
heroic figure. Joan tackled her judges valiantly and
wittily: her trial was a drama ready made, only need-
ing to be brought within theatrical limits of time and
space to be a thrilling play. But Jesus would not defend
himself. It was not that he had not a word to say for
himself, nor that he was denied the opportunity of
saying it. He was not only allowed but challenged to
defend himself. He was an experienced public speaker,
able to hold multitudes with his oratory, happy and
ready in debate and repartee, full of the illustrative
hypothetical cases beloved of lawyers (called parables
in the Gospels), and never at a loss when plied with
questions. If ever there was a full dress debate for the
forensic championship to be looked forward to with
excited confidence by the disciples of the challenged
expert it was this trial of Christ. Yet their champion
put up no fight: he went like a lamb to the slaughter,
dumb. Such a spectacle is disappointing on the stage,
which is the one thing that a drama must not be; and
when the disappointment is followed by scourging
and crucifixion it is unbearable: not even the genius
of our Poet Laureate, with all the magic of Canterbury
Cathedral for scenery, can redeem it except for people
who enjoy horror and catastrophe for their own sake
and have no intellectual expectations to be disappointed.

DIFFERENCE BETWEEN READER
AND SPECTATOR

It may be asked why the incident of the trial and execution must fail on the stage, seeing that the gospel narrative is so pathetic, and so many of us have read it without disappointment. The answer is very simple: we have read it in childhood; and children go on from horror to horror breathlessly, knowing nothing of the constitutional questions at issue. Some of them remain in this condition of intellectual innocence to the end of their lives, whilst the cleverer ones seldom reconsider the impressions they have received as little children. Most Christians, I suspect, are afraid to think about it critically at all, having been taught to consider criticism blasphemous when applied to Bible stories. Besides, there are a thousand things that will pass in a well told story that will not bear being brought to actuality on the stage. The evangelists can switch off our attention from Jesus to Peter hearing the cock crow (or the bugle blow) or to Pilate chaffering with the crowd about Barabbas; but on the stage the dumb figure cannot be got rid of: it is to him that we look for a speech that will take us up to heaven, and not to the weeping of Peter and the bawling of the mob, which become unbearable interruptions instead of skilful diversions.

For my part, when I read the story over again as an adult and as a professional critic to boot, I felt the disappointment so keenly that I have been ever since in the condition of the musician who, when he had gone to bed, heard somebody play an unresolved discord, and could not go to sleep until he had risen to play the resolution on his piano. What follows is my attempt to resolve Pilate's discord. I began with the narrative of St John, the only one of the four which represents Jesus as saying anything more than any crazy person might in the same circumstances.

PILATE. Are you the king of the Jews?

JESUS. Do you really want to know? or have those people outside put it into your head to ask me?

PILATE. Am I a Jew that I should trouble myself about you? Your own people and their priests have brought you to me for judgment. What have you done?

JESUS. My kingdom is not of this world: if it were, my followers would have fought the police and rescued me. But that sort of thing does not happen in my kingdom.

PILATE. Then you are a king?

JESUS. You say so. I came into this world and was born a common man for no other purpose than to reveal the truth. And everyone capable of receiving the truth recognizes it in my voice.

PILATE. What is truth?

JESUS. You are the first person I have met intelligent enough to ask me that question.

PILATE. Come on! no flattery. I am a Roman, and no doubt seem exceptionally intelligent to a Jew. You Jews are always talking about truth and righteousness and justice: you feed on words when you are tired of making money, or too poor to have anything else to feed on. They want me to nail you up on a cross; but as I do not yet see what particular harm you have done I prefer to nail you down to an argument. Fine words butter no parsnips in Rome. You say your vocation is to reveal the truth. I take your word for it; but I ask you what is truth?

JESUS. It is that which a man must tell even if he be stoned or crucified for telling it. I am not offering you the truth at a price for my own profit: I am offering it freely to you for your salvation at the peril of my own life. Would I do that if I were not driven by God to do it against all the protests of my shrinking flesh?

PILATE. You Jews are a simple folk. You have found only one god. We Romans have found many; and one of them is a God of Lies. Even you Jews have to admit a Father of Lies whom you call the devil, deceiving yourselves with words as usual. But he is a very potent god, is he not? And as he delights not only in lies but in all other mischief such as stonings and crucifixions of innocent men, how am I to judge whether it is he who is driving you to sacrifice yourself for a lie, or Minerva driving you to be sacrificed for the truth? I ask you again, what is truth?

JESUS. It is what you know by your experience to be true or feel in your soul must be true.

PILATE. You mean that truth is a correspondence between word and fact. It is true that I am sitting in this chair; but I am not the truth and the chair is not the truth: we are only the facts. My perception that I am sitting here may be only a dream; therefore my perception is not the truth.

JESUS. You say well. The truth is the truth and nothing else. That is your answer.

PILATE. Aye; but how far is it discoverable? We agree that it is true that I am sitting in this chair because our senses tell us so; and two men are not likely to be dreaming the same dream at the same moment. But when I rise from my chair this truth is no longer true. Truth is of the present, not of the future. Your hopes for the future are not the truth. Even in the present your opinions are not the truth. It is true that I sit in this chair. But is it true that it is better for your people that I should sit in this chair and impose on them the peace of Rome than that they should be left to slaughter oneanother in their own native savagery, as they are now clamoring to me to slaughter you?

JESUS. There is the peace of God that is beyond our understanding; and that peace shall prevail over the peace of Rome when God's hour strikes.

PILATE. Very pretty, my friend; but the hour of the gods is now and always; and all the world knows what the peace of your Jewish God Means. Have I not read it in the campaigns of Joshua? We Romans have purchased the *pax Romana* with our blood; and we prefer it as a plain understandable thing which keeps men's knives off oneanother's throats to your peace which is beyond understanding because it slaughters man woman and child in the name of your God. But that is only our opinion. It is not yours. Therefore it is not necessarily the truth. I must act on it, because a governor must act on something: he cannot loaf round the roads and talk beautifully as you do. If you were a responsible governor instead of a poetic vagrant, you would soon discover that my choice must lie, not between truth and falsehood, neither of which I can ever ascertain, but between reasonable and well informed opinion and sentimental and ill informed impulse.

JESUS. Nevertheless, opinion is a dead thing and impulse a live thing. You cannot impose on me with your reasonable and well informed opinion. If it is your will to crucify me, I can find you a dozen reasons for doing so; and your police can supply you with a hundred facts to support the reasons. If it is your will to spare me I can find you just as many reasons for that; and my disciples will supply you with more facts than you will have time or patience to listen to. That is why your lawyers can plead as well for one side as another, and can therefore plead without dishonor for the side that pays them, like the hackney charioteer who will drive you north as readily as south for the same fare.

PILATE. You are cleverer than I thought; and you are right. There is my will; and there is the will of Cæsar to which my will must give way; and there is above Cæsar the will of the gods. But these wills are in continual conflict with oneanother; therefore they are not truth; for truth is one, and cannot conflict with itself. There are conflicting opinions and conflicting wills; but there is no truth except the momentary truth that I am sitting in this chair. You tell me that you are here to bear witness to the truth! You, a vagrant, a talker, who have never had to pass a sentence nor levy a tax nor issue an edict! What have you to say that I should not have the presumption scourged out of you by my executioners?

JESUS. Scourging is not a cure for presumption, nor is it justice, though you will perhaps call it so in your report to Cæsar: it is cruelty; and that cruelty is wicked and horrible because it is the weapon with which the sons of Satan slay the sons of God is part of the eternal truth you seek.

PILATE. Leave out cruelty: all government is cruel; for nothing is so cruel as impunity. A salutary severity—

JESUS. Oh please! You must excuse me, noble Governor; but I am so made by God that official phrases make me violently sick. Salutary severity is ipecacuanha to me. I have spoken to you as one man to another, in living words. Do not be so ungrateful as to answer me in dead ones.

PILATE. In the mouth of a Roman words mean something: in the mouth of a Jew they are a cheap substitute for strong drink. If we allowed you you would fill the whole world with your scriptures and psalms and talmuds; and the history of mankind would become a tale of fine words and villainous deeds.

JESUS. Yet the word came first, before it was made flesh. The word was the beginning. The word was with God before he made us. Nay, the word was God.

PILATE. And what may all that mean, pray?

JESUS. The difference between man and Roman is but a word; but it makes all the difference. The difference between Roman and Jew is only a word.

PILATE. It is a fact.

JESUS. A fact that was first a thought; for a thought is the substance of a word. I am no mere chance pile of flesh and bone: if I were only that, I should fall into corruption and dust before your eyes. I am the embodiment of a thought of God: I am the Word made flesh: that is what holds me together standing before you in the image of God.

PILATE. That is well argued; but what is sauce for the goose is sauce for the gander; and it seems to me that if you are the Word made flesh so also am I.

JESUS. Have I not said so again and again? Have they not stoned me in the streets for saying it? Have I not sent my apostles to proclaim this great news to the Gentiles and to the very ends of the world? The Word is God. And God is within you. It was when I said this that the Jews—my own people—began picking up stones. But why should you, the Gentile, reproach me for it?

PILATE. I have not reproached you for it. I pointed it out to you.

[188]

JESUS. Forgive me. I am so accustomed to be contradicted—

PILATE. Just so. There are many sorts of words; and they are all made flesh sooner or later. Go among my soldiers and you will hear many filthy words and witness many cruel and hateful deeds that began as thoughts. I do not allow those words to be spoken in my presence. I punish those deeds as crimes. Your truth, as you call it, can be nothing but the thoughts for which you have found words which will take effect in deeds if I set you loose to scatter your words broadcast among the people. Your own people who bring you to me tell me that your thoughts are abominable and your words blasphemous. How am I to refute them? How am I to distinguish between the blasphemies of my soldiers reported to me by my centurions and your blasphemies reported to me by your High Priest?

JESUS. Woe betide you and the world if you do not distinguish!

PILATE. So you think. I am not frightened. Why do you think so?

JESUS. I do not think: I know. I have it from God.

PILATE. I have the same sort of knowledge from several gods.

JESUS. In so far as you know the truth you have it from my God, who is your heavenly father and mine. He has many names and his nature is manifold. Call him what you will: he is still Our Father. Does a father tell his children lies?

PILATE. Yes: many lies. You have an earthly father and an earthly mother. Did they tell you what you are preaching?

JESUS. Alas! no.

PILATE. Then you are defying your father and

mother. You are defying your Church. You are breaking your God's commandments, and claiming a right to do so. You are pleading for the poor, and declaring that it is easier for a camel to pass through the eye of a needle than for a rich man to enter your God's paradise. Yet you have feasted at the tables of the rich, and encouraged harlots to spend on perfume for your feet money that might have been given to the poor, thereby so disgusting your treasurer that he has betrayed you to the High Priest for a handful of silver. Well, feast as much as you please: I do not blame you for refusing to play the fakir and make yourself a walking exhibition of silly austerities; but I must draw the line at your making a riot in the temple and throwing the gold of the moneychangers to be scrambled for by your partizans. I have a law to administer. The law forbids obscenity, sedition, and blasphemy. You are accused of sedition and blasphemy. You do not deny them: you only talk about the truth, which turns out to be nothing but what you like to believe. Your blasphemy is nothing to me: the whole Jewish religion is blasphemy from beginning to end from my Roman point of view; but it means a great deal to the High Priest; and I cannot keep order in Jewry except by dealing with Jewish fools according to Jewish folly. But sedition concerns me and my office very closely; and when you undertook to supersede the Roman Empire by a kingdom in which you and not Cæsar are to occupy the throne, you were guilty of the uttermost sedition. I am loth to have you crucified; for though you are only a Jew, and a half baked young one at that, yet I perceive that you are in your Jewish way a man of quality; and it makes me uneasy to throw a man of quality to the mob, even if his quality be only a Jewish quality. For I am a patrician and therefore myself a man of quality; and hawks should not pick out hawks' eyes. I am actually condescending to parley with you at this length in the merciful hope of finding an excuse for tolerating your blasphemy and sedition. In defence you offer me nothing but an empty phrase about the truth. I am sincere in wishing to spare you; for if I do not release you I shall have to release that blackguard Barabbas, who has gone further than you and killed somebody, whereas I understand that you have only raised a Jew from the dead. So for the last time set your wits to work, and find me a sound reason for letting a seditious blasphemer go free.

JESUS. I do not ask you to set me free; nor would I accept my life at the price of Barabbas's death even if I believed that you could countermand the ordeal to which I am predestined. Yet for the satisfaction of your longing for the truth I will tell you that the answer to your demand is your own argument that neither you nor the prisoner whom you judge can prove that he is in the right; therefore you must not judge me lest you be yourself judged. Without sedition and blasphemy the world would stand still and the Kingdom of God never be a stage nearer. The Roman Empire began with a wolf suckling two human infants. If these infants had not been wiser than their fostermother your empire would be a pack of wolves. It is by children who are wiser than their fathers, subjects who are wiser than their emperors, beggars and vagrants who are wiser than their priests, that men rise from being beasts of prey to believing in me and being saved.

PILATE. What do you mean by believing in you?

JESUS. Seeing the world as I do. What else could it mean?

PILATE. And you are the Christ, the Messiah, eh?

JESUS. Were I Satan, my argument would still hold.

PILATE. And I am to spare and encourage every heretic, every rebel, every lawbreaker, every rapscallion lest he should turn out to be wiser than all the generations who made the Roman law and built up the Roman Empire on it?

JESUS. By their fruits ye shall know them. Beware how you kill a thought that is new to you. For that thought may be the foundation of the kingdom of God on earth.

PILATE. It may also be the ruin of all kingdoms, all law, and all human society. It may be the thought of the beast of prey striving to return.

JESUS. The beast of prey is not striving to return: the kingdom of God is striving to come. The empire that looks back in terror shall give way to the kingdom that looks forward with hope. Terror drives men mad: hope and faith give them divine wisdom. The men whom you fill with fear will stick at no evil and perish in their sin: the men whom I fill with faith shall inherit the earth. I say to you Cast out fear. Speak no more vain things to me about the greatness of Rome. The greatness of Rome, as you call it, is nothing but fear: fear of the past and fear of the future, fear of the poor, fear of the rich, fear of the High Priests, fear of the Jews and Greeks who are learned, fear of the Gauls and Goths and Huns who are barbarians, fear of the Carthage you destroyed to save you from your fear of it and now fear worse than ever, fear of imperial Cæsar, the idol you have yourself created, and fear of me, the penniless vagrant, buffeted and mocked, fear of everything except the rule of God: faith in nothing but blood and iron and gold. You, standing for Rome, are the universal coward: I, standing for the kingdom of God, have braved everything, lost everything, and won an eternal crown.

PILATE. You have won a crown of thorns; and you shall wear it on the cross. You are a more dangerous fellow than I thought. For your blasphemy against the god of the high priests I care nothing: you may trample their religion into hell for all I care; but you have blasphemed against Cæsar and against the Empire; and you mean it, and have the power to turn men's hearts against it as you have half turned mine. Therefore I must make an end of you whilst there is still some law left in the world.

JESUS. Law is blind without counsel. The counsel men agree with is vain: it is only the echo of their own voices. A million echoes will not help you to rule righteously. But he who does not fear you and shews you the other side is a pearl of the greatest price. Slay me and you go blind to your damnation. The greatest of God's names is Counsellor; and when your Empire is dust and your name a byword among the nations the temples of the living God shall still ring with his praise as Wonderful! Counsellor! the Everlasting Father, the Prince of Peace.

THE SACREDNESS OF CRITICISM

And so the last word remains with Christ and Handel; and this must stand as the best defence of Tolerance until a better man than I makes a better job of it.

Put shortly and undramatically the case is that a civilization cannot progress without criticism, and must therefore, to save itself from stagnation and putrefaction, declare impunity for criticism. This means impunity not only for propositions which, however novel, seem interesting, statesmanlike, and respectable, but for propositions that shock the uncritical as obscene, seditious, blasphemous, heretical, and revolutionary. That sound Catholic institution, the Devil's Advocate, must be privileged as possibly the Herald of the World to Come. The difficulty is to distinguish between the critic and the criminal or lunatic, between liberty of precept and liberty of example. It may be vitally necessary to allow a person to advocate Nudism; but it may not be expedient to allow that person to walk along Piccadilly stark naked. Karl Marx writing the death warrant of private property in the reading room of the British Museum was sacred; but if Karl Marx had sent the rent of his villa in Maitland Park to the Chancellor of the Exchequer, and shot the landlord's agents when they came to distrain on his furniture or execute a writ of ejectment, he could hardly have escaped hanging by pleading his right to criticize. Not until the criticism changes the law can the magistrate allow the critic to give effect to it. We are so dangerously uneducated in citizenship that most of us assume that we have an unlimited right to change our conduct the moment we have changed our minds. People who have a vague notion that Socialism is a state of society in which everyone gives away everything he possesses to everybody else occasionally reproach me because I, being a Socialist, do not immediately beggar myself in this fashion. People who imagined, more specifically, that a Socialist could not consistently keep a motor car, almost succeeded in making a public question of the possession of such a vehicle by a Prime Minister who at that time professed Socialism. But even if these idiots had really understood what they were talking about, they would have been wrong in supposing that a hostile critic of the existing social order either could or should behave as if he were living in his own particular Utopia. He may, at most, be a little eccentric at the cost of being indulged as slightly cracked.

On the other hand the Government, too, has not only a right but a duty of criticism. If it is to abandon once for all its savage superstition that whoever breaks the law is fair game for the torturers, and that the wrong wrought by the evildoer can be expiated and undone by a worse wrong done to him by judges and priests: if it is to substitute the doctrine of Jesus that punishment is only a senseless attempt to make a white out of two blacks, and to abolish the monstrous list of crimes and punishments by which these superstitions have been reduced to practice for routine officials, then there must be a stupendous extension of governmental criticism; for every crime will raise the essential critical question whether the criminal is fit to live at all, and if so whether he is fit to live under more or less tutelage and discipline like a soldier, or at normal liberty under an obligation to make good the damage he has cost.

For such functions as these we shall need critics educated otherwise than our judges of today; but the same may be said of all whose public functions transcend the application of a routine.

I have no doubt that the eradication of malice, vindictiveness, and Sadist libido on these terms from the personal contacts of citizens with their rulers, far from having a reassuring effect, is likely to be rather terrifying at first, as all people with any tenderness of conscience will feel the deepest misgivings as to whether they are really worth keeping alive in a highly civilized community; but that will wear off as standards of worth get established and known by practice. In the meantime the terror will act as a sort of social conscience which is dangerously lacking at present, and which none of our model educational establishments ever dreams of inculcating.

A YOT S T L AWRENCE, *22nd October, 1933*

The Cabinet Room in number ten Downing Street, Westminster, the official residence of the British Prime Minister. The illustrious holder of that office, Sir Arthur Chavender, is reading The Times on the hearth under the portrait of Walpole. The fireplace wall is covered with bookshelves; but one bit of it, on Walpole's right, is a masked door, painted with sham books and shelves, leading to the Minister's private apartments; and in the end of the same wall, on Walpole's left, is a door leading to the office of Sir Arthur's private secretary Miss Hilda Hanways. The main door is in the side wall on Walpole's right. In the opposite wall on his left are the spacious windows. Everything is on an imposing scale, including an oblong table across the middle of the room, with fourteen leather upholstered chairs, six at each side and one at each end, pushed in all along it. The presidential chair is the central one next the cold fireplace (it is mid-July); and there is a telephone and a switchboard on the table within reach of it. Sir Arthur has pulled it round and is making himself comfortable in it as he reads. At the end of the table nearest the window a silver tray, with coffee and milk for one person, indicates Sir Arthur's unofficial seat. In the corner farthest from Walpole, on his right, is a writing bureau and chair for the secretary. In the corresponding corner on his left, an armchair. There is a bluebook lying, neglected and dusty, on a half empty shelf of the bookcase within reach of the Prime Minister's seat.

Sir Arthur can hardly be much less than fifty; but his natural buoyancy makes him look younger. He has an orator's voice of pleasant tone; and his manners are very genial. In oldish clothes he has the proper aristocratic air of being carelessly but well dressed, an easy feat for him, as he is so trimly built that any clothes would look well cut on him. On the whole, a very engaging personality.

He reads The Times until his secretary hurries in from her office, with her notebook and a sheaf of letters in her hand. Her age is unknown; but she is made up to pass as reasonably young and attractive. She looks capable; but she does not carry the burden of State affairs as easily as the Prime Minister. Both are worried; but with a difference. She is worried not only by an excess of business but a sense of responsibility. He is equally worried by the excess of business; but in him enjoyment of his position leaves no doubt in his mind as to his own entire adequacy to it.

HILDA. I hear you have been asking for me, Sir Arthur. I'm so sorry to be late; but really the streets are becoming quite impassable with the crowds of unemployed. I took a taxi; but it was no use: we were blocked by a procession; and I had to get out and push my way through. [*She goes to her bureau*].

SIR ARTHUR [*rising*] What on earth good do they think they can do themselves by crowding aimlessly about Westminster and the public offices?

HILDA. Thank Goodness the police wont let them into Downing Street. [*She sits down*]. They would be all over the doorstep.

SIR ARTHUR. It's all so foolish—so ignorant, poor chaps! [*He throws The Times on the table and moves to the end chair, where his coffee is*]. They think because I'm Prime Minister I'm Divine Providence and can find jobs for them before trade revives. [*He sits down and fidgets with his papers*].

HILDA. Trafalgar Square's full. The Horse Guards parade is full. The Mall is full all the way down to Marlborough House and Buckingham Palace.

SIR ARTHUR. They have no right to be there. Trafalgar Square is not a public place: it belongs to the Commissioner of Woods and Forests. The Horse Guards parade is reserved for the military. The Mall is a thoroughfare: anyone stopping there is guilty of obstruction. What are the police thinking of? Why dont they clear them out?

HILDA. I asked the policeman who got me through to the gates why they didnt. He said "We're only too glad to have them where they cant break any windows, and where the mounted men can have a fair whack at the Hooligan Fringe when they get too obstreperous."

SIR ARTHUR. Hooligan Fringe! He got that out of the papers. It only encourages them to write them up like that.

HILDA. Sir Broadfoot Basham has come over from Scotland Yard. He is talking to Lady Chavender.

SIR ARTHUR [*rising and making for the telephone*] Yes: I telephoned for him. He really must do something to stop these meetings. It was a mistake to make a man with a name like that Chief Commissioner of Police. People think him a trampling, bashing, brutal terrorist no matter how considerately the police behave. What we need is a thoroughly popular figure. [*He takes up the telephone*] Ask Sir Broadfoot Basham to come up.

HILDA. I dont think any chief of police could be popular at present. Every day they are bludgeoning deputations of the unemployed. [*She sits down and busies herself with letters*].

[199]

SIR ARTHUR. Poor devils! I hate that part of the business. But what are the police to do? We cant have the sittings of the local authorities threatened by deputations. Deputations are frightful nuisances even in the quietest times; but just now they are a public danger.

The Chief Commissioner of Police enters by the main door. A capable looking man from the military point of view. He is a gentleman: and his manners are fairly pleasant; but they are not in the least conciliatory.

Hilda rises and pulls out a chair for him at the end of the table nearest to her and farthest from Sir Arthur; then returns to her work at her desk. Sir Arthur comes round to his side of the table.

SIR ARTHUR. Morning, Basham. Sit down. I'm devilishly busy; but you are always welcome to your ten minutes.

BASHAM [*coolly, sitting down*] Thank you. You sent for me. [*Anxiously*] Anything new?

SIR ARTHUR. These street corner meetings are going beyond all bounds.

BASHAM [*relieved*] What harm do they do? Crowds are dangerous when theyve nothing to listen to or look at. The meetings keep them amused. They save us trouble.

SIR ARTHUR. Thats all very well for you, Basham; but think of the trouble they make for me! Remember: this is a National Government, not a party one. I am up against my Conservative colleagues all the time; and they cant swallow the rank sedition that goes on every day at these meetings. Sir Dexter Rightside— you know what a regular old Diehard he is—heard a speaker say that if the police used tear gas the unemployed would give old Dexy something to cry for without any tear gas. That has brought matters to a head in the Cabinet. We shall make an Order in Council to enable you to put a stop to all street meetings and speeches.

BASHAM [*unimpressed—slowly*] If you dont mind, P.M., I had rather you didnt do that.

SIR ARTHUR. Why not?

BASHAM. Crowd psychology.

SIR ARTHUR. Nonsense! Really, Basham, if you are going to come this metaphysical rot over me I shall begin to wonder whether your appointment wasnt a mistake.

BASHAM. Of course it was a mistake. Dealing with the unemployed is not a soldier's job; and I was a soldier. If you want these crowds settled on soldierly lines, say so; and give me half a dozen machine guns. The streets will be clear before twelve o'clock.

SIR ARTHUR. Man: have you considered the effect on the bye-elections?

BASHAM. A soldier has nothing to do with elections. You shew me a crowd and tell me to disperse it. All youll hear is a noise like a watchman's rattle. Quite simple.

SIR ARTHUR. Far too simple. You soldiers never understand the difficulties a statesman has to contend with.

BASHAM. Well, whats your alternative?

SIR ARTHUR. I have told you. Arrest the sedition mongers. That will shut old Dexy's mouth.

BASHAM. So that Satan may find mischief still for idle hands to do. No, P.M.: the right alternative is mine: keep the crowd amused. You ought to know that, I think, better than most men.

SIR ARTHUR. I! What do you mean?

BASHAM. The point is to prevent the crowd doing anything, isnt it?

SIR ARTHUR. Anything mischievous: I suppose so. But—

BASHAM. An English crowd will never do anything, mischievous or the reverse, while it is listening to speeches. And the fellows who make the speeches can be depended on never to do anything else. In the first place, they dont know how. In the second, they are afraid. I am instructing my agents to press all the talking societies, the Ethical Societies, the Socialist societies, the Communists, the Fascists, the Anarchists, the Syndicalists, the official Labor Party, the Independent Labor Party, the Salvation Army, the Church Army and the Atheists, to send their best tub-thumpers into the streets to seize the opportunity.

SIR ARTHUR. What opportunity?

BASHAM. They dont know. Neither do I. It's only a phrase that means nothing: just what they are sure to rise at. I must keep Trafalgar Square going night and day. A few Labor M.P.s would help. You have a rare lot of gasbags under your thumb in the House. If you could send half a dozen of them down to the Yard, I could plant them where they would be really useful.

SIR ARTHUR [*incensed*] Basham: I must tell you that we are quite determined to put a stop to this modern fashion of speaking disrespectfully of the House of Commons. If it goes too far we shall not hesitate to bring prominent offenders to the bar of the House, no matter what their position is.

BASHAM. Arthur: as responsible head of the police, I am up against the facts all day and every day; and one of the facts is that nowadays nobody outside the party cliques cares a brass button for the House of Commons. [*Rising*] You will do what I ask you as to letting the speaking go on, wont you?

SIR ARTHUR. Well, I—er—

BASHAM. Unless you are game to try the machine guns.

SIR ARTHUR. Oh do drop that, Basham [*he returns to his chair and sits moodily*].

BASHAM. Righto! We'll let them talk. Thanks ever so much. Sorry to have taken up so much of your time: I know it's priceless. [*He hurries to the door; then hesitates and adds*] By the way, I know it's asking a lot; but if you could give us a turn in Trafalgar Square yourself—some Sunday afternoon would be best—it—

SIR ARTHUR [*springing up, thoroughly roused*] I!!!!

BASHAM [*hurriedly*] No: of course you couldnt. Only, it would do such a lot of good—keep the crowd quiet talking about it for a fortnight. However, of course it's impossible: say no more: so long. [*He goes out*].

SIR ARTHUR [*collapsing into his chair*] Well, really! Basham's losing his head. I wonder what he meant by saying that I ought to know better than most men. What ought I to know better than most men?

HILDA. I think he meant that you are such a wonderful speaker you ought to know what a magical effect a fine speech has on a crowd.

SIR ARTHUR [*musing*] Do you know, I am not at all sure that there is not something in his idea of my making a speech in Trafalgar Square. I have not done such a thing for many many years; but I have stood between the lions in my time; and I believe that if I were to tackle the unemployed face to face, and explain to them that I intend to call a conference in March next on the prospects of a revival of trade, it would have a wonderfully soothing effect.

HILDA. But it's impossible. You have a conference every month until November. And think of the time taken by the travelling! One in Paris! Two in Geneva!

One in Japan! You cant possibly do it: you will break down.

SIR ARTHUR. And shall I be any better at home here leading the House? sitting up all night in bad air listening to fools insulting me? I tell you I should have been dead long ago but for the relief of these conferences: the journeys and the change. And I look forward to Japan. I shall be able to pick up some nice old bric-a-brac there.

HILDA. Oh well! You know best.

SIR ARTHUR [*energetically*] And now to work. Work! work! work! [*He rises and paces the floor in front of the table*]. I want you to take down some notes for my speech this afternoon at the Church House. The Archbishop tells me that the Anglo-Catholics are going mad on what they call Christian Communism, and that I must head them off.

HILDA. There are those old notes on the economic difficulties of Socialism that you used at the British Association last year.

SIR ARTHUR. No: these parsons know too much about that. Besides, this is not the time to talk about economic difficulties: we're up to the neck in them. The Archbishop says "Avoid figures; and stick to the fact that Socialism would break up the family." I believe he is right: a bit of sentiment about the family always goes down well. Just jot this down for me. [*Dictating*] Family. Foundation of civilization. Foundation of the empire.

HILDA. Will there be any Hindus or Mahometans present?

SIR ARTHUR. No. No polygamists at the Church House. Besides, everybody knows that The Family means the British family. By the way, I can make a point of that. Put down in a separate line, in red capitals, "One man one wife." Let me see now: can I work that up? "One child one father." How would that do?

HILDA. I think it would be safer to say "One child one mother."

SIR ARTHUR. No: that might get a laugh—the wrong sort of laugh. I'd better not risk it. Strike it out. A laugh in the wrong place in the Church House would be the very devil. Where did you get that necklace? it's rather pretty. I havnt seen it before.

HILDA. Ive worn it every day for two months. [*Striking out the "one child" note*] Yes?

SIR ARTHUR. Then—er—what subject are we on? [*Testily*] I wish you wouldnt interrupt me: I had the whole speech in my head beautifully; and now it's gone.

HILDA. Sorry. The family.

SIR ARTHUR. The family? Whose family? What family? The Holy Family? The Royal Family? The Swiss Family Robinson? Do be a little more explicit, Miss Hanways.

HILDA [*gently insistent*] Not any particular family. THE family. Socialism breaking up the family. For the Church House speech this afternoon.

SIR ARTHUR. Yes yes yes, of course. I was in the House yesterday until three in the morning; and my brains are just so much tripe.

HILDA. Why did you sit up? The business didnt matter.

SIR ARTHUR [*scandalized*] Not matter! You really must not say these things, Miss Hanways. A full dress debate on whether Jameson or Thompson was right about what Johnson said in the Cabinet!

HILDA. Ten years ago.

SIR ARTHUR. What does that matter? The real

question: the question whether Jameson or Thompson is a liar, is a vital question of the first importance.

HILDA. But theyre both liars.

SIR ARTHUR. Of course they are; but the division might have affected their inclusion in the next Cabinet. The whole House rose at it. Look at the papers this morning! Full of it.

HILDA. And three lines about the unemployed, though I was twenty minutes late trying to shove my way through them. Really, Sir Arthur, you should have come home to bed. You will kill yourself if you try to get through your work and attend so many debates as well: you will indeed.

SIR ARTHUR. Miss Hanways: I wish I could persuade you to remember occasionally that I happen to be the leader of the House of Commons.

HILDA. Oh, what is the use of leading the House if it never goes anywhere? It just breaks my heart to see the state you come home in. You are good for nothing next morning.

SIR ARTHUR [yelling at her] Dont remind me of it: do you think I dont know? My brain is overworked: my mental grasp is stretched and strained to breaking point. I shall go mad. [Pulling himself together] However, it's no use grousing about it: I shall have a night off going to Geneva, and a week-end at Chequers. But it is hard to govern a country and do fifty thousand other things every day that might just as well be done by the Beadle of Burlington Arcade. Well, well, we mustnt waste time. Work! work! work! [He returns to his chair and sits down resolutely]. Get along with it. What were we talking about?

HILDA. The family.

SIR ARTHUR [grasping his temples distractedly] Oh

dear! Has Lady Chavender's sister-in-law been making a fuss again?

HILDA. No, no. The family. Not any real family. THE family. Socialism breaking up the family. Your speech this afternoon at the Church House.

SIR ARTHUR. Ah, of course. I am going dotty. Thirty years in Parliament and ten on the Front Bench would drive any man dotty. I have only one set of brains and I need ten. I—

HILDA [*urgently*] We must get on with the notes for your speech, Sir Arthur. The morning has half gone already; and weve done nothing.

SIR ARTHUR [*again infuriated*] How can the busiest man in England find time to do anything? It is you who have wasted the morning interrupting me with your silly remarks about your necklace. What do I care about your necklace?

HILDA. You gave it to me, Sir Arthur.

SIR ARTHUR. Did I? Ha ha ha! Yes: I believe I did. I bought it in Venice. But come along now. What about that speech?

HILDA. Yes. The family. It was about the family.

SIR ARTHUR. Well, I know that: I have not yet become a complete idiot. You keep saying the family, the family, the family.

HILDA. Socialism and the family. How Socialism will break up the family.

SIR ARTHUR. Who says Socialism will break up the family? Dont be a fool.

HILDA. The Archbishop wants you to say it. At the Church House.

SIR ARTHUR. Decidedly I am going mad.

HILDA. No: you are only tired. You were getting along all right. One man one wife: that is where you stopped.

SIR ARTHUR. One man one wife is one wife too many, if she has a lot of brothers who cant get on with the women they marry. Has it occurred to you, Miss Hanways, that the prospect of Socialism destroying the family may not be altogether unattractive?

HILDA [*despairingly*] Oh, Sir Arthur, we must get on with the notes: we really must. I have all the letters to do yet. Do try to pick up the thread. The family the foundation of the empire. The foundation of Christianity. Of civilization. Of human society.

SIR ARTHUR. Thats enough about the foundation: it wont bear any more. I must have another word to work up. Let me see. I have it. Nationalization of women.

HILDA [*remonstrating*] Oh, Sir Arthur!

SIR ARTHUR. Whats the matter now?

HILDA. Such bunk!

SIR ARTHUR. Miss Hanways: when a statesman is not talking bunk he is making trouble for himself; and Goodness knows I have trouble enough without making any more. Put this down. [*He rises and takes his platform attitude at the end of the table*]. "No, your Grace, my lords and gentlemen. Nationalize the land if you will; nationalize our industries if we must; nationalize education, housing, science, art, the theatre, the opera, even the cinema; but spare our women."

HILDA [*having taken it down*] Is that the finish?

SIR ARTHUR [*abandoning the attitude and pacing about*] No: write in red capitals under it "Rock of Ages."

HILDA. I think Rock of Ages will be rather a shock unless in connexion with something very sincere. May I suggest "The Church's One Foundation"?

SIR ARTHUR. Yes. Much better. Thank you. The family the Church's one foundation. Splendid.

Miss Flavia Chavender, 19, bursts violently into the room through the masked door and dashes to her father.

FLAVIA. Papa: I will not stand Mamma any longer. She interferes with me in every possible way out of sheer dislike of me. I refuse to live in this house with her a moment longer.

Lady Chavender follows her in, speaking as she enters, and comes between the Prime Minister and his assailant.

LADY CHAVENDER. I knew you were coming here to make a scene and disturb your father, though he has had hardly six hours sleep this week, and was up all night. I am so sorry, Arthur: she is uncontrollable.

David Chavender, 18, slight, refined, rather small for his age, charges in to the table.

DAVID [*in a childish falsetto*] Look here, Mamma. Cant you let Flavia alone? I wont stand by and see her nagged at and treated like a child of six. Nag! nag! nag! everything she does.

LADY CHAVENDER. Nag!! I control myself to the limit of human endurance with you all. But Flavia makes a study of annoying me.

FLAVIA. It's not true: I have considered you and given up all the things I wanted for you until I have no individuality left. If I take up a book you want me to read something else. If I want to see anybody you want me to see somebody else. If I choose the color of my own dress you want something different and dowdy. I cant sit right nor stand right nor do my hair right nor dress myself right: my life here is a hell.

LADY CHAVENDER. Flavia!!

FLAVIA [*passionately*] Yes, hell.

DAVID. Quite true. [*Fortissimo*] Hell.

LADY CHAVENDER [*quietly*] Miss Hanways: would you mind—

HILDA. Yes, Lady Chavender [*she rises to go*]

FLAVIA. You neednt go, Hilda. You know what I have to endure.

DAVID. Damn all this paralyzing delicacy! Damn it!

LADY CHAVENDER. Arthur—

SIR ARTHUR [*patting her*] Never mind, dear. They must be let talk. [*He returns placidly to his chair*]. It's just like the House of Commons, except that the speeches are shorter.

FLAVIA. Oh, it's no use trying to make papa listen to anything. [*She throws herself despairingly into Basham's chair and writhes*].

DAVID [*approaching Sir Arthur with dignity*] I really think, father, you might for once in a way take some slight interest in the family.

SIR ARTHUR. My dear boy, at this very moment I am making notes for a speech on the family. Ask Miss Hanways.

HILDA. Yes. Mr Chavender: Sir Arthur is to speak this afternoon on the disintegrating effect of Socialism on family life.

FLAVIA [*irresistible amusement struggling with hysterics and getting the better of them*] Ha ha! Ha ha ha!

DAVID [*retreating*] Ha ha! Haw! Thats the best—ha ha ha!

SIR ARTHUR. I dont see the joke. Why this hilarity?

DAVID. Treat the House to a brief description of this family; and you will get the laugh of your life.

FLAVIA. Damn the family!

LADY CHAVENDER. Flavia!

FLAVIA [*bouncing up*] Yes: there you go. I mustnt say damn. I mustnt say anything I feel and think, only what you feel and think. Thats family life. Scold, scold, scold!

DAVID. Squabble, squabble, squabble!

FLAVIA. Look at the unbearable way you treat me!
Look at the unbearable way you treat Papa!

SIR ARTHUR [*rising in flaming wrath*] How dare you?
Silence. Leave the room.

*After a moment of awestruck silence Flavia, rather
dazed by the avalanche she has brought down on herself,
looks at her father in a lost way; then bursts into tears
and runs out through the masked door.*

SIR ARTHUR [*quietly*] Youd better go too, my boy.

*David, also somewhat dazed, shrugs his shoulders and
goes out. Sir Arthur looks at Hilda. She hurries out
almost on tiptoe.*

SIR ARTHUR [*taking his wife in his arms affectionately*]
Treat me badly! You!! I could have killed her, poor
little devil.

*He sits down; and she passes behind him and takes the
nearest chair on his right.*

*She is a nice woman, and goodlooking; but she is
bored; and her habitual manner is one of apology for
being not only unable to take an interest in people, but
even to pretend that she does.*

LADY CHAVENDER. It serves us right, dear, for letting
them bring themselves up in the post-war fashion instead of teaching them to be ladies and gentlemen.
Besides, Flavia was right. I do treat you abominably.
And you are so good!

SIR ARTHUR. Nonsense! Such a horrid wicked thing
to say. Dont you know, my love, that you are the
best of wives? the very best as well as the very
dearest?

LADY CHAVENDER. You are certainly the best of
husbands, Arthur. You are the best of everything. I
dont wonder at the country adoring you. But Flavia
was quite right. It is the first time I have ever known
her to be right about anything. I am a bad wife and a

bad mother. I dislike my daughter and treat her badly.
I like you very much; and I treat you abominably.

SIR ARTHUR. No; no.

LADY CHAVENDER. Yes, yes. I suppose it's something wrong in my constitution. I was not born for
wifing and mothering. And yet I am very very fond
of you, as you know. But I have a grudge against your
career.

SIR ARTHUR. My career! [*Complacently*] Well, theres
not much wrong with that, is there? Of course I know
it keeps me too much away from home. That gives
you a sort of grudge against it. All the wives of successful men are a bit like that. But it's better to see too
little of a husband than too much of him, isnt it?

LADY CHAVENDER. I am so glad that you really feel
successful.

SIR ARTHUR. Well, it may sound conceited and all
that; but after all a man cant be Prime Minister and
go about with a modest cough pretending to be a
nobody. Facts are facts; and the facts in my case are
that I have climbed to the top of the tree; I am happy
in my work; and—

LADY CHAVENDER. Your what?

SIR ARTHUR. You are getting frightfully deaf, dear.
I said "my work."

LADY CHAVENDER. You call it work?

SIR ARTHUR. Brain work, dear, brain work. Do you
really suppose that governing the country is not work,
but a sort of gentlemanly diversion?

LADY CHAVENDER. But you dont govern the country,
Arthur. The country isnt governed: it just slum-
mocks along anyhow.

SIR ARTHUR. I have to govern within democratic
limits. I cannot go faster than our voters will let me.

LADY CHAVENDER. Oh, your voters! What do they

know about government? Football, prizefighting, war: that is what they like. And they like war because it isnt real to them: it's only a cinema show. War is real to me; and I hate it, as every woman to whom it is real hates it. But to you it is only part of your game: one of the regular moves of the Foreign Office and the War Office.

SIR ARTHUR. My dear, I hate war as much as you do. It makes a Prime Minister's job easy because it brings every dog to heel; but it produces coalitions; and I believe in party government.

LADY CHAVENDER [*rising*] Oh, it's no use talking to you, Arthur. [*She comes behind him and plants her hands on his shoulders*]. You are a dear and a duck and a darling; but you live in fairyland and I live in the hard wicked world. Thats why I cant be a good wife and take an interest in your career.

SIR ARTHUR. Stuff! Politics are not a woman's business: thats all it means. Thank God I have not a political wife. Look at Higginbotham! He was just ripe for the Cabinet when his wife went into Parliament and made money by journalism. That was the end of him.

LADY CHAVENDER. And I married a man with a hopelessly parliamentary mind; and that was the end of me.

SIR ARTHUR. Yes, yes, my pettums. I know that you have sacrificed yourself to keeping my house and sewing on my buttons; and I am not ungrateful. I am sometimes remorseful; but I love it. And now you must run away, I am very very very busy this morning.

LADY CHAVENDER. Yes, yes, very very busy doing nothing. And it wears you out far more than if your mind had something sensible to work on! Youll have a nervous breakdown if you go on like this. Promise me that you will see the lady I spoke to you about—if you wont see a proper doctor.

SIR ARTHUR. But you told me this woman is a doctor! [*He rises and breaks away from her*]. Once for all, I wont see any doctor. I'm old enough to do my own doctoring; and I'm not going to pay any doctor, male or female, three guineas to tell me what I know perfectly well already: that my brain's overworked and I must take a fortnight off on the links, or go for a sea voyage.

LADY CHAVENDER. She charges twenty guineas, Arthur.

SIR ARTHUR [*shaken*] Oh! Does she? What for?

LADY CHAVENDER. Twenty guineas for the diagnosis and twelve guineas a week at her sanatorium in the Welsh mountains, where she wants to keep you under observation for six weeks. That would really rest you; and I think you would find her a rather interesting and attractive woman.

SIR ARTHUR. Has she a good cook?

LADY CHAVENDER. I dont think that matters.

SIR ARTHUR. Not matter!

LADY CHAVENDER. No. She makes her patients fast.

SIR ARTHUR. Tell her I'm not a Mahatma. If I pay twelve guineas a week I shall expect three meals a day for it.

LADY CHAVENDER. Then you will see her?

SIR ARTHUR. Certainly not, if I have to pay twenty guineas for it.

LADY CHAVENDER. No, no. Only a social call, not a professional visit. Just to amuse you, and gratify her curiosity. She wants to meet you.

SIR ARTHUR. Very well, dear, very well, very well. This woman has got round you, I see. Well, she shant get round me; but to please you I'll have a look at her.

And now you really must run away. I have a frightful mass of work to get through this morning.

LADY CHAVENDER. Thank you, darling. [*She kisses him*] May I tell Flavia she is forgiven?

SIR ARTHUR. Yes. But I havnt really forgiven her. I'll never forgive her.

LADY CHAVENDER [*smiling*] Dearest. [*She kisses his fingers and goes out, giving him a parting smile as she goes through the masked door*].

Sir Arthur, left alone, looks inspired and triumphant. He addresses an imaginary assembly.

SIR ARTHUR. "My lords and gentlemen: you are not theorists. You are not rhapsodists. You are no longer young"—no, damn it, old Middlesex wont like that. "We have all been young. We have seen visions and dreamt dreams. We have cherished hopes and striven towards ideals. We have aspired to things that have not been realized. But we are now settled experienced men, family men. We are husbands and fathers. Yes, my lords and gentlemen: husbands and fathers. And I venture to claim your unanimous consent when I affirm that we have found something in these realities that was missing in the ideals. I thank you for that burst of applause: which I well know is no mere tribute to my poor eloquence, but the spontaneous and irrestible recognition of the great natural truth that our friends the Socialists have left out of their fancy pictures of a mass society in which regulation is to take the place of emotion and economics of honest human passion." Whew! that took a long breath. "They never will, gentlemen, I say they never will. They will NOT [*he smites the table and pauses, glaring round at his imaginary hearers*]. I see that we are of one mind, my lords and gentlemen. I need not labor the point." Then labor it for the next ten minutes.

That will do. That will do. [*He sits down; rings the telephone bell; and seizes the milk jug, which he empties at a single draught*].

Hilda appears at the main door.

HILDA. Did you say you would receive a deputation from the Isle of Cats this morning? I have no note of it.

SIR ARTHUR. Oh, confound it, I believe I did. I totally forgot it.

HILDA. Theyve come.

SIR ARTHUR. Bother them!

HILDA. By all means. But how am I to get rid of them? What am I to say?

SIR ARTHUR [*resignedly*] Oh, I suppose I must see them. Why do I do these foolish things? Tell Burton to shew them in.

HILDA. Burton is in his shirt sleeves doing something to the refrigerator. I'd better introduce them.

SIR ARTHUR. Oh, bundle them in anyhow. And tell them I am frightfully busy.

She goes out, closing the door softly behind her. He pushes away the breakfast tray and covers it with The Times, which he opens out to its fullest extent for that purpose. Then he collects his papers into the vacant space, and takes up a big blue one, in the study of which he immerses himself profoundly.

HILDA [*flinging the door open*] The worshipful the Mayor of the Isle of Cats.

The Mayor, thick and elderly, enters, a little shyly, followed by (a) an unladylike but brilliant and very confident young woman in smart factory-made clothes after the latest Parisian models, (b) a powerfully built loud voiced young man fresh from Oxford University, defying convention in corduroys, pullover, and unshaven black beard, (c) a thin, undersized lower middle class young man in an alderman's gown, evidently with a good conceit of himself, and (d) a sunny comfortable old chap in his Sunday best, who might be anything from a working man with a very sedentary job (say a watchman) to a city missionary of humble extraction. He is aggressively modest, or pretends to be, and comes in last with a disarming smile rather as a poor follower of the deputation than as presuming to form part of it. They group themselves at the door behind the Mayor, who is wearing his chain of office.

SIR ARTHUR [*starting from his preoccupation with important State documents, and advancing past the fireplace to greet the Mayor with charming affability*] What! My old friend Tom Humphries! How have you been all these years? Sit down. [*They shake hands, whilst Hilda deftly pulls out a chair from the end of the table nearest the door*].

The Mayor sits down, rather overwhelmed by the cordiality of his reception.

SIR ARTHUR [*continuing*] Well, well! fancy your being Mayor of—of—

HILDA [*prompting*] The Isle of Cats.

THE YOUNG WOMAN [*brightly, helping her out*] Down the river, Sir Arthur. Twenty minutes from your door by Underground.

THE OXFORD YOUTH [*discordantly*] Oh, he knows as well as you do, Aloysia. [*He advances offensively on Sir Arthur, who declines the proximity by retreating a step or two somewhat haughtily*]. Stow all this fo bunnum business, Chavender.

SIR ARTHUR. This what?

OXFORD YOUTH. Oh, chuck it. You know French as well as I do.

SIR ARTHUR. Oh, faux bonhomme, of course, yes. [*Looking him up and down*]. I see by your costume that

[217]

you represent the upper classes in the Isle of Cats.

OXFORD YOUTH. There are no upper classes in the Isle of Cats.

SIR ARTHUR. In that case, since it is agreed that there is to be no fo bunnum nonsense between us, may I ask what the dickens you are doing here?

OXFORD YOUTH. I am not here to bandy personalities. Whatever the accident of birth and the humbug of rank may have made me I am here as a delegate from the Borough Council and an elected representative of the riverside proletariat.

SIR ARTHUR [*suddenly pulling out a chair from the middle of the table—peremptorily*] Sit down. Dont break the chair. [*The Youth scowls at him and flings himself into the chair like a falling tree*]. You are all most welcome. Perhaps, Tom, you will introduce your young friends.

THE MAYOR [*introducing*] Alderwoman Aloysia Brollikins.

SIR ARTHUR [*effusively shaking her hand*] How do you do, Miss Brollikins? [*He pulls out a chair for her on the Oxford Youth's right*].

ALOYSIA. Nicely, thank you. Pleased to meet you, Sir Arthur. [*She sits*].

THE MAYOR. Alderman Blee.

SIR ARTHUR [*with flattering gravity, pressing his hand*] Ah, we have all heard of y o u, Mr Blee. Will you sit here? [*He indicates the presidential chair on the Oxford Youth's left*].

BLEE. Thank you. I do my best. [*He sits*].

THE MAYOR. Viscount Barking.

SIR ARTHUR [*triumphantly*] Ah! I thought so. A red Communist: what!

OXFORD YOUTH. Red as blood. Same red as the people's.

SIR ARTHUR. How did you get the blue out of it? The Barkings came over with the Conqueror.

OXFORD YOUTH [*rising*] Look here. The unemployed are starving. Is this a time for persiflage?

SIR ARTHUR. Camouflage, my lad, camouflage. Do you expect me to take you seriously in that get-up?

OXFORD YOUTH [*hotly*] I shall wear what I damn well please. I—

ALOYSIA. Shut up, Toffy. You promised to behave yourself. Sit down; and lets get to business.

BARKING [*subsides into his chair with a grunt of disgust*]!

SIR ARTHUR [*looking rather doubtfully at the old man, who is still standing*] Is this gentleman a member of your deputation?

THE MAYOR. Mr Hipney. Old and tried friend of the working class.

OXFORD YOUTH. Old Hipney. Why dont you call him by the name the East End knows him by? Old Hipney. Good old Hipney.

OLD HIPNEY [*slipping noiselessly into the secretary's chair at the bureau*] Dont mind me, Sir Arthur. I dont matter.

SIR ARTHUR. At such a crisis as the present, Mr Hipney, every public-spirited man matters. Delighted to meet you. [*He returns to his own chair and surveys them now that they are all seated, whilst Hilda slips discreetly out into her office*]. And now, what can I do for you, Miss Brollikins? What can I do for you, gentlemen?

THE MAYOR [*slowly*] Well, Sir Arthur, as far as I can make it out the difficulty seems to be that you cant do anything. But something's got to be done.

SIR ARTHUR [*stiffening suddenly*] May I ask why, if everything that is possible has already been done?

THE MAYOR. Well, the unemployed are—well, unemployed, you know.

SIR ARTHUR. We have provided for the unemployed. That provision has cost us great sacrifices; but we have made the sacrifices without complaining.

THE OXFORD YOUTH [*scornfully*] Sacrifices! What sacrifices? Are you starving? Have you pawned your overcoat? Are you sleeping ten in a room?

SIR ARTHUR. The noble lord enquires—

OXFORD YOUTH [*furiously*] Dont noble lord me: you are only doing it to rattle me. Well, you cant rattle me. But it makes me sick to see you rolling in luxury and think of what these poor chaps and their women folk are suffering.

SIR ARTHUR. I am not rolling, Toffy—I think that is what Miss Brollikins called you. [*To Aloysia*] Toffy is a diminutive of Toff, is it not, Miss Brollikins?

OXFORD YOUTH. Yah! Now you have something silly to talk about, youre happy. But I know what would make you sit up and do something.

SIR ARTHUR. Indeed? Thats interesting. May I ask what?

OXFORD YOUTH. Break your bloody windows.

THE MAYOR. Order! order!

ALOYSIA. Come, Toffy! you promised not to use any of your West End language here. You know we dont like it.

SIR ARTHUR. Thats right, Miss Brollikins: snub him. He is disgracing his class. As a humble representative of that class I apologize for him to the Isle of Cats. I apologize for his dress, for his manners, for his language. He must shock you every time he opens his mouth.

BLEE. We working folks know too much of bad language and bad manners to see any fun in them or think they can do any good.

THE MAYOR. Thats right.

ALOYSIA. We are as tired of bad manners as Toffy is tired of good manners. We brought Toffy here, Sir Arthur, because we knew he'd speak to you as a dock laborer would speak to you if his good manners would let him. And he's right, you know. He's rude; but he's right.

OXFORD YOUTH. Yours devotedly, Brolly. And what has his Right Honorable nibs to say to that?

SIR ARTHUR [*concentrating himself on his adversary in the House of Commons manner*] I will tell the noble lord what I have to say. He may marshal his friends the unemployed and break every window in the West End, beginning with every pane of glass in this house. What will he gain by it? Next day a score or so of his followers will be in prison with their heads broken. A few ignorant and cowardly people who have still any money to spare will send it to the funds for the relief of distress, imagining that they are ransoming their riches. You, ladies and gentlemen, will have to put your hands in your pockets to support the wives and children of the men in prison, and to pay cheap lawyers to put up perfectly useless defences for them in the police courts. And then, I suppose, the noble lord will boast that he has made me do something at last. What can I do? Do you suppose that I care less about the sufferings of the poor than you? Do you suppose I would not revive trade and put an end to it all tomorrow if I could? But I am like yourself: I am in the grip of economic forces that are beyond human control. What mortal men could do this Government has done. We have saved the people from starvation by stretching unemployment benefit to the utmost limit of our national resources. We—

OXFORD YOUTH. You have cut it down to fifteen bob

a week and shoved every man you could off it with your beastly means test.

SIR ARTHUR [*fiercely*] What do you propose? Will you take my place and put the dole up to five pounds a week without any means test?

THE MAYOR. Order! order! Why are we here? We are here because we are all sick of arguing and talking, and we want something doing. And here we are arguing and talking just as if it was an all night sitting of the Borough Council about an item of three-and-six for refreshments. If you, Sir Arthur, tell us that you cant find work for our people we are only wasting your time and our own, sitting here.

He rises. The rest, except Hipney, follow his example. Sir Arthur is only too glad to rise too.

SIR ARTHUR. At least I hope I have convinced you about the windows, Mr Mayor.

THE MAYOR. We needed no convincing. More crockery than windows will have to be broken if you gentlemen can do nothing to get us out of our present mess. But some people will say that a few thousand more to the relief funds is better than nothing. And some of the unemployed are glaziers.

SIR ARTHUR. Let us close our little talk on a more hopeful note. I assure you it has been intensely interesting to me; and I may tell you that signs of a revival of trade are not wholly wanting. Some of the best informed city authorities are of opinion that this year will see the end of the crisis. Some of them even hold that trade is already reviving. By the last returns the export of Spanish onions has again reached the 1913 level.

OXFORD YOUTH. Holy Jerusalem! Spanish onions! Come on, Brolly. [*He goes out*].

THE MAYOR. Weve got nothing out of this. We dont

run to Spanish in the Isle. [*Resignedly*] Good morning. [*He goes out*].

SIR ARTHUR [*winningly*] And do you, Miss Brollikins, feel that you have got nothing?

ALOYSIA. I feel what they feel. And I dont believe you feel anything at all. [*She goes out, followed by Blee*].

BLEE [*turning at the door*] The Mayor's wrong. Weve got something all right.

SIR ARTHUR [*brightening*] Indeed? What is it?

BLEE [*with intense contempt*] Your measure. [*He goes out*].

The Prime Minister, nettled by this gibe, resumes his seat angrily and pushes the bluebook out of his way. Then he notices that old Hipney has not budged from his seat at the secretary's bureau.

SIR ARTHUR. The deputation has withdrawn. Mr Hipney.

HIPNEY [*rising and coming to a chair at Sir Arthur's elbow, in which he makes himself comfortable with a disarmingly pleasant air of beginning the business instead of ending it*] Yes: now we can talk a bit. I been at this game now for fifty year.

SIR ARTHUR [*interested in spite of himself*] What game? Deputations?

HIPNEY. Unemployed deputations. This is my twelfth.

SIR ARTHUR. As many as that! But these crises dont come oftener than every ten years, do they?

HIPNEY. Not what you would call a crisis, perhaps. But unemployment is chronic.

SIR ARTHUR. It always blows over, doesnt it? Trade revives.

HIPNEY. It used to. We was the workshop of the world then. But you gentlemen went out of the workshop business to make a war. And while that was going

ON THE ROCKS

on our customers had to find out how to make things for themselves. Now we shall have to be their customers when weve any money to buy with.

SIR ARTHUR. No doubt that has occurred to some extent; but there is still an immense fringe of the human race growing up to a sense of the necessity for British goods.

HIPNEY. All goods is alike to that lot provided theyre the cheapest. They tell me the Italians are tapping their volcanoes for cheap power. We dont seem able to tap nothing. The east is chock full of volcanoes: they think no more of an earthquake there than you would of a deputation. A Chinese coolie can live on a penny a day. What can we do against labor at a penny a day and power for next to nothing out of the burning bowels of the earth?

SIR ARTHUR. Too true, Mr Hipney. Our workers must make sacrifices.

HIPNEY. They will if you drive em to it, Srarthur. But it's you theyll sacrifice.

SIR ARTHUR. Oh come, Mr Hipney! you are a man of sense and experience. What good would it do them to sacrifice me?

HIPNEY. Not a bit in the world, sir. But that wont stop them. Look at your self. Look at your conferences! Look at your debates! They dont do no good. But you keep on holding them. It's a sort of satisfaction to you when you feel helpless. Well, sir, if you come to helplessness there isnt on God's earth a creature more helpless than what our factories and machines have made of an English working man when nobody will give him a job and pay him to do it. And when he gets it what does he understand of it? Just nothing. Where did the material that he does his little bit of a job on come from? He dont know. What will happen to it when it goes out of the factory after he and his like have all done their little bits of jobs on it? He dont know. Where could he buy it if it stopped coming to him? He dont know. Where could he sell it if it was left on his hands? He dont know. He dont know nothing of the business that his life depends on. Turn a cat loose and itll feed itself. Turn an English working man loose and he'll starve. You have to buy him off with a scrap of dole to prevent him saying "Well, if I'm to die I may as well have the satisfaction of seeing you die first."

SIR ARTHUR. But—I really must press the point—what good will that do him?

HIPNEY. What good does backing horses do him? What good does drinking do him? What good does going to political meetings do him? What good does going to church do him? Not a scrap. But he keeps on doing them all the same.

SIR ARTHUR. But surely you recognize, Mr Hipney, that all this is thoroughly wrong—wrong in feeling—contrary to English instincts—out of character, if I may put it that way.

HIPNEY. Well, Srarthur, whatever's wrong you and your like have taken on yourselves the job of setting it right. I havnt: I'm only a poor man: a nobody, as you might say.

SIR ARTHUR. I have not taken anything on myself, Mr Hipney. I have chosen a parliamentary career, and found it, let me tell you, a very arduous and trying one: I might almost say a heartbreaking one. I have just had to promise my wife to see a doctor for brain fag. But that does not mean that I have taken it on myself to bring about the millennium.

HIPNEY [*soothingly*] Just so, Srarthur: just so. It tries you and worries you, and breaks your heart and does no good; but you keep on doing it. Theyve often wanted me to go into Parliament. And I could win the seat. Put up old Hipney for the Isle of Cats and your best man wouldnt have a chance against him. But not me: I know too much. It would be the end of me, as it's been the end of all the Labor men that have done it. The Cabinet is full of Labor men that started as red-hot Socialists; and what change has it made except that theyre in and out at Bucknam Palace like peers of the realm?

SIR ARTHUR. You ought to be in Parliament, Mr Hipney. You have the making of a first-rate debater in you.

HIPNEY. Psha! An old street corner speaker like me can debate the heads off you parliamentary gentlemen. You stick your thumbs in your waistcoat holes and wait half an hour between every sentence to think of what to say next; and you call that debating. If I did that in the Isle not a man would stop to listen to me. Mind you, I know you mean it as a compliment that I'd make a good parliamentary debater. I appreciate it. But people dont look to Parliament for talk now-adays: that game is up. Not like it was in old Gladstone's time, eh?

SIR ARTHUR. Parliament, Mr Hipney, is what the people of England have made it. For good or evil we have committed ourselves to democracy. I am here because the people have sent me here.

HIPNEY. Just so. Thats all the use they could make of the vote when they got it. Their hopes was in you; and your hopes is in Spanish onions. What a world it is, aint it, Srarthur?

SIR ARTHUR. We must educate our voters, Mr Hipney. Education will teach them to under-stand.

HIPNEY. Dont deceive yourself, Srarthur: you cant teach people anything they dont want to know. Old Dr Marx—Karl Marx they call him now—my father knew him well—thought that when he'd explained the Capitalist System to the working classes of Europe theyd unite and overthrow it. Fifty years after he founded his Red International the working classes of Europe rose up and shot one another down and blew one another to bits, and turned millions and millions of their infant children out to starve in the snow or steal and beg in the sunshine, as if Dr Marx had never been born. And theyd do it again tomorrow if they was set on to do it. Why did you set them on? All they wanted was to be given their job, and fed and made comfortable according to their notion of comfort. If youd done that for them you wouldnt be having all this trouble. But you werent equal to it; and now the fat's in the fire.

SIR ARTHUR. But the Government is not responsible for that. The Government cannot compel traders to buy goods that they cannot sell. The Government cannot compel manufacturers to produce goods that the traders will not buy. Without demand there can be no supply.

HIPNEY. Theres a powerful demand just now, if demand is what you are looking for.

SIR ARTHUR. Can you point out exactly where, Mr Hipney?

HIPNEY. In our children's bellies, Srarthur. And in our own.

SIR ARTHUR. That is not an effective demand, Mr. Hipney. I wish I had time to explain to you the inexorable laws of political economy. I—

HIPNEY [interrupting him confidentially] No use, Srarthur. That game is up. That stuff you learnt at college, that gave you such confidence in yourself, wont go down with my lot.

SIR ARTHUR [*smiling*] What is the use of saying that economic science and natural laws wont go down, Mr Hipney? You might as well say that the cold of winter wont go down.

HIPNEY. You see, you havnt read Karl Marx, have you?

SIR ARTHUR. Mr Hipney, when the Astronomer Royal tells me that it is twelve o'clock by Greenwich time I do not ask him whether he has read the nonsense of the latest flat earth man. I have something better to do with my time than to read the ravings of a half-educated German Communist. I am sorry you have wasted your own time reading such stuff.

HIPNEY. Me read Marx! Bless you, Srarthur, I am like you: I talk about the old doctor without ever having read a word of him. But I know what that man did for them as did read him.

SIR ARTHUR. Turned their heads, eh?

HIPNEY. Just that, Srarthur. Turned their heads. Turned them right round the other way to yours. I dont know whether what Marx said was right or wrong, because I dont know what he said. But I know that he puts into every man and woman that does read him a conceit that they know all about political economy and can look down on the stuff you were taught at college as ignorant oldfashioned trash. Look at that girl Aloysia Brollikins! Her father was a basket maker in Spitalfields. She's full of Marx. And as to examinations and scholarships and certificates and gold medals and the like, she's won enough of them to last your whole family for two generations. She can win them in her sleep. Look at Blee! His father was a cooper. But he managed to go through Ruskin College. You start him paying out Marx, and proving by the materialist theory of history that Capitalism is bound to develop into Communism, and that whoever doesnt know it is an ignorant nobody or a half-educated college fool; and youll realize that your college conceit is up against a Marxist conceit that beats anything you ever felt for cocksureness and despising the people that havnt got it. Look across Europe if you dont believe me. It was that conceit, sir, that nerved them Russians to go through with their Communism in 1917.

SIR ARTHUR. I must read Marx, Mr Hipney. I knew I had to deal with a sentimental revolt against unemployment. I had no idea that it had academic pretensions.

HIPNEY. Lord bless you, Srarthur, the Labor movement is rotten with book learning; and your people dont seem ever to read anything. When did an undersecretary ever sit up half the night after a hard day's work to read Karl Marx or anyone else? No fear. Your hearts are not in your education; but our young people lift themselves out of the gutter with it. Thats how you can shoot and you can ride and you can play golf; and some of you can talk the hind leg off a donkey; but when it comes to book learning Aloysia and Blee can wipe the floor with you.

SIR ARTHUR. I find it hard to believe that the Mayor ever burnt the midnight oil reading Marx.

HIPNEY. No more he didnt. But he has to pretend to, same as your people have to pretend to understand the gold standard.

SIR ARTHUR [laughing frankly] You have us there, Mr Hipney. I can make neither head nor tail of it; and I dont pretend to.

HIPNEY. Did you know the Mayor well, Srarthur? You called him your old friend Tom.

SIR ARTHUR. He took the chair for me once at an election meeting. He has an artificial tooth that looks as if it were made of zinc. I remembered him by that. [*Genially—rising*]. What humbugs we Prime Ministers have to be, Mr Hipney! You know: dont you? [*He offers his hand to signify that the conversation is over*].

MR HIPNEY [*rising and taking it rather pityingly*] Bless your innocence, Srarthur, you dont know what humbug is yet. Wait til youre a Labor leader. [*He winks at his host and makes for the door*].

SIR ARTHUR. Ha ha! Ha ha ha! Goodbye, Mr Hipney: goodbye. Very good of you to have given me so much of your time.

HIPNEY. Youre welcome to it, Srarthur. Goodbye. [*He goes out*].

Sir Arthur presses a button to summon Hilda. Then he looks at his watch, and whistles, startled to find how late it is. Hilda comes in quickly through the masked door.

SIR ARTHUR. Do you know how late it is? To work! work! work! work! Come along.

HILDA. I am afraid you cant do any work before you start for the Church House lunch. The whole morning is gone with those people from the Isle of Cats.

SIR ARTHUR. But I have mountains of work to get through. With one thing and another I havnt been able to do a thing for the last three weeks; and it accumulates and accumulates. It will crush me if I dont clear it off before it becomes impossible.

HILDA. But I keep telling you, Sir Arthur, that if you will talk to everybody for half an hour instead of letting me get rid of them for you in two minutes, what can you expect? You say you havent attended to anything for three weeks; but really you havnt attended to anything since the session began. I hate to say anything; but really, when those Isle of Cats

people took themselves off your hands almost provi-
dentially, to let that ridiculous old man talk to you
for an hour—! [*She sits down angrily*].

SIR ARTHUR. Nonsense! he didnt stay two minutes;
and I got a lot out of him. What about the letters this
morning?

HILDA. I have dealt with them: you neednt bother.
There are two or three important ones that you ought
to answer: I have put them aside for you when you
have time.

*Flavia and David dash into the room through the
masked door even more excited and obstreperous
than before, Flavia to her father's right, David to his
left.*

FLAVIA. Papa: weve been to a meeting of the unemployed with Aloysia and Toffy.

DAVID. Such a lark!

FLAVIA. We saw a police charge. David was arrested.

SIR ARTHUR. Do you mean to say that you went with
those people who were here?

FLAVIA. Yes: theyve come back to lunch with us.

SIR ARTHUR. To lunch!!!

DAVID. Yes. I say: Aloysia's a marvellous girl.

SIR ARTHUR [*determinedly*] I dont mind the girl; but
if that young whelp is coming to lunch here he must
and shall change his clothes.

DAVID. He's gone home to change and shave: he's
dotty on Flavia.

SIR ARTHUR. Why am I afflicted with such children?
Tell me at once what you have been doing. What
happened?

DAVID. The police brought the Chancellor of the
Exchequer to make a speech to the unemployed to
quiet them. The first thing we heard him say was
"Gentlemen: be patient. I promise you you will soon

see the one thing that can revive our industries and save our beloved country: a rise in prices." The mob just gave one howl and went for him. Then the police drew their batons and charged.

FLAVIA. Davy couldnt stand the way the people were knocked about. He screamed to them to stand. The inspector collared him.

SIR ARTHUR. Of course he did. Quite right. Such folly! [*To David*] How do you come to be here if you were arrested? Who bailed you?

DAVID. I asked the inspector who in hell he thought he was talking to. Then Flavia cut in and told him who we were and that old Basham was like a father to us. All he said was "You go home, sir; and take your sister with you. This is no place for you." So as I was rather in a funk by that time we collected Aloysia and Toffy and bunked for home.

SIR ARTHUR. I have a great mind to have that inspector severely reprimanded for letting you go. Three months would have done you a lot of good. Go back to the drawing room, both of you, and entertain your new friends. You know you are not allowed to come in here when I am at work. Be off with you. [*He goes back to his seat*].

FLAVIA. Well, what are we to do? Mamma sends us in on purpose to interrupt you when she thinks you have done enough.

DAVID. She says it's all we're good for.

SIR ARTHUR. A Prime Minister should have no children. Will you get out, both of you; or must I ring for Burton to throw you out?

FLAVIA. Mamma says you are to lunch, Hilda. She wants another woman to make up the party.

HILDA. Oh dear! [*rising*] You must excuse me, Sir Arthur: I must telephone to put off some people who were coming to lunch with me at The Apple Cart. And I must change my frock.

FLAVIA [*squabbling*] You neednt dress up for Brollikins, need you?

DAVID. You let Aloysia alone. You dont want Hilda to dress up for Barking, I suppose.

SIR ARTHUR [*out of patience*] Get out. Do you hear? Get out, the lot of you.

HILDA. Do come, Miss Chavender. Your father is very busy.

SIR ARTHUR [*furious*] Get OUT.

They retreat precipitately through the masked door. Sir Arthur, left alone, rests his wearied head on the table between his arms.

SIR ARTHUR. At last, a moment's peace.

The word rouses the orator in him. He raises his head and repeats it interrogatively; then tries its effect sweetly and solemnly again and again.

SIR ARTHUR. Peace?... Peace. Peace. Peace. Peace. Peace. [*Now perfectly in tune*] "Yes, your Grace, my lords and gentlemen, my clerical friends. We need peace. We English are still what we were when time-honored Lancaster described us as 'This happy breed of men.' We are above all a domestic nation. On occasion we can be as terrible in war as we have always been wise and moderate in counsel. But here, in this Church House, under the banner of the Prince of Peace, we know that the heart of England is the English home. Not the battlefield but the fireside— yes, your Grace, yes, my lords and gentlemen, yes, my clerical friends, the fire—"

He starts violently as his eye, sweeping round the imaginary assembly, lights on a woman in grey robes contemplating him gravely and pityingly. She has stolen in noiselessly through the masked door.

[233]

SIR ARTHUR. Fffff!!! Who is that? Who are you? Oh, I beg your pardon. You gave me such a— Whew!! [*He sinks back into his chair*] I didnt know there was anyone in the room.

The lady neither moves nor speaks. She looks at him with deepening pity. He looks at her, still badly scared. He rubs his eyes; shakes himself; looks again.

SIR ARTHUR. Excuse me; but are you real?

THE LADY. Yes.

SIR ARTHUR. I wish youd do something real. Wont you sit down?

THE LADY. Thank you. [*She sits down, very uncannily as it seems to him, in Basham's chair*].

SIR ARTHUR. Will you be so good as to introduce yourself? Who are you?

THE LADY. A messenger.

SIR ARTHUR. Please do not be enigmatic. My nerves are all in rags. I did not see you come in. You appeared there suddenly looking like a messenger of death. And now you tell me you are a messenger.

THE LADY. Yes: a messenger of death.

SIR ARTHUR. I thought so. [*With sudden misgiving*] You mean my death, I hope. Not my wife nor any of the children?

THE LADY [*smiling kindly*] No. Your death.

SIR ARTHUR [*relieved*] Well, thats all right.

THE LADY. You are going to die.

SIR ARTHUR. So are we all. The only question is, how soon?

THE LADY. Too soon. You are half dead already. You have been dying a long time.

SIR ARTHUR. Well, I knew I was overworking: burning the candle at both ends: killing myself. It doesnt matter. I have made my will. Everything is provided for: my wife will be comfortably off;

[234]

and the children will have as much as is good for them.

THE LADY. You are resigned?

SIR ARTHUR. No; but I cannot help myself.

THE LADY. Perhaps I can help you. I am not only a messenger. I am a healer.

SIR ARTHUR. A what?

THE LADY. A healer. One who heals the sick. One who holds off death until he is welcome in his proper time.

SIR ARTHUR. You cannot help me. I am caught in the wheels of a merciless political machine. The political machine will not stop for you. It has ground many men to pieces before their time; and it will grind me.

THE LADY. My business is with life and death, not with political machinery.

SIR ARTHUR. In that case I am afraid you can be of no use to me; so will you think it very uncivil of me if I go on with my work?

THE LADY. Shall I vanish?

SIR ARTHUR. Not unless you have something else to do. As you are a ghost, and therefore not in time but in eternity, another ten minutes or so wont cost you anything. Somehow, your presence is helping me. A presence is a wonderful thing. Would you mind sitting there and reading The Times while I work?

THE LADY. I never read the newspapers. I read men and women. I will sit here and read you. Or will that make you self-conscious?

SIR ARTHUR. My dear ghost, a public man is so accustomed to people staring at him that he very soon has no self to be conscious of. You wont upset me in the least. You may even throw in a round of applause occasionally; so that I may find out the effective bits to work up.

THE LADY. Go on. I will wait as long as you like.

SIR ARTHUR. Thank you. Now let me see where I was when you appeared. [*He takes up a scrap of paper on which he has made a memorandum*]. Ah yes: Ive got it. Peace. Yes: peace. [*Trying to make out a word*] Ence —ence—what? Oh, ensue! Of course: a good word. "My friends, lay and clerical, we must ensue peace. Yes, ensue peace. Peace. Disarmament." A burst of Pacifist applause there, perhaps. "Who says that we need a hundred battleships, gentlemen? Christian brotherhood is a safer defence than a thousand battle-ships. You have my pledge that the Government will be quite content with—with—" oh, well, my secre-tary will fill that in with whatever number of ships the Japanese are standing out for. By the way, do you think battleships are any real use now? Kenworthy says theyre not: and he was in the navy. It would be such a tremendous score for us at Geneva if we offered to scrap all our battleships. We could make up for them in aeroplanes and submarines. I should like to have the opinion of an impartial and disinterested ghost.

THE LADY. As I listen to you I seem to hear a ghost preparing a speech for his fellow ghosts, ghosts from a long dead past. To me it means nothing, because I am a ghost from the future.

SIR ARTHUR. Thats a curious idea. Of course if there are ghosts from the past there must be ghosts from the future.

THE LADY. Yes: women and men who are ahead of their time. They alone can lead the present into the future. They are ghosts from the future. The ghosts from the past are those who are behind the times, and can only drag the present back.

[236]

SIR ARTHUR. What an excellent definition of a Conservative! Thank Heaven I am a Liberal!

THE LADY. You mean that you make speeches about Progress and Liberty instead of about King and Country.

SIR ARTHUR. Of course I make speeches: that is the business of a politician. Dont you like speeches?

THE LADY. On the Great Day of Judgment the speechmakers will stand with the seducers and the ravishers, with the traffickers in maddening drugs, with those who make men drunk and rob them, who entice children and violate them.

SIR ARTHUR. What nonsense! Our sermons and speeches are the glories of our literature, and the inspired voices of our religion, our patriotism, and—of course—our politics.

THE LADY. Sermons and speeches are not religion, not patriotism, not politics: they are only the gibbering of ghosts from the past. You are a ghost from a very dead past. Why do you not die your bodily death? Is it fair for a ghost to go about with a live body?

SIR ARTHUR. This is too personal. I am afraid I cannot get on with my speech while you are there ordering my funeral. Oblige me by vanishing. Go. Disappear. Shoo!

THE LADY. I cannot vanish. [*Merrily changing her attitude*]. Shall we stop playing at ghosts, and accept one another for convenience sake as real people?

SIR ARTHUR [*shaking off his dreaminess*] Yes, lets. [*He rises and comes to her*]. We have been talking nonsense. [*He pulls out a chair. They sit close together*]. You had me half hypnotized. But first, shake hands. I want to feel that you are real.

He offers his right hand. She seizes both his hands and holds them vigorously, looking straight into his eyes.

SIR ARTHUR [*brightening*] Well, I dont know whether this is real or not; but it's electric, and very soothing and jolly. Ah-a-a-ah! [*a deep sighing breath*]. And now my dear lady, will you be good enough to tell me who the devil you are?

THE LADY [*releasing him*] Only your wife's lady doctor. Did she not tell you to expect me?

SIR ARTHUR. Of course, of course. How stupid of me! Yes, yes, yes, yes, yes, to be sure. And now I am going to be frank with you. I dont believe in doctors. Neither does my wife; but her faith in quacks is unlimited. And as I am on the verge of a nervous breakdown, she is planting every possible variety of quack on me—you will excuse the expression?—

THE LADY. I excuse everything from my patients. Go on.

SIR ARTHUR. Well, I receive them all as I am receiving you, just to gratify her, or rather to prevent her from making my life miserable. They all say the same obvious thing; and they are none of them of the slightest use. You are going to say it all over again. Can you forgive me for saying flatly that I will not pay you twenty guineas for saying it: not if you said it twenty times over?

THE LADY. Not even if I shew you how to cure yourself? The twenty guineas is an important part of the cure. It will make you take it seriously.

SIR ARTHUR. I know perfectly well how to cure myself. The cure is as simple as abc. I am Prime Minister of Great Britain. That is, I am an overworked, overworried, overstrained, overburdened, overdriven man, suffering from late hours, irregular snatched meals, no time for digestion nor for enough sleep, and having to keep my mind at full stretch all the time struggling with problems that are no longer national problems but world problems. In short, I am suffering acutely from brain fag.

THE LADY. And the cure?

SIR ARTHUR. A fortnight's golf: thats the cure. I know it all by heart. So suppose we drop it, and part friends. You see, I am really frightfully busy.

THE LADY. That is not my diagnosis. [*She rises*]. Goodbye.

SIR ARTHUR [*alarmed*] Diagnosis! Have you been diagnosing me? Do you mean that there is something else the matter with me?

THE LADY. Not something else. Something different.

SIR ARTHUR. Sit down, pray: I can spare another two minutes. Whats wrong?

THE LADY [*resuming her seat*] You are dying of an acute want of mental exercise.

SIR ARTHUR [*unable to believe his ears*] Of—of—of WHAT, did you say?

THE LADY. You are suffering from that very common English complaint, an underworked brain. To put it in one word, a bad case of frivolity, possibly incurable.

SIR ARTHUR. Frivolity! Did I understand you to say that frivolity is a common English failing?

THE LADY. Yes. Terribly common. Almost a national characteristic.

SIR ARTHUR. Do you realize that you are utterly mad?

THE LADY. Is it you or I who have piloted England on to the rocks?

SIR ARTHUR. Come come! No politics. What do you prescribe for me?

THE LADY. I take my patients into my retreat in the Welsh mountains, formerly a monastery, now much stricter and perfectly sanitary. No newspapers, no letters, no idle ladies. No books except in the afternoon as a rest from thinking.

SIR ARTHUR. How can you think without books?

THE LADY. How can you have thoughts of your own when you are reading other people's thoughts?

SIR ARTHUR [*groaning*] Oh, do talk sense. What about golf?

THE LADY. Games are for people who can neither read nor think. Men trifle with their business and their politics; but they never trifle with their games. Golf gives them at least a weekend of earnest concentration. It brings truth home to them. They cannot pretend that they have won when they have lost, nor that they made a magnificent drive when they foozled it. The Englishman is at his best on the links, and at his worst in the Cabinet. But what your country needs is not your body but your mind. And I solemnly warn you that unless you exercise your mind you will lose it. A brain underexercised is far more injurious to health than an underexercised body. You know how men become bone lazy for want of bodily exercise. Well, they become brain lazy for want of mental exercise; and if nature meant them to be thinkers the results are disastrous. All sorts of bodily diseases are produced by half used minds; for it is the mind that makes the body: that is my secret, and the secret of all the true healers. I am sorry you will not allow me to take you a little on the way back to health with me. Good morning. [*She rises*].

SIR ARTHUR. Must you go?

THE LADY. Well, you are so busy—

SIR ARTHUR [*rising*] Ah yes: I forgot. I am frightfully busy. Still, if you could spare another minute—

THE LADY. If you wish. [*She sits down*].

SIR ARTHUR [*sitting down*] You see, what makes your diagnosis so pricelessly funny to me is that as a matter of fact my life has been a completely intellectual life, and my training the finest intellectual training in the world. First rate preparatory school. Harrow. Oxford. Parliament. An Undersecretaryship. The Cabinet. Finally the Leadership of the House as Prime Minister. Intellect, intellect, all the time.

THE LADY. At Harrow you wrote Latin verses, did you not?

SIR ARTHUR. Yes, of course.

THE LADY. Do you write any now?

SIR ARTHUR. No, of course not. You dont understand. We learnt to write Latin verses not because the verses are any good—after all, it's only a trick of stringing old tags together—but because it's such a splendid training for the mind.

THE LADY. Have all the boys who made Latin verses at Harrow splendidly trained minds?

SIR ARTHUR. Yes. I unhesitatingly say yes. I dont mean, of course, that they are all geniuses; but if you go into the best society you will see that their minds are far superior to those of persons who have had no classical training.

THE LADY. You mean that they can all be trusted to say the same thing in the same way when they discuss public affairs.

SIR ARTHUR. Precisely. They are an educated class, you see.

THE LADY [*coldly, rising*] Yes: I see. I have really nothing more to say, Sir Arthur. [*She takes a card from her bag and puts it on the table*] That is the address of my retreat in Wales.

SIR ARTHUR [*rising, rather disappointed at having produced no effect*] But surely you cannot deny that a man is the better for having been put through the mill of our great educational system.

THE LADY. If a man is born with a hopelessly bad set of teeth I think it is better for him, and kinder to him, to pull them all out and replace them with a good set of artificial teeth. If some of your political colleagues had not been provided with artificial political minds in the manner you described they would have been left without any political minds at all. But in that case they would not have meddled in politics; and that, I think, would have been a public advantage. May I reserve a bedroom and a private study for you?

SIR ARTHUR. Pooh! I am not going to your retreat.

THE LADY [steadfastly] I think you are.

SIR ARTHUR. I give you up. You are factproof. I am lazy; I am idle; and I am breaking down from over-work. How logical!

THE LADY. All the idlest and laziest of my patients slave from morning to midnight trifling and tittle-tattling about great things. To a retreat, Sir Arthur: get thee to a retreat. I am never mistaken in my diagnosis. I shall telephone to ask whether my number one suite, with private bath and meditation parlor, is vacant.

SIR ARTHUR. No: I wont be rushed. Do you hear? I wont be rushed. [She is quite unshaken; and he proceeds, much less resolutely] Of course I shall have to go somewhere for a rest; and if you could really recommend it as a bracing place—

THE LADY. Bracing? What for?

SIR ARTHUR. Well, bracing, you know. Bracing.

THE LADY. Curious, how idle people are always clamouring to be braced! Like trousers.

SIR ARTHUR. Idle people! How you stick to your point! And what a humbug you are! Dont think you can impose on me with your meditation parlor and your dignified airs: I do that sort of thing myself occasionally; and you know it's no use giving tracts to a missionary. But I feel somehow that you are good for me. You are a dear delightful bighearted wrongheaded half-educated crazyboots; but a woman may be all that and yet have the right instinct as to how to flirt intellectually with a tired thinker. Will you promise to talk to me if I come?

THE LADY. I will even let you talk to me. I guarantee that in a fortnight you will begin to think before you talk. Your dead mind will come to life. I shall make a man of you. Goodbye. [*She goes out quickly through the main door*].

SIR ARTHUR [*calling after her gaily*] Ha ha! Incorrigible, incorrigible. [*He takes her card from the table, and contemplates it*]. Oh! I forgot to ask her how much a week she wants for that meditation parlor. [*He looks tragic*].

HILDA [*emerging from her office*] Anything the matter, Sir Arthur?

SIR ARTHUR. I am going into a retreat. Because my brain is underworked. Do you grasp that idea? Have you ever heard of a retreat for the mentally underworked?

HILDA. There is a very nice one at Sevenoaks that my aunt was sent to. But that is for inebriates.

SIR ARTHUR. The one I'm going to is for the mentally underworked, the thoughtless and brainless, the inveterately lazy and frivolous. Yes; the frivolous: your ears do not deceive you.

HILDA [*going to her desk*] Oh, well, theyll amuse you: you always get on well with people of that sort. Shall I pack your usual holiday books? some detective stories and Wordsworth?

SIR ARTHUR. No. You will procure all the books you can find by a revolutionary German Jew named Harry Marks—

HILDA. Dont you mean Karl Marx?

SIR ARTHUR. Thats the man. Karl Marx. Get me every blessed book by Karl Marx that you can find translated into English; and have them packed for the retreat.

HILDA. There are much newer books by Marxists: Lenin and Trotsky and Stalin and people like that.

SIR ARTHUR. Get them all. Pack the lot. By George, I'll teach Alderwoman Aloysia Brollikins to give herself airs. I'll teach her and her rabble of half-baked half-educated intellectual beggars-on-horseback that any Oxford man can beat them at their own silly game. I'll just turn Karl Marx inside-out for them. [*The household gong sounds*]. Lunch! Come on: that woman's given me an appetite. [*He goes out impetuously through the masked door*].

HILDA [*rushing after him*] No, no, Sir Arthur: the Church House! the Church House! youve forgotten that you have to lunch at [*her voice is lost in the distance*].

[244]

The same scene on the 10th *November at* 9.30 *in the morning. There is a generous fire in the grate; and the visitors wear winter clothes. Basham is on the hearthrug, warming his back and reading The Daily Herald.*

BASHAM [*amazed by what he reads*] Gosh! [*He reads further*] Wh-e-e-ew!! [*He reads still further*] Well I'll be dashed!!!

Hilda enters through the main door, and announces an explosive elderly gentleman, evidently a person of consequence, who follows her.

HILDA. Sir Dexter Rightside.

SIR DEXTER [*joining Basham on the hearth*] Ah! That you, Basham? Have you come to arrest him?

BASHAM. You may well ask. He isnt up yet. Miss Hanways: is there any sign of his getting a move on?

HILDA [*much worried*] Lady Chavender wont allow him to be disturbed. She says his speech last night at the Guildhall banquet quite tired him out. People have been ringing up and calling all the morning; but she just puts her back to his door and says that anyone who makes noise enough to waken him leaves her service that minute.

SIR DEXTER. Nonsense! He must see me. Does Lady Chavender suppose that a Prime Minister can stand the country on its head without a word of warning to his colleagues and then go to bed as if he was tired out by a day's fishing?

HILDA [*desperate*] Well, what can *I* do, Sir Dexter? [*She goes to her bureau*].

SIR DEXTER. Basham: go and break open his bedroom door.

BASHAM. I cant. I'm a policeman: I mustnt do it
without a warrant. Go and do it yourself.

SIR DEXTER. I have a devilish good mind to. Can you
conceive anything more monstrous, Basham? [*He
sits down in the chair next the end chair*]. But I said
that this would happen. I said so. When we made this
damned coalition that they call a National Government I was entitled to the Prime Ministership. I was
the Leader of the Conservative Party. I had an enormous majority in the country: the election proved
that we could have done quite well without Chavender.
But I had to give way. He humbugged us. He pretended that without his old guard of Liberals and his
ragtag and bobtail of Labor men and Socialists and
lawyers and journalists-on-the-make and used-up
trade union secretaries, and all the rest of the democratic dregs of human society, we couldnt be sure
of a majority. His golden voice was to do the trick.
He was the popular man, the safe man: I was the
unpopular Die Hard who couldnt be trusted to keep
my temper. So I stood down. I sacrificed myself. I
took the Foreign Secretaryship. Well, what price your
safe man now? How do you like your Bolshy
Premier? Who was right? the funkers and com-
promisers or the old Die Hard?

BASHAM. It's amazing. I could have sworn that if
there was a safe man in England that could be trusted
to talk and say nothing, to thump the table and do
nothing, Arthur Chavender was that man. Whats
happened to him? What does it mean? Did he go
mad at the sanatorium, do you think? Or was he mad
before that woman took him there?

SIR DEXTER. Mad! Not a bit of it. But you had better

look up that woman's record: there may be money from Moscow behind this.

BASHAM. Arthur take money! Thats going too far.

SIR DEXTER. The woman took the money. It would be waste of money to bribe Chavender: you could always trust him to say whatever he thought would please his audience without being paid for it: damned mountebank.

BASHAM. But he didnt try to please his audience at the Guildhall. They wanted some of his best soothing syrup about law and order after the attack on the Lord Mayor's Show in the afternoon by the unemployed; but according to The Daily Herald here he gave them a dose of boiling Socialism instead.

SIR DEXTER [*nervously*] By the way, Basham, I hope you have the unemployed well in hand today.

BASHAM. Quiet as lambs. Theyre all reading the papers. New editions every half-hour. Like 1914 over again.

Sir Arthur's voice is heard, singing scales. Hilda looks in.

HILDA. I think I hear Sir Arthur singing. He must have got up.

SIR DEXTER. Singing! Is this a moment for minstrelsy?

HILDA. He always sings scales after his bath [*she vanishes*].

After a final burst of solfeggi the masked door is opened vigorously and Chavender enters beaming.

SIR ARTHUR. Ah, here you are, Dexy [*he proffers his hand*].

SIR DEXTER [*like a baited bull*] Dont attempt to shake hands with me. Dont dare call me Dexy.

SIR ARTHUR. What on earth's the matter? Got out at the wrong side of the bed this morning, eh? Frightfully sorry to have kept you waiting, Basham. Whats wrong with the Foreign Secretary this time?

SIR DEXTER. This time! What do you mean by this time?

SIR ARTHUR. Well theres nothing very novel about your turning up before breakfast in a blazing rage, is there? What is it, Basham?

BASHAM. Oh come, P.M.! If you were too drunk last night at the Guildhall to know what you were saying, youd better read the papers [*he offers his paper*].

SIR ARTHUR [*keeping his hands behind his back to warm them*] I remember perfectly well what I said last night. And I drank nothing but barley water.

BASHAM [*insisting*] But look at it man. [*Quoting the headlines*] New program for winter session. Nationalization of ground rents. Nationalization of banks. Nationalization of collieries. Nationalization of transport.

SIR DEXTER [*moaning*] Nationalization of women. Why omit it? Why omit it?

BASHAM. No: nothing about women. Municipalization of urban land and the building trade, and consequent extinction of rates.

SIR DEXTER. Apostate!

BASHAM. No: nothing about the Church. Abolition of tariffs and substitution of total prohibition of private foreign trade in protected industries. State imports only, to be sold at State regulated prices.

SIR DEXTER. Rot! Incomprehensible and unheard-of rot.

BASHAM. Compulsory public service for all, irrespective of income, as in war time.

SIR DEXTER. Slavery. Call it by its proper name. Slavery.

BASHAM. Restoration of agriculture. Collective farming. Nationalization of fertilizer industries. Nitrogen from the air. Power from the tides. Britain self-supporting and blockade proof.

SIR DEXTER. Madness. Ruin to our foreign trade.

BASHAM. Ruthless extinction of parasitism.

SIR DEXTER. You dont even know the present law. You have the Verminous Persons Act. What more do you want?

BASHAM. Doubling of the surtax on unearned incomes.

SIR DEXTER. Yes: take our last penny! And when the little that the present ruinous taxation has left us is gone; when we have closed our accounts with the last tradesman and turned the last servant into the streets, where are they to find employment? Who is to pay their wages? What is to become of religion when nobody can afford pewrents or a penny to put in the plate? Even sport will not be safe: our breed of horses will be doomed; our packs of hounds sold or slaughtered; and our masters of hounds will be caddies on motor bicycles. That is to be England's future!

SIR ARTHUR. But is that all the papers have reported?

SIR DEXTER. All!!!

BASHAM. Oh come! All! Isnt that about enough?

SIR ARTHUR. But have they said nothing about our promise to restore the cuts made in the pay of the army and navy and police?

SIR DEXTER. Our promise! Whose promise?

BASHAM [interested] What was that you said? Are you going to put my men's wages up to the old figure?

SIR ARTHUR. We shall give you another five thousand men; pay the old wages with a rise of ten per cent; and double your salary.

BASHAM. Whew! That alters the case a bit.

SIR DEXTER [*rising*] Basham: you are not going to allow yourself to be corrupted like this! Are you such a dupe as to imagine that free Englishmen will tolerate such a monstrous waste of public money?

BASHAM. If I have another five thousand men and a rise on the old wages, I'll answer for the free Englishmen. If they dont like it they can lump it.

SIR DEXTER. You really believe he can keep all the monstrous promises he has made?

BASHAM. No: of course he cant. But he can keep this one. He can raise the pay of the ranks and double my salary; and that is all that concerns me. I'm a policeman, not a politician.

SIR DEXTER. Youre a mercenary gangster and a damned fool: thats what you are. [*He flings himself into the end chair*].

BASHAM [*calmly*] You seem ruffled, Sir Dexter.

Before Sir Dexter can reply, Hilda returns and announces a new visitor.

HILDA. Admiral Sir Bemrose Hotspot. [*She goes out*].

Sir Bemrose is a halfwitted admiral; but the half that has not been sacrificed to his profession is sound and vigorous.

SIR BEMROSE [*in the breeziest spirits*] Morning, Dexy. Morning, Basham. [*Slapping Sir Arthur on the back*] Splendid, Arthur! Never heard you in better form. Thats the stuff to give em. [*They shake hands cordially*].

SIR DEXTER [*sobered by his astonishment*] Rosy: have you gone mad too? Have you forgotten that you are a Conservative, and that it was as a Conservative that you were made First Lord of the Admiralty, at my personal suggestion and insistence, in this so-called National Government, which now, thank Heaven, wont last one day after the next meeting of Parliament?

SIR BEMROSE. Wont it, by Jove! It's safe for the next
five years. What the country wants is straight orders,
discipline, character, pluck, a big navy, justice for the
British sailor, no sham disarmaments, and absolute
command of the sea. If that isnt Conservatism what is
Conservatism? But mind, Arthur, I must have twelve
new aeroplane-carrying battleships. I have my eye on
Japan. And theres America. And, of course, Russia.

SIR ARTHUR. You shall have them, Rosy. Twenty-
four if you say the word.

SIR BEMROSE. Good! Then I'll answer for the House
of Commons.

SIR DEXTER. Dont be silly. What can you do with the
House of Commons, except empty it whenever you
get up to speak?

SIR BEMROSE. I leave the speaking to Arthur: it's his
job, not mine. But if there is any further attempt to
starve the navy it can give you a little surprise at
Westminster. How will you feel when you see a sub-
marine come to the surface off the terrace, and the
commander sends in word that he gives you just five
minutes before he torpedoes the whole damned Front
Bench?

SIR DEXTER. You are talking ridiculous nonsense. Do
you suppose for a moment that the navy would be
allowed to interfere in politics?

SIR BEMROSE. Who's to stop it? Where would Lenin
and Stalin and Trotsky and all that Bolshy lot have
been without the Baltic fleet and the Kronstadt sailors? Do you suppose the British navy, with its discipline and its respectable Conservative commanders,
couldnt do what these Communist scoundrels did?

SIR DEXTER. How long would the British navy survive the abolition of property in this country? tell me
that.

SIR BEMROSE. Dont talk to the navy about property. We dont live by property: we live by service. [*He takes the chair next to the presidential one, and pursues his personal grievance angrily*]. You and your confounded property owners grudge us a clerk's salary for commanding a battleship, and then dock a quarter off it for income tax. We cant set foot on shore without being rented and rated until we can hardly afford to educate our children. Thanks to Arthur, you are pledged now to give us our pay honestly free of income tax and make these lazy idle lubbers of landlords sweat for it. I call that the essence of Conservatism. Thats the way to dish these Labor chaps and Red flaggers and all the rest of the scum you have been pandering to ever since you gave them the vote. Give them whats good for them; and put their ballot papers behind the fire: thats what this country needs.

SIR ARTHUR. You see, Dexy: we have the navy and the police on our side.

SIR DEXTER. May I ask who are "we"?

SIR ARTHUR. Why, the National Government, of course. You and I, Dexy: you and I.

SIR DEXTER. It makes me sick to hear you couple my name with yours. It always did.

HILDA [*announcing*] The President of the Board of Trade. Mr Glenmorison.

Glenmorison is an easy mannered Scottish gentleman, distinctly the youngest of the party.

SIR ARTHUR. Hallo, Sandy. Sit down. Lets all sit down and have it out.

They settle themselves at the table with their backs to the fire, Sir Arthur in the middle, Glenmorison on his left, Sir Bemrose on his right, and Sir Dexter and Basham right and left respectively.

GLENMORISON. Well, Sir Arthur, when you were

letting yourself go so recklessly you might have said a word about Home Rule for Scotland. We may as well be hanged for a sheep as for a lamb.

SIR DEXTER. We! we! we! Who are we? If you mean the Cabinet, it is not responsible for the Prime Minister's frantic proceedings. He acted without consulting us. Do you suppose that if I had heard a word of this outburst of Bolshevism I should have consented to it?

SIR ARTHUR. That was why I didnt consult you.

SIR DEXTER. Psha!

SIR ARTHUR. The responsibility is mine and mine alone.

SIR BEMROSE. Not at all. I claim my share, Arthur. You got the part about the navy from me.

GLENMORISON. Same here, Sir Dexter. I claim at least two items.

SIR DEXTER. Much good may they do you. Arthur's seat is safe: anybody named Chavender can get in unopposed in this constituency because his cunning old father-in-law has every voter in the place bribed up to the neck. But your majority at the last election was seventeen: there were three recounts. Your seat's gone, anyhow.

GLENMORISON. On the contrary, Sir Dexter, it's safe for the first time in the history of Scotland.

SIR DEXTER. Safe! How? You will get the boot as a crazy Bolshevik unless you come out with me and repudiate Chavender promptly and decisively.

GLENMORISON. Oh, I'm afraid I cant do that, Sir Dexter. You see, the balance is held in my constituency by the tradesmen and shopkeepers. Their great grievance is the heavy rates. And though they are all doing middling well they think they could do better if they could raise enough capital to extend their businesses a bit. But the financiers and promoters wont look at small businesses. They are thinking in millions while my people are thinking in thousands, and mostly in only four figures at that. It's easy enough to get a couple of hundred thousand pounds if you are willing to call it a quarter of a million and pay interest on that sum. But what good is that to a man in the High Street in my constituency who wants from five to twenty thousand to extend his little business?

SIR DEXTER. Nonsense! The bank will give him an overdraft if his credit is good.

GLENMORISON. Yes; and call it in at the next slump and panic on the Stock Exchange. I can shew you half a dozen men who were forced into bankruptcy in the last panic, though they were as solvent as you or I. But Sir Arthur's proposal of panic-proof national and municipal banks, as ready and eager to find five thousand for the five thousand man as the financiers are to find a million on condition that enough of it sticks to their own fingers, is just the thing for my people. I darent say a word against it. It's an inspiration as far as my constituents are concerned. Theyre a canny lot, my people: theyd vote for the devil if he'd promise to abolish the rates and open a municipal bank. My majority fell to seventeen last time because I went to them with empty hands and a bellyful of advice to economize and make sacrifices. This bank nationalization is good business for them: theyll just jump at it.

SIR DEXTER. In short, you will make Utopian promises that you know very well will never be carried out.

GLENMORISON. You made a lot of Utopian promises, Sir Dexter, when you formed this National Government. Instead of carrying them out you told the voters to tighten their belts and save the Bank of England. They tightened their belts; and now the Bank of England is paying twelve and sixpence in the pound. Still, I admit, you pulled down my Liberal majority over my Conservative opponent from four thousand to seventeen. Ive got to pull that up again. I say nothing about the rest of the program; but I represent the small man; and on this bank business I am with Sir Arthur all the time.

HILDA [*announcing*] Sir Jafna Pandranath. [*She withdraws*].

This announcement creates a marked sensation. All five gentlemen rise as if to receive a royal personage. Sir Jafna is an elderly Cingalese plutocrat, small and slender to the verge of emaciation, elegantly dressed, but otherwise evidently too much occupied and worried by making money to get any fun out of spending it. One guesses that he must make a great deal of it; for the reverence with which he is received by the five Britons, compared with their unceremonious handling of one another, is almost sycophantic.

SIR JAFNA. Hallo! Am I breaking into a Cabinet meeting?

SIR ARTHUR. No: not a bit. Only a few friendly callers. Pray sit down.

SIR DEXTER [*offering the end chair to the visitor*] You are welcome, Sir Jafna: most welcome. You represent money; and money brings fools to their senses.

SIR JAFNA. Money! Not at all. I am a poor man. I never know from one moment to another whether I am worth thirteen millions or only three. [*He sits down. They all sit down*].

SIR BEMROSE. I happen to know, Sir Jafna, that

[255]

ON THE ROCKS

your enterprises stand at twenty millions today at the very least.

GLENMORISON. Fifty.

SIR JAFNA. How do you know? How do you know? The way I am plundered at every turn! [*To Sir Dexter*] Your people take the shirt off my back.

SIR DEXTER. My people! What on earth do you mean?

SIR JAFNA. Your land monopolists. Your blackmailers. Your robber barons. Look at my Blayport Docks reconstruction scheme! Am I a public benefactor or am I not? Have I not enough to live on and die on without troubling myself about Blayport? Shall I be any the happier when it has ten square miles of docks instead of a tuppeny-hapeny fishing harbor? What have I to gain except the satisfaction of seeing a big publicly useful thing well done, and the knowledge that without me it could not be done? Shall I not be half ruined if it fails?

SIR BEMROSE. Well, whats wrong with it, old chap?

SIR JAFNA. Rosy: you make me puke. What is wrong with it is that the owners of all the miles of land that are indispensable to my scheme, and that without it would not be worth fifteen pounds an acre, are opening their mouths so wide that they will grab sixty per cent of the profit without lifting a finger except to pocket the wealth that I shall create. I live, I work, I plan, I shatter my health and risk all I possess only to enrich these parasites, these vampires, these vermin in the commonwealth. [*Shrieking*] Yes: vermin! [*Subsiding*] You were quite right at the Guildhall last night, Arthur: you must nationalize the land and put a stop to this shameless exploitation of the financiers and entrepreneurs by a useless, idle, and predatory landed class.

SIR ARTHUR [*chuckling*]. Magnificent! I have the support of the City.

SIR JAFNA. To the last vote, to the last penny. These pirates think nothing of extorting a million an acre for land in the city. A man cannot have an address in London for his letters until he has agreed to pay them from five hundred to a thousand a year. He cant even die without paying them for a grave to lie in. Make them disgorge, Arthur. Skin them alive. Tax them twenty shillings in the pound. Make them earn their own living, damn them. [*He wipes his brow and adds, rather hysterically*] Excuse me, boys; but if you saw the Blayport estimates—! [*he can no more*].

SIR DEXTER. May I ask you to address yourself to this question not as an emotional oriental [*Sir Jafna chokes convulsively*] but as a sane man of business. If you destroy the incomes of our landed gentry where will you find the capital that exists solely through their prudent saving—their abstinence?

SIR JAFNA. Bah pooh! Pooh bah! I will find it where they find it, in the product of the labor I employ. At present I have to pay exorbitant and unnecessary wages. Why? Because out of those wages the laborer has to pay half or quarter as rent to the landlord. The laborer is ignorant: he thinks he is robbed by the landlord; but the robbed victim is me—ME! Get rid of the landlord and I shall have all the capital he now steals. In addition I shall have cheap labor. That is not oriental emotion: it is British Commonsense. I am with you, Arthur, to the last drop of my oriental blood. Nationalized land: compulsory labor: abolition of rates: strikes made criminal: I heartily endorse them all in the name of Capital and private enterprise. I say nothing about the rest of your program, Arthur;

but on these points no true Liberal can question your magnificent statesmanship.

SIR ARTHUR [*delighted*] You hear that, Dexy. Put that in your pipe and smoke it.

HILDA [*announcing*] His Grace the Duke of Domesday. [*She goes out*].

An elderly delicately built aristocrat comes in. Well preserved, but nearer 70 than 60.

THE DUKE [*surprised to see so many people*] Do I intrude, Arthur? I thought you were disengaged.

SIR ARTHUR. Not at all. Only a talk over last night. Make yourself at home.

SIR DEXTER. You come in the nick of time. Sir Jafna here has just been qualifying you as a bloodsucker, a pirate, a parasite, a robber baron and finally as vermin. Vermin! How do you like it?

THE DUKE [*calmly taking the end chair nearest the window, on Basham's left*] I wonder why the epithet robber is applied only to barons. You never hear of robber dukes; yet my people have done plenty of robbery in their time. [*With a sigh of regret*] Ah, thats all over now. The robbers have become the robbed. I wish you would create some immediate class of honest folk. I dislike your calling me vermin, Arthur.

SIR ARTHUR. I didnt. It was Jafna.

THE DUKE. Ungrateful Jafna! He is buying up my Blayport estate for next to nothing.

SIR JAFNA. Next to nothing! Holy Brahma!

THE DUKE [*continuing*] He will make millions out of it. After paying off the mortgages I shall get three and a half per cent on what is left to me out of the beggarly price he offers; and on that three and a half I shall be income-taxed and surtaxed. Jafna's grandsons will go to Eton. Mine will go to a Polytechnic.

SIR BEMROSE. Send them to Dartmouth, old chap.

Theres a career for them in the navy now that Arthur is at the helm.

SIR DEXTER. A lieutenant's pay and pension for the future Duke of Domesday! Thats the proposition, is it?

THE DUKE. He will be lucky to have any pay at all. But I shall support you in any case, Arthur. You have at last publicly admitted that the death duties are unsound in principle, and promised to abolish them. That will save us from utter extinction in three generations; and the landed classes are with you to the last man for it. Accept the humble gratitude of a pauperized duke.

SIR DEXTER. And the rest of the program. Do you swallow that too?

THE DUKE. I doubt if the rest of the program will come off. Besides, I dont pretend to understand it. By the way, Sir Jafna, I wish you would take Domesday Towers off my hands for a while. I cant afford to live in it. I cant afford even to keep it dusted. You can have it for a hundred a year.

SIR JAFNA. Too far from town.

THE DUKE. Not by aeroplane. Do think it over.

Sir Jafna shrugs his shoulders and intimates that it is hopeless. The Duke resigns himself to the expected.

SIR ARTHUR. Dexy: you are in a minority of one. The landlords are on my side. The capitalists, big and little, are on my side. The fighting services are on my side. The police are on my side. If you leave us you go out into the wilderness alone. What have you to say?

SIR DEXTER. I have to say that you are a parcel of blind fools. You are trying to scuttle the ship on the chance of each of you grabbing a share of the insurance money. But the Country will deal with you. The

Country does not want change. The Country never has wanted change. The Country never will want change. And because I will resist change while I have breath in my body I shall not be alone in England. You have all deserted me and betrayed your party; but I warn you that though I am utterly alone in this room . . .

HILDA [*reappearing*] The deputation, Sir Arthur. Theyve come back. [*She vanishes*].

The deputation enters. Hipney is not with them. Barking shaved, brilliantly dressed, and quite transfigured, is jubilant. Aloysia glows indignation. Blee and the Mayor, doggedly wearing their hats and overcoats, are gloomy, angry, and resolute. They group themselves just inside the door, glowering at the Prime Minister and his colleagues.

SIR ARTHUR [*beaming*] Gentlemen: a Labor deputation from the Isle of Cats. The one element that was lacking in our councils. You have heard the voice of the peerage, of the city, of the King's forces. You will now hear the voice of the proletariat. Sit down, ladies and gentlemen.

THE MAYOR [*rudely*] Who are you calling the proletariat? Do you take us for Communists? [*He remains standing*].

ALOYSIA. What you are going to hear, Sir Arthur, is the voice of Labor. [*She remains standing*].

BLEE. The verdict of democracy. [*He remains standing*].

EARL OF BARKING. The bleating of a bloody lot of fools. I am with you, Chavender. [*He detaches himself from the group and flings himself into Hilda's chair with intense disgust*].

SIR ARTHUR [*surprised*] Am I to understand that your colleagues are against me?

THE MAYOR. Of course we're against you. Do you expect me to go back to my people and tell them they should vote for compulsory labor and doing away with strikes?

BLEE. Arnt the workers enslaved enough already without your depriving them of that last scrap of their liberty? the only weapon they have against the capitalists?

SIR ARTHUR. My dear Mr Mayor, what is the right to strike? The right to starve on your enemy's door-step and set the whole public against you. Which of you starves first when it comes to the point?

THE MAYOR. I am not going to argue. You can beat me at that. But if you think that the British working-man will listen to compulsory labor and putting down strikes you dont know the world youre living in; and thats all about it.

SIR ARTHUR. But we need not compel the workers to work: they are working already. We shall compel the idlers. Not only your idlers but our idlers: all the idle young gentlemen who do nothing but waste their own time and your labor.

BLEE. We know. Keep all the soft jobs for your lot and the hard ones for us. Do you take us for fools?

BARKING. He does. And you a r e fools.

SIR ARTHUR. I am glad to have your lordship's support.

ALOYSIA. Support your grandparents! He wants to marry your daughter.

BARKING [*springing up*] Oh! You can hit below the belt, Aloysia. But as a matter of fact, I do want to marry your daughter, Chavender.

SIR ARTHUR. Hardly the moment to go into that now, is it?

BARKING. It was Aloysia and not I who let the cat

out of the bag. Being a cat herself she had a fellow-feeling for the animal. [*He resumes his seat*].

BLEE. Youre an aristocrat, young-fellow-me-lad. I always said that when things got serious youd turn on us and side with your own.

BARKING. Rot! Youre always bragging that you are descended from the Blee of Blayport, whoever he may have been. I shouldnt have tuppence in my pocket if my grandfather hadnt made a fortune in pork pies and bought my father's Norman title for his daughter with it. The blue blood is in your skimpy little veins: the proletarian red's in mine.

ALOYSIA. Youve too much money, Toffy.

BARKING. I havnt had all the pluck taken out of me by poverty, like you chaps. And what good will it do me to have a lot of money when I have to work like anyone else?

SIR DEXTER. Why should a man work like anyone else if he has money?

BARKING. My brother had heaps of money; but he had to go into the trenches and fight like anyone else in the war. Thats how I came into the property.

BLEE. So we're all to be slaves for the sake of setting a few loafers to work. The workers will die sooner than put up with it. I want my liberty—

BARKING. Liberty to work fourteen hours a day and bring up three children on thirtyfour shillings a week, like your brother the shopman. To hell with your filthy liberty!

BLEE [*hotly*] I—

THE MAYOR. Order! order! Dont argue with him, Blee. No good ever comes of arguing with college men. I'm not arguing with Sir Arthur: I'm telling him. The long and the short of it is that if he dont withdraw that silly new program he'll lose every vote in the Isle of Cats. And what the Isle of Cats thinks to-day, all England thinks tomorrow.

SIR JAFNA. May I speak to this gentleman? Will you introduce me, Arthur?

SIR ARTHUR [*introducing*] Sir Jafna Pandranath. The Mayor of the Isle of Cats.

SIR JAFNA. You have heard of me, Mr Mayor. You know that I am a man who knows what he is talking about. Well, I tell you that the fundamental question is not the Labor question but the Land Question.

THE MAYOR. Yes: we all know that.

SIR JAFNA. Then you will vote for Sir Arthur because he will nationalize the land for you.

BLEE [*scornfully*] Yes, with compensation! Take the land with one hand and give back its cash value to the landlords with the other! Not likely. I ask again, do you take us for fools?

SIR ARTHUR [*introducing*] Mr Alderman Blee.

THE DUKE. Enchanted. I happen to be a landlord—a duke, in fact—and I can assure you, Mr Alderman, that as the compensation will come out of my own pocket and that of my unfortunate fellow landlords in the form of income tax, surtax, and estate duties—what you call death duties—you will get all your cash back and the land as well.

THE MAYOR. Blee: I tell you, dont argue. Stick to your point. No compensation.

BLEE. Not a penny, by God.

THE DUKE. You believe in God, Mr Alderman. I am charmed to hear it.

Here the Duke is astonished to find Aloysia towering over him and pointing an accusing finger at him. At the moment of his introduction of himself as a duke, her eyes lighted up; and she has moved menacingly across the hearth towards him until she is now standing behind the vacant chair between him and Basham.

ALOYSIA. Have you ever heard of the Domesday clearances?

THE DUKE. Clearances? Which clearances do you refer to? The latest cleared me out of Domesday Towers. I can no longer afford to live there.

ALOYSIA. Dont prevaricate. You know very well what I mean. It is written in blood and tears on the pages of working class history.

SIR ARTHUR [*introducing*] Alderwoman Aloysia Brollikins. The Duke of Domesday.

THE DUKE [*rising courteously*] Wont you sit down?

ALOYSIA [*sternly*] You shall not put me out by these tricks and ceremonies. My Lord Duke: I would rather touch the hand of the most degraded criminal in London than touch yours.

THE DUKE [*collapsing into his chair*] Great heavens! Why?

ALOYSIA. Do you forget how your family drove a whole countryside of honest hardworking Scotch crofters into the sea, and turned their little farms into deer forests because you could get more shooting rents out of them in that way? Do you forget that women in childbirth were carried out by your bailiffs to die by the roadside because they clung to their ancient homesteads and ignored your infamous notices to quit? Would it surprise you to learn that I am only one of thousands of young women who have read the hideous story of this monstrous orgy of housebreaking and murder, and sworn to ourselves that never, if we can help it, will it again be possible for one wicked rich man to say to a whole population "Get off the earth."

SIR JAFNA. Admirable! What did I tell you? Hear hear!

ALOYSIA. I thank you, Sir Jafna, for shewing this man that even hardened capitalist millionaires shudder when that story is told. You will not find it in your school histories; but in the new histories, the histories of the proletariat, it has been written, not by the venal academic triflers you call historians, but by the prophets of the new order: the men in whom the word is like a burning fire shut up in their bones so that they are weary of forbearing and must speak.

THE MAYOR. Aye: in the Bible, that is.

ALOYSIA. The Domesday Clearances filled your pockets with gold to console you for the horror and remorse of your dreams: but the vengeance they cried to God for in vain is upon you now that Labor is coming to its own; and it is your turn now to get off the earth.

BLEE. And in the face of all this, you come whining for compensation! Compensation!! Compensation from us to you! From the oppressed to the oppressor! What a mockery!

ALOYSIA. It is from you that we shall exact compensation: aye, to the uttermost farthing. You are conspiring here with these capitalist bloodsuckers to rob us again of the value of what you have already stolen—to make us give you gilt edged securities in exchange for the land that no longer brings you in shooting rents; and you think we cannot see through the plot. But in vain is the net spread in sight of the bird. We shall expose you. We shall tell the story of the Domesday Clearances until the country rings with it if you dare to lift your dishonored head again in English politics. Your demand for compensation is dismissed, turned down: we spit it back in your face. The crofters whom you drove from their country to perish in a foreign land would turn in their graves at the chink of a single penny of public money in your hungry pocket. [*She tears out a chair from under the table and flops into it, panting with oratorical emotion*].

BLEE
SIR JAFNA } Good for you, Brolly!
SIR BEMROSE } [*enthused*] Hear hear! [*They hammer on the table with their knuckles*].
GLENMORISON }

THE DUKE [*very appreciative*] What a magnificent speech, Miss Brollikins! I really must insist on your shaking hands with me before we part.

ALOYSIA. Never. How dare you ask me? [*She sweeps away from him and sits down in the opposite chair at the other side of the table*].

THE DUKE [*taking the armchair*] May I not have the privilege of telling my grandchildren how I once met and shook hands with the greatest orator of my time? I assure you all these shocking things happened before I was born.

BLEE [*bawling at him*] Yes; but you still pocket the shooting rents.

THE DUKE [*brusquely*] Of course I do; and so would you too if you were in my place. [*Tenderly, to Aloysia*] I assure you, Miss Brollikins, the people make much more money out of my shooting tenants than they could as crofters: they would not go back to croftering for worlds. Wont you let bygones be bygones—except when you are exercising your wonderful gift of eloquence on the platform? Think of what y o u r ancestors were doing in those ruthless old days!

BARKING. Grabbing all they could get, like yours or mine. Whats the good of tubthumping at these johnnies, Brolly? Theyve been doing it themselves all their lives. Cant you see that compensation makes them share the loss fairly between them?

SIR BEMROSE. It's no use. These damned Liberals cant understand anything but virtuous indignation.

THE MAYOR. Who are you calling a Liberal? I represent the Labor Party.

SIR BEMROSE. Youre a No Compensation man, arnt you?

THE MAYOR. Of course I am.

SIR BEMROSE. Then youre a Liberal.

THE MAYOR. Call me what you like. I'm not arguing. I'm telling you that the Labor Party of the Isle of Cats puts down its foot and says No Compensation. Is that plain?

SIR DEXTER. I am glad we have arrived at the same conclusion from our opposite points of view, Mr Mayor. The Party I represent, the Conservative Party, will withdraw from the Coalition if there is the slightest wobbling on this point. We shall defend our property—and yours: y o u r s, Mr Mayor, to the last drop of our blood.

BASHAM [*incisively re-entering the conversation; they had forgotten him, and now turn to him in some surprise*] Our blood, you mean, dont you?

SIR DEXTER [*puzzled*] Whose blood?

BASHAM. The police's blood. You landed gentlemen never do a thing yourselves: you only call us in. I have twenty thousand constables, all full of blood, to shed it in defence of whatever the Government may decide to be your property. If Sir Arthur carries his point theyll shed it for land nationalization. If you carry yours theyll stand by your rent collectors as usual.

BLEE. The police come from the ranks of labor: dont forget that.

BASHAM. Thats not how they look at it, Blee. They feel that theyve escaped from the ranks of labor; and theyre proud of it. They have a status which they feel to be a part of the status of the Duke here.

THE DUKE. I suppose that is why they are always so civil to me.

BASHAM. In short, Mister Blee, the police are what you Socialists call class-conscious. You will find that out if you are foolish enough to fall out with them.

BLEE. Who cut their pay? Tell me that.

SIR ARTHUR. I shall restore the cuts, Mr Alderman, with a premium.

THE MAYOR. There! Now you see what comes of arguing, Blee. It only gives him his chance.

ALOYSIA. You need not warn us, Sir Broadfoot Basham, D.S.O., K.C.M.G., O.B.E. In the Class War your myrmidons will be well paid.

THE DUKE. Myrmidons!

ALOYSIA. We know too well what we have to expect from your Janissaries.

BLEE. Your bludgeoning Bashi-Bazouks.

ALOYSIA. The Class War is a fact. We face it. What we want we shall have to take; and we know it. The good of the community is nothing to you: you care only for surplus value. You will never give up your privileges voluntarily. History teaches us that: the history you never read.

THE DUKE. I assure you, my dear Héloise?

ALOYSIA. Héloise! Who are you calling Héloise?

THE DUKE. Pardon. I could not resist the French form of your charming name.

ALOYSIA [*interjects*] The cheek!

THE DUKE [*continuing*] I was merely going to point out, as between one student of history and another, that in the French Revolution it was the nobility who voluntarily abolished all their own privileges at a single sitting, on the sentimental principles they had acquired from reading the works of Karl Marx's revolutionary predecessor Rousseau. That bit of history is repeating itself today. Here is Sir Arthur offering us a program of what seems to me to be first rate Platonic Communism. I, a Conservative Duke, embrace it. Sir Jafna Pandranath here, a Liberal capitalist whose billions shame my poverty, embraces it. The Navy embraces it with the sturdy arms of Sir Bemrose Hotspot. The police are enthusiastic. The Army will be with Sir Arthur to the last man. He has the whole propertied class on his side. But the proletariat rises against him and spews out his Socialism through the eloquent lips of its Aloysia. I recall the warning my dear old father gave me when I was five years old. Chained dogs are the fiercest guardians of property; and those who attempt to unchain them are the first to be bitten.

ALOYSIA. Your Grace calls us dogs. We shall not forget that.

THE DUKE. I have found no friends better than faithful dogs, Miss Brollikins. But of course I spoke figuratively. I should not dream of calling you a dog.

ALOYSIA. No. As I am a female dog I suppose you will call me something shorter when my back is turned.

THE DUKE. Oh! Think of the names you have called me!

THE MAYOR. Well, if you will argue, Alderwoman Brollikins, there's no use my staying here. I wish I could stop your mouth as easy as I can stop my ears. Sir Arthur: youve planked down your program and weve planked down our answer. Either you drop compulsory labor and drop compensation or never shew your face in the Isle of Cats again. [*He goes out resolutely*].

BLEE. Take this from me. I am no Communist: I am a respectable Labor man, as law abiding as any man here. I am what none of you has mentioned yet: a democrat. I am just as much against Cabinet dictatorship as individual dictatorship. What I want done is the will of the people. I am for the referendum. I am for the initiative. When a majority of the people are in favor of a measure then I am for that measure.

SIR BEMROSE. Rot! The majority is never in favor of any measure. They dont know what a measure is. What they want is their orders, and as much comfort as they are accustomed to. The lower deck doesnt want to give orders, it looks to the bridge for them. If I asked my men to do my job theyd chuck me overboard; and serve me jolly well right! You just know nothing about it, because youve never had to command; and you havnt sense enough to obey and be thankful to those who have saved you the trouble of thinking for yourself and keeping you off the rocks.

BLEE. You havnt kept us off the rocks. We're on the rocks, the whole lot of us. So long, Rosy. [*He goes out*].

BARKING. Silly swine! When they are offered what they want they wont have it just because you fellows want it too. They think there must be a catch in it somewhere.

THE DUKE. There generally is. That is how you feel, Miss Brollikins, isnt it?

ALOYSIA. You dont know how I feel; and you never will. We are going to save ourselves and not be saved by you and your class. And I prefer Sir Dexter Rightside's downright outspoken opposition to your silly-clever cynicism and your sickening compliments.

THE DUKE. It is only in middle class books, Miss

Brollikins, that noblemen are always cynical and insincere. I find you a most brilliant and delightful woman. May I not tell you so? And WHAT a speaker! Will you spend a quiet week-end with me in some out-of-the-way place in the country, and let me try to convince you that a duke is a human being like yourself?

ALOYSIA [*rearing*] Are you trying to seduce me?

THE DUKE. That would be exquisite, Miss Brollikins; but I am an old and very poor man. You are young, beautiful, and probably opulent. Can you find anything seductive about me?

ALOYSIA. Yes. Youre a duke. And you have the charm of a majestic ruin, if you understand me.

BARKING [*rising*] Come on out of this, Brolly: youre only making a fool of yourself listening to that old bird buttering you up. You just dont know when to go.

ALOYSIA [*moving to the hearthrug, behind Sir Arthur*] You can go if you like. I have some business with Sir Arthur that doesnt concern you. Get out.

SIR ARTHUR. Some business with me! Public business?

ALOYSIA. Not exactly.

SIR ARTHUR. Oh! Private business?

ALOYSIA. I dont care who knows it. But perhaps you would.

BARKING. She means to marry your son David. One below the belt for you, Brolly. Ha ha! Ha ha ha ha ha! [*He goes out roaring with laughter*].

SIR ARTHUR [*after a moment of shock*] I congratulate David, Miss Brollikins. Have you arranged the date?

ALOYSIA. I havnt mentioned it to him yet. I hope all you gentlemen will remember that I was not the one that blurted this out: it was your noble viscount.

However, now it's out, I stand by it: David is a good boy; and his class is not his fault. Goodbye all. [*She goes to the door*].

THE DUKE [*rising*] And that week-end, Miss Brollikins? Or has David cut me out?

ALOYSIA. Right you are. Your Grace! I will call for you at Domesday House on Friday at half past four. As I shall bring a few friends we shall hire an omnibus from the London Transport; so you neednt trouble about a car. You wont mind my publishing an account of what happens as a special interview: you know that we Labor intelligentsia have to live by our brains. Au revoir. [*She goes out*].

THE DUKE. There is a frightful unexpectedness about these people. Where on earth shall I borrow the money to pay for the omnibus and entertain them all? [*He goes back to his chair at the end of the table and sits down*].

BASHAM. Your share will only be a few shillings, Duke; and she will reckon on having to pay for you. What girl in her class wouldnt foot the bill if she had a duke to walk out with?

THE DUKE. You reassure me, Sir Broadfoot. Thank you.

SIR DEXTER [*triumphant*] Well, Chavender? What have you to say now? When these people came in I was saying that though I was alone in this room, the people of England were on my side and always would be when it came to the point. Was I right or wrong?

SIR BEMROSE. We never meant to desert you, Dexy. You mustnt think that.

SIR ARTHUR. As you have no more intention of consulting the people of England than I have, the situation is unaltered.

SIR DEXTER. Than you have! What do you mean?

Do you think you can govern in this country without the consent of the English people?

SIR ARTHUR. No country has ever been governed by the consent of the people, because the people object to be governed at all. Even you, who ought to know better, are always complaining of the income tax.

THE DUKE. But five shillings in the pound, Arthur! Five shillings in the pound!!

SIR DEXTER. Never mind my income tax. If what you said just now means anything it means that you are going to play fast and loose with democracy: that is, you think you are going to do something that both the people and the governing class of this country are determined you shall not do. The Conservative Party, which is ten times more really democratic than you Liberals have ever been, will carry the people with it against you. How do you propose to get over that? What are you banking on? Put your cards on the table if you really have any.

SIR ARTHUR. Well, here is my ace of trumps. The people of this country, and of all the European countries, and of America, are at present sick of being told that, thanks to democracy, they are the real government of the country. They know very well that they dont govern and cant govern and know nothing about Government except that it always supports profiteering, and doesnt really respect anything else, no matter what party flag it waves. They are sick of twaddle about liberty when they have no liberty. They are sick of idling and loafing about on doles when they are not drudging for wages too beggarly to pay the rents of anything better than overcrowded one-room tenements. They are sick of me and sick of you and sick of the whole lot of us. They want to see something done that will give them decent employ-

ment. They want to eat and drink the wheat and coffee
that the profiteers are burning because they cant sell
it at a profit. They want to hang people who burn
good food when people are going hungry. They cant
set matters right themselves; so they want rulers who
will discipline them and make them do it instead of
making them do the other thing. They are ready to go
mad with enthusiasm for any man strong enough to
make them do anything, even if it is only Jew baiting,
provided it's something tyrannical, something coer-
cive, something that we all pretend no Englishman
would submit to, though weve known ever since we
gave them the vote that theyd submit to anything.

SIR DEXTER [*impatiently*] Yes, yes: we know the cant
of all the tuppeny-hapeny dictators who think themselves Mussolinis. Come down to tin tacks. How are
you going to get it through Parliament?

SIR ARTHUR. I am not going to get it through Parliament: I am going to prorogue Parliament and then
do it. When it is done I shall call a meeting of Parliament to pass an Act of Indemnity for all my proceedings.

SIR DEXTER. You cannot prorogue Parliament. Only
the King can prorogue Parliament.

SIR ARTHUR. Precisely. Kings always have prorogued
Parliament and governed without them until money
ran short.

GLENMORISON. But, man alive, it is not His Majesty
alone that you have to consider. The law courts will
not enforce your decisions if they are illegal. The
civil servants will sabotage you even if they dont flatly
disobey you.

SIR ARTHUR. We shall sidetrack them quite easily
by setting up new tribunals and special commissions
manned by officials we can depend on.

SIR DEXTER. That was how Cromwell cut off King Charles's head. His commissioners found out afterwards that they were doing it with ropes round their rascally necks.

SIR ARTHUR. A rope round a statesman's neck is the only constitutional safeguard that really safeguards. But never fear the rope. As long as we give the people an honest good time we can do just what seems good to us. The proof of the pudding will be in the eating. That will be really responsible government at last.

SIR DEXTER. So that is your game, is it? Has it occurred to you that two can play at it? What can you do that I cannot do if you drive me to it: tell me that.

SIR ARTHUR. Nothing, if you are willing to take on my job. Are you?

SIR DEXTER. The job of ruining the country and destroying the empire? My job is to prevent you from doing that. And I will prevent you.

SIR ARTHUR. Your job is to prevent me or anybody else from doing anything. Your job is to prevent the world from moving. Well, it is moving; and if you dont get out of the way something will break; and it wont be the world.

SIR DEXTER. Nothing has broken so far except the heads of the unemployed when they are encouraged by your seditious rot to rebel against the laws of nature. England is not breaking. She stands foursquare where she always stood and always will stand: the strongest and greatest land, and the birthplace of the noblest imperial race, that ever God created.

SIR ARTHUR. Loud and prolonged cheering. Come! let us both stop tub thumping and talk business. The real master of the situation is Basham here, with his fifteen thousand police.

BASHAM. Twenty thousand.

SIR ARTHUR. Well, twenty thousand. They dont stop functioning when Parliament is prorogued, do they?

BASHAM. No. At Scotland Yard we look to the Home Secretary as far as we look to anybody.

SIR ARTHUR. I can make myself Home Secretary. So that will be all right.

SIR DEXTER. Will it, by George? If you and Basham dare to try your twenty thousand police on me, do you know what I will do?

SIR ARTHUR. What?

SIR DEXTER. I will put fifty thousand patriotic young Londoners into Union Jack shirts. You say they want discipline and action. They shall have them. They shall have machine guns and automatic pistols and tear gas bombs. My Party has the money. My Party has the newspapers. My Party has the flag, the traditions, the glory that is England, the pluck, the breed, the fighting spirit. One of us is worth ten of your half starved guttersnipes and their leaders that never could afford more than a shilling for a dinner until they voted themselves four hundred a year out of our pockets.

SIR BEMROSE [*carried away*] Thats the stuff, Dexy. Now you are talking, by Jiminy.

BASHAM [*taking command of the discussion coolly*] You are all talking through your hats. The police can do nothing unless the people are on the side of the police. The police cant be everywhere: there arnt enough of them. As long as the people will call the police when anything goes wrong, and stop the runaway criminal and give evidence against him, then twenty thousand constables can keep eight million citizens in order. But if the citizens regard the policeman as their enemy—if the man who snipes a policeman in the back is not given in charge by the bystanders—if he is helped to get away—if the police cannot get a single citizen to go into the box and witness against him, where are you then? You have to double your force because the police must patrol in pairs: otherwise the men will be afraid to patrol at all. Your twenty thousand have to be reinforced up to forty thousand for their own protection; but that doesnt protect you. You would have to put two policemen standing over every ablebodied man and woman in the town to see that they behaved themselves as you want them to behave. You would need not thousands of constables but millions.

SIR DEXTER. My Union Jack men would keep order, or theyd know the reason why.

BASHAM. And who would keep t h e m in order, I should like to know: silly amateurs. And let me remind you of one thing. It seems easy to buy a lot of black shirts, or brown shirts, or red shirts, and give one to every hooligan who is out for any sort of mischief and every suburban out-of-work who fancies himself a patriot. But dont forget that the colored shirt is a uniform.

GLENMORISON. What harm is there in that? It enables a man to recognize his friends.

BASHAM. Yes; but it marks him out as an enemy in uniform; and to kill an enemy in uniform at sight is not murder: it's legitimate warfare.

SIR DEXTER. Monstrous! I should give no quarter to such an outrageous piece of sophistry.

BASHAM. In war you have to give quarter because you have to ask for it as often as to give it. It's easy to sit here and think of exterminating your opponents. But a war of extermination is a massacre. How long do you think a massacre would last in England today? Just as long as it takes a drunken man to get sick and sober.

GLENMORISON. Easy, Sir Broadfoot, easy, easy. Who is talking of extermination? I dont think you will ever induce respectable Britons to wear red-white-and-blue shirts; but surely you can have volunteers, special constables, auxiliary forces—

BASHAM [*flinching violently*] Auxiliary forces! I was in command of them in Ireland when you tried that game on the Irish, who were only a little handful of peasants in their cabbage patch. I have seen these things. I have done them. I know all about it: you know nothing about it. It means extermination; and when it comes to the point you cant go through with it. I couldnt. I resigned. You couldnt: you had to back down. And I tell you, Dexy, if you try any colored shirt hooliganism on me, I'll back the P.M. and shew you what Scotland Yard can do when it's put to it.

SIR DEXTER. Traitor!

BASHAM. Liar! Now weve called one another names how much farther has it got us?

GLENMORISON. Easy, easy: dont let us quarrel. I must support the Prime Minister, Sir Dexter, to secure my seat in Parliament. But I am a Liberal, and, as such, bound by Liberal principles. Whatever we do must be done through Parliament if I am to be a party to it. I am all for the new program; but we must draw up a parliamentary timetable for it. To carry out the program will involve the introduction of at least twelve bills. They are highly controversial bills: everyone of them will be resisted and obstructed to the very last clause. You may have to go to the country on several of them. The committee stages will last for weeks and weeks, no matter how hard you work the guillotine: there will be thousands of amendments. Then, when you have got through what is left of your

Bill and carried it, the House of Lords will turn it down; and you will have to wait two years and go through the whole job again before you can get your Bill on the statute book as an Act of Parliament. This program is not a matter of today or tomorrow. I calculate that at the very least it will take fifty years to get it through.

SIR ARTHUR. And you think the world will wait for that, Sandy?

GLENMORISON [naïvely] What else can it do?

SIR ARTHUR. It wont wait. Unless we can find a shorter way, the program will be fought out in the streets.

SIR DEXTER. And you think that in the streets you will win? You think the mob will be on your side? "Ye are many: they are few" eh? The Class War! Well, you will find out your mistake.

SIR ARTHUR. I dont believe in the Class War any more than you do, Dexy. I know that half the working class is slaving away to pile up riches, only to be smoked out like a hive of bees and plundered of everything but a bare living by our class. But what is the other half doing? Living on the plunder at second hand. Plundering the plunderers. As fast as we fill our pockets with rent and interest and profits theyre emptied again by West End tradesmen and hotel keepers, fashionable doctors and lawyers and parsons and fiddlers and portrait painters and all sorts, to say nothing of huntsmen and stablemen and gardeners, valets and gamekeepers and jockeys, butlers and housekeepers and ladies' maids and scullery maids and deuce knows who not.

THE DUKE. How true, Arthur! how profoundly true! I am with you there to the last drop of my blood.

SIR ARTHUR. Well, these parasites will fight for the

rights of property as they would fight for their own skins. Can you get a Labor member into Parliament in the places where they are in a majority? No: there is no class war: the working class is hopelessly divided against itself. But I will tell you what there is. There is the gulf between Dexy's view of the world and mine. There is the eternal war between those who are in the world for what they can get out of it and those who are in the world to make it a better place for everybody to live in.

SIR DEXTER [*rising*] I will not sit here listening to this disgusting ungentlemanly nonsense. Chavender: the coalition is dissolved. I resign. I shall take with me three quarters of the Cabinet. I shall expose the shamelessly corrupt motives of those who have supported you here today. Basham: you will get the sack the day after the King sends for me. Domesday: you have gone gaga: go home to bed and drivel where your dotage can do no harm. Rosy: you are a damned fool; and you ought to know it by this time. Pandranath: you are only a silly nigger pretending to be an English gentleman: you are found out. Good afternoon, gentlemen.

He goes out, leaving an atmosphere of awe behind him, in which the Indian is choking with indignation, and for the moment inarticulate.

SIR BEMROSE. This is awful. We cannot do without him.

SIR JAFNA [*finding his tongue*] I am despised. I am called nigger by this dirty faced barbarian whose forefathers were naked savages worshipping acorns and mistletoe in the woods whilst my people were spreading the highest enlightenment yet reached by the human race from the temples of Brahma the thousandfold who is all the gods in one. This primitive savage dares to accuse me of imitating him: me, with the blood in my veins of conquerors who have swept through continents vaster than a million dogholes like this island of yours. They founded a civilization compared to which your little kingdom is no better than a concentration camp. What you have of religion came from the east; yet no Hindu, no Parsee, no Jain, would stoop to its crudities. Is there a mirror here? Look at your faces and look at the faces of my people in Ceylon, the cradle of the human race. There you see Man as he came from the hand of God, who has left on every feature the unmistakeable stamp of the great original creative artist. There you see Woman with eyes in her head that mirror the universe instead of little peepholes filled with faded pebbles. Set those features, those eyes, those burning colors beside the miserable smudged lumps of half baked dough, the cheap commercial copies of a far away gallery of masterpieces that you call western humanity, and tell me, if you dare, that you are the original and I the imitation. Do you not fear the lightning? the earthquake? the vengeance of Vishnu? You call me nigger, sneering at my color because you have none. The jackdaw has lost his tail and would persuade the world that his defect is a quality. You have all cringed to me, not for my greater nearness to God, but for my money and my power of making money and ever more money. But today your hatred, your envy, your insolence has betrayed itself. I am nigger. I am bad imitation of that eater of unclean foods, never sufficiently washed in his person or his garments, a British islander. I will no longer bear it. The veil of your hypocrisy is rent by your own mouths: I should dishonor my country and my race by remaining here where both have been insulted. Until now I have supported the connection between India and England because I knew that in the course of nature and by the justice of Brahma it must end in India ruling England just as I, by my wealth and my brains, govern this roomful of needy imbeciles. But I now cast you off. I return to India to detach it wholly from England, and leave you to perish in your ignorance, your vain conceit, and your abominable manners. Good morning, gentlemen. To hell with the lot of you. [*He goes out and slams the door*].

SIR ARTHUR. That one word nigger will cost us India. How could Dexy be such a fool as to let it slip!

SIR BEMROSE [*very serious—rising solemnly*] Arthur: I feel I cannot overlook a speech like that. After all, we are white men.

SIR ARTHUR. You are not, Rosy, I assure you. You are walnut color, with a touch of claret on the nose. Glenmorison is the color of his native oatmeal: not a touch of white on him. The fairest man present is the Duke. He's as yellow as a Malayan headhunter. The Chinese call us Pinks. They flatter us.

SIR BEMROSE. I must tell you, Arthur, that frivolity on a vital point like this is in very bad taste. And you know very well that the country cannot do without Dexy. Dexy was at school with me before I went to Dartmouth. To desert him would be for me not only an act of political bad faith but of personal bad feeling. I must go and see him at once. [*He goes very sadly to the door*].

SIR ARTHUR. Make my apologies to Sir Jafna if you overtake him. How are we to hold the empire together if we insult a man who represents nearly seventy per cent of its population?

SIR BEMROSE. I dont agree with you, Arthur. It is for Pandy to apologize. Dexy really shares the premiership with you; and if a Conservative Prime Minister of England may not take down a heathen native when he forgets himself there is an end of British supremacy.

SIR ARTHUR. For Heaven's sake dont call him a native. You are a native.

SIR BEMROSE [*very solemnly*] Of Kent, Arthur: of Kent. Not of Ceylon. [*He goes out*].

GLENMORISON. I think I'd better clear out too. I can make allowances for Sir Dexter: he is an Englishman, and has not been trained to use his mind like us in Scotland. But that is just what gives him such a hold on the Country. We must face it: he's indispensable. I'll just go and assure him that we have no intention of breaking with him. Ta ta. Good morning, Duke. [*He goes out*].

SIR ARTHUR [*rising and strolling round to the other side of the table like a cleaned-out gambler*] That finishes me, I'm afraid.

He throws himself into the middle chair. Basham rises moodily and goes to the window to contemplate the street. The Duke comes sympathetically to Sir Arthur and sits down beside him.

THE DUKE. Oh Arthur, my dear Arthur, why didnt you play golf on your holiday instead of thinking? Didnt you know that English politics wont bear thinking about? Didnt you know that as a nation we have lost the trick of thinking? Hadnt you noticed that though in our great British Constitution there is a department for everything else in the world almost —for agriculture and health and fisheries, for home affairs and foreign affairs and education, for the exchequer and the Treasury and even the Chiltern Hundreds and the Duchy of Lancaster—we have no department for thinking? The Russians have a special Cabinet for it; and it has knocked the whole place to

pieces. Where should you and I be in Russia today?
[*He resumes his seat with a hopeless shrug*].

SIR ARTHUR. In our proper place, the dustbin. Yet
they got their ideas from us. Karl Marx thought it all
out in Bloomsbury. Lenin learnt his lesson in Holford
Square, Islington. Why can we never think out anything, nor learn any lessons? I see what has to be
done now; but I dont feel that I am the man to do it.

THE DUKE. Of course not. Not a gentleman's job.

SIR ARTHUR. It might be a duke's job, though. Why
not have a try at it?

THE DUKE. For three reasons, Arthur. First, I'm not
built that way. Second, I'm so accustomed as a duke
to be treated with the utmost deference that I simply
dont know how to assert myself and bully people.
Third, I'm so horribly hard up for pocket money
without knowing how to do without it that Ive lost all
my self-respect. This job needs a man with nothing
to lose, plenty of hard driving courage, and a complete incapacity for seeing any side of a question but
his own. A mere hereditary duke would be no use.
When Domesday Towers is sold to an American I
shall have no family seat left, and must fall back on
my political seat, which is at present on the fence.
From that eminence I shall encourage the dictator
when he arrives as far as I can without committing
myself dangerously. Sorry I can be of no use to you,
my dear Arthur.

SIR ARTHUR. What about you, Basham? You are a
man of action.

BASHAM. I have a jolly good mind to go to the King
and make him take the bit between his teeth and
arrest the lot of you.

SIR ARTHUR. Do, Basham, do. You couldnt make a
worse hash of things than we have.

THE DUKE. Theres nothing to prevent you. Look at Kemal Pasha! Look at Mussolini! Look at Hitler! Look at De Valera! Look at Franklin Roosevelt!

BASHAM. If only I had ambition enough I'd think very seriously over it. As it is, I'll go back quietly to Scotland Yard. [*He is going out when he is confronted in the doorway by Hipney*] Hallo! What the devil are you doing here?

SIR ARTHUR. I am afraid you are late, Mr Hipney. The deputation has been here. They have all gone.

HIPNEY [*seating himself beside Sir Arthur with his usual calm*] I came with them, Srarthur. I been listening on the quiet as you might say. I just came in to tell you not to mind that parliamentary lot. Theyre all the same, west end or east end, parkside or riverside. Theyll never do anything. They dont want to do anything.

BASHAM [*sitting down again in Hilda's chair*] Hipney: I may as well tell you that I have had my eye on you for some time. Take care I have no objection to your calling yourself a revolutionary Socialist: they all do that. But I suspect you of really meaning business.

HIPNEY. I do, Sir Broadfoot: I do. And if Srarthur means business, then let him come out of Parliament and keep out. It will take the life out of him and leave him a walking talking shell of a man with nothing inside. The only man that ever had a proper understanding of Parliament was old Guy Fawkes.

SIR ARTHUR. But even if he had blown that Parliament up, they would just have elected another.

HIPNEY. Yes; but it was a sort of gesture as you might say. Symbolic, I call it. Mark my words: some day there will be a statue to old Guy in Westminster on the site of the present House of Commons.

THE DUKE. Democracy, Arthur, democracy. This is what it ends in.

SIR ARTHUR [*introducing*] His Grace the Duke of Domesday, Mr Hipney.

HIPNEY. Bless you, I know his Grace. About town, as you might say, though weve never been introduced.

THE DUKE. Very much honored, Mr Hipney.

HIPNEY. No great honor, your Grace. But old Hipney can tell you something about Democracy at first hand. Democracy was a great thing when I was young and we had no votes. We talked about public opinion and what the British people would stand and what they wouldnt stand. And it had weight, I tell you, sir: it held Governments in check: it frightened the stoutest of the tyrants and the bosses and the police: it brought a real reverence into the voices of great orators like Bright and Gladstone. But that was when it was a dream and a vision, a hope and a faith and a promise. It lasted until they dragged it down to earth, as you might say, and made it a reality by giving everybody votes. The moment they gave the working men votes they found that theyd stand anything. They gave votes to the women and found they were worse than the men; for men would vote for men— the wrong men, but men all the same—but the women wouldnt even vote for women. Since then politics have been a laughing stock. Parliamentary leaders say one thing on Monday and just the opposite on Wednesday; and nobody notices any difference. They put down the people in Egypt, in Ireland, and in India with fire and sword, with floggings and hangings, burning the houses over their heads and bombing their little stores for the winter out of existence; and at the next election theyd be sent back to Parliament by working class constituencies as if they were plaster saints, while men and women like me, that had spent their lives in the service of the people, were booted out at the polls like convicted criminals. It wasnt that the poor silly sheep did it on purpose. They didnt notice: they didnt remember: they couldnt understand: they were taken in by any nonsense they heard at the meetings or read in the morning paper. You could stampede them by crying out that the Russians were coming, or rally them by promising them to hang the Kaiser, or Lord knows what silliness that shouldnt have imposed on a child of four. That was the end of democracy for me; though there was no man alive that had hoped as much from it, nor spoke deeper from his heart about all the good things that would happen when the people came to their own and had votes like the gentry. Adult suffrage: that was what was to save us all. My God! It delivered us into the hands of our spoilers and oppressors, bound hand and foot by our own folly and ignorance. It took the heart out of old Hipney; and now I'm for any Napoleon or Mussolini or Lenin or Chavender that has the stuff in him to take both the people and the spoilers and oppressors by the scruffs of their silly necks and just sling them into the way they should go with as many kicks as may be needful to make a thorough job of it.

BASHAM. A dictator: eh? Thats what you want.

HIPNEY. Better one dictator standing up responsible before the world for the good and evil he does than a dirty little dictator in every street responsible to nobody, to turn you out of your house if you dont pay him for the right to exist on the earth, or to fire you out of your job if you stand up to him as a man and an equal. You cant frighten me with a word like dictator. Me and my like has been dictated to all our lives by swine that have nothing but a snout for money, and think the world is coming to an end if anybody but themselves is given the power to do anything.

SIR ARTHUR. Steady, Mr Hipney, steady! Dont empty the baby out with the bath. If the people are to have no voice in the government and no choice of who is to govern them, it will be bad for the people.

HIPNEY. Let em have a voice. Let em have a choice. Theyve neither at present. But let it be a voice to squeal with when theyre hurt, and not to pretend they know more than God Almighty does. Give em a choice between qualified men: there's always more than one pebble on the beach; but let them be qualified men and not windbags and movie stars and soldiers and rich swankers and lawyers on the make. How are they to tell the difference between any cheap Jack and Solomon or Moses? The Jews didnt elect Moses: he just told them what to do and they did it. Look at the way they went wrong the minute his back was turned! If you want to be a leader of the people, Srarthur, youve got to elect yourself by giving us a lead. Old Hipney will follow anyone that will give him a good lead; and to blazes with your elections and your Constitution and your Democracy and all the rest of it!

THE DUKE. The police wont let him, Mr Hipney.

BASHAM [rising and planting himself between Hipney and Sir Arthur] Ha ha ha! Dont be too sure of that. I might come down on your side, Arthur, if I spotted you as a winner. Meanwhile, Hipney, I have my eye on you as a dangerous character.

SIR ARTHUR. And on me?

BASHAM. You dont matter: he does. If the proletariat comes to the top things will be more comfortable for Hipney; but they wont be more comfortable for you.

His heart is in the revolution: you have only your head in it. Your wife wouldnt like it: his would, if he has one.

HIPNEY. Not me. I'm under no woman's thumb. She's dead; and the children are grown up and off my hands. I'm free at last to put my neck in a noose if I like.

BASHAM. I wonder should I find any bombs in your house if I searched it.

HIPNEY. You would if you put them there first, Sir Broadfoot. What good would a police chief be if he couldnt find anything he wanted to find?

BASHAM. Thats a suggestion, Hipney, certainly. Isnt it rather rash of you to put it into my head?

HIPNEY. There's plenty to put it into your head if I didnt. You could do it if you liked; and you know it, Sir Broadfoot. But perhaps your conscience wouldnt let you.

BASHAM. Perhaps.

HIPNEY [rising with a chuckle] Aha! [Impressively] You take it from me, you three gentlemen: all this country or any country has to stand between it and blue hell is the consciences of them that are capable of governing it.

THE DUKE [rising] Mr Hipney: I find myself in complete agreement with you. Will you lunch with me at the Carlton?

HIPNEY. No: them big clubs is too promiscuous for the like of you and me. You come and lunch with me: I know a nice little place where the cooking's good and the company really select. You wont regret it: come along. Morning, Srarthur. Morning, Boss. [He goes out, greatly pleased].

SIR ARTHUR AND BASHAM [simultaneously] Morning. Morning.

THE DUKE. You would never have got rid of him, Arthur, if I hadnt made that move. Goodbye. Goodbye, Sir Broadfoot. [*He goes to the door*]

BASHAM. Goodbye. I wish you joy of your host.

THE DUKE. You dont appreciate him. He is absolutely unique.

BASHAM. In what way, pray?

THE DUKE. He is the only politician I ever met who had learnt anything from experience [*he goes out*].

BASHAM [*making for the door*] Well, I must be off to the Yard. The unemployed are going to have a general election to amuse them. I suppose youll be off to your constituency right away.

SIR ARTHUR [*rising*] No. I am not going to stand.

BASHAM [*returning to him in amazement*] Not stand! What do you mean? You cant chalk up a program like that and then run away.

SIR ARTHUR. I am through with parliament. It has wasted enough of my life.

BASHAM. Dont tell me you are going to take your politics into the street. You will only get your head broken.

SIR ARTHUR. Never fear: your fellows wont break my head: they have too much respect for an ex-Prime Minister. But I am not going into the streets. I am not a man of action, only a talker. Until the men of action clear out the talkers we who have social consciences are at the mercy of those who have none; and that, as old Hipney says, is blue hell. Can you find a better name for it?

BASHAM. Blackguardocracy. I should call it.

SIR ARTHUR. Do you believe in it? I dont.

BASHAM. It works all right up to a point. Dont run your head against it until the men of action get you past that point. Bye bye.

SIR ARTHUR. Bye bye. I wont.

Basham goes out through the main door. Sir Arthur drops into his chair again and looks rather sick, with his elbows on his knees and his temples on his fists. Barking and Miss Brollikins break into the room simultaneously by the private door, struggling for precedence, Sir Arthur straightens up wearily.

BARKING. I was here first. You get out and wait for your turn.

ALOYSIA. Ladies first, if you please. Sir Arthur—

BARKING [*barring her way with an arm of iron*] Ladies be damned! youre no lady. [*He comes past the table to Sir Arthur's right*]. Sir Arthur: I have proposed for the hand of your daughter Flavia; and all I can get out of her is that she is not a gold digger, and wouldnt be seen at a wedding with a lousy viscount. She wants to marry a poor man. I said I'd go over her head straight to you. You cant let her miss so good a match. Exert your authority. Make her marry me.

SIR ARTHUR. Certainly. I'll order her to marry you if you think that will get you any further. Go and tell her so, like a good boy. I'm busy.

BARKING. Righto! [*he dashes out through the masked door*].

SIR ARTHUR. Sit down, Miss Brollikins. [*She comes round to Hipney's chair; and Sir Arthur takes the Duke's chair*]. Have you consulted David?

ALOYSIA [*sitting down rather forlornly*] Of course I have. But he's obstinate. He wont look at it the right way.

SIR ARTHUR. Did he object? He should have jumped at it.

ALOYSIA. Its very nice of you to say so if you really mean it, Sir Arthur. But he has no sense. He objects to my name. He says it's ridiculous.

SIR ARTHUR. But your marriage will change it.

ALOYSIA. Yes; but he says it would be in The Times in the births marriages and deaths: Chavender and Brollikins. My name's not good enough for him. You should have heard what he said about it.

SIR ARTHUR. I hope he did not use the adjective his sister applied to poor young Barking's title.

ALOYSIA. Yes he did. The language you West End people use! I'm sure I dont know where you pick it up.

SIR ARTHUR. It doesnt mean anything, Miss Brollikins. You mustnt mind.

ALOYSIA. Would you mind calling me Aloysia, Sir Arthur? You can call me Brolly if you like; but I prefer Aloysia.

SIR ARTHUR. Certainly, Aloysia.

ALOYSIA. Thank you. I wish I could get rid of Brollikins. I'd never stoop to be ashamed of my name; but I cant deny there's something funny about it. I'm not to blame for that, am I?

SIR ARTHUR. But you can get rid of it quite easily. You can take a new name: any name you like, by deed poll. It costs only ten pounds; and David would have to pay it if it was on his account you changed. What about Bolingbroke [*he pronounces it Bullingbrook*]? Bolingbroke would be rather a nice name for The Times; and you wouldnt have to change your initials. No bother about your clothes at the laundry, for instance.

ALOYSIA. Thank you, Sir Arthur: thats a practical suggestion. At any rate it will shut David up if he talks about my name again.

SIR ARTHUR. Well, now you can run off and marry him.

ALOYSIA. But thats not all, Sir Arthur. He's such a

queer boy. He says he's never loved anyone but his sister, and that he hates his mother.

SIR ARTHUR. He had no right to tell you that he hates his mother, because as a matter of fact he doesnt. Young people nowadays read books about psycho-analysis and get their heads filled with nonsense.

ALOYSIA. Of course I know all about psycho-analysis. I explained to him that he was in love with his mother and was jealous of you. The Edipus complex, you know.

SIR ARTHUR. And what did he say to that?

ALOYSIA. He told me to go to Jericho. But I shall teach him manners.

SIR ARTHUR. Do, Aloysia. Did he make any further objection?

ALOYSIA. Well, he says his people couldnt stand my relatives.

SIR ARTHUR. Tut! the young snob! Still, snobbery is a very real thing: he made a point there, Aloysia. How did you meet it?

ALOYSIA. I said my people couldnt stand his relatives; and no more they could. I said I wasnt asking him to marry my relatives; nor was I proposing to marry his.

SIR ARTHUR. And what did he say to that?

ALOYSIA. He told me to go to hell. He's like that, you know.

SIR ARTHUR. Yes, a hasty boy.

ALOYSIA. He is, just that. But I shall cure him of it.

SIR ARTHUR [gravely] Take care, Aloysia. All young women begin by believing they can change and reform the men they marry. They cant. If you marry David he will remain David and nobody else til death do you part. If he tells you to go to hell today instead of try-ing to argue with you, he will do the same on the morning of your silver wedding.

ALOYSIA [*grimly*] We shall see.

SIR ARTHUR. May I ask whether this match is your idea or David's? So far I do not gather that he has expressed any strong feeling of—of—shall I say devotion?—to you.

ALOYSIA. We have discussed all that.

SIR ARTHUR. Satisfactorily?

ALOYSIA. I suppose so. You see, Sir Arthur, I am not like David. I am a reading thinking modern woman; and I know how to look at these things objectively and scientifically. You know the way you meet thousands of people and they mean nothing to you sexually: you wouldnt touch one of them with a barge pole. Then all of a sudden you pick out one, and feel sexy all over. If he's not nice you feel ashamed of yourself and run away. But if he is nice you say "Thats the man for me." You have had that experience yourself, havnt you?

SIR ARTHUR. Quite. The moment I saw Lady Chavender I said "Thats the woman for me."

ALOYSIA. Well, the moment I laid eyes on David I went all over like that. You cant deny that he is a nice boy in spite of his awful language. So I said—

SIR ARTHUR. "David's the man for me"?

ALOYSIA. No. I said "Evolution is telling me to marry this youth." That feeling is the only guide I have to the evolutionary appetite.

SIR ARTHUR. The what??

ALOYSIA. The evolutionary appetite. The thing that wants to develop the race. If I marry David we shall develop the race. And thats the great thing in marriage, isnt it?

SIR ARTHUR. My dear Aloysia, the evolutionary appetite may be a guide to developing the race; but it doesnt care a rap for domestic happiness. I have known the most remarkable children come of the most dreadfully unsuitable and unhappy marriages.

ALOYSIA. We have to take our chance of that, Sir Arthur. Marriage is a lottery. I think I can make David as happy as anybody ever is in this—

SIR ARTHUR. In this wicked world. Ah yes. Well, I wont press that.

ALOYSIA. I was about to say "in the capitalist phase of social development." I dont talk like your grandmother, if you will excuse me saying so.

SIR ARTHUR. I beg your pardon. I suppose I do. Have you explained this evolutionary view of the situation to David?

ALOYSIA. Of course I have. I dont treat him as a child.

SIR ARTHUR. And what did he say?

ALOYSIA. He told me to go and— Oh, I really cannot repeat what he told me to go and do. But you see how familiar we are together. I couldnt bear his being distant with me. He talks just as if we were married already.

SIR ARTHUR. Quite. But does he feel about you as you feel about him? Has he picked you out from among the thousand ladies to whom he is indifferent? To use your own expression, does he come all over like that in your presence?

ALOYSIA. He does when I get hold of him. He needs educating in these matters. I have to awaken David. But he's coming along nicely.

SIR ARTHUR. Well, if it must be it must be. I shall not withhold my blessing. That is all I can say. [*He rises: she does the same and prepares to go*]. You see, Aloysia, the effete society in which I move is based on the understanding that we shall speak and behave in the manner in which we are expected to behave.

We are hopeless when this understanding is violated. We dont know what to say or what to do. Well, you have violated it recklessly. What you have said has been unexpected to the last possible degree—

ALOYSIA. It has been true.

SIR ARTHUR. That is the climax of unexpectedness in polite society. Therefore I am at a loss. Apparently my son was not at a loss. He knows how to deal with you: I do not. I must really refer you back to him for further consideration and report.

They are about to shake hands when Lady Chavender comes in through the masked door.

LADY CHAVENDER. Still here, Miss Brollikins! I thought you had gone. [*She comes past the table to Sir Arthur's right*].

SIR ARTHUR. She wants to marry David, my dear.

LADY CHAVENDER [*calmly*] Very naturally. I think if I were in Miss Brollikins' position I should want to marry David.

ALOYSIA. I know your class point of view, Lady Chavender. You think it would be a big catch for me and a come-down for him.

LADY CHAVENDER. We both know that point of view, Miss Brollikins; but it is you, not I, that have mentioned it. Wont you sit down? [*She sits down herself in the nearest chair*].

ALOYSIA [*murmurs*] I was just going. [*She resumes her seat*].

Sir Arthur also sits.

LADY CHAVENDER. I daresay a match with you might be a very good thing for David. You seem to have all the qualities in which he is deficient. And he has been declaring for some months past that if he ever marries he will marry a factory girl.

ALOYSIA. Well, I have been a factory girl. I started

as a school teacher; but when they cut my salary I went into the factory. I organized the girls there, and became a trade union secretary. Wherever I went I rose because I couldnt keep down. But I am proletarian, bone and blood, if thats what David wants.

LADY CHAVENDER. Nobody is that in England, Miss Brollikins. We have never had a noble caste: our younger sons have always been commoners.

SIR ARTHUR. Yes, Aloysia: all British blood is blue.

ALOYSIA. Well, call it what you like. All I say is that I belong to the common working people and am proud of it; and that is what David wants, isnt it?

LADY CHAVENDER. What I said was that he wants to marry a factory girl. But I do not know what his attitude will be when a factory girl wants to marry him. Have you proposed to him?

SIR ARTHUR. Yes. He told her to go to hell.

LADY CHAVENDER. David has rather a habit of telling people to go to hell when he is too lazy to think of anything better to say. Miss Brollikins is a resolute and successful young woman. David is an irresolute and unsuccessful young man. If she has made up her mind to marry him she will probably succeed. She will have to support him; but I daresay she can do that as easily as she can support herself.

ALOYSIA. I shall expect him to work for his living.

LADY CHAVENDER. Marriage seldom fulfils all our expectations. You dont know David yet.

ALOYSIA. I will find him a job and see that he does it. I will interest him in it.

SIR ARTHUR. Splendid!

ALOYSIA [puzzled] But I cant make out you two. You havnt flared up as I thought you might; but are you for me or against me?

LADY CHAVENDER. Miss Brollikins: I am sorry; but

there are two things that I cannot bring myself to take the smallest interest in: parliamentary affairs and love affairs. They both bore me to distraction.

ALOYSIA [*to Sir Arthur*] Well, dont you take an interest in David?

SIR ARTHUR. David is at the age at which young men have to break loose from their fathers. They are very sensitive about being interfered with at that age. He would regard my taking an interest in him as parental tyranny. Therefore I am particularly careful not to take any interest in him.

ALOYSIA [*rising*] Well, you preach at me because my conversation is unexpected; but you two are the most unexpected lot I have ever been up against. What am I to understand? Will you play fair and let David take his own way?

SIR ARTHUR [*rising*] We will even let him take your way if he wishes, Aloysia.

LADY CHAVENDER [*rising*] You may leave me out of the question, Miss Brollikins. It is not my business, but my son's. I am neither his enemy nor yours.

ALOYSIA [*perplexed*] But do you think I ought to marry him?

LADY CHAVENDER. Nobody ought to marry anybody, Aloysia. But they do.

ALOYSIA. Well, thank you for calling me Aloysia, anyhow. It's about all the satisfaction I have got here.

She is about to go when David breaks in obstreperously through the masked door, and strides between the table and the window to Aloysia's left.

DAVID. Look here, Aloysia. What are you up to here? If you think you can get round me by getting round my parents, youre very much mistaken. My parents

[298]

dont care a damn what I do as long as I take myself off their hands. And I wont be interfered with. Do you hear? I wont be interfered with.

ALOYSIA. Your parents are too good for you, you uncivilized lout. Youve put me right off it by talking that way in front of your mother. If I was your mother I'd smack some manners into you.

DAVID [*appalled and imploring*] Aloysia! [*He tries to take her in his arms*].

ALOYSIA. Take your dirty hands off me [*she flings him off*]. It's off, I tell you, off. Goodbye all. [*She storms out through the main door*].

DAVID [*in loud lament to his mother*] Youve ruined my whole life. [*He goes in pursuit, crying*] Aloysia, Aloysia, wait a moment. [*With anguished intensity*] Aloysia. [*His cries recede in the distance*].

LADY CHAVENDER		He might do worse.
SIR ARTHUR	[*simultaneously*]	He might do worse.

LADY CHAVENDER. I beg your pardon. What did you say?

SIR ARTHUR. I said he might do worse.

LADY CHAVENDER. That is what I said. David is overbred: he is so fine-drawn that he is good for nothing; and he is not strong enough physically. Our breed needs to be crossed with the gutter or the soil once in every three or four generations. Uncle Theodore married his cook on principle; and his wife was my favourite aunt. Brollikins may give me goose flesh occasionally; but she wont bore me as a lady daughter-in-law would. I shall be always wondering what she will say or do next. If she were a lady I'd always know. I am so tired of wellbred people, and party politics, and the London season, and all the rest of it.

SIR ARTHUR. I sometimes think you are the only really revolutionary revolutionist I have ever met.

LADY CHAVENDER. Oh, lots of us are like that. We were born into good society; and we are through with it: we have no illusions about it, even if we are fit for nothing better. I dont mind Brollikins one bit.

SIR ARTHUR. What about Barking?

LADY CHAVENDER. I—

Barking enters through the masked door, jubilant. He comes between the pair as they rise, and claps them both on the shoulders right and left simultaneously. They flinch violently, and stare at him in outraged amazement.

BARKING. Good news, old dears! It's all right about Flavia. We may put up the banns. Hooray! [*He rubs hands gleefully*].

SIR ARTHUR. May I ask how you have got over her craze for marrying a poor man?

BARKING. Oh, that was a girlish illusion. You see, she had a glimpse today, at the unemployment meeting, of what poor men are really like. They were awfully nice to her. That did the trick. You see, what she craved for before was their rough manners, their violence, their brutality and filthy language, their savage treatment of their women folk. That was her ideal of a delightful husband. She found today that the working man doesnt realize it. I do. I am a real he-man. I called her the foulest names until she gave in. She's a dear. We shall be perfectly happy. Good old mother-in-law. [*He kisses Lady Chavender, who is too astounded to resist or speak*]. Tootle loo, Chavender. [*He slaps him on the shoulder*]. I am off to buy her a lot of presents. [*He dashes out through the main door*].

SIR ARTHUR. So thats that.

[300]

LADY CHAVENDER. The brute! How dare he kiss me? [*She rubs the place with her handkerchief*].

SIR ARTHUR. Do you realize that we two are free at last? Free, dearest: think of that! No more children. Free to give up living in a big house and to spend the remainder of our lives as we please. A cottage near a good golf links seems to be indicated. What would you like?

LADY CHAVENDER. But your political career? Are you really going to give up that?

SIR ARTHUR. It has given me up, dearest. Arnt you glad?

LADY CHAVENDER. Arthur: I cant bear this.

SIR ARTHUR. Cant bear what?

LADY CHAVENDER. To see you discouraged. You have never been discouraged before: you have always been so buoyant. If this new departure is to do nothing for you but take away your courage and high spirits and selfconfidence, then in Heaven's name go back to your old way of life. I will put up with anything rather than see you unhappy. That sort of unhappiness kills; and if you die I'll die too. [*She throws herself into a chair and hides her face on the table*].

SIR ARTHUR. Dont fuss, dearest: I'm not unhappy. I am enjoying the enormous freedom of having found myself out and got myself off my mind. That looks like despair; but it is really the beginning of hope, and the end of hypocrisy. Do you think I didnt know, in the days of my great speeches and my roaring popularity, that I was only whitewashing the slums? I did it very well—I dont care who hears me say so—and there is always a sort of artistic satisfaction in doing a thing very well, whether it's getting a big Bill through the House, or carrying a big meeting off its feet, or winning a golf championship. It was all very jolly;

and I'm still a little proud of it. But even if I had not
had you here to remind me that it was all hot air, I
couldnt help knowing as well as any of those damned
Socialists that though the West End of London was
chockful of money and nice people all calling one
another by their Christian names, the lives of the
millions of people whose labor was keeping the whole
show going were not worth living. I knew it quite
well; but I was able to put it out of my mind because
I thought it couldnt be helped and I was doing the
best that could be done. I know better now: I know
that it can be helped, and how it can be helped. And
rather than go back to the old whitewashing job, I'd
seize you tight round the waist and make a hole in the
river with you.

LADY CHAVENDER [*rising*] Then why, dearest love,
dont you—

SIR ARTHUR. Why dont I lead a revolt against it all?
Because I'm not the man for the job, darling; and
nobody knows that better than you. And I shall hate
the man who will carry it through for his cruelty and
the desolation he will bring on us and our like.

*Shouting, as of an excited mob suddenly surging into
the street; and a sound of breaking glass and police
whistling.*

LADY CHAVENDER. What on earth is that?

Hilda comes from her office and runs to the window.

LADY CHAVENDER [*joining her*] What is going on,
Hilda?

HILDA. The unemployed have broken into Downing
Street; and theyre breaking the windows of the
Colonial Office. They think this side is only private
houses.

SIR ARTHUR [*going to see*] Yes: they always break the
wrong windows, poor devils!

HILDA. Oh! here come the mounted police.

SIR ARTHUR. Theyve splendid horses, those fellows.

HILDA. The people are all running away. And they cant get out: theyre in a cul-de-sac. Oh, why dont they make a stand, the cowards?

LADY CHAVENDER. Indeed I hope they wont. What are you thinking of, Hilda?

SIR ARTHUR. Men are like that, Hilda. They always run away when they have no discipline and no leader.

HILDA. Well, but cant the police let them run away without breaking their heads? Oh look: that policeman has just clubbed a quite old man.

SIR ARTHUR. Come away: it's not a nice sight. [*He draws her away, placing himself between her and the window*].

HILDA. It's all right when you only read about it in the papers; but when you actually see it you want to throw stones at the police.

Defiant singing through the tumult.

LADY CHAVENDER [*looking out*] Someone has opened the side gate and let them through into the Horse Guards Parade. They are trying to sing.

SIR ARTHUR. What are they singing? The Red Flag?

LADY CHAVENDER. No. I dont know the tune. I caught the first two words. "England, arise."

HILDA [*suddenly hysterical*] Oh, my God! I will go out and join them [*she rushes out through the main door*].

LADY CHAVENDER. Hilda! Hilda!

SIR ARTHUR. Never mind, dear: the police all know her: she'll come to no harm. She'll be back for tea. But what she felt just now other girls and boys may feel tomorrow. And just suppose—!

LADY CHAVENDER. What?

SIR ARTHUR. Suppose England really did arise!

[303]

Unemployed England, however, can do nothing but continue to sing, as best it can to a percussion accompaniment of baton thwacks, Edward Carpenter's verses

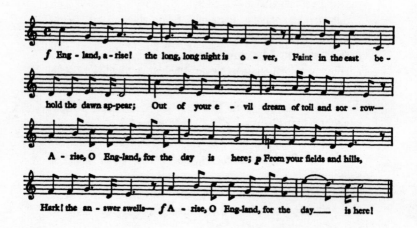

f Eng - land, a - rise! the long, long night is o - ver, Faint in the east be -

hold the dawn ap-pear; Out of your e - vil dream of toil and sor - row—

A - rise, O Eng-land, for the day is here; p From your fields and hills,

Hark! the an - swer swells— f A - rise, O Eng-land, for the day___ is here!

Geneva:
Another Political Extravaganza

WITH

Preface

Composition begun 11 February 1936; completed 4 April 1936, extensively revised prior to publication in 1939. Revised for third printing, 1940, and for French translation, 1946. Additional act in Standard Edition (*Geneva, Cymbeline Refinished, & Good King Charles*), 1947. First presented in Polish at the Teatr Polski, Warsaw, on 25 July 1938. First presented in English at the Festival Theatre, Malvern, on 1 August 1938.

Begonia Brown   *Eileen Beldon*
The Jew   *Donald Eccles*
A Newcomer   *Maitland Moss*
The Widow   *Phyllis Gill*
A Journalist   *Wilson Barrett*
The Bishop   *H. R. Hignett*
Commissar Posky   *J. O. Twiss*
The Secretary of the League of Nations
   Cyril Gardiner
Sir Orpheus Midlander   *Ernest Thesiger*
The Judge   *Donald Wolfit*
The Betrothed   *Kenneth Villiers*
Bardo Bombardone   *Cecil Trouncer*
Ernest Battler   *Norman Wooland*
The Deaconess   *Marie Ault*
General Flanco de Fortinbras   *R. Stuart Lindsell*

Period—The present. Geneva

ACT I *The Office of the International Institute for Intellectual Co-operation. A May morning*

ACT II *Office of the Secretary of the League of Nations. Late afternoon*
ACT III *Lounge of a Fashionable Restaurant overlooking the Lake of Geneva. Afternoon (some time later)*
ACT IV *A Salon in the Old Palace of the Hague. Ten a.m.*

Preface

Contents

When I had lived for 58 years free from the fear that war could come to my doorstep, the thing occurred. And when the war to end war had come to a glorious victory, it occurred again, worse than ever. I have now lived through two "world wars" without missing a meal or a night's sleep in my bed, though they have come near enough to shatter my windows, break in my door, and wreck my grandfather clock, keeping me for nine years of my life subject to a continual apprehension of a direct hit next time blowing me and my household to bits.

I cannot pretend that this troubled me much: people build houses and live on the slopes of Etna and Vesuvius and at the foot of Stromboli as cheerfully as on Primrose Hill. I was too old to be conscribed for military service; and the mathematical probabilities were enormously against a bomb coming my way; for at the worst of the bombardments only from ten to fifteen inhabitants of these islands were killed by air raids every day; and a dozen or so out of fortyfive millions is not very terrifying even when each of us knows that he or she is as likely as not to be one of the dozen. The risk of being run over by a motor bus, which townsmen run daily, is greater.

HOODWINKED HEROISM

It was this improbability which made pre-atomic air raiding futile as a means of intimidating a nation, and enabled the government of the raided nation to prevent the news of the damage reaching beyond its immediate neighborhood. One night early in the resumed war I saw, from a distance of 30 miles, London burning for three hours. Next morning I read in the newspapers that a bomb had fallen on the windowsill of a city office, and been extinguished before it exploded. Returning to London later on I found that half the ancient city had been levelled to the ground, leaving only St. Paul's and a few church towers standing. The wireless news never went beyond "some damage and a few casualties in Southern England" when in fact leading cities and seaports had been extensively wrecked. All threatening news was mentioned only in secret sessions of parliament, hidden under heavy penalties until after the victory. In 1941, after the Dunkirk rout, our position was described by the Prime Minister to the House of Commons in secret session as so desperate that if the enemy had taken advantage of it we should have been helplessly defeated; and it is now the fashion to descant dithyrambically on the steadfast heroism with which the nation faced this terrible emergency. As a matter of fact the nation knew nothing about it. Had we been told, the Germans would have overheard and rushed the threatened invasion they were bluffed into abandoning. Far from realizing our deadly peril, we were exulting in the triumph of our Air Force in "the Battle of Britain" and in an incident in South America in which three British warships drove one German one into the river Plate. Rather than be interned with his crew the German captain put to sea again against hopeless odds; scuttled his ship; and committed suicide. The British newspapers raved about this for weeks as a naval victory greater than Salamis, Lepanto, and Trafalgar rolled into one.

Later on our flight from Tobruk to the border of Egypt did not disturb us at home: it was reported as a trifling setback, whilst trumpery captures of lorries or motor bicycles by British patrols figured as victories. After major engagements German losses were given in figures: Allies' losses were not given at all, the impression left being that the Allies had killed or taken tens of thousands of Axis troops without suffering any casualties worth mentioning. Only by listening to the German broadcasts, similarly cooked, could the real facts and fortunes of the war be estimated. Of course the truth leaked out months later; but it produced only a fresh orgy of bragging about our heroic fortitude in the face of the deadly peril we knew nothing of.

All this was necessary and inevitable. It was dangerous to tell the truth about anything, even about the weather. The signposts on the roads had to be taken down and hidden lest they should help an invader to find his way. It was a crime to give an address with a date, or to scatter a few crumbs for the birds. And it was an act of heroic patriotism to drop a bomb weighing ten thousand pounds on dwellings full of women and children, or on crowded railway trains. Our bombing of foreign cities not only in Germany but in countries which we claimed to be "liberating" became so frightful that at last the word had to be given to two of our best broadcasters of war reports to excuse them on the ground that by shortening the war they were saving the lives of thousands of British soldiers.

Meanwhile nobody noticed how completely war, as an institution, had reduced itself to absurdity. When Germany annexed Poland in 1939, half of it was snatched out of her jaws by Soviet Russia. The British Commonwealth having bound itself to maintain inviolate the frontiers of Poland as they were left after the fighting of 1914–18 with a Polish corridor cut right through Prussia to the Baltic, was committed to declare war on Germany and Russia simultaneously. But the British people and their rulers were in no mood to black out their windows and recommence the Four Years War in defence of this distant and foreign corridor. Being, as usual, unprepared for war, we tried to appease Germany and yet keep the peace with Soviet Russia.

ENGLAND FRIGHTENED AND GREAT

Nations should always be prepared for war, just as people with any property to leave should always have made their wills. But as most of them never do make their wills, and the rest seldom keep them revised and up to date, States, however militarist, are never fully prepared for war. England will do nothing outside her routine until she is thoroughly frightened; but when England is frightened England is capable of anything. Philip II of Spain frightened her. Louis XIV of France frightened her. Napoleon frightened her. Wilhelm II of the German Reich frightened her. But instead of frightening the wits out of her they frightened the wits into her. She woke up and smashed them all. In vain did the Kaiser sing *Deutschland über Alles*, and Hitler claim that his people were the Herrenvolk created by God to rule the earth. The English were equally convinced that when Britain first at Heaven's command arose from out the azure main she was destined to rule the waves, and make the earth her footstool. This is so natural to Englishmen that they are unconscious of it, just as they cannot taste water because it is always in their mouths. Long before England first sang Rule Britannia at Cliveden she had annihilated Philip's Invincible Armada to the music of the winds and waves, and, after being defeated again and again by General Luxemburg, made hay of the French armies at Blenheim, Ramillies, and Malplaquet to the senseless gibberish of Lillibullerobullenalah. She not only took on Hitler singlehanded without a word to the League of Nations nor to anyone else, but outfought him, outbragged him, outbullied him, outwitted him in every trick and turn of warfare, and finally extinguished him and hanged his accomplices.

ENGLAND SECURE AND LAZY

The drawback to England's capacity for doing impossible things when in danger is her incapacity for doing possible things (except repeating what was done last time) in security. The prefabrication in England of harbors for France and planting them there as part of the baggage of the allied invading armies, was a feat which still seems incredible even now that it has actually been achieved; yet during the 20 years armistice England could not bridge the Severn below Gloucester, harness the Pentland tides, nor tap the volcanic fires of the earth's boiling core, much less mechanize the coalmines or even design an alphabet capable of saving billionsworth of British time, ink, and paper, by spelling English speech sounds unequivocally and economically. The moment the Cease Fire is sounded England forgets all the lessons of the war and proves the truth of Dr Inge's old comment on the Anglo-Irish situation as illustrating the difficulty of driving in double harness people who remember nothing with people who forget nothing. Still, as forgetful people who act in the present can master vindictive people who only brood on the past there is much to be said for England's full share of human thoughtlessness. It is sometimes better not to think at all than to think intensely and think wrong.

Statesmen who know no past history are dangerous because contemporary history cannot be ascertained. No epoch is intelligible until it is completed and can be seen in the distance as a whole, like a mountain. The victorious combatants in the battle of Hastings did not know that they were inaugurating feudalism for four centuries, nor the Red Roses on Bosworth Field and the Ironsides at Naseby know that they were exchanging it for Whig plutocracy. Historians and newspaper editors can see revolutions three centuries off but not three years off, much less three hours. Had

Marx and Engels been contemporaries of Shakespear they could not have written the Communist Manifesto, and would probably have taken a hand, as Shakespear did, in the enclosure of common lands as a step forward in civilization.

HISTORY STOPS YESTERDAY: STATECRAFT WORKS BLINDFOLD

This is why history in our schools stops far short of the present moment, and why statesmen, though they can learn the lessons of history from books, must grope their way through daily emergencies within the limits of their ignorance as best they can. If their vision is vulgar and vindictive the guesses they make may be worse than the war. That vision has not widened nor that ability grown of late. But the perils of the situation have increased enormously. Men are what they were; but war has become many times more destructive, not of men, who can be replaced, but of the plant of civilization, the houses and factories, the railways and airways, the orchards and furrowed fields, and the spare subsistence which we call capital, without which civilized mankind would perish. Even the replacement of the slain is threatened because the latest bombs are no respecters of sex; and where there are no women there will soon be no warriors. In some of the air raids, more women were killed than men. The turning point of the war was the siege of Stalingrad, written up by the newspapers more dithyrambically than any siege in history since the siege of Troy. But when the Greeks captured Troy they had the city for their pains as well as the glory. When the Red Army triumphed at Stalingrad they had nothing but festering corpses to bury, heaps of rubble to clear away, and a

host of prisoners to feed. Meanwhile the British and
American armies were "liberating" French cities,
Dutch cities, Belgian cities, Italian cities: that is, they
were destroying them exactly as they were destroying
German cities, and having to house and feed their
surviving inhabitants after wrecking their water mains,
electric power stations and railway communications.
From the national point of view this was conquest,
glory, patriotism, bravery, all claiming to be necessary for security. From the European wider angle it
was folly and devilment, savagery and suicide. The
ready money collected for it (wars cannot be fought
on credit) was called Savings: a barefaced wicked lie.
All the belligerents have been bled white, and will find,
when they claim their "savings" back from their
governments, that their Chancellors of the Exchequer
will reply, like the juvenile spendthrift exhorted to
pay his debts by Richelieu in Lytton's play, "Wil-
lingly, your Eminence: where shall I borrow the
money?"; for not a farthing of it (say 12 millions shot
away every day for six years) remains; and all of it
that achieved its purpose of ruin has imposed on us
the added burden of repairing what we have destroyed.

So much for England frightened into fighting. The
question now is has war become frightful enough to
frighten her out of it? In the last months the bombs
launched by young British warriors from airplanes
at the risk of their lives grew to such prodigious weight
and destructiveness that they wrecked not merely
houses but whole streets, and scattered blazing phos-
phorus and magnesium on such a scale that the
victims, chiefly women with children who could not
escape by flight as a few of the men did, were stifled
by having nothing to breathe but white hot air, and

then burnt to cinders and buried under the piles of rubble that had been their houses. We rained these monster bombs on Germany until the destruction of their railways and munition factories made retaliation in kind impossible. Our flame throwing from tanks finished the fugitives.

WE SPLIT THE ATOM

But the resources of decivilization were not exhausted. When we were exulting in our demolition of cities like Cologne and Hamburg we were very considerably frightened by the descent on London of new projectiles, unmanned yet aimed and guided, which demolished not only streets but districts. And when we and our allies "liberated" German-occupied territory (blowing its cities to smithereens largely in the process) we discovered that the manufacture of these new horrors had been planned for on such a scale that but for their capture in time the tables might have been turned on us with a vengeance.

But we had another card up our sleeve: this time a trump so diabolical that when we played it the war, which still lingered in Japan, was brought to an abrupt stop by an Anglo-American contrivance which may conceivably transform the globe into a cloud of flaming gas in which no form of life known to us could survive for a moment. That such explosions have visibly occurred on other stars (called novas) is vouched for by our astronomers, who have seen them with their naked eyes and studied their photographs and spectrographs for years past. When England and the United States of North America got ahead of Germany and Japan with this terrific weapon all their opponents at once surrendered at discretion.

AN AMORAL VICTORY

This time there could be no sustainable pretence of a moral victory, though plenty were made as usual; for nothing yet discovered has cured mankind of lying and boasting. It was what Wellington called Waterloo, a very near thing; for had the Germans not concentrated on the jet propulsion of pilotless aeroplanes instead of on the atomic bomb, they might have contrived it before us and made themselves masters of the situation if not of the world. They may yet cheapen and improve on it. Or they may discover a gas lighter than air, deadly but not destructive. And then where shall we be? Ethical victories endure. Discoveries cannot be guaranteed for five minutes.

Still, though the victory was not a triumph of Christianity it was a triumph of Science. American and British scientists, given *carte blanche* in the matter of expense, had concentrated on a romantic and desperate search for a means of harnessing the mysterious forces that mould and hold atoms into metals, minerals, and finally into such miracles as human geniuses, taking some grains of metal and a few salts purchasable at the nearest oil-shop and fashioning with them the head of Shakespear, to say nothing of my own. It is already known that the energy that makes uranium out of molecules, escapes by slow radiation and both kills and cures living organisms, leaving behind it not radium but lead. If this disintegration could be speeded up to instantaneousness it would make a heat so prodigious that a couple of morsels of uranium dropped from a plane and timed to collide and disintegrate above a city could convert that city and its inhabitants into a heap of flaming gas in a fraction of a second. The experiment was tried on two Japanese cities. Four square miles of them vanished before the experimenters could say Jack Robinson.

There is no getting away from the fact that if another world war be waged with this new weapon there may be an end of our civilization and its massed populations. Even for those philosophers who are of opinion that this would not be any great loss there is a further possibility. An atomic bomb attached to a parachute and exploded in the air would devastate only as many square miles as it was meant to; but if it hung fire and exploded in the earth it might start a continuous process of disintegration in which our planet would become a *nova* to astronomers on Mars, blazing up and dimming out, leaving nothing of it and of us in the sky but a gaseous nebula.

It seems that if "the sport of kings" is to continue it must be fought under Queensberry rules classing atomic bombs with blows below the belt, and barring them. But it was the British refusal to bar aerial bombardment that made the air battles of the world war lawful; and these air battles had already reduced war to economic absurdity before the atomic bomb came into action. War had become logical: enemies were massacred or transported: wayleave was abolished. Thus the victors were left with the terror of their own discovery, and the vanquished with the hope that they may soon discover for themselves how to disintegrate uranium or perhaps some other element with ten times its energy. And two of the great allies, England and America, flatly refuse to share the secret of the new bomb with Russia, the third. Villages in India are still wiped out to "larn" their mostly harmless inhabitants not to snipe at British soldiers. The alarm is general: the cry of all hands, the triumphant even

more than the subjugated, is that there must be an end
of war. But all the other cries are as warlike as ever.
The victorious Allies agree in demanding that Germans and Japanese must be treated as Catholic Ireland
was treated by England in the seventeenth century.

Some of them are now consoling themselves with
the hope that the atomic bomb has made war impossible. That hope has often been entertained before.
Colonel Robinson, in *The Nineteenth Century And
After*, has given a list of previous discoveries, dating
back to B.C., which have developed the technique of
killing from the single combats of the Trojan war,
fought man to man, to artillery operations and. air
raids in which the combatants are hundreds of miles
apart on the ground or thousands of feet up in the air
dropping bombs and flying away at a speed of ten
miles per second, never seeing one another nor the
mischief they do. At every development it is complained that war is no longer justifiable as a test of
heroic personal qualities, and demonstrated that it has
become too ruinous to be tolerated as an institution.
War and imperialist diplomacy persist none the less.

CIVILIZATION'S WILL TO LIVE ALWAYS
DEFEATED BY DEMOCRACY

Mankind, though pugnacious, yet has an instinct
which checks it on the brink of selfdestruction. We
are still too close to the time when men had to fight
with wild beasts for their lives and with one another
for their possessions, and when women had to choose
fighters for their mates to protect them from robbery
and rapine at their work as mothers, nurses, cooks,
and kitchen gardeners. There are still places in the
world where after tribal battles the victors eat the

vanquished and the women share the feast with the warriors. In others foreign explorers, visitors, and passengers are killed as strangers. The veneer of civilization which distinguishes Europeans from these tribesmen and their wives is dangerously thin. Even English ladies and gentlemen "go Fantee" occasionally. Christmas cards will not prevent them from using atomic bombs if they are again frightened and provoked. But the magnitude of the new peril rouses that other instinct, stronger finally than pugnacity, that the race must not perish. This does not mean that civilization cannot perish. Civilizations have never finally survived: they have perished over and over again because they failed to make themselves worth their cost to the masses whom they enslaved. Even at home they could not master the art of governing millions of people for the common good in spite of people's inveterate objection to be governed at all. Law has been popularly known only as oppression and taxation, and politics as a clamor for less government and more liberty. That citizens get better value for the rates and taxes they pay than for most other items in their expenditure never occurs to them. They will pay a third of their weekly earnings or more to an idle landlord as if that were a law of nature; but a collection from them by the rate collector they resent as sheer robbery: the truth being precisely the reverse. They see nothing extravagant in basing democracy on an assumption that every adult native is either a Marcus Aurelius or a combination of Saint Teresa and Queen Elizabeth Tudor, supremely competent to choose any tinker tailor soldier sailor or any good-looking well dressed female to rule over them. This insane prescription for perfect democracy of course makes democracy impossible and the adventures of

Cromwell, Napoleon, Hitler, and the innumerable conquistadores and upstart presidents of South American history inevitable. There never has been and never will be a government which is both plebiscitary and democratic, because the plebs do not want to be governed, and the plutocrats who humbug them, though they are so far democratic that they must for their own sakes keep their slaves alive and efficient, use their powers to increase their revenues and suppress resistance to their appropriation of all products and services in excess of this minimum. Substitute a plebeian government, and it can only carry on to the same point with the same political machinery, except that the plunder goes to the Trade Unions instead of to the plutocrats. This may be a considerable advance; but when the plebeian government attempts to reorganize production collectively so as to increase the product and bring the highest culture within the reach of all who are capable of it, and make the necessary basic material prosperity general and equal, the dread and hatred of government as such, calling itself Liberty and Democracy, reasserts itself and stops the way. Only when a war makes collective organization compulsory on pain of slaughter, subjugation, and nowadays extinction by bombs, jet propelled or atomic, is any substantial advance made or men of action tolerated as Prime Ministers. The first four years of world war forced us to choose a man of action as leader; but when the armistice came we got rid of him and had a succession of premiers who could be trusted to do nothing revolutionary. Our ideal was "a commonplace type with a stick and a pipe and a half bred black and tan." Even Franklin Roosevelt won his first presidential election more by a photograph of himself in the act of petting a baby than by his political program, which few understood: indeed he only half understood it himself. When Mr Winston Churchill, as a man of action, had to be substituted for the *fainéants* when the war was resumed, his big cigars and the genial romantic oratory in which he glorified the war maintained his popularity until the war was over and he opened the General Election campaign by announcing a domestic policy which was a hundred years out of fashion, and promised nothing to a war weary proletariat eager for a Utopia in which there should be no military controls and a New World inaugurated in which everybody was to be both employed and liberated.

Mr Churchill at once shared the fate of Lloyd George; and the Utopians carried the day triumphantly. But the New World proved the same as the old one, with the same fundamental resistance to change of habits and the same dread of government interference surviving in the adult voter like the child's dread of a policeman.

It may be asked how it is that social changes do actually take place under these circumstances. The reply is that other circumstances create such emergencies, dangers, and hardships, that the very people who dread Government action are the first to run to the Government for a remedy, crying that "something must be done." And so civilization, though dangerously slowed down, forces its way piecemeal in spite of stagnant ignorance and selfishness.

Besides, there are always ancient constitutions and creeds to be reckoned with; and these are not the work of adult suffrage, but inheritances from feudal and ecclesiastical systems which had to provide law and order during the intervals between dominating personalities, when ordinary governments had to mark

time by doing what was done last time until the next
big boss came along and became a popular idol, worshipped at the polls by 99 per cent majorities.

All the evidence available so far is to the effect that
since the dawn of history there has been no change in
the natural political capacity of the human species.
The comedies of Aristophanes and the Bible are at
hand to convince anyone who doubts this. But this
does not mean that enlightenment is impossible.
Without it our attempts at democracy will wreck our
civilization as they have wrecked all the earlier civilizations we know of. The ancient empires were not
destroyed by foreign barbarians. They assimilated
them easily. They destroyed themselves: their col-
lapse was the work of their own well meaning native
barbarians. Yet these barbarians, like our own at
present, included a percentage of thinkers who had
their imaginations obsessed by Utopias in which perfectly wise governments were to make everybody
prosperous and happy. Their old men saw visions
and their young men dreamed dreams just as they
do now. But they were not all such fools as to believe
that their visions and dreams could be realized by
Tom, Dick, and Harriet voting for Titus Oates, Lord
George Gordon, Horatio Bottomley, Napoleon, or
Hitler. My experience as an enlightener, which is considerable, is that what is wrong with the average
citizen is not altogether deficient political capacity.
It is largely ignorance of facts, creating a vacuum into
which all sorts of romantic antiquarian junk and cast-
off primitive religion rushes. I have to enlighten sects
describing themselves as Conservatives, Socialists,
Protestants, Catholics, Communists, Fascists, Fabians,
Friends (Quakers), Ritualists; all bearing labels which
none of them can define, and which indicate tenets

which none of them accept as practical rules of life and many of them repudiate with abhorrence when they are presented without their labels. I was baptized as a member of the then established Protestant Episcopal Church in Ireland. My religious education left me convinced that I was entitled to call myself a Protestant because I believed that Catholics were an inferior species who would all go to hell when they died; and I daresay the Roman Catholic children with whom I was forbidden to play believed that the same eternity of torment awaited me in spite of Pope Pius the Ninth's humane instruction to them to absolve me on the plea of invincible ignorance. We were both taught to worship "a tenth rate tribal deity" of the most vindictive, jealous, and ruthless pugnacity, equally with his Christlike son. Just so today Conservatives know nothing of the Tory creed, but are convinced that the rulers of Russia are bloodstained tyrants, robbers and murderers, and their subjects slaves without rights or liberties. All good Russians believe equally that the capitalist rulers of the Western pluto cracies are ruthless despots out for nothing but exploiting labor in pursuit of surplus value, as Marx called rent, interest, and profit. They group themselves in political parties and clubs in which none of them knows what he or she is talking about. Some of them have Utopian aspirations and have read the prophets and sages, from Moses to Marx, and from Plato to Ruskin and Inge; but a question as to a point of existing law or the function of a County Council strikes them dumb. They are more dangerous than simpletons and illiterates because on the strength of their irrelevant schooling they believe themselves politically educated, and are accepted as authorities on political subjects accordingly.

Now this political ignorance and delusion is curable by simple instruction as to the facts without any increase of political capacity. I am ending as a sage with a very scrappy and partial knowledge of the world. I do not see why I should not have begun with it if I had been told it all to begin with: I was more capable of it then than I am now in my dotage. When I am not writing plays as a more or less inspired artist I write political schoolbooks in which I say nothing of the principles of Socialism or any other Ism (I disposed of all that long ago), and try to open my readers' eyes to the political facts under which they live. I cannot change their minds; but I can increase their knowledge. A little knowledge is a dangerous thing; but we must take that risk because a little is as much as our biggest heads can hold; and a citizen who knows that the earth is round and older than six thousand years is less dangerous than one of equal capacity who believes it is a flat groundfloor between a first floor heaven and a basement hell.

INCOMPETENT GOVERNMENTS ARE THE CRUELLEST

The need for confining authority to the instructed and capable has been demonstrated by terrible lessons daily for years past. As I write, dockfulls of German prisoners of war, male and female, are being tried on charges of hideous cruelties perpetrated by them at concentration camps. The witnesses describe the horrors of life and death in them; and the newspapers class the accused as fiends and monsters. But they also publish photographs of them in which they appear as ordinary human beings who could be paralleled from any crowd or army.

These Germans had to live in the camps with their prisoners. It must have been very uncomfortable and dangerous for them. But they had been placed in authority and management, and had to organize the feeding, lodging, and sanitation of more and more thousands of prisoners and refugees thrust upon them by the central government. And as they were responsible for the custody of their prisoners they had to be armed to the teeth and their prisoners completely disarmed. Only eminent leadership, experience, and organizing talent could deal with such a situation.

Well, they simply lacked these qualities. They were not fiends in human form; but they did not know what to do with the thousands thrown on their care. There was some food; but they could not distribute it except as rations among themselves. They could do nothing with their prisoners but overcrowd them within any four walls that were left standing, lock them in, and leave them almost starving to die of typhus. When further overcrowding became physically impossible they could do nothing with their unwalled prisoners but kill them and burn the corpses they could not bury. And even this they could not organize frankly and competently: they had to make their victims die of illusage instead of by military law. Under such circumstances any miscellaneous collection of irresistibly armed men would be demoralized; and the natural percentage of callous toughs among them would wallow in cruelty and in the exercise of irresponsible authority for its own sake. Man beating is better sport than bear baiting or cock fighting or even child beating, of which some sensational English cases were in the papers at home at the time. Had there been efficient handling of the situation by the authorities (assuming this to have been possible) none of these atrocities would have occurred. They occur in every war when the troops get out of hand.

HITLER

The German government was rotten at the centre as well as at the periphery. The Hohenzollern monarchy in Germany, with an enormous military prestige based on its crushing defeat of the Bonapartist French Army in 1871 (I was fifteen at the time, and remember it quite well) was swept away in 1918 by the French Republic. The rule of the monarch was succeeded by the rule of anybody chosen by everybody, supposed, as usual, to secure the greatest common measure of welfare, which is the object of democracy, but which really means that a political career is open to any adventurer. It happened that in Munich in 1930 there was a young man named Hitler who had served in the Four Years War. Having no special military talent he had achieved no more as a soldier than the Iron Cross and the rank of corporal. He was poor and what we call no class, being a Bohemian with artistic tastes but neither training nor talent enough to succeed as an artist, and was thus hung up between the bourgeoisie for which he had no income and the working class for which he had no craft. But he had a voice and could talk, and soon became a beer cellar orator who could hold his audience. He joined a cellar debating society (like our old Cogers Hall) and thereby brought its numbers up to seven. His speeches soon attracted considerable reinforcements and established him as a leading spirit. Much of what he spouted was true. As a soldier he had learnt that disciplined men can make short work of mobs; that party parliaments on the British model neither could nor would abolish the poverty that was so bitter to him; that the Treaty of Versailles under which Germany, defeated and sub-jected far beyond the last penny she could spare, could be torn up clause by clause by anyone with a big enough army to intimidate the plunderers; and that Europe was dominated economically by a plutocracy of financiers who had got the whip hand even of the employers. So far he was on solid ground, with un-questionable facts to support him. But he mixed the facts up with fancies such as that all plutocrats are Jews; that the Jews are an accursed race who should be exterminated as such; that the Germans are a chosen race divinely destined to rule the world; and that all she needs to establish her rule is an irresistible army. These delusions were highly flattering to Hans, Fritz, and Gretchen at large as well as to the beer drinkers in the cellar; and when an attempt was made to silence the new Hitlerites by hired gangsters, Hitler organized a bodyguard for himself so effectively that the opposition was soon sprawling in the street.

With this stock in trade Hitler found himself a born leader, and, like Jack Cade, Wat Tyler, Essex under Elizabeth Tudor, Emmet under Dublin Castle, and Louis Napoleon under the Second Republic, im-agined he had only to appear in the streets with a flag to be acclaimed and followed by the whole population. He tried the experiment with a general from the Four Years War at his side and such converts to his vogue and eloquence as his beer cellar orations had made. With this nucleus he marched through the streets. A rabble gathered and followed to see the fun, as rabbles always will in cities. In London I have seen thousands of citizens rushing to see why the others were rushing, and to find out why. It looked like a revolutionary *émeute*. On one occasion it was a runaway cow. On another it was Mary Pickford, "World's Sweetheart" of the old silent films, driving to her hotel in a taxi.

For a moment Hitler may have fancied that a success like that of Mussolini's march to Rome (he went by train) was within his grasp. He had the immediate precedent of Kurt Eisner's successful *Putsch* to encourage him. But Eisner was not resisted. When Hitler and his crowd came face to face with the Government troops they did not receive him as the grognards of the Bourbon army received Napoleon on his return from Elba. They opened fire on him. His rabble melted and fled. He and General Ludendorff had to throw themselves flat on the pavement to avoid the bullets. He was imprisoned for eight months for his escapade, not having frightened the Government enough to be considered worth killing as Cade, Tyler, and Essex were killed. In prison, he and his companion-secretary Hess, wrote a book entitled *Mein Kampf* (My Struggle, My Program, My Views or what you please).

Like Louis Napoleon he had now learnt his lesson: namely, that *Putsches* are a last desperate method, not a first one, and that adventurers must come to terms with the captains of finance and industry, the bankers, and the Conservatives who really control the nations wherever the people choose what rulers they please, before he can hope to be accepted by them as a figure head. Hitler had sufficient histrionic magnetism to strike this bargain even to the extent of being made perpetual chancellor of the German Realm with more than royal honors, though his whole stock-in-trade was a brazen voice and a doctrine made up of scraps of Socialism, mortal hatred of the Jews, and complete contempt for pseudo-democratic parliamentary mobocracy.

PSEUDO MESSIAH AND MADMAN

So far he was the creature and tool of the plutocracy. But the plutocracy had made a bad bargain. The moment it made Hitler a figure head, popular idolatry made a prophet and a hero of him, and gave him a real personal power far in excess of that enjoyed by any commercial magnate. He massacred all his political rivals not only with impunity but with full parliamentary approval. Like St Peter on a famous earlier occasion the German people cried "Thou art the Christ", with the same result. Power and worship turned Hitler's head; and the national benefactor who began by abolishing unemployment, tearing up the Treaty of Versailles, and restoring the selfrespect of sixty millions of his fellow countrymen, became the mad Messiah who, as lord of a Chosen Race, was destined to establish the Kingdom of God on earth— a German kingdom of a German God—by military conquest of the rest of mankind. Encouraged by spineless attempts to appease him he attacked Russia, calculating that as a crusader against Soviet Communism he would finally be joined by the whole Capitalist West.

But the Capitalist West was much too shortsighted and jealous to do anything so intelligent. It shook hands with Stalin and stabbed Hitler in the back. He put up a tremendous fight, backed by his fellow adventurers in Italy and Spain; but, being neither a Julius Cæsar nor a Mahomet, he failed to make his initial conquests welcome and permanent by improving the condition of the inhabitants. On the contrary he made his name execrated wherever he conquered. The near West rose up against him, and was joined by the mighty far West of America. After twelve years of

killing other people he had to kill himself, and leave
his accomplices to be hanged.

The moral for conquerors of empires is that if they
substitute savagery for civilization they are doomed.
If they substitute civilization for savagery they make
good, and establish a legitimate title to the territories
they invade. When Mussolini invaded Abyssinia and
made it possible for a stranger to travel there without
being killed by the native Danakils he was rendering
the same service to the world as we had in rendering
by the same methods (including poison gas) in the
north west provinces of India, and had already completed in Australia, New Zealand, and the Scottish
Highlands. It was not for us to throw stones at Musso,
and childishly refuse to call his puppet king Emperor.
But we did throw stones, and made no protest when his
star was eclipsed and he was scandalously lynched in
Milan. The Italians had had enough of him; for he,
too, was neither a Cæsar nor a Mahomet.

Contemplating the careers of these two poor devils
one cannot help asking was their momentary grandeur
worth while? I pointed out once that the career of
Bourrienne, Napoleon's valet-secretary for a while,
was far longer, more fortunate, easier and more comfortable in every commonsense way, than that of
Napoleon, who, with an interval of one year, was
Emperor for fourteen years. Mussolini kept going for
more than twenty. So did Louis Napoleon, backed by
popular idolization of his uncle, who had become a
national hero, as Hitler will become in Germany
presently. Whether these adventurers would have been
happier in obscurity hardly matters; for they were kept
too busy to bother themselves about happiness; and
the extent to which they enjoyed their activities and
authority and deification is unknown. They were

finally scrapped as failures and nuisances, though they all began by effecting some obvious reforms over which party parliaments had been boggling for centuries. Such successes as they had were reactions from the failures of the futile parliamentary talking shops, which were themselves reactions from the bankruptcies of incompetent monarchs, both mobs and monarchs being products of political idolatry and ignorance. The wider the suffrage, the greater the confusion. "Swings to the Left" followed by "swings to the Right" kept the newspapers and the political wind-bags amused and hopeful. We are still humbugging ourselves into the belief that the swings to the Left are democratic and those to the Right imperial. They are only swings from failure to failure to secure sub-stantial democracy, which means impartial govern-ment for the good of the governed by qualified rulers. Popular anarchism defeats them all.

Upstart dictators and legitimate monarchs have not all been personal failures. From Pisistratus to Porfirio, Ataturk, and Stalin, able despots have made good by doing things better and much more promptly than parliaments. They have kept their heads and known their limitations. Ordinary mortals like Nero, Paul of Russia, our James the Second, Riza Khan in Iran, and some of the small fry of degenerate hereditary tribal chiefs like Theebaw in Burma have gone crazy and become worse nuisances than mad dogs. Lord Acton's dictum that power corrupts gives no idea of the extent to which flattery, deference, power, and apparently unlimited money, can upset and demoral-ize simpletons who in their proper places are good fellows enough. To them the exercise of authority is not a heavy and responsible job which strains their mental capacity and industry to the utmost, but a delightful sport to be indulged for its own sake, and asserted and reasserted by cruelty and monstrosity.

DEMOCRACY MISUNDERSTOOD

Democracy and equality, without which no State can achieve the maximum of beneficence and stability, are still frightfully misunderstood and confused. Popular logic about them is, like most human logic, mere association of ideas, or, to call it by the new name invented by its monstrous product Pavlov, conditional reflex. Government of the people for the people, which is democracy, is supposed to be achievable through government by the people in the form of adult suffrage, which is finally so destructive of democracy that it ends in a reaction into despot-idolatry. Equality is supposed to mean similarity of political talent, which varies as much as musical or mathematical or military capacity from individual to individual, from William Rufus to Charles II, from Nero to Marcus Aurelius, from Monmouth and Prince Charlie to Alexander and Napoleon. Genuine democracy requires that the people shall choose their rulers, and, if they will, change them at sufficient intervals; but the choice must be limited to the public spirited and politically talented, of whom Nature always provides not only the necessary percentage, but superfluity enough to give the people a choice. Equality, which in practice means intermarriageability, is based on the hard facts that the greatest genius costs no more to feed and clothe and lodge than the narrowest minded duffer, and at a pinch can do with less, and that the most limited craftsman or laborer who can do nothing without direction from a thinker, is, if worth employing at all, as necessary and important socially as the ablest director. Equality between them is either equality of income and of income only or an obvious lie.

Equality of income is practicable enough: any sporting peer with his mind bounded by the race-course can dine on equal terms with an astronomer whose mental domain is the universe. Their children are intermarriageable without misalliance. But when we face the democratic task of forming panels of the persons eligible for choice as qualified rulers we find first that none of our tests are trustworthy or sufficient, and finally that we have no qualified rulers at all, only bosses. The rule of vast commonwealths is beyond the political capacity of mankind at its ablest. Our Solons, Cæsars and Washingtons, Lenins, Stalins and Nightingales, may be better than their best competitors; but they die in their childhood as far as statesmanship is concerned, playing golf and tennis and bridge, smoking tobacco and drinking alcohol as part of their daily diet, hunting, shooting, coursing, reading tales of murder and adultery and police news, wearing fantastic collars and cuffs, with the women on high heels staining their nails, daubing their lips, painting their faces: in short, doing all sorts of things that are child's play and not the exercises or recreations of statesmen and senators. Even when they have read Plato, the Gospels, and Karl Marx, and to that extent know what they have to do, they do not know how to do it, and stick in the old grooves for want of the new political technique which is evolving under pressure of circumstances in Russia. Their attempts at education and schooling end generally in boy farms and concentration camps with flogging blocks, from which the prisoners when they adolesce emerge as trained prejudiced barbarians with a hatred of learning and discipline, and a dense ignorance of what life is to nine tenths of their compatriots.

"GREAT MEN"

Here and there, however, cases of extraordinary faculty shew what mankind is capable of within its existing framework. In mathematics we have not only Newtons and Einsteins, but obscure illiterate "lightning calculators," to whom the answers to arithmetical and chronological problems that would cost me a long process of cyphering (if I could solve them at all) are instantly obvious. In grammar and scripture I am practically never at a loss; but I have never invented a machine, though I am built like engineers who, though they are never at a loss with machinery, are yet so unable to put descriptions of their inventions into words that they have to be helped out by patent agents of no more than common literary ability. Mozart, able in his infancy to do anything he pleased in music, from the simplest sonata to the most elaborate symphony or from the subtlest comic or tragic opera to fugal settings of the Mass, resembled millions of Austrians who could not to save their lives hum a line of *Deutschland über Alles* nor compose a bar of music playable by one finger, much less concerted for 30 different orchestral instruments. In philosophy we spot Descartes and Kant, Swift and Schopenhauer, Butler and Bergson, Richard Wagner and Karl Marx, Blake and Shelley, Ruskin and Morris, with dozens of uncrucified Jesuses and saintly women in every generation, look like vindictive retaliators, pugnacious sportsmen, and devout believers in ancient tribal idols. The geniuses themselves are steeped in vulgar superstitions and prejudices: Bunyan and Newton

astound us not only by their specific talents but by
their credulity and Bible fetichism. We prate gravely
of their achievements and faculties as attainments of
mankind, as if every Italian were Michael Angelo and
Raphael and Dante and Galileo rolled into one, every
German a Goethe, and every Englishman a compound
of Shakespear and Eddington. Of this folly we have
had more than enough. The apparent freaks of nature
called Great Men mark not human attainment but
human possibility and hope. They prove that though
we in the mass are only child Yahoos it is possible for
creatures built exactly like us, bred from our unions
and developed from our seeds, to reach the heights of
these towering heads. For the moment, however, when
we are not violently persecuting them we are like
Goldsmith's villagers, wondering how their little heads
can carry all they know and ranking them as passing
rich on four hundred pounds a year when they are
lucky enough to get paid for their work instead of
persecuted.

WE CAN AND MUST LIVE LONGER

Considering now that I have lived fourteen years
longer than twice as long as Mozart or Mendelssohn,
and that within my experience men and women,
especially women, are younger at fifty than they were
at thirty in the middle of the nineteenth century, it is
impossible to resist at least a strong suspicion that the
term of human life cannot be fixed at seventy years or
indeed fixed at all. If we master the art of living instead of digging our graves with our teeth as we do at
present we may conceivably reach a point at which the
sole cause of death will be the fatal accident which is
statistically inevitable if we live long enough. In short,

it is not proved that there is such a thing as natural death: it is life that is natural and infinite.

How long, then, would it take us to mature into competent rulers of great modern States instead of, as at present, trying vainly to govern empires with the capacity of village headmen. In my Methuselah cycle I put it at three hundred years: a century of childhood and adolescence, a century of administration, and a century of oracular senatorism.

But nobody can foresee what periods my imaginary senators will represent. The pace of evolutionary development is not constant: the baby in the womb recapitulates within a few months an evolution which our biologists assure us took millions of years to acquire. The old axiom that Nature never jumps has given way to a doubt whether Nature is not an incorrigible kangaroo. What is certain is that new faculties, however long they may be dreamt of and desired, come at last suddenly and miraculously like the balancing of the bicyclist, the skater, and the acrobat. The development of homo sapiens into a competent political animal may occur in the same way.

THE NEXT DISCOVERY

Meanwhile here we are, with our incompetence armed with atomic bombs. Now power civilizes and develops mankind, though not without having first been abused to the point of wiping out entire civilizations. If the atomic bomb wipes out ours we shall just have to begin again. We may agree on paper not to use it as it is too dangerous and destructive; but tomorrow may see the discovery of that poisonous gas lighter than air and capable before it evaporates through the stratosphere of killing all the inhabitants of a city without damaging its buildings or sewers or water supplies or railways or electric plants. Victory might then win cities if it could repopulate them soon enough, whereas atomic bombing leaves nothing for anyone, victor or vanquished. It is conceivable even that the next great invention may create an overwhelming interest in pacific civilization and wipe out war. You never can tell.

AYOT SAINT LAWRENCE, *1945*

[ACT I]

A May morning in Geneva, in a meagrely equipped office with secondhand furniture, much the worse for wear, consisting of a dingy writing table with an old typewriter on it in the middle of the room, a revolving chair for the typist, an old press which has not been painted or varnished for many years, and three chairs for visitors against the wall near the door. The stove, an undecorated iron one of the plainest sort, designed rather for central heating in a cellar than for an inhabited apartment, is to the typist's right, the press facing it at the opposite side on the typist's left. The door is beside the press. The window is behind the typist.

A young Englishwoman is seated in the revolving chair. From the state of the table she seems to have been working at the compilation of a card index, as there are cards scattered about, and an open case to put them in, also a pile of foolscap from which she has been copying the card inscriptions. But at present she is not at work. She is smoking and reading an illustrated magazine with her heels on the table. A thermos flask, a cup and saucer, and a packet of cigarettes are beside her on a sliding shelf drawn out from the table. She is a self-satisfied young person, fairly attractive and well aware of it. Her dress, though smartly cut, is factory made ; and her speech and manners are London suburban.

Somebody knocks at the door. She hastily takes her heels off the table; jumps up; throws her cigarette into the stove; snatches the things off the sliding shelf and

hides them in the press; finally resumes her seat and looks
as busy as possible.

THE TYPIST [*calling*] Entrez, s'il vous plaît.

A middle-aged gentleman of distinguished appearance,
with a blond beard and moustache, top hatted, frock
coated, and gloved, comes in. He contemplates the room
and the young woman with evident surprise.

HE. Pardon, mademoiselle: I seek the office of the
International Committee for Intellectual Co-
operation.

SHE. Yes: thats quite all right. Take a seat, please.

HE [*hesitating*] Thank you; but my business is of
great importance: I must see your chief. This is not
the head office, is it?

SHE. No: the head office is in Paris. This is all there
is here. Not much of a place, is it?

HE. Well, I must confess that after visiting the magnificent palace of the International Labor Office and
the new quarters of the Secretariat, I expected to find
the Committee for Intellectual Co-operation lodged
in some imposingly monumental structure.

SHE. Oh, isnt it scandalous? I wish youd write to
the papers about it. Do please sit down.

HE. Thank you. [*He is about to take one of the chairs*
from the wall].

SHE. No, not that one: one of its legs isnt safe: it's
there only for show. Will you please take the other?

HE. Can the Committee not afford you a new chair?

SHE. It cant afford anything. The intellectual budget
is the interest on two million paper francs that one is
glad to get threepence for: they used to be tuppence.
So here I am in one rotten little room on the third
floor of a tumbledown old house full of rats. And

as to my salary I should be ashamed to name it. A Church charity would be ashamed to pay it.

HE. I am utterly astounded. [*He takes a sound chair from the wall; places it near the office table; and sits down*]. The intellectual co-operation of sixty nations must be a very extensive business. How can it possibly be conducted in this bare little place?

SHE. Oh, I conduct it all right. It's never in a hurry, you know.

HE. But really—pardon me if I am taking too much of your time—

SHE. Oh, thats quite all right. I'm only too glad to have a bit of chat with somebody. Nobody ever comes in here: people dont seem to know that the Committee exists.

HE. Do you mean that you have nothing to do?

SHE. Oh no. I tell you I have to do all the intellectual co-operation. I have to do it singlehanded too: I havnt even an office boy to help me. And theres no end to the work. If it werent, as I say, that theres no hurry about it, I should never get through it. Just look here at this nice little job theyve given me! A card index of all the universities with the names and addresses of their bursars and their vice chancellors. And there is a correspondence about the protection of professional titles that takes up half my time.

HE. And do they call that intellectual co-operation?

SHE. Well, what else would you call it?

HE. It is mere compilation. How are the intellectual giants who form your committee bringing the enormous dynamic force of their brains, their prestige, their authority, to bear on the destinies of the nations? What are they doing to correct the mistakes of our ignorant politicians?

SHE. Well, we have their names on our notepaper,

you know. What more can they do? You cant expect them to sit in this little hole talking to people. I have never seen one of them.

HE. So they leave it all to you?

SHE. Oh, I wouldnt say all. Theres the head office in Paris, you know, and some offices in other countries. I suppose they do their bit; and anyhow we all do a lot of writing to oneanother. But I must say it's as dull as ditchwater. When I took the job I thought it was going to be interesting, and that I'd see all the great men. I am ambitious, you know: I won a London County Council scholarship. I wanted a job that would draw out my faculties, if you understand me. But theres nothing to do here that any common typist couldnt do. And nobody ever comes near the place. Oh, it is dull.

HE. Shall I give you an interesting job, mademoiselle? One that would get you appreciated and perhaps a little talked about?

SHE. I'll just jump at it—if it is all right.

HE. How all right?

SHE. Morally, you know. No hanky panky. I am respectable; and I mean to keep respectable.

HE. I pledge you my word that my intentions are completely honorable.

SHE. Well, what about the pay? And how long will the job last? The work here may be dull; and the pay is just short of starvation; but I have the appointment for 25 years certain; and I darent give it up for anything chancy. You dont know what it is to be out of a job.

HE. I shall not ask you to give up your post here. On the contrary, it is essential that you should keep it. But I think I can make it more interesting for you. And I should of course make you a suitable present if at any time you found that your emoluments here were insufficient.

SHE. They are. But I mustnt take bribes, you know.

HE. You need not. Any friendly service I may be able to render will be entirely independent of your official work here.

SHE. Look here: I dont half like this. Whats the game?

THE JEW. I must begin by explaining that I am a Jew.

SHE. I dont believe you. You dont look like one.

THE JEW. I am not a primitive Hittite. You cannot draw my nose in profile by simply writing down the number six. My hair is not black, nor do I wear it in excessively oiled ringlets. I have all the marks of a German blond. German is my native language: in fact I am in every sense a German. But I worship in the synagogue; and when I worship I put my hat on, whereas a German takes it off. On this ground they class me as a non-Aryan, which is nonsense, as there is no such thing as an Aryan.

SHE. I'm so glad to hear you say that. The Germans here say that I am an Aryan; but I tell them I am nothing of the kind: I'm an Englishwoman. Not a common Englishwoman, of course: I'm a Camberwell woman; and though the west end may turn up its nose at Camberwell, Camberwell is better than Peckham any day in the week.

THE JEW. No doubt. I have not been there.

SHE. I never could abide Peckham people. They are disliked everywhere. It's instinctive, somehow. Havnt you noticed it?

THE JEW. All peoples are disliked in the lump. The English are disliked: the Germans are disliked: the French are disliked. The Protestants are disliked; and all their hundreds of sects dislike oneanother. So are the Catholics, the Jesuits, the Freemasons. You tell me that the inhabitants of Peckham are disliked: no doubt they deserve it.

SHE. They do.

THE JEW. Some of the greatest men have disliked the human race. But for Noah, its Creator would have drowned it. Can we deny that He had good reasons for disliking it? Can I deny that there are good reasons for disliking Jews? On the contrary, I dislike most of them myself.

SHE. Oh, dont say that. Ive known lots of quite nice Jews. What I say is why pick on the Jews, as if they were any worse than other people?

THE JEW. That is precisely my business here today. I find you most intelligent—most sympathetic.

SHE. Come now! none of that. Whats the game?

THE JEW. I have been assaulted, plundered, and driven from my native soil by its responsible ruler. I, as a ruined individual, can do nothing. But the League of Nations can act through its Committee for Intellectual Co-operation. The Committee can act through the permanent court of International Justice at the Hague, which is also an organ of the League. My business here is to ask the Committee to apply to the court for a warrant against the responsible ruler. I charge him with assault and battery, burglary—

SHE. Burglary! Did they break into your house?

THE JEW. I cannot speak of it. Everything I treasured. Wrecked! Smashed! Defiled! Never will I forgive: never can I forget.

SHE. But why didnt you call the police?

THE JEW. Mademoiselle: the police did it. The Government did it. The Dictator who controls the police is responsible before Europe! before civilization! I look to the League of Nations for redress. It

alone can call unrighteous rulers to account. The
initiative must be taken by its Committee for Intellectual Co-operation: that is, for the moment, by you,
mademoiselle.

SHE. But what can I do? I cant go out and collar
your unrighteous ruler.

THE JEW. No, mademoiselle. What you must do is to
write to the International Court, calling on it to issue a
warrant for the arrest of my oppressor on a charge of
attempting to exterminate a section of the human race.

SHE. Well, it seems like taking a lot on myself, doesnt
it?

THE JEW. Not at all. You will be acting, not for
yourself, but for the intellect of Europe. I assure you
it is the correct course.

SHE. But I'm not sure that I know how to write a
letter with all those police court things in it.

THE JEW. It is quite simple. But if you will allow
me I will draft the letter for you.

SHE. Oh I say, Mister Jew, I dont like this.

THE JEW. Then write the letter yourself. I am sure
you will do it perfectly. It will be an opportunity for
you to shew the Committee what you are made of.

SHE. Well, look here. I have a particular friend, an
American journalist. Would you mind if I shewed him
your draft before I send it off?

THE JEW. An American journalist! Excellent, excellent. By all means submit my draft to him and ask him
to correct it if necessary. My English is German
English, and may leave something to be desired.

SHE. Yes: thatll be splendid. Thank you ever so much.

THE JEW. Not at all. [*Rising*] I will bring the draft
in the course of the afternoon. Au revoir, then.

SHE. Au revoir.

They shake hands cordially. Meanwhile the door is

*opened by an obstinate-looking middle-aged man of
respectable but not aristocratic appearance, speaking
English like a shopkeeper from the provinces, or perhaps,
by emigration, the dominions.*

NEWCOMER. Can I see the boss, miss?

SHE [*with haughty nonchalance in a would-be distinguished accent startlingly unlike her unaffected deference to the gentlemanlike Jew*] I am sorry. Our chiefs are
scattered over Europe, very eminent persons, you
know. Can I do anything?

NEWCOMER [*looking at the Jewish gentleman*] I'm
afraid I'm interrupting.

THE JEW. Not at all: my business is finished. [*Clicking
his heels and bowing*] Until the afternoon, mademoiselle. Monsieur— [*He bows to the newcomer, and
goes out*].

SHE. You can sit down.

NEWCOMER. I will keep you only a minute, miss.
[*He sits and takes out some notes he has made*].

SHE. Be as quick as you can, please. I am busy this
morning.

NEWCOMER. Yes: you have the brainwork of the
world on your shoulders here. When any of the nations
goes off the rails, this is the place to have it put back.
Thats so, isnt it?

SHE [*with aplomb*] Undoubtedly.

NEWCOMER. Well, it's like this. In my country weve
had an election. We thought it lay between our usual
people: the National Party and the Labor Party;
but it was won by an upstart kind of chap who called
himself a Business Democrat. He got a clear majority
over the Nationals and the Labor Party; so it was
up to him to form a Government. And what do you
suppose the fellow did when he became Prime
Minister?

SHE [*bored*] Cant imagine, I'm sure.

NEWCOMER. He said he had been returned to power as a business democrat, and that the business part of it meant that he was not to waste time, but to get the nation's work done as quickly as possible.

SHE. Quite, quite. Nothing to complain of in that, is there?

NEWCOMER. Wait. I'm going to astonish you. He said the country had decided by its democratic vote that it should be governed by him and his party for the next five years, and that no opposition could be tolerated. He said the defeated minority must step down and out instead of staying there to obstruct and delay and annoy him. Of course the Opposition werent going to stand that: they refused to leave the Chamber. So he adjourned the House until next day; and when the Opposition turned up the police wouldnt let them in. Most of them couldnt get as far as the doors, because the Prime Minister had organized a body of young men called the Clean Shirts, to help the police.

SHE. Well?

NEWCOMER. Well!!! Is that all you have to say to me?

SHE. What do you expect me to say? It seems all right to me. It's what any man of business would do. Wouldnt you?

NEWCOMER. Of course I should do it in business; but this is politics.

SHE. Well! arnt politics business?

NEWCOMER. Of course theyre not. Just the opposite. You know that, dont you?

SHE. Oh, quite, quite.

NEWCOMER. What I say is, business methods are business methods; and parliamentary methods are parliamentary methods.

SHE [*brightly*] "And never the twain shall meet," as Kipling puts it.

NEWCOMER. No: I dont hold with Kipling. Too imperialist for me. I'm a democrat.

SHE. But not a business democrat, if I follow you.

NEWCOMER. No, no: not a business democrat. A proper democrat. I'm all for the rights of minorities.

SHE. But I always thought that democracy meant the right of the majority to have its way.

NEWCOMER. Oh no: that would be the end of all liberty. You have nothing to say against liberty, I hope.

SHE. I have nothing to say against anything. I am not here to discuss politics with everyone who walks into my office. What do you want?

NEWCOMER. Well, heres a Prime Minister committing high treason and rebellion and breach of privilege; levying armed forces against the Crown; violating the constitution; setting up a dictatorship and obstructing the lawful ingress of duly elected members to the legislative Chamber. Whats to be done with him?

SHE. Quite simple. I shall apply to the International Court at the Hague for a warrant for his arrest on all those charges. You can look in at the end of the week, when the answer from the Hague will have arrived. You will supply me with the man's name and the particulars—

NEWCOMER [*putting his notes on the table before her*] Here they are, miss. By Gosh, thats a splendid idea.

SHE. Thank you. That is all. Good morning.

NEWCOMER [*rising and going to the door*] Well, you know how to do business here: theres no mistake about that. Good morning, miss.

As he is going out the door opens in his face; and a

widow comes in: a Creole lady of about forty, with the remains of a gorgeous and opulent southern beauty. Her imposing style and dress at once reduce the young lady of the office to nervous abjection.

THE WIDOW. Are you the president of the Intellectual Co-operation Committee of the League of Nations?

NEWCOMER. No, maam. This lady will do all you require [*he goes out*].

THE WIDOW. Am I to take that seriously? My business is important. I came here to place it before a body of persons of European distinction. I am not prepared to discuss it with an irresponsible young woman.

SHE. I am afraid I dont look the part, do I? I am only the staff, so to speak. Still, anything I can do I shall be most happy.

THE WIDOW. But where are your chiefs?

SHE. Ah, there you have me. They live all over the world, as you might say.

THE WIDOW. But do they not come here to attend to their business?

SHE. Well, you see, there is really nothing for them to attend to. It's only intellectual business, you know.

THE WIDOW. But do they not take part in the Assembly of the League?

SHE. Some of them have been, once. Nobody ever goes to the Assembly twice if they can help it.

THE WIDOW. But I must see somebody—somebody of importance.

SHE. Well, I'm sorry. Theres nobody but me. I can do whatever is necessary. Did you by any chance want a warrant from the International Court at the Hague?

THE WIDOW. Yes: that is exactly what I do want. A death warrant.

SHE. A what?!!

THE WIDOW. A death warrant. I will sit down, if you will allow me.

SHE. Oh please—

THE WIDOW [*sitting down*] Do you see that? [*She takes an automatic pistol from her bag, and throws it on the table*].

SHE. Oh, thats not allowed in Geneva. Put it up quick. Somebody might come in.

THE WIDOW [*replacing the pistol in her bag*] This is the most absurd place. In my country everybody carries a gun.

SHE. What country, may I ask?

THE WIDOW. The Republic of the Earthly Paradise.

SHE. My mother has a school prize called The Earthly Paradise. What a coincidence!

THE WIDOW. Then you know that the Earthly Paradise is one of the leading States in the world in culture and purity of race, and that its capital contained more than two thousand white inhabitants before the last revolution. There must be still at least fifteen hundred left.

SHE. But is it a member of the League?

THE WIDOW. Of course it is. And allow me to remind you that by its veto it can put a stop to all action by the League until its affairs are properly attended to.

SHE. Can it? I didnt know that. Of course I shall be only too pleased to apply for a warrant; but I'd rather not call it a death warrant. Death warrant sounds a bit thick, if you understand me. All you need do is to give me a list of the charges you make against— well, against whoever it is.

THE WIDOW. Simply one charge of the wilful murder

of my late husband by the President of the Earthly Paradise.

SHE. Surely if a president kills anyone it's an execution; but if anyone kills a president it's an assassination.

THE WIDOW. And is not that just the state of things the League of Nations is here to put a stop to?

SHE. Oh, dont ask me. All I know about the League is that it pays my salary. Just give me the gentleman's name and who he murdered. Murder stories are thrillingly interesting.

THE WIDOW. You would not think so if you lived in a country where there is at least one murder in every family.

SHE. What an awful place! Is it as barbarous as that?

THE WIDOW. Barbarous! Certainly not. The Earthly Paradise is the most civilized country in the world. Its constitution is absolutely democratic: every president must swear to observe it in every particular. The Church is abolished: no moral authority is recognized except that of the people's will. The president and parliament are elected by adult suffrage every two years. So are all the judges and all the officials, even the road sweepers. All these reforms, which have made The Earthly Paradise the most advanced member of the League of Nations, were introduced by my late husband the sixth president. He observed the constitution strictly. The elections were conducted with absolute integrity. The ballot was secret. The people felt free for the first time in their lives. Immediately after the elections the budget was passed providing for two years. My husband then prorogued the Parliament until the end of that period, and governed the country according to his own ideas whilst the people enjoyed themselves and made money in their own ways without any political disturbances or arguments. He was re-elected three times, and is now known in the Paradise as the father of his country.

SHE. But you said he was murdered, and that the president murdered him. How could that be if he was the president? He couldnt murder himself.

THE WIDOW. Unhappily he had certain weaknesses. He was an affectionate husband: I may even say an uxorious one; but he was very far from being faithful to me. When he abolished the Church he would have abolished marriage also if public opinion would have stood for it. And he was much too indulgent to his enemies. Naturally, whenever he won an election his opponent raised an army and attempted a revolution; for we are a high spirited race and do not submit to the insult of defeat at the polls. But my husband was a military genius. He had no difficulty in putting down these revolutions; but instead of having his opponent shot in the proper and customary way, he pardoned him and challenged him to try again as often as he pleased. I urged him again and again not to trifle with his own safety in this way. Useless: he would not listen to me. At last I found out the reason. He was carrying on an intrigue with his opponent's wife, my best friend. I had to shoot her—shoot her dead—my dearest friend [*she is overcome with emotion*].

SHE. Oh, you shouldnt have done that. That was going a little too far, wasnt it?

THE WIDOW. Public opinion obliged me to do it as a selfrespecting wife and mother. God knows I did not want to do it: I loved her: I would have let her have ten husbands if I had had them to give. But what can you do against the etiquette of your class? My brothers had to fight duels and kill their best friends because it was etiquette.

SHE. But where were the police? Werent you tried for it?

THE WIDOW. Of course I was tried for it; but I pleaded the unwritten law and was acquitted. Unfortunately the scandal destroyed my husband's popularity. He was defeated at the next election by the man he had so foolishly spared. Instead of raising an army to avenge this outrage, my husband, crushed by the loss of his mistress, just moped at home until they came and shot him. They had come to shoot me; and [*with a fresh burst of tears*] I wish to Heaven they had; but I was out at the time; so they thought they might as well shoot my husband as there was nobody else to shoot.

SHE. What a dreadful thing for you!

THE WIDOW. Not at all. It served him right, absolutely. He never spoke to me after I had to kill the woman we both loved more than we loved oneanother. I believe he would have been only too glad if they had shot me; and I dont blame him. What is the use of the League of Nations if it cannot put a stop to such horrors?

SHE. Well, it's not the League's business, is it?

THE WIDOW. Not the League's business! Do you realize, young woman, that if the League does not bring the murderer of my husband to justice my son will be obliged to take up a blood feud and shoot the murderer with his own hands, though they were at the same school and are devoted to oneanother? It is against Nature, against God: if your committee does not stop it I will shoot every member of it, and you too. [*She rises*]. Excuse me. I can bear no more of this: I shall faint unless I get into the fresh air. [*She takes papers and a card from her bag and throws them on the table*]. There are the particulars. This is my card.

Good morning. [*She goes as abruptly as she came in*].

SHE. [*rising*] Good—

But the widow has gone and the young office lady, greatly upset, drops back into her seat with a prolonged Well!!!!!

A smart young American gentleman looks in.

THE GENTLEMAN. Say, baby: who is the old girl in the mantilla? Carmen's grandmother, eh? [*He sits on the table edge, facing her, on her right*].

SHE. A murderess. Her dearest friend. She had to. Horrible. Theyve shot her husband. She says she will shoot me unless the League stops it.

HE. Grand! Fine!

SHE. Is that all you care? Well, look at my morning's work! Persecutions, revolutions, murders, all sorts. The office has been full of people all the morning. We shant have it all to ourselves any more.

HE. No, baby; but I shall have some dough to spend. I have been kicking my heels here for months faking news for my people when there was no news. And here you hand me a mouthful. What a scoop for me, honey! You are a peach. [*He kisses her*].

Someone knocks at the door.

SHE. Shsh! Someone knocking.

They separate hastily, he going to the stove and she composing herself in her chair.

HE. Come in! Entrez! Herein!

A gaitered English bishop enters. He is old, soft, gentle and rather infirm.

THE BISHOP. Excuse me; but does anyone here speak English?

HE [*putting on all the style he is capable of*] My native language, my lord. Also this lady's. [*Exchange of bows*]. Will you take a pew, my lord?

BISHOP [*sitting*] Thank you. Your stairs are some-

what trying to me: I am not so young as I was; and
they tell me I must be careful not to overstrain my
heart. The journey to Geneva is a terrible one for a
man of my years. Nothing but the gravest emergency
could have forced me to undertake it.

HE. Is the emergency one in which we can have the
honor of assisting you, my lord?

BISHOP. Your advice would be invaluable to me;
for I really dont know what to do or where to go here.
I am met with indifference—with apathy—when I
reveal a state of things that threatens the very
existence of civilized society, of religion, of the family,
of the purity of womanhood, and even, they tell me,
of our commercial prosperity. Are people mad? Dont
they know? Dont they care?

HE. My! my! my! [*He takes a chair to the end of the
table nearest the stove*] Pray be seated, my lord. What
has happened?

BISHOP [*sinking into the chair*] Sir: they are actually
preaching Communism in my diocese. Commun-
ism!!! My butler, who has been in the palace for
forty years, a most devoted and respectable man,
tells me that my footman—I am the only bishop in
England who can afford to keep a footman now—that
my footman is a cell.

HE. A sell? You mean that he has disappointed you?

BISHOP. No: not that sort of cell. C.E. double L. A
communist cell. Like a bee in a hive. Planted on me
by the Communists to make their dreadful propaganda in my household! And my grandson at Oxford
has joined a Communist club. The Union—the
Oxford Union—has raised the red flag. It is dreadful.
And my granddaughter a nudist! I was graciously
allowed to introduce my daughters to good Queen
Victoria. If she could see my granddaughter she

would call the police. Is it any wonder that I have a weak heart? Shock after shock. My own footman, son of the most respectable parents, and actually an Anglo-Catholic!

HE. I can hardly believe it, my lord. What times we are living in!

SHE [*with her most official air*] Surely this is a case for the International Court at the Hague, my lord.

BISHOP. Yes, yes. An invaluable suggestion. The Court must stop the Bolshies from disseminating their horrible doctrines in England. It is in the treaties.

He is interrupted by the entrance of a very smart Russian gentleman, whom he receives with pleased recognition.

BISHOP [*rising*] Ah, my dear sir, we meet again. [*To the others*] I had the pleasure of making this gentleman's acquaintance last night at my hotel. His interest in the Church of England kept us up talking long after my usual hour for retirement. [*Shaking his hand warmly*] How do you do, my dear friend? how do you do?

RUSSIAN. Quite well, thank you, my lord. Am I interrupting your business?

BISHOP. No no no no: I beg you to remain. You will help: you will sympathize.

RUSSIAN. You are very kind, my lord: I am quite at your service.

BISHOP [*murmuring gratefully as he resumes his seat*] Thank you. Thank you.

RUSSIAN. Let me introduce myself. I am Commissar Posky of the Sovnarkom and Politbureau, Soviet delegate to the League Council.

BISHOP [*aghast, staggering to his feet*] You are a Bolshevik!

COMMISSAR. Assuredly.

The Bishop faints. General concern. The men rush to him.

COMMISSAR. Do not lift him yet. He will recover best as he is.

SHE. I have some iced lemonade in my thermos. Shall I give him some?

BISHOP [*supine*] Where am I? Has anything happened?

HE. You are in the office of the Intellectual Co-operation Committee in Geneva. You have had a slight heart attack.

COMMISSAR. Lie still, comrade. You will be quite yourself presently.

BISHOP [*sitting up*] It is not my heart. [*To the Commissar*] It is moral shock. You presented yourself to me yesterday as a cultivated and humane gentleman, interested in the Church of England. And now it turns out that you are a Bolshie. What right had you to practise such a cruel imposture on me? [*He rises: the Commissar helps him*] No: I can rise without assistance, thank you. [*He attempts to do so, but collapses into the arms of the Commissar*].

COMMISSAR. Steady, comrade.

BISHOP [*regaining his seat with the Commissar's assistance*] Again I must thank you. But I shudder at the touch of your bloodstained hands.

COMMISSAR. My hands are not bloodstained, comrade. I have not imposed on you. You have not quite recovered yet, I think. I am your friend of last night. Dont you recognize me?

BISHOP. A Bolshie! If I had known, sir, I should have repudiated your advances with abhorrence.

HE [*again posting himself at the stove*] Russia is a member of the League, my lord. This gentleman's standing here is the same as that of the British Foreign Secretary.

BISHOP [*intensely*] Never. Never.

SHE [*airily*] And what can we do for you, Mr Posky?
I'm sorry I cant offer you a chair. That one isnt safe.

COMMISSAR. Pray dont mention it. My business
will take only a moment. As you know, the Soviet
Government has gone as far as possible in agreeing
not to countenance or subsidize any propaganda of
Communism which takes the form of a political conspiracy to overthrow the British National Government.

BISHOP. And in violation of that agreement you
have corrupted my footman and changed him from an
honest and respectable young Englishman into a Cell.

COMMISSAR. Have we? I know nothing of your
footman. If he is intelligent enough to become a
Communist, as so many famous Englishmen did long
before the Russian revolution, we cannot prevent
him. But we do not employ him as our agent nor support him financially in any way.

HE. But what, then, is your difficulty, Comrade
Posky?

COMMISSAR. We have just discovered that there is
a most dangerous organization at work in Russia,
financed from the British Isles, having for its object
the overthrow of the Soviet system and the substitution of the Church of England and the British Constitution.

BISHOP. And why not, sir? Why not? Could any
object be more desirable, more natural? Would you
in your blind hatred of British institutions and of all
liberty of thought and speech, make it a crime to advocate a system which is universally admitted to be the
the best and freest in the world?

COMMISSAR. We do not think so. And as the obligation to refrain from this sort of propaganda is recipro-
cal, you are bound by it just as we are.

HE. But what is this seditious organization you have just discovered?

COMMISSAR. It is called the Society for the Propagation of the Gospel in Foreign Parts. It has agents everywhere. They call themselves missionaries.

BISHOP. I cannot bear this: the man is insane. I subscribe to the Society almost beyond my means. It is a body of the highest respectability and piety.

COMMISSAR. You are misinformed: its doctrines are of the most subversive kind. They have penetrated to my own household. My wife is a busy professional woman, and my time is taken up altogether by public work. We are absolutely dependent for our domestic work on our housekeeper Feodorovna Ballyboushka. We were ideally happy with this excellent woman for years. In her youth she was a udarnik, what you call a shock worker.

BISHOP. You are all shock workers in Russia now. You have seen the effect on me?

COMMISSAR. That was in the early days of the revolution, when she was young and ardent. Now she is elderly; and her retirement into domestic service suits her years and her helpful and affectionate temperament. Two months ago an extraordinary change came over her. She refused to do any work that was not immediately necessary, on the ground that the end of the world is at hand. She declared that she was in a condition which she described as "saved," and interrupted my work continually with attempts to save me. She had long fits of crying because she could not bear the thought of my wife spending eternity in hell. She accused the Soviets of being the hornets prophesied in the Book of Revelation. We were about to have her certified as insane—most reluctantly; for we loved our dear Ballyboushka—when we discovered

that she had been hypnotized by this illegal Society. I
warned our Secret Police, formerly known to you as
the Gay Pay Ooh. They followed up the clue and
arrested four missionaries.

BISHOP. And shot them. Christian martyrs! All who
fall into the hands of the terrible Gay Pay Ooh
are shot at once, without trial, without the ministra-
tions of the Church. But I will have a memorial service
said for them. To that extent at last I can defeat your
Godless tyranny.

COMMISSAR. You are quite mistaken: they have
not been shot. They will be sent back to England:
that is all.

BISHOP [passionately] What right had you to arrest
them? How dare you arrest Englishmen? How dare
you persecute religion?

COMMISSAR. They have been very patiently examined by our official psychologists, who report that
they can discover nothing that could reasonably be
called religion in their minds. They are obsessed with
tribal superstitions of the most barbarous kind. They
believe in human sacrifices, in what they call the remis-
sion of sins by the shedding of blood. No man's life
would be safe in Russia if such doctrines were propagated there.

BISHOP. But you dont understand. Oh, what dreadful ignorance!

COMMISSAR. Let us pass on to another point. Our
police have found a secret document of your State
Church, called the Thirty-nine Articles.

BISHOP. Secret! It is in the Prayer Book!

COMMISSAR. It is not read in church. That fact
speaks for itself. Our police have found most of the
articles incomprehensible; but there is one, the eighteenth, which declares that all Russians are to be held

accursed. How would you like it if our chief cultural institution, endowed by our government, the Komintern, were to send its agents into England to teach that every Englishman is to be held accursed?

BISHOP. But surely, surely, you would not compare the Komintern to the Church of England!!

COMMISSAR. Comrade Bishop: the Komintern is the State Church in Russia exactly as the Church of England is the State Church in Britain.

The Bishop slides to the floor in another faint.

SHE. Oh! He's gone off again. Shall I get my thermos?

HE. I should break things to him more gently, Mr Posky. People die of shock. He maynt recover next time. In fact, he maynt recover this time.

COMMISSAR. What am I to do? I have said nothing that could possibly shock any educated reasonable person; but this man does not seem to know what sort of world he is living in.

SHE. He's an English bishop, you know.

COMMISSAR. Well? Is he not a rational human being?

SHE. Oh no: nothing as common as that. I tell you he's a bishop.

BISHOP. Where am I? Why am I lying on the floor? What has happened?

HE. You are in the Intellectual Co-operation Bureau in Geneva; and you have just been told that the Russian Komintern is analogous to the Church of England.

BISHOP [*springing to his feet unaided, his eyes blazing*] I still have life enough left in me to deny it. Karl Marx—Antichrist—said that the sweet and ennobling consolations of our faith are opium given to the poor to enable them to endure the hardships of that state of

[362]

life to which it has pleased God to call them. Does your Komintern teach that blasphemy or does it not?

COMMISSAR. Impossible. There are no poor in Russia.

BISHOP. Oh! [*he drops dead*].

HE [*feeling his pulse*] I am afraid you have shocked him once too often, Comrade. His pulse has stopped. He is dead.

POSKY. Was he ever alive? To me he was incredible.

SHE. I suppose my thermos is of no use now. Shall I ring up a doctor?

HE. I think you had better ring up the police. But I say, Mr Posky, what a scoop!

COMMISSAR. A scoop? I do not understand. What is a scoop?

HE. Read all the European papers tomorrow and youll see.

[ACT II]

*Office of the secretary of the League of Nations. Except
for the small writing table at which the secretary is seated
there is no office furniture. The walls are covered with
engraved prints or enlarged photographs of kings, presidents, and dictators, mostly in military uniforms. Above
these bellicose pictures the cornice is decorated with a row
of plaster doves in low relief. There is one large picture in
oils, representing a lifesize Peace, with tiny figures, also
in military uniforms, kneeling round her feet and bowing
their heads piously beneath the wreath which she offers
them. This picture faces the secretary from the other side
of the room as he sits at his table with his back to the
window presenting his left profile to anyone entering
from the door, which is in the middle of the wall between
them. A suite of half a dozen chairs is ranged round the
walls, except one, which stands near the writing table for
the convenience of people interviewing the secretary.*

*He is a disillusioned official with a habit of dogged
patience acquired in the course of interviews with distinguished statesmen of different nations, all in a condition of invincible ignorance as to the spirit of Geneva and
the constitution of the League of Nations, and each with
a national axe to grind. On this occasion he is rather
exceptionally careworn. One pities him, as he is of a refined type, and, one guesses, began as a Genevan idealist.
Age fifty or thereabouts.*

*There is a telephone on the table which he is at
present using.*

THE SECRETARY. Yes: send her up instantly. Remind me of her name. What?!... Ammonia? Nonsense! that cant be her name. Spell it...V E?... Oh, *B* E. Do you mean to say that her name is Begonia? Begonia Brown?... Farcical.

He replaces the receiver as Begonia enters. She is the Intellectual Co-operation typist. She is in walking dress, cheap, but very smart.

THE SECRETARY. Miss Brown?

BEGONIA [*with her best smile*] Yes.

THE SECRETARY. Sit down.

BEGONIA [*complying*] Kew [*short for Thank you*].

THE SECRETARY [*gravely*] You have heard the news, no doubt?

BEGONIA. Oh yes. Jack Palamedes has won the dancing tournament. I had ten francs on him; and I have won a hundred. Had you anything on?

THE SECRETARY [*still more gravely*] I am afraid you will think me very ignorant, Miss Brown; but I have never heard of Mr Palamedes.

BEGONIA. Fancy that! He's the talk of Geneva, I assure you.

THE SECRETARY. There are other items of news, Miss Brown. Germany has withdrawn from the League.

BEGONIA. And a good riddance, if you ask me. My father lost a lot of money through the war. Otherwise —you wont mind my telling you—youd never have got me slaving at a typewriter here for my living.

THE SECRETARY. No doubt. A further item is that the British Empire has declared war on Russia.

BEGONIA. Well, what could you expect us to do with those awful Bolshies? We should have done it long ago. But thank goódness we're safe in Geneva, you and I.

THE SECRETARY. We are safe enough everywhere, so far. The war is one of sanctions only.

BEGONIA. More shame for us, say I. I should give those Bolshies the bayonet: thats the way to talk to scum of that sort. I cant contain myself when I think of all the murder and slavery of them Soviets— [*correcting herself*] those Soviets.

THE SECRETARY. In consequence Japan has declared war on Russia and is therefore in military alliance with Britain. And the result of that is that Australia, New Zealand and Canada have repudiated the war and formed an anti-Japanese alliance with the United States under the title of the New British Federation. South Africa may join them at any moment.

BEGONIA [*flushing with indignation*] Do you mean that theyve broken up our dear Empire?

THE SECRETARY. They have said nothing about that.

BEGONIA. Oh, then thats quite all right. You know, when I was at school I was chosen five times to recite on Empire Day; and in my very first year, when I was the smallest child there, I presented the bouquet to King George's sister, who came to our prize giving. Say a word against the Empire, and you have finished with Begonia Brown.

THE SECRETARY. Then you went to school, did you?

BEGONIA. Well, of course: what do you take me for? I went to school for seven years and never missed a single day. I got fourteen prizes for regular attendance.

THE SECRETARY. Good God!

BEGONIA. What did you say?

THE SECRETARY. Nothing. I was about to tell you

what has happened in Quetzalcopolis, the chief seaport of the Earthly Paradise.

BEGONIA. I know. In Central America, isnt it?

THE SECRETARY. Yes. The mob there has attacked the British Consulate, and torn down the British flag.

BEGONIA [*rising in a fury*] Insulted the British flag!!!

THE SECRETARY. They have also burnt down three convents and two churches.

BEGONIA. Thats nothing: theyre only Catholic churches. But do you mean to say that they have dared to touch the British flag?

THE SECRETARY. They have. Fortunately it was after hours and the staff had gone home. Otherwise they would assuredly have been massacred.

BEGONIA. Dirty swine! I hope the British fleet will not leave a stone standing or a nigger alive in their beastly seaport. Thatll teach them.

THE SECRETARY. There is only one other trifle of news. The little Dominion of Jacksonsland has declared itself an independent republic.

BEGONIA. It ought to be ashamed of itself. Republics are a low lot. But dont you be anxious about that: the republicans will soon be kicked out. The people may be misled for a while; but they always come back to king and country.

THE SECRETARY. And now, Miss Brown, I must ask you whether you fully realize that all this is your doing?

BEGONIA. Mine!

THE SECRETARY. Yours and nobody else's. In every one of these cases, it was your hand that started the series of political convulsions which may end in the destruction of civilization.

BEGONIA [*flattered*] Really? How?

THE SECRETARY. Those letters that you sent to the Court of International Justice at the Hague—

BEGONIA. Oh, of course. Yes. Fancy that!

THE SECRETARY. But did you not know what you were doing? You conducted the correspondence with very remarkable ability—more, I confess, than I should have given you credit for. Do you mean to tell me that you did not foresee the consequences of your action? That you did not even read the newspapers to see what was happening?

BEGONIA. I dont read political news: it's so dry. However, I seem to be having a big success; and I wont pretend I am not gratified.

THE SECRETARY. Unfortunately the Powers do not consider it a success. They are blaming me for it.

BEGONIA. Oh, if there is any blame I am ready to take it all on myself.

THE SECRETARY. That is very magnanimous of you, Miss Brown.

BEGONIA. Not so magnanimous either: thank you all the same. I tell you I back the Empire; and the Empire will back me. So dont be uneasy.

THE SECRETARY. You are very possibly right. And now may I ask you a personal question? How did you become interested in the League of Nations? How did you get this post of yours, which has placed the world's destiny so unexpectedly in your hands?

BEGONIA. Was I interested in the League? Let me see. You know that there is a Society called the League of Nations Union, dont you?

THE SECRETARY. I do. I shudder whenever I think of it.

BEGONIA. Oh, theres no harm in it. I'd never heard of it until last year, when they opened a branch in Camberwell with a whist drive. A friend gave me a ticket for it. It was opened by the Conservative candidate: an innocent young lad rolling in money. He saw that I was a cut above the other girls there, and picked me for his partner when he had to dance. I told him I'd won a County Council scholarship and was educated and knew shorthand and a bit of French and all that, and that I was looking out for a job. His people fixed me up for Geneva all right. A perfect gentleman I must say: never asked so much as a kiss. I was disappointed.

THE SECRETARY. Disappointed at his not kissing you?

BEGONIA. Oh no: there were plenty of kisses going from better looking chaps. But he was a bit of a sucker; and I thought he had intentions; and of course he would have been a jolly good catch for me. But when his people got wind of it they packed him off for a tour round the Empire, and got me this job here—to keep me out of his way, I suppose. Anyhow here I am, you see.

THE SECRETARY. Were you examined as to your knowledge and understanding of the Covenant of the League, and its constitution?

BEGONIA. No. They didnt need to examine me to find out that I was educated. I had lots of prizes and certificates; and there was my L.C.C. scholarship. You see, I have such a good memory: examinations are no trouble to me. Theres a book in the office about the League. I tried to read it; but it was such dry stuff I went to sleep over it.

THE SECRETARY [rising] Well, Miss Brown, I am glad to have made your acquaintance, and delighted to learn that though you have produced a first class political crisis, including what promises to be a world war, and made an amazing change in the constitution of the British Empire all in the course of a single morning's work, you are still in high spirits and in fact rather proud of yourself.

BEGONIA [*she has also risen*] Oh, I am not a bit proud; and I'm quite used to being a success. You know, although I was always at the top of my class at school, I never pretended to be clever. Silly clever, I call it. At first I was frightened of the girls that went in for being clever and having original ideas and all that sort of crankiness. But I beat them easily in the examinations; and they never got anywhere. That gave me confidence. Wherever I go I always find that lots of people think as I do. The best sort of people always do: the real ladies and gentlemen, you know. The others are oddities and outsiders. If you want to know what real English public opinion is, keep your eye on me. I'm not a bit afraid of war: remember that England has never lost a battle, and that it does no harm to remind the foreigners of it when they get out of hand. Good morning. So pleased to have met you.

They shake hands; and he goes to the door and opens it for her. She goes out much pleased with herself.

THE SECRETARY [*ruminating dazedly*] And thats England! [*The telephone rings. He returns to the table to attend to it*]. Yes? . . . Which Foreign Secretary? Every hole and corner in the Empire has its own Foreign Secretary now. Do you mean the British Foreign Secretary, Sir Orpheus Midlander? . . . Well, why didnt you say so? Shew him up at once.

Sir Orpheus comes in. He is a very welldressed gentleman of fifty or thereabouts, genial in manner, quickwitted in conversation, altogether a pleasant and popular personality.

THE SECRETARY. Do sit down. I cant say how I feel about your being dragged here all the way from London in Derby week.

SIR O. [*sitting*] Well, my friend, it's you who have dragged me. And I hope you wont mind my asking you what on earth you think you have been doing? What induced you to do it?

THE SECRETARY. I didnt do it. It was done by the Committee for Intellectual Co-operation.

SIR O. The what??! I never heard of such a body.

THE SECRETARY. Neither did I until this business was sprung on me. Nobody ever heard of it. But I find now that it is part of the League, and that its members are tremendous swells with European reputations. Theyve all published translations from the Greek or discovered new planets or something of that sort.

SIR O. Ah yes: outside politics: I see. But we cant have literary people interfering in foreign affairs. And they must have held meetings before taking such an outrageous step as this. Why were we not told? We'd have squashed them at once.

THE SECRETARY. They are quite innocent: they know no more about it than I did. The whole thing was done by a young woman named Begonia Brown.

SIR O. Begonia Brown! But this is appalling. I shall be personally compromised.

THE SECRETARY. You! How?

SIR O. This woman—it must be the same woman; for there cant be another female with such a name in the world—she's engaged to my nephew.

THE SECRETARY. She told me about it. But I had no idea the man was your nephew. I see how awkward it is for you. Did you ever talk to her about it?

SIR O. I! I never set eyes on her in my life. I remember her ridiculous name: thats all.

THE SECRETARY. Were you in the habit of discussing foreign affairs with your nephew?

SIR O. With Benjy! You might as well discuss Einstein's general theory of relativity with a blue behinded ape. I havnt exchanged twenty words with the boy since I tipped him when he was going from Eton to Oxford.

THE SECRETARY. Then I cant understand it. Her correspondence with the Hague Court has been conducted with remarkable ability and in first-rate style. The woman herself is quite incapable of it. There must be somebody behind her. Can it be your nephew?

SIR O. If, as you say, the work shews political ability and presentable style, you may accept my assurance that Sue's boy has nothing to do with it. Besides, he is at present in Singapore, where the native dancing girls are irresistible.

The telephone rings.

THE SECRETARY. Excuse me. Yes?... Hold on a moment. [*To Sir O.*] The Senior Judge of the Court of International Justice at the Hague is downstairs. Hadnt you better see him?

SIR O. By all means. Most opportune.

THE SECRETARY [*into the telephone*] Send him up.

SIR O. Have you had any correspondence about this business?

THE SECRETARY. Correspondence!!! I havnt read one tenth of it. The Abyssinian war was a holiday job in comparison. Weve never had anything like it before.

The Senior Judge enters. He is a Dutchman, much younger than a British judge: under forty, in fact, but very grave and every inch a judge.

THE SECRETARY. I am desolate at having brought your honor all the way from the Hague. A word from you would have brought me there and saved you the trouble. Have you met the British Foreign Secretary, Sir Orpheus Midlander?

JUDGE. I have not had that pleasure. How do you do, Sir Midlander?

SIR O. How do you do?

They shake hands whilst the Secretary places a chair for the judge in the middle of the room, between his table and Sir Orpheus. They all sit down.

JUDGE. I thought it best to come. The extraordinary feature of this affair is that I have communicated with all the members of the Intellectual Committee; and every one of them denies any knowledge of it. Most of them did not know that they are members.

SIR O. Do you mean to say that it is all a hoax?

JUDGE. It may be that someone was hoaxing the Court. But now that the applications for warrants have been made public, the Court must take them seriously. Otherwise it would cut a ridiculous figure in the eyes of Europe.

SIR O. But surely such a procedure was never contemplated when the Powers joined the League?

JUDGE. I do not think anything was contemplated when the Powers joined the League. They signed the Covenant without reading it, to oblige President Wilson. The United States then refused to sign it to disoblige President Wilson, also without reading it. Since then the Powers have behaved in every respect as if the League did not exist, except when they could use it for their own purposes.

SIR O. [*naïvely*] But how else could they use it?

JUDGE. They could use it to maintain justice and order between the nations.

SIR O. There is nothing we desire more. The British Empire stands for justice and order. But I must tell you that the British Foreign Office would take a very grave view of any attempt on the part of the Court to do anything without consulting us. I need not remind you that without us you have no powers. You have no police to execute your warrants. You cant put the Powers in the dock: you havnt got a dock.

JUDGE. We have a court room at the Hague which can easily be provided with a dock if you consider such a construction necessary, which I do not. We have employees to whom we can assign police duties to any necessary extent.

SIR O. Pooh! You cant be serious. You have no jurisdiction.

JUDGE. You mean that our jurisdiction is undefined. That means that our jurisdiction is what we choose to make it. You are familiar with what you call judge-made law in England. Well, Sir Midlander, the judges of the Court of International Justice are not nonentities. We have waited a long time for a case to set us in motion. You have provided us with four cases; and you may depend on us to make the most of them. They will affirm our existence, which is hardly known yet. They will exercise our power, which is hardly felt yet. All we needed was a *cause célèbre*; and Miss Begonia Brown has found several for us very opportunely.

SIR O. My dear sir: Miss Brown is a nobody.

JUDGE. Unless the highest court can be set in motion by the humblest individual justice is a mockery.

SIR O. Of course I agree with that—in principle. Still, you know, there are people you can take into court and people you cant. Your experience at the bar—

JUDGE [*interrupting him sharply*] I have had no experience at the bar. Please remember that you are not now in England, where judges are only worn-out barristers, most of whom have forgotten any sense of law they may ever have acquired.

SIR O. How very odd! I own I was surprised to find the judicial bench represented by so young a man; and I am afraid I must add that I prefer our British system. We should have had no trouble with a British judge.

JUDGE. Why should you have any trouble with me? I am simply a Judge, first and last. To me it is a continual trouble and scandal that modern statesmen are slipping back, one after another, from the reign of law based on the eternal principle of justice, to the maintenance of governments set up by successful demagogues or victorious soldiers, each of whom has his proscription list of enemies whom he imprisons, exiles, or murders at his pleasure until he is himself overcome by an abler rival and duly proscribed, imprisoned, exiled or assassinated in his turn. Such a state of things is abhorrent to me. I have spent years in trying to devise some judicial procedure by which these law-breakers can be brought to justice. Well, the Intellectual Co-operation Committee—of the existence of which I must confess I was entirely ignorant—has found the procedure; and the Court will back it up to the utmost of its powers.

SIR O. I am afraid you are a bit of an idealist.

JUDGE. Necessarily. Justice is an ideal; and I am a judge. What, may I ask, are you?

SIR O. I! Oh, only a much harassed Foreign Secretary. You see my young friend—if you will allow me to call you so—justice, as you say, is an ideal, and a very fine ideal too; but what I have to deal with is Power; and Power is often a devilishly ugly thing. If any of these demagogue dictators issues a warrant for your arrest or even an order for your execution, you will be arrested and shot the moment you set foot in their country. You may even be kidnapped and carried there: remember Napoleon and the Duc d'Enghien. But if you issue a warrant or pronounce a sentence against one of them Europe will just laugh at you, because you have no power. It will be as futile as a decree of excommunication.

JUDGE. Would you like to be excommunicated?

SIR O. Hardly a serious question, is it?

JUDGE. Very serious.

SIR O. My dear sir, it couldnt happen.

JUDGE. Pardon me: it could.

SIR O. [*obstinately*] Pardon me: it couldnt. Look at the thing practically. To begin with I am not a Roman Catholic. I am a member of the Church of England; and down at my place in the country the Church living is in my gift. Without my subscription the churchwardens could not make both ends meet. The rector has no society except what he gets in my house.

JUDGE. The rector is a freeholder. If you are a notoriously evil liver, he can refuse to admit you to Communion.

SIR O. But I am not a notoriously evil liver. If the rector suggested such a thing I should have him out of his rectory and in a lunatic asylum before the end of the week.

JUDGE. Suppose the rector were prepared to risk that! Suppose the war of 1914 were renewed, and you were responsible for sending the young men of your country to drop bombs on the capital cities of Europe! Suppose your rector, as a Christian priest, took the view that you were in a condition of mortal sin and refused you Communion! Suppose, if you wish, that you had him locked up as a lunatic! Would you like it?

SIR O. Suppose the villagers burnt down his rectory

and ducked him in the horse pond to teach him a little British patriotism! How would he like it?

JUDGE. Martyrdom has its attractions for some natures. But my question was not whether he would like it, but whether you would like it.

SIR O. I should treat it with contempt.

JUDGE. No doubt; but would you like it?

SIR O. Oh, come! Really! Really!

JUDGE. Believe me, Sir Midlander, you would not like it. And if the International Court, moved by the Committee for Intellectual Co-operation, were to deliver an adverse judgment on you, you would not like it. The man whom the Hague condemns will be an uncomfortable man. The State which it finds to be in the wrong will be an uncomfortable State.

SIR O. But you cant enforce anything. You have no sanctions.

JUDGE. What, exactly, do you mean by sanctions, Sir Midlander?

SIR O. I mean what everybody means. Sanctions, you know. That is plain English. Oil, for instance.

JUDGE. Castor oil?

SIR O. No no: motor oil. The stuff you run your aeroplanes on.

JUDGE. Motor oil is a sanction when you withhold it. Castor oil is a sanction when you administer it. Is there any other difference?

SIR O. [smiling] Well, that has never occurred to me before; but now you mention it there is certainly an analogy. But in England the castor oil business is just one of those things that are not done. Castor oil is indecent. Motor oil is all right.

JUDGE. Well, you need not fear that the Hague will resort to any other sanction than the sacredness of justice. It will affirm this sacredness and make the necessary applications. It is the business of a judge to see that there is no wrong without a remedy. Your Committee for Intellectual Co-operation has been appealed to by four persons who have suffered grievous wrongs. It has very properly referred them to the International Court. As president of that court it is my business to find a remedy for their wrongs; and I shall do so to the best of my ability even if my decisions should form the beginning of a new code of international law and be quite unprecedented.

SIR O. But, my dear sir, what practical steps do you propose to take? What steps can you take?

JUDGE. I have already taken them. I have fixed a day for the trial of the cases, and summoned the plaintiffs and defendants to attend the court.

THE SECRETARY. But the defendants are the responsible heads of sovereign States. Do you suppose for a moment that they will obey your summons?

JUDGE. We shall see. That, in fact, is the object of my experiment. We shall see. [*He rises*] And now I must ask you to excuse me. Sir Midlander: our interview has been most instructive to me as to the attitude of your country. Mr Secretary: you are very good to have spared me so much of your valuable time. Good afternoon, gentlemen. [*He goes out*].

SIR O. What are we to do with men like that?

THE SECRETARY. What are they going to do with us? That is the question we have to face now.

SIR O. Pooh! They cant do anything, you know, except make speeches and write articles. They are free to do that in England. British liberty is a most useful safety valve.

THE SECRETARY. I was on his honor's side myself once, until my official experience here taught me how hopeless it is to knock supernationalism—

SIR O. Super what? Did you say supernaturalism?

THE SECRETARY. No. Supernationalism.

SIR O. Oh, I see. Internationalism.

THE SECRETARY. No. Internationalism is nonsense.
Pushing all the nations into Geneva is like throwing
all the fishes into the same pond: they just begin eating
oneanother. We need something higher than nationalism: a genuine political and social catholicism. How
are you to get that from these patriots, with their
national anthems and flags and dreams of war and
conquest rubbed into them from their childhood?
The organization of nations is the organization of
world war. If two men want to fight how do you
prevent them? By keeping them apart, not by bringing them together. When the nations kept apart war
was an occasional and exceptional thing: now the
League hangs over Europe like a perpetual warcloud.

SIR O. Well, dont throw it at my head as if I dis-
agreed with you.

THE SECRETARY. I beg your pardon. I am worried
by this crisis. Let us talk business. What are we to do
with Begonia Brown?

SIR O. Do with her! Squash her, impudent little
slut. She is nobody: she doesnt matter.

*The conversation is abruptly broken by the irruption of
Begonia herself in a state of ungovernable excitement.*

BEGONIA. Have you heard the news? [*Seeing Sir
Orpheus*] Oh, I beg your pardon: I didnt know you
were engaged.

THE SECRETARY. This is Sir Orpheus Midlander,
the British Foreign Secretary, Miss Brown.

BEGONIA. Oh, most pleased to meet you, Sir Orpheus.
I know your nephew. We are quite dear friends [*she
shakes Sir O.'s hand effusively*]. Have you heard the
news? Lord Middlesex is dead.

[379]

SIR O. Indeed? Let me see. Middlesex? I dont attach any significance to the news. He must have been a backwoodsman. Remind me about him.

BEGONIA. His son is Lord Newcross.

SIR O. Oh! Then Newcross goes to the Lords to succeed his father. That means a by-election in Camberwell.

BEGONIA. Yes; and the Conservatives want me to stand.

BOTH GENTLEMEN. What!!!

BEGONIA. Dont you think I ought to? I have been a lot in the papers lately. It's six hundred a year for me if I get in. I shall be the patriotic candidate; and the Labor vote will be a split vote; for the Communists are putting up a candidate against the Labor man; and the Liberals are contesting the seat as well. It will be just a walk-over for me.

SIR O. But my nephew is the Government candidate. Has he not told you so?

BEGONIA. Oh, thats quite all right. He has withdrawn and proposed me. He'll pay my election expenses.

SIR O. I thought he was in Singapore.

BEGONIA. So he is. It's all been done by cable. Ive just this minute heard it. You see, dear Billikins is not very bright; and he'd better not be here to muddle everything up. [*She sits*].

SIR O. But will his committee accept you?

BEGONIA. Only too glad to get a candidate that will do them credit. You see, no matter how carefully they coached Bill for the public meetings he made the most awful exhibition of himself. And he knew it, poor lamb, and would never have gone in for it if his mother hadnt made him.

SIR O. And do you think you will be able to make a

better impression at the meetings? You are not a politician, are you?

BEGONIA. The same as anybody else, I suppose. I shall pick up all the politics I need when I get into the House; and I shall get into the House because there are lots of people in Camberwell who think as I do. You bet I shall romp in at the head of the poll. I am quite excited about it. [*To the Secretary*] You were so kind to me just now that I thought you had a right to know before anyone else. [*To Sir O.*] And it's splendid news for the Government, isnt it, Sir Orpheus?

SIR O. Thrilling, Miss Brown.

BEGONIA. Oh, do call me Begonia. We're as good as related, arnt we?

SIR O. I am afraid so.

BEGONIA. I am sure to get in, arnt I?

SIR O. If your three opponents are foolish enough to go to the poll, it's a cert.

BEGONIA. Yes: isnt it? I wonder would you mind lending me my fare to London. I dont like taking money off Billikins. I will pay you when my ship comes home: the six hundred a year, you know.

SIR O. Will a five pound note be any use [*he produces one*]?

BEGONIA [*taking it*] Thanks ever so much: itll just see me through. And now I must toddle off to my little constituency. I have barely time to pack for the night train. Goodbye, Mr Secretary [*They shake hands*]; and [*to Sir O. effusively*] thanks ever so much, and au revoir. [*She goes out*].

THE SECRETARY. What an amazing young woman! You really think she will get in?

SIR O. Of course she will. She has courage, sincerity, good looks, and big publicity as the Geneva heroine. Everything that our voters love.

THE SECRETARY. But she hasnt a political idea in her head.

SIR O. She need not have. The Whips will pilot her through the division lobby until she knows the way. She need not know anything else.

THE SECRETARY. But she is a complete ignoramus. She will give herself away every time she opens her mouth.

SIR O. Not at all. She will say pluckily and sincerely just what she feels and thinks. You heard her say that there are lots of people in Camberwell who feel and think as she does. Well, the House of Commons is exactly like Camberwell in that respect.

THE SECRETARY. But can you contemplate such a state of things without dismay?

SIR O. Of course I can. I contemplated my nephew's candidature without dismay.

THE SECRETARY. The world is mad. Quite mad.

SIR O. Pooh! you need a cup of tea. Nothing wrong with the world: nothing whatever.

THE SECRETARY [resignedly sitting down and speaking into the telephone] Tea for two, please.

⌈ACT III⌉

Afternoon in the lounge of a fashionable restaurant over-looking the Lake of Geneva. Three tea tables, with two chairs at each, are in view. There is a writing table against the wall. The Secretary is seated at the centre table, reading a magazine. The American journalist comes in flourishing a cablegram.

THE JOURNALIST. Heard the news, boss?

THE SECRETARY. What news? Anything fresh from the Hague?

THE JOURNALIST. Yes. The International Court has abolished Intellectual Co-operation [*he seats himself at the next table on the Secretary's left*].

THE SECRETARY. What!

THE JOURNALIST. They have had enough of it. The Court also finds the big Powers guilty of flagrant contempt of the League Covenant.

THE SECRETARY. So they are, of course. But the League was doing as well as could be expected until Dame Begonia took a hand in it. By the way, have you heard the latest about her?

THE JOURNALIST. No. She has dropped me completely since she became a Dame of the British Empire.

THE SECRETARY. Well, at a fashion demonstration in the Albert Hall, some blackshirt thought it would be a good joke to pretend to forget her name and call her Mongolia Muggins. Sixteen newspapers quoted this; and Begonia took an action against every one of them.

They settled with her for three hundred apiece. Begonia must have netted at least four thousand.

THE JOURNALIST. And to think I might have married that girl if only I had had the foresight to push myself on her!

THE SECRETARY. Ah! A great opportunity missed: she would have made a most comfortable wife. Pleasant-looking, good-natured, able to see everything within six inches of her nose and nothing beyond. A domestic paragon: a political idiot. In short, an ideal wife.

The widow enters on the arm of Sir Orpheus Midlander. She still carries her handbag, heavy with the weight of her pistol.

SIR O. I assure you, señora, this is the only place in Geneva where you can be perfectly happy after a perfect tea.

THE WIDOW. It is easy for you to be happy. But think of this weight continually hanging on my arm, and reminding me at every moment of my tragic destiny.

SIR O. Oh, you must allow me to carry it for you. I had no idea it was heavy. Do you keep all your money in it?

THE WIDOW. Money! No: it is this [*she takes the weapon from it and throws it on the nearest table on the Secretary's right. The pair seat themselves there*].

SIR O. Good gracious! What do you carry that for? It is against the law in Geneva.

THE WIDOW. There is no longer any law in Geneva. The Hague has abolished the Intellectual Committee, leaving my husband's murder still unexpiated. That throws me back on the blood feud. Properly this is the business of my son. I cabled him to shoot the usurping president at once. But the boy is a shameless dastard.

SIR O. A bastard!

THE WIDOW. No: I wish he were: he has disgraced

[384]

me. A dastard, a coward. He has become a Communist, and pretends that the blood feud is a bourgeois tradition, contrary to the teachings of Karl Marx.

SIR O. Well, so much the better. I can hardly believe that Marx taught anything so entirely reasonable and proper as that it is wrong to shoot a president; but if he did I must say I agree with him.

THE WIDOW. But public opinion in the Earthly Paradise would never tolerate such a monstrous violation of natural justice as leaving the murder of a father unavenged. If our relatives could be murdered with impunity we should have people shooting them all over the place. Even cousins five times removed have to be avenged if they have no nearer relative to take on that duty.

SIR O. Dear me! But if your son wont, he wont; and there is an end to it. A very happy end, if I may say so.

THE WIDOW. An end of it! Nothing of the sort. If my son will not shoot the president, I shall have to do it myself. The president has two brothers who will shoot me unless I stay in this ghastly Europe instead of returning to my beloved Earthly Paradise.

SIR O. To me as an Englishman, all this seems ridiculous. You really need not shoot him.

THE WIDOW. You dont know how strong public opinion is in the Earthly Paradise. You couldnt live there if you defied it. And then there is my own sense of right and wrong. You mustnt think I have no conscience.

SIR O. People have such extraordinary consciences when they have not been educated at an English public school! [*To the secretary*] Talking of that, have you read the Prime Minister's speech in the debate on the League last night?

THE SECRETARY [*illhumoredly*] Yes. Half about Harrow as a nursery for statesmen, and the other half about the sacredness of treaties. He might have shewn some consideration for me.

SIR O. But, my dear fellow, in what way could his speech have possibly hurt you? He has made that speech over and over again. You know very well that after a certain age a man has only one speech. And you have never complained before.

THE SECRETARY. Well, he had better get a new speech, and stop talking about the sacredness of treaties. Will you fellows in London never take the trouble to read the Covenant of the League? It entirely abolishes the sacredness of treaties. Article 26 expressly provides for the revision and amendment both of the treaties and the League itself.

SIR O. But how can that be? Surely the League was created to see the Treaty of Versailles carried out. With what other object would we have joined it?

THE SECRETARY [*desperately*] Oh, there is no use talking to you. You all come here to push your own countries without the faintest notion of what the League is for; and I have to sit here listening to foreign ministers explaining to me that their countries are the greatest countries in the world and their people God's chosen race. You are supposed to be international statesmen; but none of you could keep a coffee stall at Limehouse because you would have to be equally civil to sailors of all nations.

SIR O. Nerves, my dear boy, nerves. I sometimes feel like that myself. I tell my wife I am sick of the whole business, and am going to resign; but the mood passes.

The Jew enters, in animated conversation with the quondam newcomer. The rest become discreetly silent, but keep their ears open.

THE JEW. My good sir, what is your grievance compared to mine? Have you been robbed? Have you been battered with clubs? gassed? massacred? Have you been commercially and socially ruined? Have you been imprisoned in concentration camps commanded by hooligans? Have you been driven out of your country to starve in exile?

THE NEWCOMER. No; but if the people vote for it there is no violation of democratic principle in it. Your people voted ten to one for getting rid of the Jews. Hadnt they the right to choose the sort of people they would allow to live in their own country? Look at the British! Will they allow a yellow man into Australia? Look at the Americans! Will they let a Jap into California? See what happened to the British Government in 1906 when it wanted to let Chinese labor into Lancashire!

THE JEW. Your own country! Who made you a present of a piece of God's earth?

THE NEWCOMER. I was born on it, wasnt I?

THE JEW. And was not I born in the country from which I have been cast out?

THE NEWCOMER. You oughtnt to have been born there. You ought to have been born in Jerusalem.

THE JEW. And you, my friend, ought never to have been born at all. You claim a right to shut me out of the world; but you burn with indignation because you yourself have been shut out of your trumpery little parliament.

THE NEWCOMER. Easy! easy! dont lose your temper. I dont want to shut you out of the world: all I say is that you are not in the world on democratic principles; but I ought to be in parliament on democratic principles. If I shoot a Jew, thats murder; and I ought to be hanged for it. But if I vote for a Jew, as I often have, and he is elected and then not let into Parliament, what becomes of democracy?

THE JEW. The question is not what becomes of democracy but what becomes of you? You are not less rich, less happy, less secure, less well or badly governed because you are making speeches outside your Parliament House instead of inside it. But to me the persecution is a matter of life and death.

THE NEWCOMER. It's a bit hard on you, I admit. But it's not a matter of principle.

THE WIDOW [*to the Jew*] Do you know what I would do if I were a president?

THE JEW. No, madam. But it would interest me to hear it.

THE WIDOW. I would shoot every Jew in the country: that is what I would do.

THE JEW. Pray why?

THE WIDOW. Because they crucified my Savior: that is why. I am a religious woman; and when I meet a God murderer I can hardly keep my hands off my gun.

THE JEW. After all, madam, your Savior was a Jew.

THE WIDOW. Oh, what a horrible blasphemy! [*she reaches for her pistol*].

Sir Orpheus seizes her wrist. The Secretary secures her left arm.

THE WIDOW [*struggling*] Let me go. How dare you touch me? If you were Christians you would help me to kill this dirty Jew. Did you hear what he said?

SIR O. Yes, yes, señora: I heard. I assure you he did not mean to blaspheme. Ethnologically, you know, he was right. Only ethnologically, of course.

THE WIDOW. I do not understand that long word. Our Savior and his Virgin Mother were good Catholics, were they not?

SIR O. No doubt, señora, no doubt. We are all good
Catholics, I hope, in a sense. You will remember that
our Savior was of the house of King David.

THE WIDOW. You will be telling me next that King
David was a Jew, I suppose.

SIR O. Well, ethnologically—

THE WIDOW. Eth no fiddlesticks. Give me my gun.

SIR O. I think you had better let me carry it for you,
señora. You shall have it when this gentleman has
gone.

THE NEWCOMER. Give it to the police. That woman
is not safe.

THE WIDOW. I spit upon you.

SIR O. The police would arrest her for carrying arms.

THE WIDOW. Three men and a Jew against one disarmed woman! Cowards.

THE JEW. Fortunate for you, madam, and for me. But
for these three gentlemen you would soon be awaiting
death at the hands of the public executioner; and I
should be a corpse.

THE JOURNALIST. A cadaver. Put it nicely. A
cadaver.

THE WIDOW. Do you believe that any jury would
find me guilty for ridding the world of a Jew?

THE JEW. One can never be quite certain, madam. If
there were women on the jury, or some Jews, your
good looks might not save you.

THE WIDOW. Women on juries are an abomination.
Only a Jew could mention such a thing to a lady [*she
gives up the struggle and resumes her seat*].

*The Commissar comes in with Begonia and the Judge,
of whom she has evidently made a conquest.*

BEGONIA [*to the Secretary*] Good evening, boss.
Cheerio, Sir Orpheus. You remember me, señora.
You know the judge, boss.

THE SECRETARY. Do me the honor to share my table, your honor.

THE JUDGE. Thank you. May I introduce Commissar Posky. [*He seats himself on the Secretary's left*].

THE SECRETARY. We have met. Pray be seated.

THE JOURNALIST. Take my place, Commissar. I must get on with my work. [*He retires to the writing table, where he sits and sets to work writing his press messages, withdrawing from the conversation, but keeping his ears open*].

THE COMMISSAR [*taking the vacated seat beside the Newcomer*] I thank you.

THE SECRETARY. There is room for you here, Dame Begonia [*indicating chair on his right*].

BEGONIA [*taking it*] There is always room at the top.

THE COMMISSAR. I represent the Soviet.

THE WIDOW [*exploding again*] Another Jew!!!

THE SECRETARY. No, no. You have Jews on the brain.

THE WIDOW. He is a Bolshevist. All Bolshevists are Jews. Do you realize that if I lived under the horrible tyranny of the Soviet I should be shot?

THE JEW. I take that to be a very striking proof of the superior civilization of Russia.

THE COMMISSAR. Why should we shoot her, comrade?

THE JEW. She has just tried to shoot me.

THE COMMISSAR. We do not shoot Jews as such: we civilize them. You see, a Communist State is only possible for highly civilized people, trained to Communism from their childhood. The people we shoot are gangsters and speculators and exploiters and scoundrels of all sorts who are encouraged in other countries in the name of liberty and democracy.

THE NEWCOMER [*starting up*] Not a word against liberty and democracy in my presence! Do you hear?

THE COMMISSAR. And not a word against Communism in mine. Agreed?

THE NEWCOMER [*sits down sulkily*] Oh, all right.

THE COMMISSAR [*continuing*] I find it very difficult to accustom myself to the exaggerated importance you all attach to sex in these western countries. This handsome lady, it seems, has some lover's quarrel with this handsome gentleman.

THE WIDOW. A lover's quarrel!!!

THE COMMISSAR. In the U.S.S.R. that would be a triviality. At the very worst it would end in a divorce. But here she tries to shoot him.

THE WIDOW. You are mad. And divorce is a deadly sin: only Bolsheviks and Protestants would allow such an infamy. They will all go to hell for it. As to my loving this man, I hate, loathe, and abhor him. He would steal my child and cut it in pieces and sprinkle its blood on his threshold. He is a Jew.

THE COMMISSAR. Come to Russia. Jews do not do such things there. No doubt they are capable of anything when they are corrupted by Capitalism.

THE JEW. Lies! lies! Excuses for robbing and murdering us.

THE COMMISSAR. For that, comrade, one excuse is as good as another. I am not a Jew; but the lady may shoot me because I am a Communist.

THE WIDOW. How can I shoot you? They have stolen my gun. Besides, shooting Communists is not a religious duty but a political one; and in my country women do not meddle in politics.

THE COMMISSAR. Then I am safe.

BEGONIA [*recovering from her astonishment at the shooting conversation*] But dont you know, señora, that you mustnt go about shooting people here? It may be all right in your country; but here it isnt done.

THE WIDOW. Where I am is my country. What is right in my country cannot be wrong in yours.

SIR O. Ah, if you were a Foreign Secretary—

THE SECRETARY. If you were the secretary of the League of Nations—

SIR O. You would make the curious discovery that one nation's right is another nation's wrong. There is only one way of reconciling all the nations in a real league, and that is to convert them all to English ideas.

THE COMMISSAR. But all the world is in revolt against English ideas, especially the English themselves. The future is for Russian ideas.

THE NEWCOMER. Where did Russia get her ideas? From England. In Russia Karl Marx would have been sent to Siberia and flogged to death. In England he was kept in the British Museum at the public expense and let write what he liked. England is the country where, as the poet says, "A man may say the thing he wills—"

THE JUDGE. Pardon me: that is an illusion. I have gone into that question; and I can assure you that when the British Government is alarmed there are quite as many prosecutions for sedition, blasphemy and obscenity as in any other country. The British Government has just passed a new law under which any person obnoxious to the Government can be imprisoned for opening his mouth or dipping his pen in the ink.

SIR O. Yes; but whose fault is that? Your Russian propaganda. Freedom of thought and speech is the special glory of Britain; but surely you dont expect us to allow your missionaries to preach Bolshevism, do you?

THE COMMISSAR [laughing] I dont expect any government to tolerate any doctrine that threatens its existence or the incomes of its rulers. The only difference is that in Russia we dont pretend to tolerate such doctrines; and in England you do. Why do you give yourselves that unnecessary and dangerous trouble?

THE NEWCOMER. Karl Marx was tolerated in England: he wouldnt have been tolerated in Russia.

THE COMMISSAR. That was a weakness in the British system, not a virtue. If the British Government had known and understood what Marx was doing, and what its effect was going to be on the mind of the world, it would have sent him to prison and destroyed every scrap of his handwriting and every copy of his books. But they did not know where to strike. They persecuted poor men for making profane jokes; they suppressed newspapers in England as well as in Ireland; they dismissed editors who were too independent and outspoken; they burnt the books of novelists who had gone a little too far in dealing with sex; they imprisoned street corner speakers on charges of obstructing traffic; and all the time they were providing Karl Marx with the finest reading room in the world whilst he was writing their death warrants.

SIR O. Those warrants have not yet been executed in England. They never will be. The world may be jolted out of its tracks for a moment by the shock of a war as a railway train may be thrown off the rails; but it soon settles into its old grooves. You are a Bolshevik; but nobody would know it. You have the appearance, the dress, the culture of a gentleman: your clothes might have been made within half a mile of Hanover Square.

THE COMMISSAR. As a matter of fact they were: I buy them in London.

SIR O. [triumphant] You see! You have given up all this Marxian nonsense and gone back to the capitalist system. I always said you would.

THE COMMISSAR. If it pleases you to think so, Sir Orpheus, I shall do nothing to disturb your happiness. Will you be so good as to convey to your Government my great regret and that of the Soviet Cabinet that your bishop should have died of his personal contact with Russian ideas. I blame myself for not having been more considerate. But I had never met that kind of man before. The only other British Bishop I had met was nearly seven feet high, an athlete, and a most revolutionary preacher.

SIR O. That is what makes the Church of England so easy to deal with. No types. Just English gentlemen. Not like Catholic priests.

THE WIDOW. Oh, Sir Orpheus! You, of all men, to insult my faith!

SIR O. Not at all, not at all, I assure you. I have the greatest respect for the Catholic faith. But you cannot deny that your priests have a professional air. They are not like other men. Our English clergy are not like that. You would not know that they were clergy at all if it were not for their collars.

THE WIDOW. I call that wicked. A priest should not be like other men.

THE COMMISSAR. Have you ever tried to seduce a priest, madam?

THE WIDOW. Give me my gun. This is monstrous. Have Bolsheviks no decency?

THE NEWCOMER. I knew a priest once who—

THE SECRETARY. No, please. The subject is a dangerous one.

THE COMMISSAR. All subjects are dangerous in Geneva, are they not?

THE JUDGE. Pardon me. It is not the subjects that are dangerous in Geneva, but the people.

THE WIDOW. Jews! Bolsheviks! Gunmen!

THE JEW. What about gunwomen? Gunmolls they are called in America. Pardon my reminding you.

THE WIDOW. You remind me of nothing that I can decently mention.

THE NEWCOMER. Hullo, maam! You know, ladies dont say things like that in my country.

THE WIDOW. They do in mine. What I have said I have said.

THE JUDGE. When the International Court was moved to action by the enterprise of my friend Dame Begonia, it found that the moment the League of Nations does anything on its own initiative and on principle, it produces, not peace, but threats of war or secession or both which oblige it to stop hastily and do nothing until the Great Powers have decided among themselves to make use of it as an instrument of their oldfashioned diplomacy. That is true, Mr Secretary, is it not?

THE SECRETARY. It is too true. Yet it is not altogether true. Those who think the League futile dont know what goes on here. They dont know what Geneva means to us. The Powers think we are nothing but their catspaw. They flout us openly by ignoring the Covenant and making unilateral treaties that should be made by us. They have driven us underground as if we were a criminal conspiracy. But in little ways of which the public knows nothing we sidetrack them. We sabotage them. We shame them. We make things difficult or impossible that used to be easy. You dont know what the atmosphere of Geneva is. When I came here I was a patriot, a Nationalist, regarding my appointment as a win for my own country in the diplomatic game. But the atmosphere of Geneva changed me. I am now an Internationalist. I am the ruthless enemy of every nation, my own included. Let me be frank. I hate the lot of you.

ALL THE OTHERS. Oh!

THE SECRETARY. Yes I do. You the Jew there: I hate you because you are a Jew.

THE JEW. A German Jew.

THE SECRETARY. Worse and worse. Two nationalities are worse than one. This gunwoman here: I hate her because she is heaven knows what mixture of Spaniard and Indian and savage.

THE WIDOW. Men with red blood in them do not hate me.

THE SECRETARY. You, Sir Orpheus, are an amiable and honest man. Well, I never hear you talking politics without wanting to shoot you.

SIR O. Dear me! Fortunately I have the lady's gun in my pocket. But of course I dont believe you.

THE SECRETARY. If you had the Geneva spirit you would believe me. This Russian here: I hate him because his Government has declared for Socialism in a single country.

THE COMMISSAR. You are a Trotskyite then?

THE SECRETARY. Trotsky is nothing to me; but I hate all frontiers; and you have shut yourself into frontiers.

THE COMMISSAR. Only because infinite space is too much for us to manage. Be reasonable.

THE SECRETARY. On this subject I am not reasonable. I am sick of reasonable people: they see all the reasons for being lazy and doing nothing.

THE NEWCOMER. And what price me? Come on. Dont leave me out.

THE SECRETARY. You! You are some sort of half-Americanized colonist. You are a lower middle-class politician. Your pose is that of the rugged individualist, the isolationist, at bottom an Anarchist.

THE NEWCOMER. Anarchist yourself. Anyhow I have more common sense than you: I dont hate all my fellow creatures.

THE SECRETARY. You are all enemies of the human race. You are all armed to the teeth and full of patriotism. Your national heroes are all brigands and pirates. When it comes to the point you are all cut-throats. But Geneva will beat you yet. Not in my time, perhaps. But the Geneva spirit is a fact; and a spirit is a fact that cannot be killed.

ALL THE REST. But—'

THE SECRETARY [*shouting them down*] I am not going to argue with you: you are all too damnably stupid.

SIR O. Are you sure you are quite well this afternoon? I have always believed in you and supported you as England's truest friend at Geneva.

THE SECRETARY. You were quite right. I am the truest friend England has here. I am the truest friend of all the Powers if they only knew it. That is the strength of my position here. Each of you thinks I am on his side. If you hint that I am mad or drunk I shall hint that you are going gaga and that it is time for the British Empire to find a younger Foreign Secretary.

SIR O. Gaga!!!

THE SECRETARY. I cannot afford to lose my job here. Do not force me to fight you with your own weapons in defence of my hardearned salary.

THE WIDOW [*to Sir O.*] The best weapon is in your hands. You stole it from me. In my country he would now be dead at your feet with as many holes drilled through him as there are bullets in the clip.

THE SECRETARY. In your country, señora, I might have fired first.

THE WIDOW. What matter! In either case honor would be satisfied.

THE SECRETARY. Honor! The stock excuse for making a corpse.

THE JOURNALIST. A cadaver.

THE WIDOW. Thank you.

THE SECRETARY. A slovenly unhandsome corse. I am quoting Shakespear.

THE WIDOW. Then Shakespear, whoever he may be, is no gentleman.

THE SECRETARY. Judge: you hear what we have to contend with here. Stupidity upon stupidity. Geneva is expected to make a league of nations out of political blockheads.

THE JUDGE. I must rule this point against you. These people are not stupid. Stupid people have nothing to say for themselves: these people have plenty to say for themselves. Take Sir Midlander here for example. If you tell me he is stupid the word has no meaning.

SIR O. Thank you, my dear Judge, thank you. But for Heaven's sake dont call me clever or I shall be defeated at the next election. I have the greatest respect for poetry and the fine arts and all that sort of thing; but please understand that I am not an intellectual. A plain Englishman doing my duty to my country according to my poor lights.

THE JUDGE. Still, doing it with ability enough to have attained Cabinet rank in competition with hundreds of other successful and ambitious competitors.

SIR O. I assure you I am not ambitious. I am not competitive. I happen to be fairly well off; but the money was made by my grandfather. Upon my honor I dont know how I got landed where I am. I am quite an ordinary chap really.

THE JUDGE. Then you have risen by sheer natural ordinary superiority. However, do not be alarmed: all

I claim for the purposes of my argument is that you are not a born fool.

SIR O. Very good of you to say so. Well, I will let it go at that.

THE JUDGE. At the other extreme, take the case of this passionate and attractive lady, whose name I have not the pleasure of knowing.

THE JEW. Try Dolores.

THE WIDOW. I suppose you think you are insulting me. You are simply making a fool of yourself. My name is Dolores.

SIR O. I guessed it, señora. In my undergraduate days I used to quote Oscar Wilde's famous poem.

"We are fain of thee still, we are fain.
O sanguine and subtle Dolores
Our Lady of pain."

THE JOURNALIST. Swinburne, Sir Orpheus.

SIR O. Was it Swinburne? Well, it does not matter: it was one of the literary set.

THE WIDOW. It sounds well; but English is not my native language. I do not understand the first line. "We are fain of thee still: we are fain." What does fain mean?

SIR O. Ah well, never mind, señora, never mind. We are interrupting his honor the Judge. [To the Judge] You were about to say—?

THE JUDGE. I was about to point out that whatever is the matter with this lady it is not stupidity. She speaks several languages. Her intelligence is remarkable: she takes a point like lightning. She has in her veins the learning of the Arabs, the courage and enterprise of the Spanish conquistadores, the skyward aspiration of the Aztecs, the selfless devotion to divine purposes of the Jesuit missionaries, and the readiness of them all to face death in what she conceives to be her social duty. If we have been actually obliged to disarm her to prevent her from sacrificing this harmless Jewish gentleman as her ancestors would have sacrificed him to the God Quetzalcoatl on the stepped altars of Mexico, it is not because she is stupid.

THE WIDOW. I hardly follow you, however intelligent you may think me. But I am proud of having Aztec blood in my veins, though I should never dream of insulting Quetzalcoatl by sacrificing a Jew to him.

THE JUDGE. As to the Jewish gentleman himself, I need not dwell on his case as he has been driven out of his native country solely because he is so thoughtful and industrious that his fellow-countrymen are hopelessly beaten by him in the competition for the conduct of business and for official positions. I come to our democratic friend here. I do not know what his business is—

THE NEWCOMER. I'm a retired builder if you want to know.

THE JUDGE. He has had ability enough to conduct a builder's business with such success that he has been able to retire at his present age, which cannot be far above fifty.

THE NEWCOMER. I am no millionaire, mind you. I have just enough to do my bit on the Borough Council, and fight the enemies of democracy.

THE JUDGE. Precisely. That is the spirit of Geneva. What you lack is not mind but knowledge.

THE NEWCOMER. My wife says I'm pigheaded. How is that for a testimonial?

THE JUDGE. A first rate one, sir. Pigs never waver in their convictions, never give in to bribes, arguments, nor persuasions. At all events you are wise enough to be dissatisfied with the existing world order, and as anxious to change it as anybody in Geneva.

THE NEWCOMER. The world's good enough for me. Democracy is what I want. We were all for democracy when only the privileged few had votes. But now that everybody has a vote, women and all, where's democracy? Dictators all over the place! and me, an elected representative, kept out of parliament by the police!

THE JUDGE. I come to our Russian friend. He must be a man of ability, or he could not be a Commissar in a country where nothing but ability counts. He has no fears for the future, whereas we are distracted by the continual dread of war, of bankruptcy, of poverty. But there is no evidence that he is a superman. Twenty years ago he would have been talking as great nonsense as any of you.

THE REST [except the Russian and Begonia] Nonsense!

THE JUDGE. Perhaps I should have said folly; for folly is not nonsensical: in fact the more foolish it is, the more logical, the more subtle, the more eloquent, the more brilliant.

SIR O. True. True. I have known men who could hold the House of Commons spellbound for hours; but most unsafe. Mere entertainers.

BEGONIA. My turn now, I suppose. I see you are looking at me. Well, all politics are the same to me: I never could make head or tail of them. But I draw the line at Communism and atheism and nationalization of women and doing away with marriage and the family and everybody stealing everybody's property and having to work like slaves and being shot if you breathe a word against it all.

THE JUDGE. You are intelligent enough, well-meaning enough, to be against such a state of things, Dame Begonia, are you?

BEGONIA. Well, of course I am. Wouldnt anybody?

THE JUDGE. It does you the greatest credit.

THE COMMISSAR. But allow me to remark—

THE JUDGE. Not now, Mr. Posky, or you will spoil my point, which is that Dame Begonia's sympathies and intentions are just the same as yours.

BEGONIA. Oh! I never said so. I hate his opinions.

THE COMMISSAR. I must protest. The lady is a bourgeoise: I am a Communist. How can there be the smallest sympathy between us? She upholds the dictatorship of the capitalist, I the dictatorship of the proletariat.

THE JUDGE. Never mind your opinions: I am dealing with the facts. It is evident that the lady is wrong as to the facts, because the inhabitants of a country conducted as she supposes Russia to be conducted would all be dead in a fortnight. It is evident also that her ignorance of how her own country is conducted is as complete as her ignorance of Russia. None of you seem to have any idea of the sort of world you are living in. Into the void created by this ignorance has been heaped a groundwork of savage superstitions: human sacrifices, vengeance, wars of conquest and religion, falsehoods called history, and a glorification of vulgar erotics and pugnacity called romance which transforms people who are naturally as amiable, as teachable, as companionable as dogs, into the most ferocious and cruel of all the beasts. And this, they say, is human nature! But it is not natural at all: real human nature is in continual conflict with it; for amid all the clamor for more slaughter and the erection of monuments to the great slaughterers the cry for justice, for mercy, for fellowship, for peace, has never been completely silenced: even the worst villainies must pretend to be committed for its sake.

SIR O. Too true: oh, too true. But we must take the world as we find it.

THE JUDGE. Wait a bit. How do you find the world? You find it sophisticated to the verge of suicidal insanity. This makes trouble for you as Foreign Secretary. Why not cut out the sophistication? Why not bring your economics, your religion, your history, your political philosophy up to date? Russia has made a gigantic effort to do this; and now her politicians are only about fifty years behind her philosophers and saints whilst the rest of the civilized world is from five hundred to five thousand behind it. In the west the vested interests in ignorance and superstition are so overwhelming that no teacher can tell his young pupils the truth without finding himself starving in the street. The result is that here we despair of human nature, whereas Russia has hopes that have carried her through the most appalling sufferings to the forefront of civilization. Then why despair of human nature when it costs us so much trouble to corrupt it? Why not stop telling it lies? Are we not as capable of that heroic feat as the Russians?

THE COMMISSAR. Apparently not. There are qualities which are produced on the Russian soil alone. There may be a future for the western world if it accepts the guidance of Moscow; but left to its childish self it will decline and fall like all the old capitalist civilizations.

SIR O. Let me tell you, Mr Posky, that if ever England takes to Communism, which heaven forbid, it will make a first-rate job of it. Downing Street will not take its orders from Moscow. Moscow took all its ideas from England, as this gentleman has told you. My grandfather bought sherry from John Ruskin's father; and very good sherry it was. And John

Ruskin's gospel compared with Karl Marx's was like boiling brandy compared with milk and water.

THE JEW. Yes; but as the British would not listen to Ruskin he produced nothing. The race whose brains will guide the world to the new Jerusalem is the race that produced Karl Marx, who produced Soviet Russia.

THE JUDGE. Race! Nonsense! You are all hopeless mongrels pretending to be thoroughbreds. Why not give up pretending?

SIR O. I am not pretending. I am an Englishman: an Englishman from the heart of England.

THE JUDGE. You mean a British islander from Birmingham, the choicest breed of mongrels in the world. You should be proud of your cross-fertilization.

SIR O. At least I am not a Frenchman nor a negro.

THE JUDGE. At least you are not a Scot, nor an Irishman, nor a man of Kent, nor a man of Devon, nor a Welshman—

SIR O. One of my grandmothers was a Welsh girl. Birmingham is nearer the Welsh border than a Cockney concentration camp like London.

THE JUDGE. In short, you are a mongrel.

THE WIDOW. What is a mongrel? I thought it was a cheap kind of dog.

THE JUDGE. So it is, madam. I applied the word figuratively to a cheap kind of man: that is, to an enormous majority of the human race. It simply indicates mixed ancestry.

THE WIDOW. Ah, that is the secret of the unique distinction of the upper class in the Earthly Paradise. My blood is a blend of all that is noblest in history: the Maya, the Aztec, the Spaniard, the Mexican, the—

THE SECRETARY [*flinging away his pen, with which he*

has been making notes of the discussion]. You see, Judge. If you knock all this nonsense of belonging to superior races out of them, they only begin to brag of being choice blends of mongrel. Talk til you are black in the face: you get no good of them. In China the Manchus have given up binding the women's feet and making them cripples for life; but we still go on binding our heads and making fools of ourselves for life.

THE JUDGE. Yes, but do not forget that as lately as the nineteenth century the world believed that the Chinese could never change. Now they are the most revolutionary of all the revolutionists.

THE JEW [*to the Widow*] May I ask have you any engagement for dinner this evening?

THE WIDOW. What is that to you, pray?

THE JEW. Well, would you care to dine with me?

THE WIDOW. Dine with you! Dine with a Jew!

THE JEW. Only a Jew can appreciate your magnificent type of beauty, señora. These Nordics, as they ridiculously call themselves, adore girls who are dolls and women who are cows. But wherever the Jew dominates the theatre and the picture gallery—and he still dominates them in all the great capitals in spite of persecution—your type of beauty is supreme.

THE WIDOW. It is true. You have taste, you Jews. You have appetites. You are vital, in your oriental fashion. And you have boundless ambition and indefatigable pertinacity: you never stop asking for what you want until you possess it. But let me tell you that if you think you can possess me for the price of a dinner, you know neither your own place nor mine.

THE JEW. I ask nothing but the pleasure of your company, the luxury of admiring your beauty and experiencing your sex appeal, and the distinction of being seen in public with you as my guest.

THE WIDOW. You shall not get them. I will not accept your dinner.

THE JEW. Not even if I allow you to pay for it?

THE WIDOW. Is there any end to your impudence? I have never dined with a Jew in my life.

THE JEW. Then you do not know what a good dinner is. Come! Try dining with a Jew for the first time in your life.

THE WIDOW [*considering it*] It is true that I have nothing else to do this evening. But I must have my gun.

SIR O. [*taking the pistol from his pocket*] Well, as we seem to have got over the Anti-Semite difficulty I have no further excuse for retaining your property. [*He hands her the pistol*].

THE WIDOW [*replacing it in her handbag*] But remember. If you take the smallest liberty—if you hint at the possibility of a more intimate relation, you are a dead man.

THE JEW. You need have no fear. If there are any further advances they must come from yourself.

THE WIDOW. I could never have believed this.

BEGONIA. Geneva is like that. You find yourself dining with all sorts.

SIR O. By the way, Mr. Posky, have you anything particular to do this evening? If not, I should be glad if you would join me at dinner. I want to talk to you about this funny Russian business. You need not dress.

THE COMMISSAR. I will dress if you will allow me. They are rather particular about it now in Moscow.

BEGONIA. Well I never! Fancy a Bolshie dressing!

THE JUDGE. May I suggest, gracious Dame, that you and I dine together?

BEGONIA. Oh, I feel I am imposing on you: I have dined with you three times already. You know, I am a little afraid of you, you are so deep and learned and what I call mental. I may be a Dame of the British Empire and all that; but I am not the least bit mental; and what attraction you can find in my conversation I cant imagine.

THE SECRETARY. Geneva is so full of mental people that it is an inexpressible relief to meet some cheerful person with absolutely no mind at all. The Judge can have his pick of a hundred clever women in Geneva; but what he needs to give his brain a rest is a soft-bosomed goose without a political idea in her pretty head.

BEGONIA. Go on: I am used to it. I know your opinion of me: I am the only perfect idiot in Geneva. But I got a move on the League; and thats more than you ever could do, you old stick-in-the-mud.

THE WIDOW. Take care, señorita! A woman should not wear her brains on her sleeve as men do. She should keep them up it. Men like to be listened to.

BEGONIA. I have listened here until I am nearly dead. Still, when men start talking you can always think of something else. They are so taken up with themselves that they dont notice it.

THE WIDOW. Do not give away the secrets of our sex, child. Be thankful, as I am, that you have made sure of your next dinner.

THE JOURNALIST. What about my dinner?

THE SECRETARY. You had better dine with me. You can tell me the latest news.

THE JUDGE. I can tell you that. The trial of the dictators by the Permanent Court of International Justice has been fixed for this day fortnight.

THE REST. Where?

THE JUDGE. At the Hague, in the old palace.

THE SECRETARY. But the trial will be a farce. The dictators wont come.

THE JUDGE. I think they will. You, Sir Orpheus, will, I presume, be present with a watching brief from the British Foreign Office.

SIR O. I shall certainly be present. Whether officially or not I cannot say.

THE JUDGE. You will all be present, I hope. May I suggest that you telephone at once to secure rooms at the Hague. If you wait until the news becomes public you may find yourselves crowded out.

All except the Judge and the Secretary rise hastily and disappear in the direction of the hotel bureau.

THE SECRETARY. You really think the dictators will walk into the dock for you?

THE JUDGE. We shall see. There will be no dock. I shall ask you to act as Clerk to the Court.

THE SECRETARY. Impossible.

THE JUDGE. It seems so now; but I think you will.

THE SECRETARY. Well, as Midlander is coming I shall certainly be there to hear what he may say. But the dictators? Bombardone? Battler? How can you make them come? You have not a single soldier. Not even a policeman.

THE JUDGE. All the soldiers and police on earth could not move them except by the neck and heels. But if the Hague becomes the centre of the European stage all the soldiers and police in the world will not keep them away from it.

THE SECRETARY [*musing*] Hm! Well—[*he shakes his head and gives it up*].

THE JUDGE [*smiles*] They will come. Where the spotlight is, there will the despots be gathered.

[ACT IV]

A salon in the old palace of the Hague. On a spacious dais a chair of State, which is in fact an old throne, is at the head of a table furnished with chairs, writing materials, and buttons connected with telephonic apparatus. The table occupies the centre of the dais. On the floor at both sides chairs are arranged in rows for the accommodation of spectators, litigants, witnesses, etc. The tall windows admit abundance of sunlight and shew up all the gilding and grandeur of the immovables. The door is at the side, on the right of the occupant of the chair of state, at present empty. The formal arrangement of the furniture suggests a sitting or hearing or meeting of some kind. A waste paper basket is available.

The Secretary of the League of Nations has a little central table to himself in front of the other. His profile points towards the door. Behind him, in the front row of chairs are the Jew, the Commissar and the Widow. In the opposite front row are Begonia and a cheerful young gentleman, powerfully built, with an uproarious voice which he subdues to conversational pitch with some difficulty. Next to him is the quondam Newcomer. They are all reading newspapers. Begonia and her young man have one excessively illustrated newspaper between them. He has his arm round her waist and is shamelessly enjoying their physical contact. The two are evidently betrothed.

THE JEW. Do you think anything is really going to happen, Mr Secretary?

THE SECRETARY. Possibly not. I am here to be able to report from personal knowledge whether any notice has been taken of the summonses issued by the court.

THE BETROTHED. The judge himself hasnt turned up.

THE SECRETARY [*looking at his watch*] He is not due yet: you have all come too early.

THE BETROTHED. We came early to make sure of getting seats. And theres not a soul in the bally place except ourselves.

Sir Orpheus comes in.

SIR ORPHEUS. What! Nobody but ourselves! Dont they admit the public?

THE SECRETARY. The public is not interested, it seems.

BEGONIA. One free lance journalist looked in; but she went away when she found there was nothing doing.

THE BETROTHED. The doors are open all right. All are affectionately invited.

SIR ORPHEUS [*seating himself next Begonia*] But what a dreadful fiasco for our friend the judge! I warned him that this might happen. I told him to send special invitations to the press, and cards to all the leading people and foreign visitors. And here! not a soul except ourselves! All Europe will laugh at him.

THE SECRETARY. Yes, but if the affair is going to be a fiasco the fewer people there are to witness it the better.

BEGONIA. After all, theres more than half a dozen of us. Quite a distinguished audience I call it. Remember, you are the Foreign Secretary, Nunky. You are an honorable, Billikins. And I'm not exactly a nobody.

THE BETROTHED [*kissing her hand*] My ownest and bestest, you are a Dame of the British Empire. The

Camberwell Times has celebrated your birthday by a poem hailing you as the Lily of Geneva; but on this occasion only, you are not the centre of European interest. The stupendous and colossal joke of the present proceedings is that this court has summoned all the dictators to appear before it and answer charges brought against them by the Toms, Dicks, Harriets, Susans and Elizas of all nations.

THE WIDOW. Pardon me, young señor. I am neither Susan nor Eliza.

THE BETROTHED. Present company excepted, of course, señora. But the point—the staggering paralyzing, jolly bally breath-bereaving point of our assembly today is that the dictators have been summoned and that they wont come. Young Johnny Judge has no more authority over them than his cat.

THE NEWCOMER. But if they wont come, gentlemen, what are we here for?

THE BETROTHED. To see the fun when Johnny Judge comes and finds nothing doing, I suppose.

THE WIDOW. Is he not late? We seem to have been waiting here for ages.

THE SECRETARY [*looking at his watch*] He is due now. It is on the stroke of ten.

The Judge, in his judicial robe, enters. They all rise. He is in high spirits and very genial.

THE JUDGE [*shaking hands with Sir Orpheus*] Good morning, Sir Midlander. [*He passes on to the judicial chair, greeting them as he goes*] Good morning, ladies and gentlemen. Good morning, mademoiselle. Good morning, señora. Good morning. Good morning. [*Takes his seat*] Pray be seated.

They all sit, having bowed speechlessly to his salutations.

THE JUDGE. Any defendants yet, Mr Secretary?

THE SECRETARY. None, your Honor. The parties on your left are all plaintiffs. On your right, Sir Orpheus Midlander has a watching brief for the British Foreign Office. The lady, Dame Begonia Brown, represents the Committee for Intellectual Co-operation. The young gentleman is the public.

THE JUDGE. An impartial spectator, eh?

THE BETROTHED. No, my lord. Very partial to the girl. Engaged, in fact.

THE JUDGE. My best congratulations. May I warn you all that the instruments on the table are microphones and televisors? I have arranged so as to avoid a crowd and make our proceedings as unconstrained and comfortable as possible; but our apparent privacy is quite imaginary.

General consternation. They all sit up as in church.

BEGONIA. But they should have told us this when we came in. Billikins has been sitting with his arm round my waist, whispering all sorts of silly things. Theyll be in The Camberwell Times tomorrow.

THE JUDGE. I'm sorry. You should have been warned. In the International Court no walls can hide you, and no distance deaden your lightest whisper. We are all seen and heard in Rome, in Moscow, in London, wherever the latest type of receiver is installed.

BEGONIA. Heard! You mean overheard.

THE WIDOW. And overlooked. Our very clothes are transparent to the newest rays. It is scandalous.

THE JUDGE. Not at all, señora. The knowledge that we all live in public, and that there are no longer any secret places where evil things can be done and wicked conspiracies discussed, may produce a great improvement in morals.

THE WIDOW. I protest. All things that are private are not evil; but they may be extremely indecent.

BEGONIA. We'd better change the subject, I think.

THE BETROTHED. What about the dictators, my lord? Do you really think any of them will come?

THE JUDGE. They are not under any physical compulsion to come. But every day of their lives they do things they are not physically compelled to do.

SIR ORPHEUS. That is a fact, certainly. But it is hardly a parliamentary fact.

A telephone rings on the Judge's desk. He holds down a button and listens.

THE JUDGE. You will not have to wait any longer, Sir Midlander. [*Into the telephone*] We are waiting for him. Shew him the way. [*He releases the button*]. The very first dictator to arrive is Signor Bombardone.

ALL THE REST. Bombardone!!!

The Dictator enters, dominant, brusque, every inch a man of destiny.

BOMBARDONE. Is this the so-called International Court?

THE JUDGE. It is.

BBDE. My name is Bombardone. [*He mounts the dais; takes the nearest chair with a powerful hand and places it on the Judge's left; then flings himself massively into it*] Do not let my presence embarrass you. Proceed.

THE JUDGE. I have to thank you, Signor Bombardone, for so promptly obeying the summons of the court.

BBDE. I obey nothing. I am here because it is my will to be here. My will is part of the world's will. A large part, as it happens. The world moves towards internationalism. Without this movement to nerve you you would have never have had the audacity to summon me. Your action is therefore a symptom of the movement of civilization. Wherever such a symptom can be detected I have a place: a leading place.

SIR ORPHEUS. But pardon me, Signor: I understand that you are a great nationalist: How can you be at once a nationalist and an internationalist?

BBDE. How can I be anything else? How do you build a house? By first making good sound bricks. You cant build it of mud. The nations are the bricks out of which the future world State must be built. I consolidated my country as a nation: a white nation. I then added a black nation to it and made it an empire. When the empires federate, its leaders will govern the world; and these leaders will have a superleader who will be the ablest man in the world: that is my vision. I leave you to imagine what I think of the mob of bagmen from fifty potty little foreign States that calls itself a League of Nations.

JUDGE. Your country is a member of that League, Signor.

BBDE. My country has to keep an eye on fools. The scripture tells us that it is better to meet a bear in our path than a fool. Fools are dangerous; and the so-called League of Nations is a League of Fools; therefore the wise must join it to watch them. That is why all the effective Powers are in the League, as well as the little toy republics we shall swallow up in due time.

THE ÇI-DEVANT NEWCOMER. Steady on, mister. I dont understand.

BBDE. [*contemptuously to the Judge*] Tell him that this is a court of people who understand, and that the place of those who do not understand is in the ranks of silent and blindly obedient labor.

NEWCOMER. Oh, thats your game, is it? Who are you that I should obey you? What about democracy?

BBDE. I am what I am: you are what you are; and in virtue of these two facts I am where I am and you are where you are. Try to change places with me: you may as well try to change the path of the sun through the heavens.

THE NEWCOMER. You think a lot of yourself, dont you? I ask you again: what about democracy?

An unsmiling middle aged gentleman with slim figure, erect carriage, and resolutely dissatisfied expression, wanders in.

THE DISSATISFIED GENTLEMAN. Is this the sitting of the department of international justice?

BBDE. [*springing up*] Battler, by all thats unexpected!

BATTLER [*equally surprised*] Bombardone, by all thats underhand!

BBDE. You thought you could steal a march on me, eh?

BATTLER. You have ambushed me. Fox!

BBDE. [*sitting down*] Undignified, Ernest. Undignified.

BATTLER. True, Bardo. I apologize. [*He takes a chair from behind Sir Orpheus, and mounts the dais to the right of the Judge, who now has a dictator on each side of him*] By your leave, sir. [*He sits*].

JUDGE. I thank you, Mr Battler, for obeying the summons of the court.

BATTLER. Obedience is hardly the word, sir.

JUDGE. You have obeyed. You are here. Why?

BATTLER. That is just what I have come to find out. Why are you here, Bardo?

BBDE. I am everywhere.

THE BETROTHED [*boisterously*] Ha ha! Ha ha ha! Dam funny, that.

THE JUDGE. I must ask the public not to smile.

NEWCOMER [*who has no sense of humor*] Smile! He was not smiling: he laughed right out. With all respect to your worship we are wasting our time talking nonsense. How can a man be everywhere? The other gentleman says he came here to find out why he came here. It isnt sense. These two gents are balmy.

[415]

BBDE. Pardon me. What does balmy mean?

NEWCOMER. Balmy. Off your chumps. If you want it straight, mad.

BBDE. You belong to the lower orders, I see.

NEWCOMER. Who are you calling lower orders? Dont you know that democracy has put an end to all that?

BBDE. On the contrary, my friend, democracy has given a real meaning to it for the first time. Democracy has thrown us both into the same pair of scales. Your pan has gone up: mine has gone down; and nothing will bring down your pan while I am sitting in the other. Democracy has delivered you from the law of priest and king, of landlord and capitalist, only to bring you under the law of personal gravitation. Personal gravitation is a law of nature. You cannot cut its head off.

NEWCOMER. Democracy can cut your head off. British democracy has cut off thicker heads before.

BBDE. Never. Plutocracy has cut off the heads of kings and archbishops to make itself supreme and rob the people without interference from king or priest; but the people always follow their born leader. When there is no leader, no king, no priest, nor any body of law established by dead kings and priests, you have mob law, lynching law, gangster law: in short, American democracy. Thank your stars you have never known democracy in England. I have rescued my country from all that by my leadership. I am a democratic institution.

NEWCOMER. Gosh. You democratic! Youve abolished democracy, you have.

BBDE. Put my leadership to the vote. Take a plebiscite. If I poll less than 95 per cent of the adult nation I will resign. If that is not democracy what is democracy?

NEWCOMER. It isnt British democracy.

BATTLER. British democracy is a lie. I have said it.

NEWCOMER. Oh, dont talk nonsense, you ignorant foreigner. Plebiscites are unEnglish, thoroughly un-English.

BEGONIA. Hear hear!

SIR O. May I venture to make an observation?

BATTLER. Who are you?

SIR O. Only a humble Englishman, listening most respectfully to your clever and entertaining conversation. Officially, I am the British Foreign Secretary.

Both Leaders rise and give Fascist salute. Sir Orpheus remains seated, but waves his hand graciously.

BBDE. I must explain to the court that England is no longer of any consequence apart from me. I have dictated her policy for years [*he sits*].

BATTLER. I have snapped my fingers in England's face on every issue that has risen between us. Europe looks to me, not to England. [*He also resumes his seat*].

SIR O. You attract attention, Mr Battler: you certainly do attract attention. And you, Signor Bombardone, are quite welcome to dictate our policy as long as it is favorable to us. But the fact is, we are mostly unconscious of these triumphs of yours in England. I listen to your account of them with perfect complacency and—I hope you will not mind my saying so—with some amusement. But I must warn you that if your triumphs ever lead you to any steps contrary to the interests of the British Empire we shall have to come down rather abruptly from triumphs to facts; and the facts may not work so smoothly as the triumphs.

BATTLER. What could you do, facts or no facts?

SIR O. I dont know.

BATTLER.⎫
BBDE. ⎬ You dont know!!!
      ⎭

SIR O. I dont know. Nor do you, Mr Battler. Nor you, signor.

BBDE. Do you mean that I do not know what you could do, or that I do not know what I should do.

SIR O. Both, signor.

BBDE. What have you to say to that, Ernest?

BATTLER. I should know what to do: have no doubt about that.

SIR O. You mean that you would know what to do when you knew what England was going to do?

BATTLER. I know already what you could do. Nothing. I tore up your peace treaty and threw the pieces in your face. You did nothing. I took your last Locarno pact and marched 18,000 soldiers through it. I threw down a frontier and doubled the size and power of my realm in spite of your teeth. What did you do? Nothing.

SIR O. Of course we did nothing. It did not suit us to do anything. A child of six could have foreseen that we should do nothing; so you shook your fist at us and cried "Do anything if you dare." Your countrymen thought you a hero. But as you knew you were quite safe, we were not impressed.

BBDE. You are quite right, Excellency. It was your folly and France's that blew Ernest up the greasy pole of political ambition. Still, he has a flair for power; and he has my example to encourage him. Do not despise Ernest.

BATTLER. I have never concealed my admiration for you, Bardo. But you have a failing that may ruin you unless you learn to keep it in check.

BBDE. And what is that, pray?

BATTLER. Selfconceit. You think yourself the only great man in the world.

BBDE. [calm] Can you name a greater?

BATTLER. There are rivals in Russia, Arabia, and Iran.

BBDE. And there is Ernest the Great. Why omit him?

BATTLER. We shall see. History, not I, must award the palm.

JUDGE. Let us omit all personalities, gentlemen. Allow me to recall you to the important point reached by Sir Midlander.

SIR O. What was that, my lord?

JUDGE. When you were challenged as to what your country would do in the event of a conflict of interest, you said frankly you did not know.

SIR O. Well, I dont.

BATTLER. And you call yourself a statesman!

SIR O. I assure you I do not. The word is hardly in use in England. I am a member of the Cabinet, and in my modest amateur way a diplomatist. When you ask me what will happen if British interests are seriously menaced you ask me to ford the stream before we come to it. We never do that in England. But when we come to the stream we ford it or bridge it or dry it up. And when we have done that it is too late to think about it. We have found that we can get on without thinking. You see, thinking is very little use unless you know the facts. And we never do know the political facts until twenty years after. Sometimes a hundred and fifty.

JUDGE. Still, Sir Midlander, you know that such an activity as thought exists.

SIR O. You alarm me, my lord. I am intensely reluctant to lose my grip of the realities of the moment and sit down to think. It is dangerous. It is unEnglish. It leads to theories, to speculative policies, to dreams and visions. If I may say so, I think my position is a more comfortable one than that of the two eminent leaders who are gracing these proceedings by their presence here today. Their remarks are most entertaining: every sentence is an epigram: I, who am only a stupid Englishman, feel quite abashed by my commonplaceness. But if you ask me what their intentions are I must frankly say that I dont know. Where do they stand with us? I dont know. But they know what England intends. They know what to expect from us. We have no speculative plans. We shall simply stick to our beloved British Empire, and undertake any larger cares that Providence may impose on us. Meanwhile we should feel very uneasy if any other Power or combinations of Powers were to place us in a position of military or naval inferiority, especially naval inferiority. I warn you—I beg you—do not frighten us. We are a simple wellmeaning folk, easily frightened. And when we are frightened we are capable of anything, even of things we hardly care to remember afterwards. Do not drive us in that direction. Take us as we are; and let be. Pardon my dull little speech. I must not take more of your time.

BATTLER. Machiavelli!

BBDE. A most astute speech. But it cannot impose on us.

JUDGE. It has imposed on both of you. It is a perfectly honest speech made to you by a perfectly honest gentleman; and you both take it as an outburst of British hypocrisy.

BEGONIA. A piece of damned cheek, I call it. I wont sit here and listen to my country being insulted.

THE BETROTHED. Hear hear! Up, Camberwell!

BATTLER. What does he mean by "Up, Camberwell!"? What is Camberwell?

BEGONIA. Oh! He doesnt know what Camberwell is!

THE SECRETARY. Camberwell, Mr Battler, is a part

of London which is totally indistinguishable from any other part of London, except that it is on the south side of the Thames and not on the north.

BEGONIA. What do you mean—indistinguishable? It maynt be as distangay as Mayfair; but it's better than Peckham anyhow.

BBDE. Excuse my ignorance; but what is Peckham?

BEGONIA. Oh! He doesnt know what Peckham is. These people dont know anything.

THE SECRETARY. Peckham is another part of London, adjacent to Camberwell and equally and entirely indistinguishable from it.

BEGONIA. Dont you believe him, gentlemen. He is saying that just to get a rise out of me. The people in Camberwell are the pick of south London society. The Peckham people are lower middle class: the scum of the earth.

BATTLER. I applaud your local patriotism, young lady; but I press for an answer to my question. What does "Up, Camberwell!" mean?

JUDGE. I think it is the south London equivalent to "Heil, Battler!"

BBDE. Ha ha ha! Ha ha! Good.

BATTLER. Am I being trifled with?

JUDGE. You may depend on me to keep order, Mr Battler. Dame Begonia is making a most valuable contribution to our proceedings. She is shewing us what we really have to deal with. Peace between the Powers of Europe on a basis of irreconcilable hostility between Camberwell and Peckham: that is our problem.

SIR O. Do not deceive yourself, my lord. Fire a shot at England; and Camberwell and Peckham will stand shoulder to shoulder against you.

BATTLER. You hear, Bardo. This Englishman is threatening us.

SIR O. Not at all. I am only telling you what will happen in certain contingencies which we sincerely wish to avoid. I am doing my best to be friendly in manner, as I certainly am in spirit. I respectfully suggest that if an impartial stranger were present his impression would be that you two gentlemen are threatening me: I might almost say bullying me.

BBDE. But we are. We shall not be thought the worse of at home for that. How are we to keep up the self-respect of our people unless we confront the rest of the world with a battle cry? And—will you excuse a personal criticism?

SIR O. Certainly. I shall value it.

BBDE. You are very kind: you almost disarm me. But may I say that your technique is out of date? It would seem amusingly quaint in a museum, say in the rooms devoted to the eighteenth century; but of what use is it for impressing a modern crowd? And your slogans are hopelessly obsolete.

SIR O. I do not quite follow. What, exactly, do you mean by my technique?

BBDE. Your style, your gestures, the modulations of your voice. Public oratory is a fine art. Like other fine arts, it cannot be practised effectively without a laboriously acquired technique.

SIR O. But I am an experienced public speaker. My elocution has never been complained of. Like other public speakers I have taken pains to acquire a distinct articulation; and I have had the best parliamentary models before me all through my public life. I suppose—now that you put it in that way—that this constitutes a technique; but I should be sorry to think that there is anything professional about it.

BATTLER. Yes; but what a technique! I contemplated it at first with amazement, then with a curiosity which obliged me to study it—to find out what it could possibly mean. To me the object of public speaking is to propagate a burning conviction of truth and importance, and thus produce immediate action and enthusiastic faith and obedience. My technique, like that of my forerunner opposite, was invented and perfected with that object. You must admit that it has been wonderfully successful: your parliaments have been swept away by the mere breath of it; and we ourselves exercise a personal authority unattainable by any king, president, or minister. That is simple, natural, reasonable. But what is your technique? What is its object? Apparently its object is to destroy conviction and to paralyze action. Out of the ragbag of stale journalism and Kikkeronian Latin—

SIR O. I protest. I beg. I ask the court to protect me.

THE JUDGE. What is the matter? Protect you from what?

SIR O. From these abominable modern mispronunciations. Kikkeronian is an insult to my old school. I insist on Sisseronian.

THE BETROTHED. Hear hear!

BBDE. Take care, Ernest. This is part of the British technique. Your were talking of something really important. That is dangerous. He switches you off to something of no importance whatever.

SIR O. I did not intend that, I assure you. And I cannot admit that the modern corruption of our old English pronunciation of the classics is a matter of no importance. It is a matter of supreme importance.

JUDGE. We do not question its importance, Sir Midlander; but it is outside the jurisdiction of this court; and we must not allow it to divert us from our proper business. I recall you to a specific charge of a specific crime against a specific section of the community. It is a crime of the most horrible character to drop a bomb upon a crowded city. It is a crime only a shade less diabolical to strew the sea, the common highway of all mankind, with mines that will shatter and sink any ship that stumbles on them in the dark. These abominable crimes are being committed by young men—

SIR O. Under orders, my lord, and from patriotic motives.

JUDGE. No doubt. Suppose a young man picks your pocket, and, on being detected, alleges, first that somebody told him to do it, and second that he wanted your money to pay his income tax—a highly patriotic motive—would you accept that excuse?

SIR O. Ridiculous! Remember, sir, that if our young heroes are the killers, they are also the killed. They risk their own lives.

JUDGE. Let us then add a third plea to our pickpocket's defence. He runs the same risk of having his pocket picked as you. Would you accept that plea also?

SIR O. My lord: I abhor war as much as you do. But, damn it, if a fellow is coming at me to cut my throat, I must cut his if I can. Am I to allow him to kill me and ravish my wife and daughters?

JUDGE. I think that under such circumstances a plea of legitimate defence might be allowed. But what has a tussle with a murderer and a ravisher to do with laying a mine in the high seas to slaughter innocent travellers whose intentions towards yourself, your wife, and your daughters, if they have any intentions, are entirely friendly? What has it to do with dropping a bomb into the bed of a sleeping baby or a woman in childbirth?

SIR O. One feels that. It is terrible. But we cannot help its happening. We must take a practical view. It is like the London traffic. We know that so many children will be run over and killed every week. But we cannot stop the traffic because of that. Motor traffic is a part of civilized life. So is coalmining. So is railway transport. So is flying. The explosions in the mines, the collisions of the trains, the accidents in the shunting yards, the aeroplane crashes, are most dreadful; but we cannot give up flying and coalmining and railway travelling on that account. They are a part of civilized life. War is a part of civilized life. We cannot give it up because of its shocking casualties.

JUDGE. But the mine explosions and railway collisions and aeroplane crashes are not the objects of the industry. They are its accidents. They occur in spite of every possible precaution to prevent them. But war has no other object than to produce these casualties. The business and purpose of a coalminer is to hew the coal out of the earth to keep the home fires burning. But the soldier's business is to burn the homes and kill their inhabitants. That is not a part of civilization: it is a danger to it.

COMMISSAR. Come, Comrade Judge: have you never sentenced a criminal to death? Has the executioner never carried out your sentence? Is not that a very necessary part of civilization?

JUDGE. I sentence persons to death when they have committed some crime which has raised the question whether they are fit to live in human society, but not until that question has been decided against them by a careful trial at which they have every possible legal assistance and protection. This does not justify young men in slaughtering innocent persons at random. It would justify me in sentencing the young men to death if they were brought to trial. What we are here to investigate is why they are not brought to trial.

SIR O. But really, they only obey orders.

THE JUDGE. Why do you say "only"? The slaughter of human beings and the destruction of cities are not acts to be qualified by the word only. Why are the persons who give such atrocious orders not brought to trial?

SIR O. But before what court?

JUDGE. Before this court if necessary. There was a time when I might have answered "Before the judgment seat of God". But since people no longer believe that there is any such judgment seat, must we not create one before we are destroyed by the impunity and glorification of murder?

BBDE. Peace may destroy you more effectually. It is necessary for the cultivation of the human character that a field should be reserved for war. Men decay when they do not fight.

THE WIDOW. And when they fight they die.

BBDE. No no. Only a percentage, to give zest and reality to the conflict.

THE JUDGE. Would you describe a contest of a man against a machine gun, or a woman in childbirth against a cloud of mustard gas, as a fight?

BBDE. It is a peril: a deadly peril. And it is peril that educates us, not mere bayonet fencing and fisticuffs. Nations never do anything until they are in danger.

THE JEW. Is there not plenty of danger in the world without adding the danger of poison gas to it?

BBDE. Yes: there is the danger of getting your feet wet. But it has not the fighting quality that gives war its unique power over the imagination, and through the imagination over the characters and powers of mankind.

THE WIDOW. You have been a soldier. Are you the better for it? Were you not glad when your wounds took you out of the trenches and landed you in a hospital bed?

BBDE. Extremely glad. But that was part of the experience. War is not all glory and all bravery. You find out what a rotten coward you are as well as how brave you are. You learn what it is to be numbed with misery and terror as well as how to laugh at death. Ask my understudy here. He too has been a soldier. He knows.

BATTLER. We all begin as understudies, and end, perhaps, as great actors. The army was a school in which I learnt a good deal, because whoever has my capacity for learning can learn something even in the worst school. The army is the worst school, because fighting is not a whole-time-job, and in the army they pretend that it is. It ends in the discharged soldier being good for nothing until he recovers his civilian sense and the habit of thinking for himself. No, cousin: I am a man of peace; but it must be a voluntary peace, not an intimidated one. Not until I am armed to the teeth and ready to face all the world in arms is my Pacifism worth anything.

SIR O. Admirable! Precisely our British position.

NEWCOMER. I'm British. And what I say is that war is necessary to keep down the population.

BBDE. This man is a fool. War stimulates population. The soldier may go to his death; but he leaves behind him the pregnant woman who will replace him. Women cannot resist the soldier: they despise the coward. Death, the supreme danger, rouses life to its supreme ecstasy of love. When has a warlike race ever lacked children?

THE BETROTHED. Very romantic and all that, old man; but this notion of man on the battlefield and woman in the home wont wash nowadays. Home was a safe place when Waterloo was fought; but today the home is the bomber's favorite mark. The soldier is safe in his trench while the woman is being blown to smithereens by her baby's cot. Kill the women; and where will your population be? Egad, you wont have any population at all.

BATTLER. This man is not a fool. If the object of war is extermination, kill the women: the men do not matter.

BBDE. The object of war is not extermination: it is the preservation of man's noblest attribute, courage. The utmost safety for women, the utmost peril for men: that is the ideal.

THE BETROTHED. I say, signor: do you take any precautions against assassination?

BBDE. I do not encourage it; but it is one of the risks of my position. I live dangerously. It is more intense than living safely.

NEWCOMER. Your worship: these gentlemen are talking nonsense.

JUDGE. All politicians talk nonsense. You mean, I presume, that it is not the sort of nonsense you are accustomed to.

NEWCOMER. No I dont. I am accustomed to hear statesmen talking proper politics. But this about living dangerously is not proper politics: it's nonsense to me. Am I to cross the street without looking to see whether there is a bus coming? Are there to be no red and green lights? Am I to sleep in a smallpox hospital? Am I to cross the river on a tight rope instead of on a bridge? Am I to behave like a fool or a man of sense?

BBDE. You would be a much more wonderful man if you could walk on a tight rope instead of requiring several feet of solid pavement, costing years of labor to construct.

SIR O. Do you seriously propose that we should be ruled by an aristocracy of acrobats?

BBDE. Is it more impossible than your British aristocracy of foxhunters?

SIR O. Signor: acrobats are not foxhunters.

BBDE. And gentlemen are not acrobats. But what a pity!

THE NEWCOMER. Oh, whats the use of talking to you people? Am I dreaming? Am I drunk?

BBDE. No: you are only out of your depth, my friend. And now to business. Strength. Silence. Order. I am here to meet my accusers, if any.

JUDGE. You are accused, it seems, of the murder and destruction of liberty and democracy in Europe.

BBDE. One cannot destroy what never existed. Besides, these things are not my business. My business is government. I give my people good government, as far as their folly and ignorance permit. What more do they need?

THE NEWCOMER. Why am I locked out of the parliament of Jacksonsland, to which I have been lawfully elected: tell me that.

BBDE. Presumably because you want to obstruct its work and discredit its leaders. Half a dozen such obstructionists as you could spin out to two years the work I do in ten minutes. The world can endure you no longer. Your place is in the dustbin.

THE NEWCOMER. I give up. You are too much for me when it comes to talking. But what do I care? I have my principles still. Thats my last word. Now go on and talk yourself silly.

BBDE. It is your turn now, cousin.

BATTLER. Do I stand accused? Of what, pray?

THE JEW [springing up] Of murder. Of an attempt to exterminate the flower of the human race.

BATTLER. What do you mean?

THE JEW. I am a Jew.

BATTLER. Then what right have you in my country? I exclude you as the British exclude the Chinese in Australia, as the Americans exclude the Japanese in California.

JEW. Why do the British exclude the Chinese? Because the Chinaman is so industrious, so frugal, so trustworthy, that nobody will employ a white British workman or caretaker if there is a yellow one within reach. Why do you exclude the Jew? Because you cannot compete with his intelligence, his persistence, his foresight, his grasp of finance. It is our talents, our virtues, that you fear, not our vices.

BATTLER. And am I not excluded for my virtues? I may not set foot in England until I declare that I will do no work there and that I will return to my own country in a few weeks. In every country the foreigner is a trespasser. On every coast he is confronted by officers who say you shall not land without your passport, your visa. If you are of a certain race or color you shall not land at all. Sooner than let German soldiers march through Belgium England plunged Europe into war. Every State chooses its population and selects its blood. We say that ours shall be Nordic, not Hittite: that is all.

JEW. A Jew is a human being. Has he not a right of way and settlement everywhere upon the earth?

BATTLER. Nowhere without a passport. That is the law of nations.

JEW. I have been beaten and robbed. Is that the law of nations?

BATTLER. I am sorry. I cannot be everywhere; and all my agents are not angels.

THE JEW [triumphantly] Ah! Then you are NOT God

Almighty, as you pretend to be. [*To the Judge*] Your honor: I am satisfied. He has admitted his guilt. [*He flings himself back into his seat*].

BATTLER. Liar. No Jew is ever satisfied. Enough. You have your warning. Keep away; and you will be neither beaten nor robbed. Keep away, I tell you. The world is wide enough for both of us. My country is not.

THE JEW. I leave myself in the hands of the court. For my race there are no frontiers. Let those who set them justify themselves.

BBDE. Mr President: if you allow Ernest to expatiate on the Jewish question we shall get no further before bed-time. He should have waited for a lead from me before meddling with it, and forcing me to banish the Jews lest my people should be swamped by the multitudes he has driven out. I say he should have waited. I must add that I have no use for leaders who do not follow me.

BATTLER. I am no follower of yours. When has a Nordic ever stooped to follow a Latin Southerner?

BBDE. You forget that my country has a north as well as a south, a north beside whose mountains your little provincial Alps are molehills. The snows, the crags, the avalanches, the bitter winds of those mountains make men, Ernest, MEN! The trippers' paradise from which you come breeds operatic tenors. You are too handsome, Ernest: you think yourself a blond beast. Ladies and gentlemen, look at him! Is he a blond beast? The blondest beast I know is the Calabrian bull. I have no desire to figure as a blond beast; but I think I could play the part more plausibly than Ernest if it were my cue to do so. I am everything that you mean by the word Nordic. He is a born Southerner; and the south is the south, whether it be the south of the Arctic circle or the south of the equator.

Race is nothing: it is the number of metres above sealevel that puts steel into men. Our friend here was born at a very moderate elevation. He is an artist to his finger tips; but his favorite play as a boy was not defying avalanches. As to our races, they are so mixed that the whole human race must be descended from Abraham; for everybody who is alive now must be descended from everybody who was alive in Abraham's day. Ernest has his share in Abraham.

BATTLER. This is an intolerable insult. I demand satisfaction. I cannot punch your head because you are at least two stone heavier than I; but I will fight you with any weapon that will give me a fair chance against you.

THE JUDGE. Gentlemen: you are at the Hague, and in a Court of Justice. Duels are out of date. And your lives are too valuable to be risked in that way.

BBDE. True, your Excellency. I admit that Ernest's ancestors are totally unknown. I apologize.

BATTLER. I dont want an apology. I want satisfaction. You shall not rob me of it by apologizing. Are you a coward?

BBDE. We are both cowards, Ernest. Remember 1918. All men are cowards now.

BATTLER [*rising*] I shall go home.

WIDOW [*rising*] You shall not. Here at least we have come to the real business of this court; and you want to run away from it. If a man of you stirs I shall shoot [*Panic*].

BBDE. Hands up, Ernest [*politely holding up his own*].

THE WIDOW. Listen to me. In my country men fight duels every day. If they refuse they become pariahs: no one will visit them or speak to them: their women folk are driven out of society as if they were criminals.

BATTLER. It was so in my country. But I have stopped it.

JUDGE. Yet you want to fight a duel yourself.

BATTLER. Not for etiquette. For satisfaction.

THE WIDOW. Yes: that is what men always want. Well, look at me. I am a murderess [*general consternation*]. My husband wanted satisfaction of another kind. He got it from my dearest friend; and etiquette obliged me to kill her. In my dreams night after night she comes to me and begs me to forgive her; and I have to kill her again. I long to go mad; but I cannot: each time I do this dreadful thing I wake up with my mind clearer and clearer, and the horror of it deeper and more agonizing.

BATTLER [*flinching*] Stop this. I cannot bear it.

BBDE. Who is this woman? What right has she to be here?

WIDOW. My name is Revenge. My name is Jealousy. My name is the unwritten law that is no law. Until you have dealt with me you have done nothing.

JUDGE. You have a specific case. State it.

WIDOW. My husband has been murdered by his successor. My son must murder him if there is to be no redress but the blood feud; and I shall dream and dream and kill and kill. I call on you to condemn him.

BBDE. And condemn you.

WIDOW. I shall condemn myself. Pass your sentence on me; and I shall execute it myself, here in this court if you will.

JUDGE. But do you not understand that the judgments of this court are followed by no executions? They are moral judgments only.

WIDOW. I understand perfectly. You can point the finger of the whole world at the slayer of my husband and say "You are guilty of murder." You can put the same brand on my forehead. That is all you need do, all you can do. Then my dreams will cease and I shall kill myself. As for him, let him bear the brand as best he can.

JUDGE. That is the justice of this court. I thank you, señora, for your comprehension of it.

BATTLER [*distressed by the narrative*] I cannot bear this. Order that woman not to kill herself.

BBDE. No. If she has a Roman soul, who dares forbid her?

JUDGE. My authority does not go so far, Mr Battler.

BATTLER. Your authority goes as far as you dare push it and as far as it is obeyed. What authority have I? What authority has Bardo? What authority has any leader? We command and are obeyed: that is all.

BBDE. That is true, signor judge. Authority is a sort of genius: either you have it or you have not. Either you are obeyed or torn to pieces. But in some souls and on some points there is an authority higher than any other. Of such is the Roman soul; and this is one of the points on which the Roman soul stands firm. The woman's life is in her own hands.

BATTLER. No: I tell you I cannot bear it. Forbid her to kill herself or I will leave the court.

JUDGE. Señora: I forbid you to kill yourself. But I will sentence the slayer of your husband when his offence is proved; and by that act I will deliver you from your dreams.

WIDOW. I thank your Honor [*she sits down*].

JUDGE. Are you satisfied, Mr Battler?

BATTLER. I also thank your Honor. I am satisfied [*he resumes his seat; but his emotion has not yet quite subsided*].

BBDE. No duel then?

BATTLER. Do not torment me. [*Impatiently*] Bardo: you are a damned fool.

BBDE. [*hugely amused*] Ha ha! [*To the Judge*] The incident is closed.

An attractive and very voluble middleaged English lady enters. She is dressed as a deaconess and carries a handbag full of tracts.

DEACONESS. May I address the court? [*She goes on without waiting for a reply*]. I feel strongly that it is my duty to do so. There is a movement in the world which is also a movement in my heart. It is a movement before which all war, all unkindness, all uncharitableness, all sin and suffering will disappear and make Geneva superfluous. I speak from personal experience. I can remember many witnesses whose experience has been like my own. I——

BBDE. [*thundering at her*] Madam: you have not yet received permission to address us.

DEACONESS [*without taking the slightest notice of the interruption*] It is so simple! and the happiness it brings is so wonderful! All you have to do is to open your heart to the Master.

BATTLER. What master? I am The Master.

BBDE. There are others, Ernest.

DEACONESS. If you knew what I was, and what I am, all that you are doing here would seem the idlest trifling.

BATTLER [*shouting*] Who is the Master? Name him.

DEACONESS. Not so loud, please. I am not deaf; but when one is listening to the inner voice it is not easy to catch external noises.

BATTLER. I am not an external noise. I am the leader of my people. I may become leader of many peoples. Who is this Master of whom you speak?

DEACONESS. His beloved name, sir, is Jesus. I am

sure that when you were a child your mother taught you to say "All hail the power of Jesu's name."

THE BETROTHED. "Let angels prostrate fall."

BEGONIA. Now shut up, Billikins. I wont have you laughing at religion.

BBDE. In Ernest's country, madam, they say Heil Battler. He has abolished Jesus.

DEACONESS. How can you say that? Jesus is stronger than ever. Jesus is irresistible. You can perhaps unify your countrymen in love of yourself. But Jesus can unite the whole world in love of Him. He will live when you are dust and ashes. Can you find the way to my heart as Jesus has found it? Can you make better men and women of them as Jesus can? Can——

BATTLER. I have made better men and women of them. I live for nothing else. I found them defeated, humiliated, the doormats of Europe. They now hold up their heads with the proudest; and it is I, Battler, who have raised them to spit in the faces of their oppressors.

DEACONESS. Jesus does not spit in people's faces. If your people are really raised up, really saved, it is Jesus who has done it; and you, sir, are only the instrument.

NEWCOMER [rising] A point of order, mister. Is this a court of justice or is it not? Are we to be interrupted by every dotty female who starts preaching at us? I protest.

DEACONESS. It is no use protesting, my friend. When He calls you must follow.

NEWCOMER. Rot. Where are the police?

THE JUDGE. The peculiarity of this court, sir, is that there are no police. The lady is raising a point of general importance: one we must settle before we can come to any fruitful conclusions here. I rule that Jesus is a party in this case.

NEWCOMER. You are as dotty as she is. I say no more. [*He resumes his seat sulkily*].

THE JEW. A party in what capacity, may I ask? I speak as a Jew, if Mr Battler will permit me.

THE JUDGE. In the capacity of a famous prophet who laid down the law in these words, "This commandment I give unto you, that ye love one another." Are you prepared to love one another?

ALL EXCEPT SIR O. [*vociferously*] No.

SIR O. Not indiscriminately.

THE BRITISH CONTINGENT. Hear hear!

SIR O. What about the Unlovables? Judas Iscariot, for instance?

DEACONESS. If he had loved the Master he would not have betrayed Him. What a proof of the truth of my message!

BBDE. Do you love Ernest here?

DEACONESS. Why of course I do, most tenderly.

BATTLER. Woman: do not presume.

BBDE. Ha! ha! ha!

DEACONESS. Why should I not love you? I am your sister in Christ. What is there to offend you in that? Is not this touchiness a great trouble to you? You can easily get rid of it. Bring it to Jesus. It will fall from you like a heavy burden; and your heart will be light, oh, so light! You have never been happy. I can see it in your face.

BBDE. He practises that terrible expression for hours every day before the looking glass; but it is not a bit natural to him. Look at my face: there you have the real thing.

DEACONESS. You have neither of you the light in your eyes of the love of the Master. There is no happiness in these expressions that you maintain so industriously. Do you not find it very tiresome to have to be making faces all day? [*Much laughter in the British section*].

BATTLER. Is this to be allowed? The woman is making fun of us.

DEACONESS. I cannot make fun. But God has ordained that when men are childish enough to fancy that they are gods they become what you call funny. We cannot help laughing at them.

BBDE. Woman: if you had ever had God's work to do you would know that He never does it Himself. We are here to do it for Him. If we neglect it the world falls into the chaos called Liberty and Democracy, in which nothing is done except talk while the people perish. Well, what you call God's work, His hardest work, His political work, cannot be done by everybody: they have neither the time nor the brains nor the divine call for it. God has sent to certain persons this call. They are not chosen by the people: they must choose themselves: that is part of their inspiration. When they have dared to do this, what happens? Out of the Liberal democratic chaos comes form, purpose, order and rapid execution.

NEWCOMER. Yes, the executions come along all right. We know what dictators are.

BBDE. Yes: the triflers and twaddlers are swept away. This trifler and twaddler here can see nothing but his own danger, which raises his twaddle to a squeak of mortal terror. He does not matter. His selfchosen ruler takes him by the scruff of the neck and flings him into some island or camp where he and his like can trifle and twaddle without obstructing God's effectives. Then comes this pious lady to bid me turn to God. There is no need: God has turned to me; and to the best of my ability I shall not fail Him, in spite of all the Democratic Liberal gabblers. I have spoken. Now it is your turn, Ernest, if you have anything left to say.

BATTLER. You have said it all in your oldfashioned way, perhaps more clearly than I could have said it. But this woman's old fairy tales do not explain me, Ernest Battler, born a nobody, and now in command above all kings and kaisers. For my support is no dead Jew, but a mighty movement in the history of the world. Impelled by it I have stretched out my hand and lifted my country from the gutter into which you and your allies were trampling it, and made it once more the terror of Europe, though the danger is in your own guilty souls and not in any malice of mine. And mark you, the vision does not stop at my frontiers, nor at any frontier. Do not mistake me: I am no soldier dreaming of military conquests: I am what I am, and have done what I have done, without winning a single battle. Why is this? Because I have snapped my fingers in the face of all your Jewish beliefs and Roman traditions, your futile treaties and halfhearted threats, and the vulgar abuse you have spat at me from your platforms and newspapers like the frightened geese you are. You must all come my way, because I march with the times, and march as pioneer, not as camp follower. As pioneer I know that the real obstacle to human progress is the sort of mind that has been formed in its infancy by the Jewish Scriptures. That obstacle I must smash through at all costs; and so must you, Bardo, if you mean to be yourself and not the tool of that accursed race.

COMMISSAR. I must intervene. Are we here to discuss the Jewish problem? If so, I have no business here: my country has solved it. And we did not solve it by badinage.

BBDE. Badinage! Are our proceedings to be described as badinage by a Bolshevist?

SECRETARY. You see how hopeless it is for us to get any further. You have only to say the word Jew to Herr Battler or the word Bolshevist to Signor Bombardone, and they cease to be reasonable men. You have only to say Peckham to the representative of the Intellectual Committee of the League of Nations to reveal her as an irreconcilable belligerent. You have—

BEGONIA. Whats that he called me? It sounded awful. What does it mean, Uncle O?

SIR O. I understood the secretary to imply that however large-minded your view of the brotherhood of mankind, you must make an exception in the case of Peckham.

BEGONIA. Okay. No Peckham for me. And mind: on that point I am a representative woman. Sorry I interrupted. Carry on, old man.

SECRETARY. I thank you, Dame Begonia. I must add, with great respect for the British Foreign Secretary, that you have only to say British Empire to discover that in his view the rest of the world exists only as a means of furthering the interests of that geographical expression.

SIR O. Surely the British Empire is something more than a geographical expression. But of course with me the British Empire comes first.

SECRETARY. Precisely. And as a common basis of agreement this lady has proposed the policy of the Sermon on the Mount.

DEACONESS. Love oneanother. It is so simple.

SECRETARY. It turns out that we do not and cannot love oneanother—that the problem before us is how to establish peace among people who heartily dislike oneanother, and have very good reasons for doing so: in short, that the human race does not at present consist exclusively or even largely of likeable persons.

DEACONESS. But I assure you, that does not matter. There is a technique you have not learnt.

SIR O. What! More techniques! Madam: before your arrival, I was accused of having a technique. Can we not keep on the plain track of commonsense?

DEACONESS. But this one is so simple. You have spites. You have hatreds. You have bad tempers. All you have to do is to bring them to Jesus. He will relieve you of them. He will shew you that they are all imaginary. He will fill your hearts with love of Himself; and in that love there is eternal peace. I know so many cases. I know by my own experience.

SECRETARY. You are an amiable lady; and no doubt there are, as you say, other cases—

DEACONESS. Oh, I was not an amiable lady. I was a perfect fiend, jealous, quarrelsome, full of imaginary ailments, as touchy as Mr Battler, as bumptious as Signor Bombardone—

BATTLER. Pardon. What does touchy mean?

BBDE. I am unacquainted with the word bumptious. What am I to understand by it?

DEACONESS. Look within, look within, and you will understand. I brought it all to Jesus; and now I am happy: I am what the gentleman is kind enough to describe as amiable. Oh, why will you not do as I have done? It is so simple.

BBDE. It is made much simpler by the fact that you are protected by an efficient body of policemen with bludgeons in their pockets, madam. You have never had to govern.

DEACONESS. I have had to govern myself, sir. And I am now governed by Jesus.

JUDGE. Allow the lady the last word, Mr Leader. Proceed, Mr Secretary.

SECRETARY. No: I have said enough. You know now

what an impossible job I have here as secretary to the
League of Nations. To me it is agony to have to listen
to all this talk, knowing as I do that nothing can come
of it. Have pity on me. Let us adjourn for lunch.

JUDGE. Oh, it is not lunch time yet, Mr Secretary.
We have been here less than an hour.

SECRETARY. It seems to me twenty years.

JUDGE. I am sorry, Mr Secretary. But I am waiting
for the arrival of a defendant who has not yet appeared,
General Flanco de Fortinbras, who is accused of
having slaughtered many thousands of his fellow
countrymen on grounds that have never been clearly
stated.

BBDE. But he has not yet been elected Leader. He is a
mere soldier.

COMMISSAR. Half Europe describes him as your valet.

BBDE. I do not keep valets. But in so far as Flanco is
striving to save his country from the horrors of Communism he has my sympathy.

COMMISSAR. Which includes the help of your guns
and soldiers.

BBDE. I cannot prevent honest men from joining in a
crusade, as volunteers, against scoundrels and assas-
sins.

JUDGE. You also, Mr Battler, sympathize with General
Flanco?

BATTLER. I do. He has accepted my definite offer to
Europe to rid it of Bolshevism if the western states
will co-operate.

JUDGE. And you, Sir Midlander, can of course assure
General Flanco of British support?

SIR O. [rising] Oh, no, no, no. I am amazed at such a
misunderstanding. The British Empire has maintained the strictest neutrality. It has merely recognized
General Flanco as a belligerent.

BBDE. Flanco will not come. I have not authorized him to come.

General Flanco de Fortinbras enters at the door. He is a middle aged officer, very smart, and quite conventional.

FLANCO. Pardon. Is this the International Court?

JUDGE. It is.

FLANCO. My name is Flanco de Fortinbras—General Flanco de Fortinbras. I have received a summons.

JUDGE. Quite so, General. We were expecting you. You are very welcome. Pray be seated.

The secretary places a chair between the judge and Bombardone. Flanco crosses to it.

JUDGE [*before Flanco sits down*] You know these gentlemen, I think.

FLANCO [*sitting down carelessly*] No. But I have seen many caricatures of them. No introduction is necessary.

THE JUDGE. You recognize also the British Foreign Secretary, Sir Orpheus Midlander.

Flanco immediately rises; clicks his heels; and salutes Sir Orpheus with a distinguished consideration that contrasts very significantly with his contemptuous indifference to the two leaders. Sir Orpheus, as before, waves a gracious acknowledgment of the salute. Flanco resumes his seat.

FLANCO. I have come here because it seemed the correct thing to do. I am relieved to find that His Excellency the British Foreign Secretary agrees with me.

BBDE. In what capacity are you here, may I ask?

FLANCO. Do I seem out of place between you and your fellow talker opposite? A man of action always is out of place among talkers.

BBDE. Inconceivable nothingness that you are, do you dare to class me as a talker and not a man of action?

FLANCO. Have you done anything?

BBDE. I have created an empire.

FLANCO. You mean that you have policed a place infested by savages. A child could have done it with a modern mechanized army.

BBDE. Your little military successes have gone to your head. Do not forget that they were won with my troops.

FLANCO. Your troops do fairly well under my command. We have yet to see them doing anything under yours.

BBDE. Ernest: our valet has gone stark mad.

FLANCO. Mr Battler may be a useful civilian. I am informed that he is popular with the lower middle class. But the fate of Europe will not be decided by your scraps of Socialism.

JUDGE. May I recall you to the business of the court, gentlemen. General: you are charged with an extraordinary devastation of your own country and an indiscriminate massacre of its inhabitants.

FLANCO. That is my profession. I am a soldier; and my business is to devastate the strongholds of the enemies of my country, and slaughter their inhabitants.

NEWCOMER. Do you call the lawfully constituted democratic government of your country its enemies?

FLANCO. I do, sir. That government is a government of cads. I stand for a great cause; and I have not talked about it, as these two adventurers talk: I have fought for it: fought and won.

JUDGE. And what, may we ask, is the great cause?

FLANCO. I stand simply for government by gentlemen against government by cads. I stand for the religion of gentlemen against the irreligion of cads. For me there are only two classes, gentlemen and cads: only

two faiths: Catholics and heretics. The horrible
vulgarity called democracy has given political power
to the cads and the heretics. I am determined that the
world shall not be ruled by cads nor its children
brought up as heretics. I maintain that all spare
money should be devoted to the breeding of gentlemen. In that I have the great body of public opinion
behind me. Take a plebiscite of the whole civilized
world; and not a vote will be cast against me. The
natural men, the farmers and peasants, will support
me to a man, and to a woman. Even the peasants whom
you have crowded into your towns and demoralized
by street life and trade unionism, will know in their
souls that I am the salvation of the world.

BBDE. A Saviour, no less! Eh?

FLANCO. Do not be profane. I am a Catholic officer
and gentleman, with the beliefs, traditions, and duties
of my class and my faith. I could not sit idly reading
and talking whilst the civilization established by that
faith and that order was being destroyed by the mob.
Nobody else would do anything but read seditious
pamphlets and talk, talk, talk. It was necessary to fight,
fight, fight to restore order in the world. I undertook
that responsibility and here I am. Everybody understands my position: nobody understands the pamphlets, the three volumes of Karl Marx, the theories of
idealists, the ranting of the demagogues: in short, the
caddishness of the cads. Do I make myself clear?

BBDE. Am I a cad? Is Ernest here a cad?

FLANCO. You had better not force me to be personal.

BBDE. Come! Face the question. Are we cads or
gentlemen? Out with it.

FLANCO. You are certainly not gentlemen. You are
freaks.

BATTLER. Freaks!

[445]

BBDE. What is a freak?

JUDGE. An organism so extraordinary as to defy classification.

BBDE. Good. I accept that.

BATTLER. So do I. I claim it.

JUDGE. Then, as time is getting on, gentlemen, had we not better come to judgment?

BATTLER. Judgment!

BBDE. Judgment!

BATTLER. What do you mean? Do you presume to judge me?

BBDE. Judge me if you dare.

FLANCO. Give judgment against me and you pass out of history as a cad.

BATTLER. You have already passed out of history as a Catholic: that is, nine tenths a Jew.

BBDE. The bee in your bonnet buzzes too much, Ernest. [*To the Judge*] What is the law?

JUDGE. Unfortunately there is no law as between nations. I shall have to create it as I go along, by judicial precedents.

BATTLER. In my country I create the precedents.

BBDE. Well said, Ernest. Same here.

JUDGE. As you are not judges your precedents have no authority outside the operations of your police. You, Mr Battler, are here to answer an accusation made against you by a Jewish gentleman of unlawful arrest and imprisonment, assault, robbery, and denial of his right to live in the country of his birth. What is your defence?

BATTLER. I do not condescend to defend myself.

JEW. You mean that you have no defence. You cannot even find a Jewish lawyer to defend you, because you have driven them all from your country and left it with no better brains than your own. You have

[446]

employed physical force to suppress intellect. That is the sin against the Holy Ghost. I accuse you of it.

JUDGE. What have you to say to that, Mr Battler?

BATTLER. Nothing. Men such as I am are not to be stopped by academic twaddle about intellect. But I will condescend to tell this fellow from the Ghetto that to every superior race that is faithful to itself a Messiah is sent.

DEACONESS. Oh, how true! If only you would accept him!

JUDGE. I understand you to plead divine inspiration, Mr Battler.

BATTLER. I say that my power is mystical, not rational.

BBDE. Ernest: take care. You are walking on a razor's edge between inspiration and the madness of the beggar on horseback. We two are beggars on horseback. For the credit of leadership let us ride carefully. Leadership, we two know, is mystical. Then let us not pretend to understand it. God may choose his leaders; but he may also drop them with a crash if they get out of hand. Tell yourself that every night before you get into bed, my boy; and you may last a while yet.

Loud applause from the British section.

BATTLER. Physician, cure yourself. You need not prescribe for me.

JUDGE. This is very edifying, gentlemen; and I thank you both in the name of all present. May I ask whether this divine guidance of which you are conscious has any limits? Does it not imply a world State with Mr Battler or Signor Bombardone or the British Foreign Office at its head?

FLANCO. Certainly not in my country. A frontier is a frontier; and there must be no monkeying with it. Let these gentlemen manage their own countries and leave us to manage ours.

JUDGE. Is that your view, Mr Battler?

BATTLER. No. I believe that the most advanced race, if it breeds true, must eventually govern the world.

JUDGE. Do you agree, Sir Midlander?

SIR O. With certain reservations, yes. I do not like the term "advanced race." I greatly mistrust advanced people. In my experience they are very difficult to work with, and often most disreputable in their private lives. They seldom attend divine service. But if you will withdraw the rather unfortunate word "advanced" and substitute the race best fitted by its character—its normal, solid, everyday character—to govern justly and prosperously, then I think I agree.

JUDGE. Precisely. And now may we have your opinion, Signor Leader?

BBDE. In principle I agree. It is easy for me to do so, as my people, being a Mediterranean people, can never be subject to northern barbarians, though it can assimilate and civilize them in unlimited numbers.

JUDGE. Has the Russian gentleman anything to say?

COMMISSAR. Nothing. These gentlemen talk of their countries. But they do not own their countries. Their people do not own the land they starve in. Their countries are owned by a handful of landlords and capitalists who allow them to live in it on condition that they work like bees and keep barely enough of the honey to keep themselves miserably alive. Russia belongs to the Russians. We shall look on whilst you eat each other up. When you have done that, Russia—Holy Russia—will save the soul of the world by teaching it to feed its people instead of robbing them.

FLANCO. Did your landlords ever rob the people as

your bureaucracy now robs them to build cities and factories in the desert and to teach children to be atheists? Your country is full of conspiracies to get the old order back again. You have to shoot the conspirators by the dozen every month.

COMMISSAR. That is not many out of two hundred million people, General. Think of all the rascals you ought to shoot!

JUDGE. Pray, gentlemen, no more recriminations. Let us keep to the point of the superior race and the divine leadership. What is to happen if you disagree as to which of you is the divinely chosen leader and the superior race?

BBDE. My answer is eight million bayonets.

BATTLER. My answer is twelve million bayonets.

JUDGE. And yours, Sir Midlander?

SIR O. This sort of talk is very dangerous. Besides, men do not fight with bayonets nowadays. In fact they do not fight at all in the old sense. Mr Battler can wipe out London, Portsmouth, and all our big provincial cities in a day. We should then be obliged to wipe out Hamburg and all the eastern cities from Munster to Salzburg. Signor Bombardone can wipe out Tunis, Nice, Algiers, Marseilles, Toulouse, Lyons, and every city south of the Loire, and oblige the French, headed by the British fleet, to wipe out Naples, Venice, Florence, Rome, and even Milan by return of post. The process can go on until the European stock of munitions and air pilots is exhausted. But it is a process by which none of us can win, and all of us must lose frightfully. Which of us dare take the responsibility of dropping the first bomb?

BATTLER. Our precautions against attack from the air are perfect.

SIR O. Ours are not, unfortunately. Nobody believes

in them. I certainly do not. You must allow me to doubt the efficiency of yours.

JUDGE. And your precautions, Signor? Are they efficient?

BBDE. They do not exist. Our strength is in our willingness to die.

JUDGE. That seems to complicate murder with suicide. However, am I to take it that you are all provided with the means to effect this destruction, and to retaliate in kind if they are used against you?

SIR O. What else can we do, sir?

JUDGE. I find myself in a difficulty. I have listened to you all and watched you very attentively. You seem to me to be personally harmless human beings, capable of meeting one another and chatting on fairly pleasant terms. There is no reason why you should not be good neighbors. So far, my work of building up a body of international law by judicial precedent would seem to be simple enough. Unfortunately when any question of foreign policy arises you confront me with a black depth of scoundrelism which calls for nothing short of your immediate execution.

The Leaders and the British contingent, except the Newcomer, rise indignantly.

NEWCOMER. Hear hear! Hear hear! Hear hear! SIR O. Scoundrelism! BATTLER. Execution! BOMBARDONE. You are mad.

JUDGE. If you dislike the word execution I am willing to substitute liquidation. The word scoundrelism and its adjectives I cannot withdraw. Your objective is domination: your weapons fire and poison, starvation and ruin, extermination by every means known to science. You have reduced one another to such a condition of terror that no atrocity makes you recoil and say that you will die rather than commit it. You call this patriotism, courage, glory. There are a thousand good things to be done in your countries. They remain undone for hundreds of years; but the fire and the poison are always up to date. If this be not scoundrelism what is scoundrelism? I give you up as hopeless. Man is a failure as a political animal. The creative forces which produce him must produce something better. [*The telephone rings*]. Pardon me a moment. [*Changing countenance and holding up his hand for silence*] I am sorry to have to announce a very grave piece of news. Mr Battler's troops have invaded Ruritania.

General consternation. All rise to their feet except Battler, who preserves an iron calm.

JUDGE. Is this true, Mr Battler?

BATTLER. I am a man of action, not a dreamer. While you have been talking my army has been doing. Bardo: the war for the mastery of the world has begun. It is you and I, and, I presume, our friend Fortinbras, against the effete so-called democracies of which the people of Europe and America are tired.

BBDE. Ernest: you have done this without consulting me. I warned you a year ago, when you were negotiating with a relative of Sir Orpheus here, that I could not afford another war.

FLANCO. Neither can I.

All sit down gradually, greatly relieved, except Battler.

BATTLER [*rising in great agitation*] Bardo: are you going to betray me? Remember the axis. Dare you break it?

BBDE. Damn the axis! Do you suppose I am going to ruin my country to make you emperor of the universe? You should know me better [*He resumes his seat majestically*].

BATTLER. This is the most shameless betrayal in

human history. General Flanco: you owe your victory to my aid. Will you be such a monster of ingratitude as to desert me now?

FLANCO. I owe my victory equally to the aid of Signor Bombardone and to the masterly non-intervention policy of Sir Orpheus Midlander. I cannot prove ungrateful to either of them.

BATTLER. Well, traitors as you are, I can do without you. I can conquer Ruritania single-handed, no thanks to either of you. But where should I be if the British were not afraid to fight. Fortunately for me they do not believe in what they call brute force. [*He sits*].

SIR O. [*rising*] Pardon me. It is true that we abhor brute force, and are willing to make any sacrifice for the sake of peace—or almost any sacrifice. We understood that this was your attitude also. But I had the honor of informing you explicitly—very explicitly, Mr Battler—that Ruritania is, so to speak, our little sister, and that if you laid a finger on her we should—pardon me if in my indignant surprise at your breach of the peace I am unable to adhere to the language of diplomacy—we should be obliged to knock the stuffing out of you. That is our British method of meeting brute force.

BATTLER. What! You will fight?

SIR O. Fight, Mr Battler! We shall wipe you off the face of the earth. [*He resumes his seat*].

BATTLER. Then I am alone: *contra mundum*. Well, I have never failed yet.

FLANCO. Because you have never fought yet.

BATTLER. We shall see. I shall sweep through Ruritania like a hurricane.

COMMISSAR. Do so by all means, Comrade Battler. When you have finished you will settle with me how much of it you may keep.

BATTLER. What! You too! So the encirclement is complete.

SIR ORPHEUS. No! I cannot permit that expression. Outflanked if you like. Hemmed in if you will have it so. I will even go so far as to say surrounded. But encircled, NO.

NEWCOMER. It puts the kybosh on Battlerism anyhow.
The telephone rings again.

ALL EXCEPT THE JUDGE. Hush. Let us hear the news. The news. The news. [*They listen with strained attention*]. Sh-sh-sh-sh-sh-.

JUDGE. What? Say that again: I must take it down: I do not understand. [*Writing as he listens*] "Astronomers report that the orbit of the earth is jumping to its next quantum. Message received at Greenwich from three American observatories. Humanity is doomed." Thank you. Goodbye. Can anyone explain this? Why is humanity doomed?

SECRETARY. It is intelligible enough, and very serious indeed.

JUDGE. It is not intelligible to me. Will you kindly explain?

SECRETARY. The orbit of the earth is the path in which it travels round the sun. As the sun is 93 million miles distant it takes us a year to get round.

JUDGE. We all know that. But the message says that the orbit is jumping to its next quantum. What does quantum mean?

SECRETARY. When orbits change they dont change gradually. They suddenly jump by distances called quantums or quanta. Nobody knows why. If the earth is jumping to a wider orbit it is taking us millions of miles further away from the sun. That will take us into the awful cold of space. The icecaps that we have on the north and south poles will spread over the whole earth. Even the polar bears will be frozen stiff. Not a trace of any sort of life known to us will be possible on this earth.

THE JEW [*rising and hurrying to the door*] Excuse me.

COMMISSAR. No use running away, my friend. The icecap will overtake you wherever you go.

SECRETARY. Let him alone. The shock has made him ill.

THE JEW. No: not that. I must telephone [*he goes out*].

JUDGE [*rising*] Fellow citizens: this is the end. The end of war, of law, of leaders and foreign secretaries, of judges and generals. A moment ago we were important persons: the fate of Europe seemed to depend on us. What are we now? Democracy, Fascism, Communism: how much do they matter? Your totalitarian Catholic Church: does it still seem so very totalitarian?

FLANCO. Do not blaspheme at such a moment, sir. You tell us that nothing matters. Ten minutes ago the judgment of God seemed far off: now we stand at the gates of purgatory. We have to organize absolution for millions of our people; and we have barely priests enough to do it, even if we have no converts to deal with; and we shall have many converts. We Catholics know what to do; and I have no more time to spend trifling here with men who know nothing and believe nothing. [*He moves towards the door. He stops to hear Sir O.*]

SIR O. One moment, I beg of you. This rumor must be contradicted at all costs.

COMMISSAR. How can you contradict a scientific fact?

SIR O. It must be contradicted—officially contradicted. Think of the consequences if it is believed! People will throw off all decency, all prudence. Only the Jews, with the business faculty peculiar to their race, will profit by our despair. Why has our Jewish friend just left us? To telephone, he said. Yes; but to whom is he telephoning? To his stockbroker, gentlemen. He is instructing his stockbroker to sell gilt-edged in any quantity, at any price, knowing that if this story gets about before settling day he will be able to buy it for the price of waste paper and be a millionaire until the icecap overtakes him. It must not be. I will take the necessary steps in England. The Astronomer Royal will deny this story this afternoon. You two gentlemen must see to it at once that it is officially denied in your countries.

COMMISSAR. Suppose your Astronomer Royal refuses to tell a lie. Remember: he is a man of science, not a politician.

SIR O. He is an Englishman, sir, and has some common sense. He will do his duty. Can I depend on the rest of you gentlemen?

BBDE. Can you depend on the icecap? I must go home at once. There will be a rush to the equator. My country stands right in the way of that rush. I must stop it at our frontier at any cost.

COMMISSAR. Why? Will it matter?

BBDE. I will not tolerate disorder. I will not tolerate fear. We shall die decently, stoically, steadfast at our posts, like Romans. Remember: we shall not decay: we shall stand to all eternity in cold storage. When we are discovered by some explorer from another star or another race that can live and breathe at absolute zero, he shall find my people erect at their posts like the Pompeian sentinel. You also, Ernest, must— What! Crying!! For shame, man! The world looks to us for leadership. Shall it find us in tears?

BATTLER. Let me alone. My dog Blonda will be

frozen to death. My doggie! My little doggie! [*He breaks down, sobbing convulsively*].

NEWCOMER. Oh, come, old man. Dont take it so hard. I used to keep dogs myself; but I had to give it up: I couldnt bear the shortness of their lives. Youd have had to lose your little doggie some day.

Battler takes out his handkerchief and controls himself; but the Deaconess bursts into tears.

BEGONIA. Oh for God's sake, dont you start crying. You will set us all off. It's hard enough on us without that.

THE SECRETARY. Yes, maam. Take your trouble to Jesus; and set all the women a good example.

DEACONESS. But in heaven I shall lose my Jesus. There He will be a king; and there will be no more troubles and sorrows and sins to bring to Him. My life has been so happy since I found Him and came to Him a year ago! He made heaven for me on earth; and now that is all over. I cannot bear it. [*Her tears overcome her*].

NEWCOMER. Oh come come! This wont do, you know. All you people seem to think you were going to live for ever. Well, you werent. Our numbers are up; but so they were before, sooner or later. I dont complain: I havnt had such a bad time of it; and I am ready to depart, as the poet says, if it must be. In fact I must depart now and cheer up the missus. [*He rises to go*].

DEACONESS. Oh, sir, do you believe this? May it not be untrue?

NEWCOMER [*gravely*] No: it's true all right enough. If it were a priest's tale or a superstition out of the Bible I shouldnt give a snap of my fingers for it. But Science cannot be wrong. Weve got to face it. Good morning, gents.

The Newcomer goes out; and his departure breaks up the court. The Leaders and the General rise and come forward together.

DEACONESS [*to Flanco*] Oh, General, is Science always right?

FLANCO. Certainly not: it is always wrong. But I await the decision of the Church. Until that is delivered the story has no authority.

SIR O. May I suggest that you use all your influence at Rome to obtain an immediate decision from the Church against this story?

FLANCO. You shock me. The Church cannot be influenced. It knows the truth as God knows it, and will instruct us accordingly. Anyone who questions its decision will be shot. My business is to see to that. After absolution, of course. Good morning. [*He goes out*].

WIDOW. He at least has something to offer to men about to die.

COMMISSAR. Dope.

JUDGE. Why not, if they die comforted?

BATTLER. Men must learn to die undeluded.

BBDE. Flanco is dead; but he does not know it. History would have kicked him out were not History now on its deathbed.

BEGONIA. I must say I thought the general a perfect gentleman. I never wanted to kick him while he was speaking. I wanted to kick you two all the time.

THE BETROTHED. Steady, Gonny, steady! Mustnt be rude, you know.

BEGONIA. Oh, what does it matter now? As we shall all be frozen stiff presently we may as well have the satisfaction of speaking our minds until then.

THE BETROTHED. Take it easy, dear. Have a choc.

BEGONIA. No, thank you.

[457]

THE BETROTHED. I say, Uncle O: this is the first time she has ever refused a choc.

SIR O. Our valuations have changed, naturally.

THE BETROTHED. Mine havnt. You know, uncle, I think theres something in your notion of selling out and having a tremendous spree before the icecaps nip us. How does that strike you, Gonny?

BEGONIA. I dont pretend it might not have appealed to me before I represented Intellectual Co-operation. But I am a Dame of the British Empire now; and if I must die I will die like a Dame. [*She goes out*].

SIR O. Go with her, sir. And mind you behave yourself.

THE BETROTHED. Well, it does seem rather a pity. However— [*He shrugs resignedly and goes out*].

SIR O. [*to the Commissar*] Do you, sir, understand what is going to happen? My classical education did not include science.

COMMISSAR. I await instructions. The Marxian dialectic does not include the quantum theory. I must consult Moscow. [*He goes out*].

SIR O. Have these men no minds of their own? One of them must consult Rome: the other must consult Moscow. You two gentlemen fortunately have no one but yourselves to consult. Can I rely on you to do your utmost to stifle this appalling news while I return to London to consult the Cabinet?

BBDE. You can rely on nothing but this. The news has just been broadcast to all the world through the arrangements made for publicity in this court. According to you, the result will be that the people will throw off all decency and repudiate all leadership. I say that the people will want a leader as they have never wanted one before. I have taught them to order their lives: I shall teach them to order their deaths.

The magnitude of the catastrophe is the measure of the leader's greatness.

SIR O. You always have a speech which sounds equal to the occasion. In England that gift would make you Prime Minister. But your very excitable countrymen may run wild.

BBDE. In that case I can do nothing but fall at the head of an attempt to stem the rush. At least one man shall stand for human courage and dignity when the race expires.

SIR O. Yes: that is a very fine attitude and quite a correct one. But have you nothing better to propose than an attitude?

BBDE. Has anyone anything better to propose than an attitude?

SIR O. I suppose not; but I feel strongly that a burst of sincerity would be a great relief.

BBDE. [*to Battler*] Give him his burst of sincerity, Ernest. Cry for your dog again. Good morning, gentlemen. [*He goes to the door*].

BATTLER [*calling after him*] You will have the honor of sharing my little dog's fate. But nobody will weep for you, Bardo.

BBDE. I hope not. I do not deal in tears. [*He strides out*].

BATTLER. What an actor!

SECRETARY. You should be a good judge of that. You have done a good deal in that line yourself.

BATTLER. We all have. But I claim to have done a little good with my acting. I will not have my work undone. We shall not stand in statuesque attitudes in Bardo's manner: we shall work to the last, and set an example to the new race of iceproof men who will follow us.

SIR O. Still, you know, it's no use going on making motor cars that you know will never run.

BATTLER. Yes: when the alternative is to wring our hands in despair or get drunk. We cannot work for ourselves to the last moment; but we can all work for honor. [*He goes out*].

SIR O. Wonderful luck that man has! His dog will get him into all the headlines. [*He goes out*].

JUDGE [*to the Deaconess and the widow*] Ladies: I am afraid there is nothing more to be done here.

DEACONESS [*rising*] None of you understands what this means to me, because none of you has learnt how to live. You are souls in torment, as I was until six months ago. And now I must die when I have only just learnt to live. Excuse me: I cannot bear to speak of it [*she goes out distractedly*].

JUDGE. She, at least, values her life.

SECRETARY. Yes: she belongs to some movement or other.

WIDOW [*taking her pistol from her handbag and rising*] I killed my best friend with this. I kept it to kill myself. It is useless now: God will execute His own judgment on us all. [*She throws it into the waste paper basket*]. But He is merciful; for I shall never dream again. And [*to the Secretary*] I do n o t belong to any movement.

He bows; and she goes out.

SECRETARY. Can you switch off?

JUDGE [*going to the table and turning a masterswitch*] No one can hear us now. [*Returning*] Can this thing be true?

SECRETARY. No. It is utter nonsense. If the earth made a spring to a wider orbit half a minute would carry us to regions of space where we could not breathe and our blood would freeze in our veins.

JUDGE. Yet we all believed it for the moment.

SECRETARY. You have nothing to do but mention the

quantum theory, and people will take your voice for the voice of Science and believe anything. It broke up this farce of a trial, at all events.

JUDGE. Not a farce, my friend. They came, these fellows. They blustered: they defied us. But they came. They came.